A-Level Year 1 & AS

Chemistry

The Complete Course for AQA

Let's face it, Chemistry is a tough subject. You'll need to get to grips with a lot of difficult concepts, and have plenty of practical skills up your lab-coat sleeve.

But don't worry — this brilliant CGP book covers everything you'll need for the new AQA courses. It's packed with clear explanations, exam practice, advice on maths skills and practical investigations... and much more!

It even includes a free Online Edition to read on your PC, Mac or tablet.

How to get your free Online Edition

Go to **cgpbooks.co.uk/extras** and enter this code...

1735 5328 5463 4414

This code will only work once. If someone has used this book before you, they may have already claimed the Online Edition.

Contents

How to use this book

Learning Objectives
- These tell you exactly what you need to learn, or be able to do, for your exams.
- There's a specification reference at the bottom that links to the AQA specification.

Exam Tips
There are tips throughout the book to help with all sorts of things to do with answering exam questions.

Tips
These are here to help you understand the theory.

- Be able to apply IUPAC rules for nomenclature to name and draw the structure of organic compounds limited to chains and rings with up to six carbon atoms each.

Specification Reference 3.3.1.1

Exam Tip
Always double check that you've spelled the IUPAC names of compounds correctly in exams — if you don't spell them right, you won't get the marks.

Tip: These stems come up again and again in chemistry so it's really important that you know all of them.

Figure 1: August Kekulé was one of the first scientists to recognise the need for a way to systematically name molecules.

3. Nomenclature

Nomenclature is just a fancy word for naming organic compounds. You have to follow a strict set of rules for naming, but it's dead handy — this way anyone anywhere can know what compound you're talking about.

Naming alkanes
The IUPAC system for naming organic compounds is the agreed international language of chemistry. Years ago, organic compounds were given whatever names people fancied, such as acetic acid and ethylene. But these names caused confusion between different countries.

The IUPAC system means scientific ideas can be communicated across the globe more effectively. So it's easier for scientists to get on with testing each other's work, and either support or dispute new theories.

You need to be able to name straight-chain and branched alkanes using the IUPAC system for naming organic compounds.

Straight-chain alkanes
There are two parts to the name of a straight-chain alkane. The first part — the stem — states how many carbon atoms there are in the molecule (see Figure 1 on page 176). The second part is always "-ane". It's the "-ane" bit that lets people know it's an alkane.

┌ Example
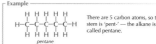

There are 5 carbon atoms, so the stem is 'pent-' — the alkane is called pentane.

pentane

Branched alkanes
Branched alkanes have side chains. These are the carbon atoms that aren't part of the longest continuous chain. To name branched alkanes you first need to count how many carbon atoms are in the longest chain and work out the stem (just like you would for a straight-chain alkane). Once you've done that you can name the side chains.

The side chains are named according to how many carbon atoms they have (see Figure 3 on page 177) and which carbon atom they are attached to. If there's more than one side chain in a molecule, you place them in alphabetical order. So but- groups come before eth- groups, which come before meth- groups.

┌ Examples

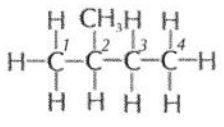

The longest continuous carbon chain is 4 carbon atoms, so the stem is butane.
There's one side chain, which has one carbon atom, so it's a methyl group.
It's joined to the main carbon chain at the 2nd carbon atom, so it's a 2-methyl group.
The alkane is called 2-methylbutane.

2-methylbutane

---

3. Measuring Reaction Rates

Understanding all about the rates of chemical reactions is a really important part of chemistry. You need to know how to measure reaction rate as well.

Calculating reaction rates
Rate of reaction is the change in the amount of a reactant or product over time. The units of reaction rate will be 'change you're measuring ÷ unit of time' (e.g. g s⁻¹ or cm³ s⁻¹). Here's a simple formula for finding the rate of a reaction:

$$\text{rate of reaction} = \frac{\text{amount of reactant used or product formed}}{\text{time}}$$

Measuring the rate of a reaction
If you want to find the rate of a reaction, you need to be able to follow the reaction as it's occurring. Although there are quite a few ways to follow reactions, not every method works for every reaction. You've got to pick a property that changes as the reaction goes on. Here are a few examples:

REQUIRED PRACTICAL 3

Time taken for a precipitate to form
You can use this method when the product's a precipitate that clouds a solution.

┌ Example
When you mix colourless sodium thiosulfate solution and colourless hydrochloric acid solution, a yellow precipitate of sulfur is formed:

$$Na_2S_2O_{3(aq)} + 2HCl_{(aq)} \rightarrow 2NaCl_{(aq)} + SO_{2(g)} + S_{(s)}$$

You can stand a conical flask on top of a white tile with a black mark on it. Then you add fixed volumes of the reactant solutions to the flask and start a stopwatch. Look through the solutions to observe the mark on the tile. As the precipitate forms, the mark will become harder to see clearly. Stop the timer when the mark is no longer visible. The reading on the timer is recorded as the time taken for the precipitate to form.

Stopwatch

A mark is made on a tile underneath the reaction vessel, which is visible through the initial reaction mixture.

Sodium thiosulfate and hydrochloric acid solution.

A yellow sulfur precipitate forms which clouds the solution.

Figure 1: Experimental setup for measuring reaction rate by monitoring the time taken for a precipitate to form.

You can repeat this reaction for solutions at different temperatures to investigate how temperature affects reaction rate. Use a water bath to gently heat both solutions to the desired temperature before mixing them. The volumes and concentrations of the solutions must be kept the same each time. The results should show that the higher the temperature, the less time it takes for the mark to disappear and the faster the rate of the reaction gets.

Learning Objectives:
- Understand the meaning of the term rate of reaction.
- Investigate how the rate of a reaction changes with temperature (Required Practical 3).

Specification Reference 3.1.5.3

Tip: Carrying out experiments can be hazardous so you should always do a risk assessment before beginning.

Tip: If the same person uses the same mark each time you can compare the reaction rate, because roughly the same amount of precipitate will have been formed when the mark is obscured. But this method is subjective — different people might not agree on exactly when the mark has 'disappeared'.

Tip: In this experiment, temperature is the independent variable because you're changing it to see what happens. Time is the dependent variable because that's what you're measuring. See page 1 for more about this.

Required Practicals
- As part of your course, you'll be expected to do a set of Required Practicals. You'll be tested on your knowledge of them in your exams too.
- Information about these practicals is marked with a Required Practical stamp.

Practical Skills
- There are some key practical skills you'll not only need to use in your Required Practicals, but you could be tested on in the exams too.
- There's a Practical Skills section at the front of this book with loads of information on how to plan experiments and analyse data.

Examples
These are here to help you understand the theory.

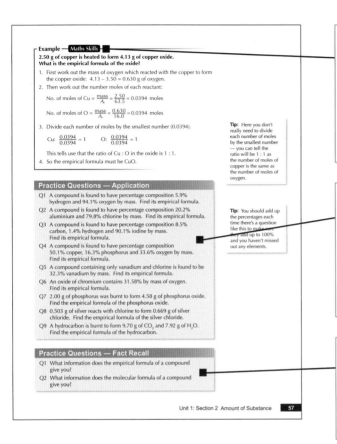

Maths Skills

There's a range of maths skills you could be expected to apply in your exams.

- Examples that show these maths skills in action are marked up like this.
- There's also a maths skills section at the back of the book.

Practice Questions — Application

- Annoyingly, the examiners expect you to be able to apply your knowledge to new situations — these questions are here to give you plenty of practice at doing this.
- All the answers are in the back of the book (including any calculation workings).

Practice Questions — Fact Recall

- There are a lot of facts you need to learn — these questions are here to test that you know them.
- All the answers are in the back of the book.

Exam-style Questions

- Practising exam-style questions is really important — you'll find some at the end of each section.
- They're the same style as the ones you'll get in the real exams — some will test your knowledge and understanding and some will test that you can apply your knowledge.
- All the answers are in the back of the book, along with a mark scheme to show you how you get the marks.

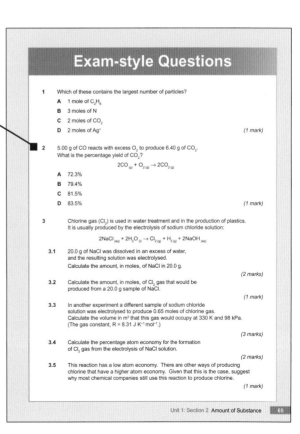

Exam Help

There's a section at the back of the book stuffed full of things to help with your exams.

Glossary

There's a glossary at the back of the book full of all the definitions you need to know for your exams, plus loads of other useful words.

Published by CGP

Editors:
Mary Falkner, Katherine Faudemer, Gordon Henderson, Emily Howe, Paul Jordin,
Rachel Kordan, Sophie Scott, Ben Train.

Contributors:
Ian H. Davis, John Duffy, Emma Grimwood, Lucy Muncaster, Derek Swain.

ISBN: 978 1 78294 321 1

With thanks to Glenn Rogers and Jamie Sinclair for the proofreading.
With thanks to Jan Greenway for the copyright research.
AQA Specification reference points are adapted and reproduced by permission of AQA.

Printed by Elanders Ltd, Newcastle upon Tyne.
Clipart from Corel®

Practical Skills

1. Planning Experiments

You'll get to do loads of practicals in class during this course, which is great. Unfortunately, you can also get tested on how to carry out experiments in your exams. The first thing you need is a good plan...

Initial Planning

Scientists solve problems by suggesting answers and then doing experiments that test their ideas to see if the evidence supports them. Being able to plan experiments that will give you valid and accurate results (see page 9) is a very important part of this process. Here's how you go about it:

First, you have to identify what question you are trying to answer. This is the **aim** of your experiment. It could be something like 'the aim of this experiment is to determine how temperature affects the rate of this reaction'. You can then make a **prediction** — a specific testable statement about what will happen in the experiment, based on observation, experience or a **hypothesis** (a suggested explanation for a fact or observation).

The next step is to identify what the independent and dependent **variables** (see below) are for your experiment. You can then decide what **data** you need to collect and how to collect it. This means working out what **equipment** would be appropriate to use (see page 2) — it needs to be the right size and have the right level of sensitivity.

Next you write out a detailed **method** for your experiment. As part of this, you'll need to do a **risk assessment** and plan any safety precautions. This ensures that you minimise the risk of any dangers there might be in your experiment, such as harmful chemicals you might be using. Your method will also need to include details of what steps you are going to take to control any other variables (see below) which may affect your results.

Finally, it's time to carry out the experiment — by following your method you can gather evidence to address the aim of your experiment.

Variables

You probably know this all off by heart, but it's easy to get mixed up sometimes. So here's a quick recap. A **variable** is a quantity that has the potential to change, e.g. temperature, mass or volume. There are two types of variable commonly referred to in experiments:

Independent variable — the thing that you change in an experiment.

Dependent variable — the thing that you measure in an experiment.

As well as the independent and dependent variables, you need to think of all the other variables that could affect the result of the experiment and plan ways to keep each of them the same. These other variables are called **control variables**.

You could investigate the effect of temperature on the rate of a reaction using the apparatus in Figure 1, below:

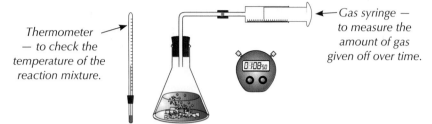

Thermometer — to check the temperature of the reaction mixture.

Gas syringe — to measure the amount of gas given off over time.

Figure 1: *Apparatus for measuring the rate of a reaction.*

- The independent variable is the temperature.
- The dependent variable is the amount of gas produced.
- For this experiment to be a fair test, all other variables must be kept the same. This includes the concentration and volume of solutions, the masses of solids, the pressure, the presence or absence of a catalyst, the surface area of any solid reactants, and the time over which the gas is collected.

Risks, hazards and ethical considerations

When you plan an experiment, you need to think about how you're going to make sure that you work safely. The first step is to identify all the hazards that might be involved in your experiment (e.g. dangerous chemicals or naked flames).

Then you need to come up with ways to reduce the risks that these hazards pose. This means things like wearing goggles and a lab coat to do any reactions that produce nasty gases, or heating anything flammable with a water bath or electric heater (rather than over a flame).

You need to make sure you're working ethically too. This is most important if there are other people or animals involved. You have to put their welfare first.

Choosing equipment

When you're planning an experiment, you should always plan to use equipment that is appropriate for the experiment you're doing.

Example

If you want to measure the amount of gas produced in a reaction, you need to make sure you use apparatus which will collect the gas, without letting any escape.

The equipment that you use needs to be the right size for your experiment too.

Example

If you're using a gas syringe to measure the volume of a gas produced by a reaction, it needs to be big enough to collect all the gas, or the plunger will be pushed out of the end. You might need to do some rough calculations to work out what size of equipment to use.

Figure 2: *Hazard symbols on bottles of chemicals can tell you if a chemical is dangerous, for example if it is flammable or toxic.*

Tip: Check the hazard data for all the chemicals when you are planning your experiment, so you can include any appropriate safety precautions in your plan.

The equipment also needs to have the right level of sensitivity.

Example

If you want to measure out 3.8 g of a substance, you need a balance that measures to the nearest tenth of a gram, not the nearest gram. If you want to measure out 6 cm^3 of a solution, you need to use a measuring cylinder that has a scale marked off in steps of 1 cm^3, not one that only has markings every 10 cm^3.

Tip: If you want to measure out a solution really accurately (e.g. 20.0 cm^3 of solution) you'll need to use a burette or a pipette.

Methods

When you come to write out your method, you need to keep all of the things on the preceding pages in mind.

The method must be clear and detailed enough for anyone to follow — it's important that other people can recreate your experiment and get the same results. Make sure your method includes:

■ All the substances needed and what quantity of each to use.

■ How to control variables.

■ The exact apparatus needed
(a diagram is often helpful to show the set-up).

■ Any safety precautions that should be taken.

■ What data to collect and how to collect it.

Evaluating experiment plans

If you ever need to evaluate the plan for someone else's experiment, you need to think about the same sorts of things that you would if you were designing the experiment yourself:

■ Does the experiment actually test what it sets out to test?

■ Is the method clear enough for someone else to follow?

■ Apart from the independent and dependent variables, is everything else going to be properly controlled?

■ Are the apparatus and techniques appropriate for what's being measured? Will they be used correctly?

■ Are enough repeated measurements going to be taken?

■ Is the experiment going to be conducted safely?

Exam Tip
This is the sort of thing you could be asked to do in an exam as a written test of your practical skills — either to evaluate an experiment plan, or to spot any issues with a small bit of it, e.g. the safety precautions.

2. Data

When you're planning an experiment you need to think carefully about what things you're going to change, what things you're going to measure, and how you're going to record your results.

Types of data

Experiments always involve some sort of measurement to provide data. There are different types of data — and you need to know what they are.

1. Discrete data

You get discrete data by counting — a discrete variable can only have certain values on a scale. E.g. the number of bubbles produced in a reaction would be discrete (see Figure 1). You can't have 1.25 bubbles. That'd be daft. Shoe size is another good example of a discrete variable.

2. Continuous data

A continuous variable can have any value on a scale. For example, the volume of gas produced or the mass of products from a reaction. You can never measure the exact value of a continuous variable.

3. Categoric data

A categoric variable has values that can be sorted into categories. For example, the colours of solutions might be blue, red and green (see Figure 2). Or types of material might be wood, steel, glass.

4. Ordered (ordinal) data

Ordered data is similar to categoric, but the categories can be put in order. For example, if you classified reactions as 'slow', 'fairly fast' and 'very fast' you'd have ordered data.

Tables of data

It's a good idea to set up a table to record the results of your experiment. Make sure that you include enough rows and columns to record all the data you need. You might also need to include a column for processing your data (e.g. working out an average).

Each column should have a heading so that you know what's going to be recorded where. In the column heading, you should include the units — this is to avoid having to write them repeatedly below.

Figure 1: *An acid-carbonate reaction. The number of bubbles produced is discrete data, but the volume of gas produced is continuous data.*

Figure 2: *Different coloured solutions. Colour is a type of categoric data.*

Temp. / °C	Time / s	Volume of gas evolved / cm³				Average volume of gas evolved / cm³
		Run 1	Run 2	Run 3	Run 4	
	10	8.1	8.4	8.2	8.1	
20	20	19.8	19.6	20.0	19.4	
	30	29.5	29.9	20.2	30.0	

Figure 3: *Table of results*

Calculating means

A mean is just an **average** of your repeated results. It's normally more **precise** than an individual result because it helps to balance out any random errors in your data (see page 11).

To calculate the mean result for a data point, first remove any anomalous results. Then add up all the other measurements from each repeat and divide by the number of (non-anomalous) measurements.

Tip: There's more about dealing with data (e.g. using the right number of significant figures and converting units) in the Maths Skills section on pages 256 to 262.

Example — **Maths Skills**

The average volume of gas evolved at each time point for the table in Figure 3 is:

- After 10 seconds: $(8.1 + 8.4 + 8.2 + 8.1) \div 4 = \mathbf{8.2\ cm^3}$
- After 20 seconds: $(19.8 + 19.6 + 20.0 + 19.4) \div 4 = \mathbf{19.7\ cm^3}$
- After 30 seconds: The result at 30 seconds in Run 3 is anomalously low, so ignore it when calculating the mean. $(29.5 + 29.9 + 30.0) \div 3 = \mathbf{29.8\ cm^3}$

Tip: Have a look at page 7 for more on anomalous results.

Types of graphs and charts

You'll often be expected to make a graph of your results. Graphs make your data easier to understand — so long as you choose the right type.

Bar charts

You should use a bar chart when one of your data sets is categoric or ordered data, like in Figure 4.

Tip: Use simple scales when you draw graphs — this'll make it easier to plot points.

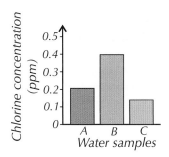

Figure 4: Bar chart to show chlorine concentration in water samples.

Pie charts

Pie charts are normally used to display categoric data, like in Figure 5.

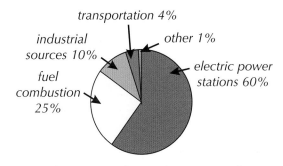

Figure 5: Pie chart to show sources of a country's sulfur dioxide emissions.

Exam Tip
Whatever type of graph you make, you'll only get full marks if you:

1. Choose a sensible scale — don't do a tiny graph in the corner of the paper.

2. Label both axes — including units.

3. Plot your points accurately — using a sharp pencil.

Scatter graphs

Scatter graphs, like the graphs shown in Figures 6 and 7, are great for showing how two sets of continuous data are related (or correlated — see page 7).

Don't try to join up all the points on a scatter graph — you should draw a line of best fit to show the trend of the data instead. A line of best fit can be a straight line, like the example in Figure 6...

Tip: A line of best fit should have about half of the points above it and half of the points below. You should ignore any anomalous results, like the one circled in Figure 6 — there's more about anomalous results coming up on page 7.

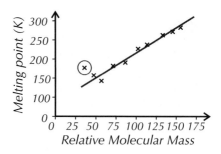

Figure 6: Scatter graph showing the relationship between M_r and melting point of some alcohols.

...or a curve, like the example in Figure 7.

Exam Tip
If you're asked to <u>sketch</u> a graph in an exam, you only need to show the labelled axes and the general shape of the line. You don't need to plot the values and draw the line accurately for a sketch graph.

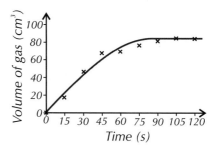

Figure 7: Scatter graph to show volume of gas evolved against time.

3. Analysing Results

Once you've got your results nicely presented you can start to draw a conclusion. But be careful — you may have a graph showing a lovely correlation, but that doesn't always tell you as much as you might think.

Anomalous results

Anomalous results are ones that don't fit in with the other values — this means they are likely to be wrong. They're often caused by experimental errors, e.g. if a drop in a titration is too big and shoots past the end point, or if a syringe plunger gets stuck whilst collecting gas produced in a reaction. When looking at results in tables or graphs, you need to check if there are any anomalies — you ignore these results when calculating means or drawing a line of best fit.

Tip: Even though you ignore anomalies when you're calculating means and drawing lines of best fit, if possible you should try to find an explanation for why they happened (and include it in your write-up).

Examples — Maths Skills

The table below shows the titre volume of a number of titrations.

Titration Number	1	2	3	4
Titre Volume (cm³)	15.20	15.30	15.70	15.25

Titre 3 isn't concordant with (doesn't match) the other results, so you need to ignore that one and just use the other three.

$$\text{mean} = \frac{15.20 + 15.30 + 15.25}{3} = 15.25 \text{ cm}^3$$

The graph below shows the volume of oxygen evolved against time for a rate of reaction experiment.

The result at 30 seconds doesn't fit with the other results, so you should ignore it when drawing the line of best fit.

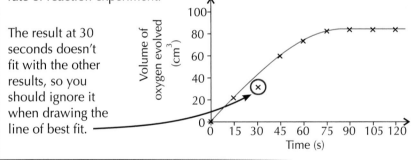

Tip: In titrations, saying that your results are concordant means that they're all within 0.1 cm³ of each other.

Tip: Saying that one result 'isn't concordant' with the other results is just another way of saying that it's an anomalous result.

Scatter graphs and correlation

Correlation describes the relationship between two variables — usually the independent one and the dependent one. Data can show positive correlation, negative correlation or no correlation. A scatter graph can show you how two variables are correlated:

Positive correlation
As one variable increases the other also increases.

Negative correlation
As one variable increases the other decreases.

No correlation
There is no relationship between the variables.

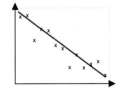
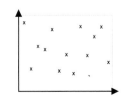

Correlation and cause

Ideally, only two quantities would ever change in any experiment — everything else would remain constant. But in experiments or studies outside the lab, you can't usually control all the variables. So even if two variables are correlated, the change in one may not be causing the change in the other. Both changes might be caused by a third variable.

— Example —

Some studies have found a correlation between drinking chlorinated tap water and the risk of developing certain cancers. So some people argue that this means water shouldn't have chlorine added. But it's hard to control all the variables between people who drink tap water and people who don't. It could be many lifestyle factors. Or, the cancer risk could be affected by something else in tap water — or by whatever the non-tap water drinkers drink instead.

Drawing conclusions

The data should always support the conclusion. This may sound obvious, but it's easy to jump to conclusions. Conclusions have to be specific — not make sweeping generalisations.

— Example —

The rate of an enzyme-controlled reaction was measured at 10 °C, 20 °C, 30 °C, 40 °C, 50 °C and 60 °C. All other variables were kept constant, and the results are shown in Figure 1.

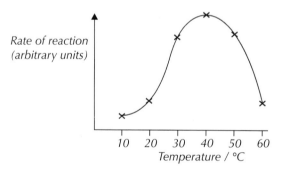

Figure 1: *Graph to show the effect of temperature on the rate of an enzyme-controlled reaction.*

A science magazine concluded from this data that this enzyme works best at 40 °C. The data doesn't support this exact claim. The enzyme could work best at 42 °C or 47 °C, but you can't tell from the data because increases of 10 °C at a time were used. The rate of reaction at in-between temperatures wasn't measured. All you know is that it's faster at 40 °C than at any of the other temperatures tested.

Also, the experiment only gives information about this particular enzyme-controlled reaction. You can't conclude that all enzyme-controlled reactions happen faster at a particular temperature — only this one. And you can't say for sure that doing the experiment at, say, a different constant pressure wouldn't give a different optimum temperature.

6. Evaluations and Errors

Now that you've drawn some conclusions from your experiment, you can consider how accurate those conclusions could be.

Evaluations

There are a few terms that you need to understand. They'll be useful when you're evaluating how convincing your results are.

1. Valid results

Valid results answer the original question. For example, if you haven't controlled all the variables your results won't be valid, because you won't be testing just the thing you wanted to.

2. Accurate results

Accurate results are those that are really close to the true answer.

3. Precise results

The smaller the amount of spread of your data around the mean (see page 11), the more **precise** it is. Calculating a mean (average) result from your repeats will increase the precision of your result, because it helps to reduce the effect of random errors on the answer (see page 17).

4. Repeatable results

Your results are **repeatable** if you get the same results when you repeat the experiment using the same method and the same equipment. You really need to repeat your readings at least three times to demonstrate that your results really are repeatable.

Tip: Results that fulfil all of these criteria are sometimes referred to as being reliable.

5. Reproducible results

Your results are **reproducible** if other people get the same results when they repeat your experiment.

Uncertainty

Any measurements you make will have **uncertainties** (or **errors**) in them, due to the limits of the sensitivity of the equipment.

Uncertainties are usually written with a ± sign, e.g. ±0.05 cm. The ± sign tells you the actual value of the measurement is likely to lie somewhere between your reading minus the uncertainty value and your reading plus the uncertainty value.

The uncertainty will be different for different pieces of equipment.

Figure 1: A conical flask where the graduations have an uncertainty of ±5%.

> **Example**
>
> Pieces of equipment such as pipettes and volumetric flasks will have uncertainties that depend on how well made they are.
>
> The manufacturers provide these uncertainty values — they're usually written on the equipment somewhere (see Figure 1).

For any piece of equipment you use that has a **scale**, the uncertainty will be **half** the **smallest increment** the equipment can measure, in either direction.

Example

The scale on a 50 cm³ burette usually has marks every 0.1 cm³. You should be able to tell which mark the level's closest to, so any reading you take won't be more than 0.05 cm³ out. So the uncertainty on your burette readings is ±0.05 cm³.

The level in the burette shown in Figure 2 is between the 44.9 cm³ and 45.0 cm³ marks. It's closer to 45.0 — so the level is between 44.95 and 45.0. So a reading of 45.0 cm³ can't have an uncertainty of more than 0.05 cm³.

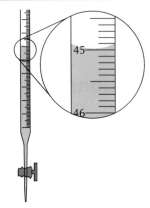

Figure 2: *Reading a volume from a burette.*

Tip: When you combine uncertainties, the overall uncertainty should be given to the same number of decimal places as the measurement.

If you use two readings to work out a measurement, you'll need to combine their uncertainties. For example, if you find a temperature change by subtracting a final temperature from an initial temperature, the uncertainty for the temperature change is the uncertainty for both readings added together.

Uncertainty on a mean

The uncertainty on a **mean** is equal to half the range of the measured values:

$$\text{uncertainty on a mean} = \frac{\text{largest measurement} - \text{smallest measurement}}{2}$$

Percentage uncertainty

If you know the **uncertainty** (or **error**) in a reading that you've taken, you can use it to calculate the percentage uncertainty in your measurement:

Tip: The same formula works for finding the percentage uncertainty on a <u>mean</u> value — just divide the uncertainty on the mean by the mean and multiply the result by 100.

$$\text{percentage uncertainty} = \frac{\text{uncertainty}}{\text{reading}} \times 100$$

Examples — Maths Skills

The EMF of an electrochemical cell is measured as 0.42 V. The voltmeter has an uncertainty of ±0.01 V. Find the percentage uncertainty on the EMF.

Percentage uncertainty is $\frac{0.01}{0.42} \times 100 = \textbf{2.4 \%}$.

In a titration a burette with an uncertainty of ±0.05 cm³ is used. The initial reading on the burette is 0.0 cm³. The final reading is 21.2 cm³. Calculate the percentage uncertainty on the titre value.

The titre value is $21.2 - 0.0 = 21.2$ cm³. The uncertainty on each burette reading is ±0.05 cm³. Two readings have been combined to find the titre value, so the total uncertainty is $0.05 + 0.05 = \pm 0.1$ cm³.

So, percentage uncertainty on the titre value

$= \frac{0.1}{21.2} \times 100 = 0.472 = \textbf{0.5\% (to 1 d.p)}$

Tip: Percentage uncertainty means you can directly compare the degree of uncertainty in different measurements as a proportion of the total measurement.

Percentage uncertainty is useful because it tells you how significant the uncertainty in a reading is in comparison to its size — e.g. an uncertainty of ±0.1 g is more significant when you weigh out 0.2 g of a solid than when you weigh out 100.0 g.

You can reduce uncertainty in your measurements by using the most sensitive equipment available. There's not much you can do about this at school or college though — you're stuck with whatever's available.

But there are other ways to lower the uncertainty in experiments. The larger the reading you take with a piece of equipment, the smaller the percentage uncertainty on that reading will be. Here's a quick example:

Example

If you measure out 5 cm³ of liquid in a measuring cylinder with an uncertainty of ±1 cm³ the percentage uncertainty is $(1 \div 5) \times 100 = 20\%$.

But if you measure 10 cm³ of liquid in the same measuring cylinder the percentage uncertainty is $(1 \div 10) \times 100 = 10\%$. You've just halved the percentage uncertainty.

So you can reduce the percentage uncertainty of this experiment by using a larger volume of liquid.

You can apply the same principle to other measurements too. For example, if you weigh out a small mass of a solid, the percentage uncertainty will be larger than if you weighed out a larger mass using the same balance.

Types of error

Errors in your results can come from a variety of different sources.

Random errors

Random errors cause readings to be spread about the true value due to the results varying in an unpredictable way. You get random error in all measurements and no matter how hard you try, you can't correct them. The tiny errors you make when you read a burette are random — you have to estimate the level when it's between two marks, so sometimes your figure will be above the real one and sometimes below.

Repeating an experiment and finding the mean of your results helps to deal with random errors. The results that are a bit high will be cancelled out by the ones that are a bit low. So your results will be more precise.

Systematic errors

Systematic errors cause each reading to be different to the true value by the same amount, i.e. they shift all of your results. They may be caused by the set-up or the equipment you're using. If the 10.00 cm³ pipette you're using to measure out a sample for titration actually only measures 9.95 cm³, your sample will be 0.05 cm³ too small every time you repeat the experiment.

Repeating your results won't get rid of any systematic errors, so your results won't get more accurate. The best way to get rid of systematic errors is to carefully calibrate any equipment you're using, if possible.

Tip: 'Calibration' is when you mark a scale on a measuring instrument or check the scale by measuring a known value.

Learning Objectives:

- Understand that an atom consists of a nucleus containing protons and neutrons surrounded by electrons.
- Be able to describe the properties of protons, neutrons and electrons in terms of relative charge and relative mass.
- Know the meaning of mass number (*A*) and atomic (proton) number (*Z*).
- Be able to determine the number of protons, neutrons and electrons in atoms and ions using mass number, atomic number and charge.
- Be able to explain the existence of isotopes.

Specification Reference 3.1.1.1, 3.1.1.2

Tip: The mass of an electron is negligible compared to a proton or a neutron — so you can usually ignore it.

Tip: You can find the symbols and atomic numbers for each element using the periodic table. The other number in the periodic table isn't the mass number though — it's the relative atomic mass, which is a bit different. (See page 17 for more on relative atomic mass.)

1. The Atom

Atoms are the basis of all of chemistry. You learned about them at GCSE and they're here again. They're super important.

The structure of the atom

All elements are made of **atoms**. Atoms are made up of 3 types of particle — **protons**, **neutrons** and **electrons**. Figure 1 shows how they are arranged in the atom.

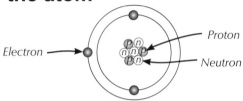

Figure 1: *The atom.*

Electrons have –1 charge. They whizz around the nucleus in orbitals, which take up most of the volume of the atom. Most of the mass of the atom is concentrated in the **nucleus**, although the diameter of the nucleus is rather titchy compared to the whole atom. The nucleus is where you find the protons and neutrons. The mass and charge of these subatomic particles is really small, so relative mass and relative charge are used instead. Figure 2 shows the relative masses and charges of protons, neutrons and electrons.

Subatomic particle	Relative mass	Relative charge
Proton	1	+1
Neutron	1	0
Electron, e^-	$\frac{1}{2000}$	–1

Figure 2: *Relative masses and charges of subatomic particles.*

Mass number and atomic number

You can figure out the number of protons, neutrons and electrons in an atom from the nuclear symbol.

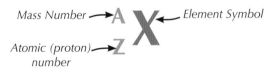

Figure 3: *Nuclear symbol.*

Mass number

This is the total number of protons and neutrons in the nucleus of an atom.

Atomic (proton) number

This is the number of protons in the nucleus of an atom — it identifies the element. All atoms of the same element have the same number of protons. Sometimes the atomic number is left out of the nuclear symbol, e.g. ^{7}Li. You don't really need it because the element's symbol tells you its value.

Atoms

For neutral atoms, which have no overall charge, the number of electrons is the same as the number of protons. The number of neutrons is just mass number minus atomic number (top minus bottom in the nuclear symbol). Figure 4 shows some examples.

Nuclear symbol	Atomic number, Z	Mass number, A	Protons	Electrons	Neutrons
$_{3}^{7}Li$	3	7	3	3	$7 - 3 = 4$
$_{35}^{79}Br$	35	79	35	35	$79 - 35 = 44$
$_{12}^{24}Mg$	12	24	12	12	$24 - 12 = 12$

Figure 4: *Calculating the number of neutrons in atoms.*

Ions

Atoms form **ions** by gaining or losing electrons. Ions have different numbers of protons and electrons — negative ions have more electrons than protons, and positive ions have fewer electrons than protons. For example:

┌─ Examples ─────────────────────────────

Br^- is a negative ion

The negative charge means that there's 1 more electron than there are protons. Br has 35 protons (see table above), so Br^- must have 36 electrons. The overall charge $= + 35 - 36 = -1$.

Mg^{2+} is a positive ion

The 2+ charge means that there's 2 fewer electrons than there are protons. Mg has 12 protons (see table above), so Mg^{2+} must have 10 electrons. The overall charge $= +12 - 10 = +2$.

Tip: Ions are easy to spot because they've always got a $^+$ or a $^-$ next to them. If they've got a $^+$ it means they've lost electrons; if it's a $^-$ then they've gained electrons. If there's a number next to the sign it means more than one electron has been lost or gained. For example, $^{3+}$ means 3 electrons have been lost, and $^{2-}$ means that 2 have been gained.

Isotopes

Isotopes of an element are atoms with the same number of protons but different numbers of neutrons.

┌─ Examples ─────────────────────────────

Chlorine-35 and chlorine-37 are examples of isotopes. They have different mass numbers, so they have different numbers of neutrons. Their atomic numbers are the same — both isotopes have 17 protons and 17 electrons.

Chlorine-35: $_{17}^{35}Cl$ **Chlorine-37:** $_{17}^{37}Cl$

$35 - 17 = 18$ neutrons $37 - 17 = 20$ neutrons

Here's another example — naturally occurring magnesium consists of 3 isotopes.

^{24}Mg (79%)	^{25}Mg (10%)	^{26}Mg (11%)
12 protons	12 protons	12 protons
12 neutrons	13 neutrons	14 neutrons
12 electrons	12 electrons	12 electrons

Figure 5: *Subatomic particles in Mg isotopes.*

Tip: You can show isotopes in different ways. For example, the isotope of magnesium with 12 neutrons can be shown as:

Magnesium-24,

^{24}Mg **or** $_{12}^{24}Mg$

The number and arrangement of the electrons decides the chemical properties of an element. Isotopes have the same configuration of electrons, so they have the same chemical properties. Isotopes of an element do have slightly different physical properties though, e.g. different densities and rates of diffusion. This is because physical properties tend to depend more on the mass of the atom.

Q1 Aluminium has the nuclear symbol: $^{27}_{13}\text{Al}$

    a) How many protons does an atom of aluminium have?

    b) How many electrons does an atom of aluminium have?

    c) How many neutrons does an atom of aluminium have?

Q2 A potassium atom has 19 electrons and 20 neutrons.

    a) How many protons does a potassium ion have?

    b) What is the mass number of a potassium atom?

    c) Write the nuclear symbol for potassium.

    d) Potassium can form ions with a charge of 1+.
       How many electrons does one of these potassium ions have?

Q3 Calcium has the nuclear symbol: $^{40}_{20}\text{Ca}$
It forms Ca^{2+} ions.

    a) How many electrons does a Ca^{2+} ion have?

    b) How many neutrons does a Ca^{2+} ion have?

Q4 Isotope X has 41 protons and 52 neutrons.
Identify which element isotope X is an isotope of.
Write the nuclear symbol of isotope X.

Q5 This question relates to the atoms or ions A to D:

    A $^{16}_{8}\text{O}^{2-}$ B $^{17}_{7}\text{N}$ C $^{20}_{10}\text{Ne}$ D $^{18}_{8}\text{O}$

Identify the similarity for each of the following pairs.

    a) A and C.

    b) A and D.

    c) B and C.

    d) B and D.

    e) Which two of the atoms or ions are isotopes of each other?
       Explain your reasoning.

Exam Tip
In your exams you'll probably have to look at the periodic table to find the nuclear symbol of an element — you won't usually be given it in the question like this.

Tip: Here we mean similarities in the numbers of protons, neutrons or electrons between the two atoms or ions.

Practice Questions — Fact Recall

Q1 Name the three types of particle found in an atom.

Q2 State where in the atom each of these particles would be found.

Q3 Give the relative masses of these particles.

Q4 What is a mass number?

Q5 What is an atomic number?

Q6 How can you work out the number of neutrons an atom has?

Q7 What are isotopes?

Q8 Why do isotopes have the same chemical properties?

Q9 Explain why isotopes can have different physical properties.

2. Atomic Models

Models of the atom are useful for understanding loads of ideas in chemistry. But the accepted model of the atom has changed throughout history.

Learning Objective:
- Appreciate that knowledge and understanding of atomic structure has evolved over time.

Specification Reference 3.1.1.1

Dalton's and Thomson's models

The **model** of the atom you need to know (the one on page 12) is one of the currently accepted ones. But in the past, completely different models were accepted, because they fitted the evidence available at the time. As scientists did more experiments, new evidence was found and the models were modified to fit it.

At the start of the 19th century John Dalton described atoms as solid spheres (see Figure 1) and said that different spheres made up the different elements.

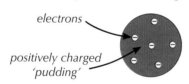

atoms of one element

atoms of another element

Figure 1: Dalton's model of the atom.

Tip: A model is a simplified description of a real-life situation. Scientists use models to help make complicated real-world science easier to explain or understand.

In 1897 J. J. Thomson concluded from his experiments that an atom must contain even smaller, negatively charged particles — electrons. The 'solid sphere' idea of atomic structure had to be changed. The new model was known as the 'plum pudding model' — see Figure 2.

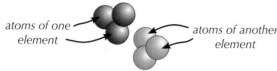

electrons

positively charged 'pudding'

Figure 2: Thomson's model of the atom.

Rutherford's model

In 1909 Ernest Rutherford and his students Hans Geiger and Ernest Marsden conducted their famous gold foil experiment. They fired alpha particles (which are positively charged) at a very thin sheet of gold. From the plum pudding model, they were expecting most of the alpha particles to be deflected slightly by the positive 'pudding' that made up most of an atom. In fact, most of the alpha particles passed straight through the gold atoms and a very small number were deflected backwards. So the plum pudding model couldn't be right.

So Rutherford came up with an idea that could explain this new evidence — the nuclear model of the atom (see Figure 4). In this, there's a tiny, positively charged nucleus at the centre, surrounded by a 'cloud' of negative electrons. Most of the atom is empty space.

Figure 3: Thomson and Rutherford worked together at Cambridge University.

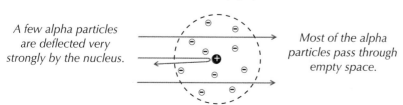

A few alpha particles are deflected very strongly by the nucleus.

Most of the alpha particles pass through empty space.

Figure 4: Rutherford's model of the atom.

Bohr's model

Scientists realised that electrons in a 'cloud' around the nucleus of an atom, as Rutherford described, would quickly spiral down into the nucleus, causing the atom to collapse. Niels Bohr proposed a new model of the atom with four basic principles:

- Electrons only exist in fixed orbits (shells) and not anywhere in between.
- Each shell has a fixed energy.
- When an electron moves between shells electromagnetic radiation is emitted or absorbed.
- Because the energy of shells is fixed, the radiation will have a fixed frequency.

Figure 6: *Rutherford and Bohr worked together at the University of Manchester.*

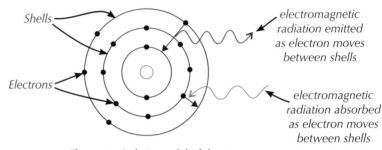

Shells

Electrons

electromagnetic radiation emitted as electron moves between shells

electromagnetic radiation absorbed as electron moves between shells

Figure 5: *Bohr's model of the atom.*

The frequencies of radiation emitted and absorbed by atoms were already known from experiments. The Bohr model fitted these observations.

Other atomic models

Scientists later discovered that not all the electrons in a shell had the same energy. This meant that the Bohr model wasn't quite right, so they refined it to include sub-shells (see page 25). The refined model fitted observations even better than Bohr's original model. We now know that the refined Bohr model is not perfect either — but it's still widely used to describe atoms because it is simple and explains many observations from experiments, like bonding and ionisation energy trends.

The most accurate model we have today is based on quantum mechanics. The quantum model explains some observations that can't be accounted for by the Bohr model, but it's a lot harder to get your head round and visualise. Scientists use whichever model is most relevant to whatever they're investigating.

Practice Questions — Fact Recall

Q1 Describe how J. J. Thomson's model of the atom was different from Dalton's model.

Q2 Explain how Rutherford's gold foil experiment provided evidence that Thomson's model was wrong.

Q3 Describe Rutherford's model of the atom.

Q4 Describe the main features of Bohr's model of the atom.

3. Relative Mass

The actual mass of an atom is very, very tiny. Don't worry about exactly how tiny for now, but it's far too small to weigh. So you usually talk about the mass of an atom compared to the mass of one carbon atom instead — this is its relative mass. You need to know about relative atomic mass, relative isotopic mass and relative molecular mass.

Relative atomic mass

The relative atomic mass, A_r, is the average mass of an atom of an element on a scale where an atom of carbon-12 is exactly 12. The relative atomic mass of each element is shown in the periodic table (see Figure 1).

Relative isotopic mass

Relative isotopic mass is the mass of an atom of an isotope of an element on a scale where an atom of carbon-12 is exactly 12.

Calculating relative atomic mass

Relative isotopic mass is usually a whole number (at AS and A-level anyway). Relative atomic mass is an average, so it's not usually a whole number.

┌─ **Example** ── **Maths Skills** ────────────────────

A natural sample of chlorine contains a mixture of ^{35}Cl and ^{37}Cl, whose relative isotopic masses are 35 and 37. 75% of the sample is ^{35}Cl and 25% is ^{37}Cl. You need to take these percentages into account when you work out the relative atomic mass of chlorine.

Relative atomic mass $= \dfrac{(35 \times 75) + (37 \times 25)}{100}$ ← isotopic masses × percentages

← total percentage
(75% ^{35}Cl + 25% ^{37}Cl)

Relative atomic mass = 35.5

Relative molecular mass

The relative molecular mass, M_r, is the average mass of a molecule on a scale where an atom of carbon-12 is exactly 12. To find the M_r, just add up the relative atomic mass values of all the atoms in the molecule.

┌─ **Example** ── **Maths Skills** ────────────────────

Calculating the relative molecular mass of C_2H_6O.
In one molecule of C_2H_6O there are 2 atoms of carbon, 6 of hydrogen and 1 of oxygen. The relative atomic masses (A_r) of each atom are shown in Figure 2.

6 H atoms A_r of H

M_r of $C_2H_6O = (2 \times 12.0) + (6 \times 1.0) + (1 \times 16.0) = 46.0$

2 C atoms A_r of C   1 O atom A_r of O

Calculating the relative molecular mass of C_4H_{10}.
In one molecule of C_4H_{10} there are 4 atoms of carbon and 10 of hydrogen.

M_r of $C_4H_{10} = (4 \times 12.0) + (10 \times 1.0) = 58.0$

Learning Objectives:
- Be able to define relative atomic mass (A_r) and relative molecular mass (M_r) in terms of ^{12}C.
- Understand that the term relative formula mass is used for ionic compounds.

Specification Reference 3.1.2.1

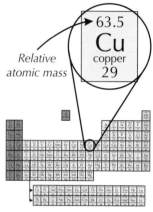

Figure 1: Location of relative atomic masses on the periodic table.

Tip: You could turn the percentages into decimals and multiply instead. For the chlorine example, 75% = 0.75 and 25% = 0.25, so the relative atomic mass is $(35 \times 0.75) + (37 \times 0.25)$ = 35.5

Atom	A_r
Carbon (C)	12.0
Hydrogen (H)	1.0
Oxygen (O)	16.0
Calcium (Ca)	40.1
Fluorine (F)	19.0

Figure 2: Table of relative atomic masses.

Relative formula mass

Tip: Relative molecular mass and relative formula mass are basically the same thing — it's just that ionic compounds aren't made of molecules so they can't have a molecular mass. You work them out the same way though.

Relative formula mass is the average mass of a formula unit on a scale where an atom of carbon-12 is exactly 12. It's used for compounds that are ionic (or giant covalent, such as SiO_2). To find the relative formula mass, just add up the relative atomic masses (A_r) of all the ions in the formula unit.

Examples — Maths Skills

Calculating the relative formula mass of CaF_2.
The formula unit of CaF_2 contains one Ca^{2+} ion and two F^- ions.

A_r of Ca (there's only one calcium ion)

$$M_r \text{ of } CaF_2 = 40.1 + (2 \times 19.0) = 78.1$$

2 ions of F^-   *A_r of F*

Calculating the relative formula mass of $CaCO_3$.
In the $CaCO_3$ formula unit, there is one Ca^{2+} ion and one CO_3^{2-} ion. The CO_3^{2-} ion contains 1 carbon atom and 3 oxygen atoms, so the A_r values of all these atoms need to be included in the calculation.

$$M_r \text{ of } CaCO_3 = 40.1 + 12.0 + (3 \times 16.0) = 100.1$$

Tip: The relative atomic masses (A_r) of all of the elements in these examples are shown in Figure 2.

Practice Questions — Application

Use the periodic table to help you answer Questions 1-3.

Q1 Find the relative atomic mass of the following elements:
 a) Rubidium
 b) Mercury
 c) Zinc

Q2 Find the relative molecular mass of the following compounds:
 a) NH_3
 b) CO_2
 c) $C_2H_4O_6N_2$

Q3 Find the relative formula mass of the following compounds:
 a) $CaCl_2$
 b) $MgSO_4$
 c) NaOH

Q4 A sample of tungsten is 0.1% ^{180}W, 26.5% ^{182}W, 14.3% ^{183}W, 30.7% ^{184}W and 28.4% ^{186}W. Calculate the A_r of tungsten.

Q5 A sample of zirconium is 51.5% ^{90}Zr, 11.2% ^{91}Zr, 17.1% ^{92}Zr, 17.4% ^{94}Zr and 2.8% ^{96}Zr. Calculate the A_r of zirconium.

Exam Tip
It's really important that you can calculate relative molecular mass (and relative formula mass). It crops up in loads of different calculations, so you need to be really confident that you can do it correctly.

Practice Questions — Fact Recall

Q1 What is relative atomic mass?
Q2 What is relative molecular mass?
Q3 What is relative formula mass?

4. The Mass Spectrometer

A mass spectrometer is a machine used to analyse elements or compounds. You need to know how a time of flight (TOF) mass spectrometer works.

How a mass spectrometer works

A mass spectrometer can give you information about the relative atomic mass of an element and the relative abundance of its isotopes, or the relative molecular mass of a molecule if you use it to analyse a compound.

There are four things that happen when a sample is squirted into a time of flight (TOF) mass spectrometer:

1. Ionisation

The sample needs to be ionised before it enters the mass spectrometer. Two ways doing this are:

Electrospray ionisation, — in this method the sample is dissolved in a solvent and pushed through a small nozzle at high pressure. A high voltage is applied to it, causing each particle to gain an H^+ ion. The solvent is then removed, leaving a gas made up of positive ions.

Electron impact ionisation — in this method, the sample is vaporised and an 'electron gun' is used to fire high energy electrons at it. This knocks one electron off one each particle, so they become +1 ions.

2. Acceleration

The positive ions are accelerated by an electric field. The electric field gives the same kinetic energy to all the ions. The lighter ions experience a greater acceleration — they're given as much energy as the heavier ions, but they're lighter, so they accelerate more.

3. Ion drift

Next, the ions enter a region with no electric field. They drift through it at the same speed as they left the electric field. So the lighter ions will be drifting at higher speeds.

4. Detection

Because lighter ions travel through the drift region at higher speeds, they reach the detector in less time than heavier ions. The detector detects the current created when the ions hit it and records how long they took to pass through the spectrometer. This data is then used to calculate the mass/charge values needed to produce a mass spectrum (see next page).

Learning Objectives:

- Know that the mass spectrometer gives accurate information about relative isotopic mass and also about the relative abundance of isotopes.
- Understand the principles of a simple time of flight (TOF) mass spectrometer, limited to ionisation, acceleration to give all ions constant kinetic energy, ion drift, ion detection and data analysis.
- Be able to interpret simple mass spectra of elements.
- Know that mass spectrometry can be used to identify elements.

Specification Reference 3.1.1.2

Tip: The particles need to be ionised when they're put into the mass spectrometer, otherwise they couldn't be accelerated by the electric field or detected by the ion detector.

Figure 1: *Electrospray ionisation apparatus.*

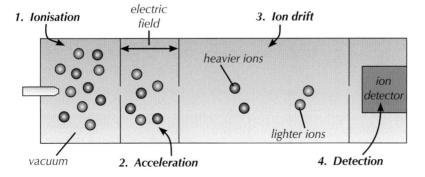

Figure 2: *Diagram showing how a TOF mass spectrometer works.*

Interpreting a mass spectrum

A **mass spectrum** is a type of chart produced by a mass spectrometer. It shows information about the sample that was passed through the mass spectrometer.

If the sample is an element, each line will represent a different isotope of the element (see Figure 3). The y-axis gives the abundance of ions, often as a percentage. For an element, the height of each peak gives the **relative isotopic abundance** (the relative amount of each isotope present in a sample). The x-axis units are given as a 'mass/charge' ratio. Since the charge on the ions is mostly 1+, you can usually assume the x-axis is simply the relative isotopic mass.

Tip: Mass/charge is often shown as *m/z*.

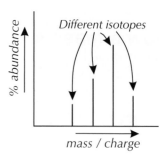

Figure 3: The mass spectrum of an element

Example — Maths Skills

The mass spectrum produced when a sample of chlorine is passed through a mass spectrometer is shown below.

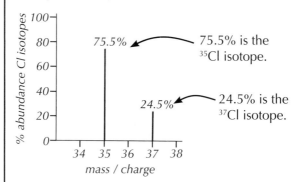

75.5% is the ^{35}Cl isotope.

24.5% is the ^{37}Cl isotope.

There are two peaks, so there are two isotopes of chlorine.

One peak has a mass/charge ratio of 35, so the relative isotopic mass of one isotope is 35. (Since the chlorine ions produced in a mass spectrometer have a charge of 1+ (Cl^+) and $35 \div 1 = 35$.)

The other peak has a mass/charge ratio of 37, so the relative isotopic mass of the other isotope is 37.

So, from the mass spectrum you can tell that there are two isotopes present, ^{35}Cl and ^{37}Cl. 75.5% of the sample is ^{35}Cl. 24.5% of the sample is ^{37}Cl.

Tip: The mass spectrometer produces ions by removing an electron, so the ions it produces are always positive — even for substances like chlorine which normally form negative ions.

Practice Question — Application

Q1 The mass spectrum for a sample of copper is shown below.

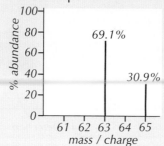

a) How many isotopes of copper were in the sample?

b) Give the relative isotopic mass of each isotope.

c) Give the relative isotopic abundance of each isotope.

Identifying elements

Mass spectrometry can be used to identify elements. Elements with different isotopes produce more than one line in a mass spectrum because the isotopes have different masses. This produces characteristic patterns which can be used as 'fingerprints' to identify certain elements.

> **Tip:** Many elements only have one stable isotope. They can still be identified in a mass spectrum by looking for a line at their relative atomic mass.

Example

Magnesium has three isotopes with the percentage abundances shown in the table below. If a sample being analysed contains magnesium, this isotopic distribution will show up in the mass spectrum.

Mg isotopes	% Abundance
^{24}Mg	79
^{25}Mg	10
^{26}Mg	11

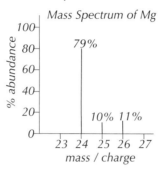

Mass Spectrum of Mg

Figure 4: The Phoenix Mars lander probe. The Phoenix lander had a mass spectrometer that was used to analyse dust on the surface of Mars.

Practice Question — Application

Q1 The table below shows the relative abundance of the stable isotopes of three elements.

Magnesium		Silicon		Indium	
^{24}Mg	79.0%	^{28}Si	92.2%	^{113}In	4.3%
^{25}Mg	10.0%	^{29}Si	4.7%	^{115}In	95.7%
^{26}Mg	11.0%	^{30}Si	3.1%		

The mass spectrum for a sample of an unknown element is shown on the right.

For each element listed in the table above, explain why the mass spectrum suggests that the unknown substance is unlikely to be that element.

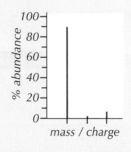

Practice Questions — Fact Recall

Q1 Name the four stages that a sample goes through in a time of flight mass spectrometer.

Q2 How does a time of flight mass spectrometer separate different ions?

Q3 What does the x-axis of a mass spectrum show?

Q4 Assuming all the ions in a sample have a charge of +1, how can you tell from the mass spectrum of an element how many isotopes are present in the sample?

Learning Objectives:
- Be able to calculate relative atomic mass from isotopic abundance, limited to mononuclear ions.
- Know that mass spectrometry can be used to determine relative molecular mass.

Specification Reference 3.1.1.2

5. Using Mass Spectra

Once you've analysed a sample in a mass spectrometer, you can use the mass spectrum that the sample produces to find out about what's in it.

Calculating relative atomic mass

You need to know how to calculate the relative atomic mass (A_r) of an element from a mass spectrum.

- Step 1: For each peak, read the % relative isotopic abundance from the y-axis and the relative isotopic mass from the x-axis. Multiply them together to get the total relative mass for each isotope.
- Step 2: Add up these totals.
- Step 3: Divide by 100 (since percentages were used).

Example — Maths Skills

Here's how to calculate A_r for magnesium, using the mass spectrum below:

Step 1:

Total mass of 1st isotope: $79 \times 24 = 1896$

Total mass of 2nd isotope: $10 \times 25 = 250$

Total mass of 3rd isotope: $11 \times 26 = 286$

Step 2:

$1896 + 250 + 286 = 2432$

Step 3:

$2432 \div 100 = 24.32$

So A_r (Mg) = 24.3 (to 3 s.f.)

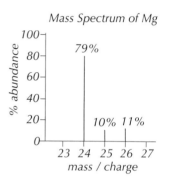

Mass Spectrum of Mg

Tip: Remember — the relative isotopic mass for each isotope is the same as its mass/charge value.

If the relative abundance is not given as a percentage, the total abundance may not add up to 100. In this case, don't panic. Just do steps 1 and 2 as above, but then divide by the total relative abundance instead of 100.

Example — Maths Skills

Here's how to calculate A_r for neon, using the mass spectrum below:

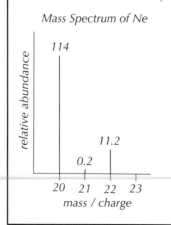

Mass Spectrum of Ne

Step 1:

Total mass of 1st isotope: $114 \times 20 = 2280$

Total mass of 2nd isotope: $0.2 \times 21 = 4.2$

Total mass of 3rd isotope: $11.2 \times 22 = 246.4$

Step 2:

$2280 + 4.2 + 246.4 = 2530.6$

Step 3:

$2530.6 \div (114 + 0.2 + 11.2) = 20.18...$

So A_r (Ne) = 20.2 (to 3 s.f.)

— total relative abundance

Tip: To find the total relative abundance, you just add up the relative abundances of all the isotopes in the sample.

Q1 Use the mass spectrum below to calculate the A_r of bromine.

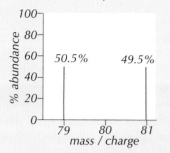

Q2 Use the mass spectrum below to calculate the A_r of boron.

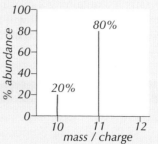

Exam Tip
Remember to check whether the y-axis shows relative abundance or percentage abundance before you start your calculation.

Q3 Use the mass spectrum below to calculate the A_r of lithium.

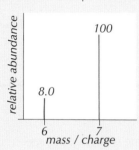

Q4 Use the mass spectrum below to calculate the A_r of gallium.

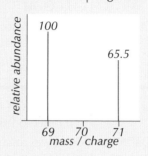

Calculating relative molecular mass

You can also get a mass spectrum for a molecular sample. A molecular ion, $M^+_{(g)}$, is formed when 1 electron is removed from the molecule. This gives a peak in the spectrum with a mass/charge ratio equal to the M_r of the molecule. This can be used to help identify an unknown compound. There's more about using mass spectra to identify compounds on page 246.

Tip: If a compound contains any atoms with more than one common isotope (e.g. chlorine), individual molecules will have different masses — so you'll get more than one molecular ion peak in its mass spectrum. But it's unlikely that this will come up in your exams, unless the examiners are feeling really mean.

┌─ **Example** ─────────────────────

A sample of an unknown alcohol was analysed in a mass spectrometer. The mass/charge ratio of its molecular ion was 46.0.

The M_r values of the first few alcohols are:

Alcohol	M_r
Methanol CH_3OH	$12.0 + (4 \times 1.0) + 16.0 = 32.0$
Ethanol C_2H_5OH	$(2 \times 12.0) + (6 \times 1.0) + 16.0 = 46.0$
Propanol C_3H_7OH	$(3 \times 12.0) + (8 \times 1.0) + 16.0 = 60.0$
Butanol C_4H_9OH	$(4 \times 12.0) + (10 \times 1.0) + 16.0 = 74.0$

The mass/charge ratio of the molecular ion on a mass spectrum is equal to the M_r value of the compound being analysed.
So the unknown alcohol must be ethanol ($M_r = 46.0$).

Tip: Some types of mass spectrometer produce spectra with many smaller peaks, representing fragment ions created when the molecular ion breaks up. You don't need to know about these fragmentation patterns for this course.

If you have a mixture of compounds with different M_r values, you'll get a peak for the molecular ion of each one.

┌─ **Example** ─────────────────────────────────────

A sample containing a mixture of ethanol ($M_r = 46.0$)
and butanol ($M_r = 74.0$) will produce a mass spectrum
with peaks at $m/z = 46.0$ and $m/z = 74.0$.

└──

Practice Questions — Application

Q1 Give the mass/charge ratio of the molecular ion formed when each of the following compounds is passed through a mass spectrometer.
   a) C_3H_6O
   b) $CH_3CH_2CHCH_2$
   c) CH_3CH_2COOH

Q2 A sample of an unknown gas was passed through a time of flight mass spectrometer. The spectrum produced had a peak with $m/z = 28$. Which of the following cannot be the gas contained in the sample?
   A   Nitrogen (N_2)
   B   Ethene (CH_2CH_2)
   C   Methylamine (CH_3NH_2)
   D   Carbon monoxide (CO)

Q3 A compound was analysed using a time of flight mass spectrometer. Its molecular ion produced a peak with $m/z = 34$ on the mass spectrum. Which of the following compounds could be responsible for this peak?
   A   Ethane (CH_3CH_3)
   B   Fluoromethane (CH_3F)
   C   Carbon dioxide (CO_2)
   D   Hydrogen cyanide (HCN)

Q4 A list of compounds and a mass spectrum are shown below. A mixture is known to contain a combination of some of the compounds listed. The mixture was analysed in a time of flight mass spectrometer and produced the peaks shown on the mass spectrum.

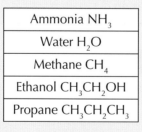

| Ammonia NH_3 |
| Water H_2O |
| Methane CH_4 |
| Ethanol CH_3CH_2OH |
| Propane $CH_3CH_2CH_3$ |

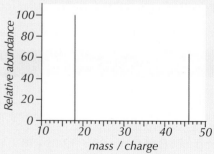

Which of the compounds listed must make up the mixture?

Figure 1: A scientist using a mass spectrometer to analyse a sample in a research lab.

6. Electronic Structure

Electronic structure is all about how electrons are arranged in atoms.

Learning Objective:
- Know the electron configurations of atoms and ions up to $Z = 36$ in terms of shells and sub-shells (orbitals) s, p and d.

  Specification Reference 3.1.1.3

Electron shells

In the currently accepted model of the atom, electrons have fixed energies. They move around the nucleus in certain regions of the atom called **shells** or **energy levels**. Each shell is given a number called the principal quantum number. The further a shell is from the nucleus, the higher its energy and the larger its principal quantum number — see Figure 1.

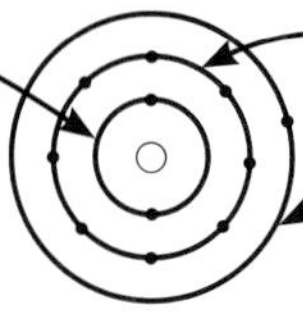

1st electron shell.
Principal quantum number = 1
This shell has the lowest energy.

2nd electron shell.
Principal quantum number = 2

3rd electron shell.
Principal quantum number = 3
This shell has the highest energy.

Figure 1: *A sodium atom.*

Experiments show that not all the electrons in a shell have exactly the same energy. The atomic model explains this — shells are divided up into **sub-shells**. Different electron shells have different numbers of sub-shells, which each have a different energy. Sub-shells can be s sub-shells, p sub-shells, d sub-shells or f sub-shells.

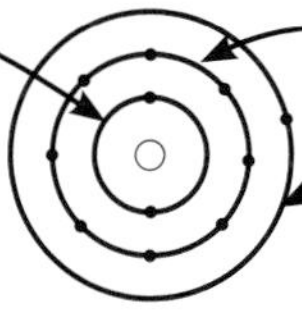

1st shell contains one sub-shell, 1s

The 4th shell contains four sub-shells, 4s, 4p, 4d and 4f.

2nd shell contains two sub-shells, 2s and 2p.

3rd shell contains three sub-shells, 3s, 3p and 3d.

Figure 2: *A sodium atom.*

Tip: Don't get confused by notation like 2s or 4f. The letter shows what type of sub-shell it is, the number shows what shell it's in. So 3p means a p sub-shell in the 3rd electron shell.

The sub-shells have different numbers of **orbitals** which can each hold up to 2 electrons. The table on the right shows the number of orbitals in each sub-shell. You can use it to work out the number of electrons that each shell can hold.

Sub-shell	Number of orbitals	Maximum electrons
s	1	$1 \times 2 = 2$
p	3	$3 \times 2 = 6$
d	5	$5 \times 2 = 10$
f	7	$7 \times 2 = 14$

Exam Tip
The f subshell has been included here so you know all the details of the first four shells. But in your exams you <u>won't</u> be asked to give the electron configuration of any atom that goes past the d subshell.

Example

The third shell contains 3 sub-shells: 3s, 3p and 3d.
- An s sub-shell contains 1 orbital, so can hold 2 electrons (1×2).
- A p sub-shell contains 3 orbitals, so can hold 6 electrons (3×2).
- A d sub-shell contains 5 orbitals, so can hold 10 electrons (5×2).

So the total number of electrons the third shell can hold is $2 + 6 + 10 = 18$

The table on the right shows the number of electrons that the first four electron shells can hold.

Shell	Sub-shells	Total number of electrons	
1st	1s	2	= 2
2nd	2s 2p	$2 + (3 \times 2)$	= 8
3rd	3s 3p 3d	$2 + (3 \times 2) + (5 \times 2)$	= 18
4th	4s 4p 4d 4f	$2 + (3 \times 2) + (5 \times 2) + (7 \times 2)$	= 32

Exam Tip
Make sure you learn how many electrons each shell and sub-shell can hold — you won't get far with electronic structures if you don't know these numbers.

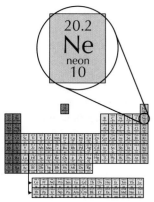

Figure 3: Neon has the atomic number 10, so an atom of neon must have 10 electrons.

Tip: Sub-shell notation is the 'standard' way of showing electron configurations. The other ways can be useful for showing the information in a different way, but if you're just asked to give 'the electron configuration' in an exam question, it will be the sub-shell notation they want.

Showing electron configurations

The number of electrons that an atom or ion has, and how they are arranged, is called its **electron configuration**. Electron configurations can be shown in different ways. For example, an atom of neon has 10 electrons — two electrons are in the 1s sub-shell, two are in the 2s sub-shell and six are in the 2p sub-shell. You can show this electron configuration in three ways...

1. Sub-shell notation

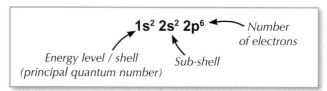

2. Arrows in boxes

Each of the boxes represents one orbital. Each of the arrows represents one electron. The up and down arrows represent the electrons spinning in opposite directions. Two electrons can only occupy the same orbital if they have opposite spin.

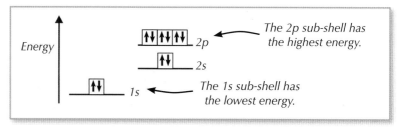

3. Energy level diagrams

These show the energy of the electrons in different orbitals, as well as the number of electrons and their arrangement.

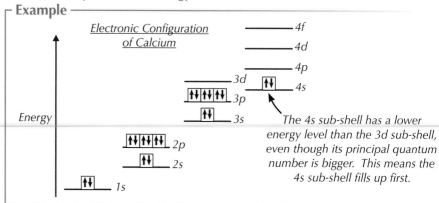

Working out electron configurations

You can figure out most electron configurations pretty easily, so long as you know a few simple rules:

Rule 1

Electrons fill up the lowest energy sub-shells first.

┌ **Example** ─────────────────────────────

Electronic Configuration of Calcium

4f
4d
4p
3d
3p
4s
3s

The 4s sub-shell has a lower energy level than the 3d sub-shell, even though its principal quantum number is bigger. This means the 4s sub-shell fills up first.

Energy

2p
2s

1s

Rule 2

Electrons fill orbitals in a sub-shell singly before they start sharing.

Examples

	1s	2s	2p			1s	2s	2p

Nitrogen   [↑↓] [↑↓] [↑][↑][↑]   Oxygen   [↑↓] [↑↓] [↑↓][↑][↑]

Tip: Elements with their outer electrons in an s sub-shell are called s block elements. Elements with their outer electrons in a p sub-shell are called p block elements. The configurations of d block elements (transition metals) are covered on the next page.

Rule 3

For the configuration of ions from the s and p blocks of the periodic table, just add or remove the electrons to or from the highest energy occupied sub-shell.

Examples

Mg atom: $1s^2 \, 2s^2 \, 2p^6 \, 3s^2$ Cl atom: $1s^2 \, 2s^2 \, 2p^6 \, 3s^2 \, 3p^5$

Mg^{2+} ion: $1s^2 \, 2s^2 \, 2p^6$ Cl^- ion: $1s^2 \, 2s^2 \, 2p^6 \, 3s^2 \, 3p^6$

Shortened electron configurations

Noble gas symbols in square brackets, such as [Ar], are sometimes used as shorthand in electron configurations. E.g. calcium ($1s^2 \, 2s^2 \, 2p^6 \, 3s^2 \, 3p^6 \, 4s^2$) can be written as $[Ar]4s^2$, where $[Ar] = 1s^2 \, 2s^2 \, 2p^6 \, 3s^2 \, 3p^6$.

Tip: Writing electron configurations using noble gas symbols can save time. Just make sure you've got your head around sub-shell notation before you start to use it — otherwise you're likely to get confused.

Practice Questions — Application

Q1 Use sub-shell notation to show the full electron configurations of the elements listed below.

a) Lithium

b) Titanium

c) Gallium

d) Nitrogen

Q2 Draw arrows in boxes to show the electron configurations of the elements listed below.

a) Calcium

b) Nickel

c) Sodium

d) Oxygen

Q3 Draw energy level diagrams to show the electron configurations of the elements listed below.

a) Magnesium

b) Argon

c) Carbon

d) Arsenic

Q4 Use sub-shell notation to show the full electron configurations of the ions listed below.

a) Na^+

b) O^{2-}

c) Al^{3+}

d) S^{2-}

Q5 Which elements have the electron configurations given below?

a) $[Ar]3d^{10} \, 4s^2 \, 4p^5$

b) $[Ne]3s^2 \, 3p^3$

c) $[Ar]3d^3 \, 4s^2$

Exam Tip
If a question asks you to give the <u>full</u> configuration, that means 'don't use the noble gas shorthand or you'll lose marks'.

Electron configuration of transition metals

Chromium (Cr) and copper (Cu) are badly behaved. They donate one of their
4s electrons to the 3d sub-shell. It's because they're happier with a more
stable full or half-full d sub-shell.

So, the electron configuration of a Cr atom is: $1s^2 \, 2s^2 \, 2p^6 \, 3s^2 \, 3p^6 \, 3d^5 \, 4s^1$
(not ending in $3d^4 \, 4s^2$ as you'd expect).

And the electron configuration of a Cu atom is: $1s^2 \, 2s^2 \, 2p^6 \, 3s^2 \, 3p^6 \, 3d^{10} \, 4s^1$
(rather than finishing with $3d^9 \, 4s^2$).

Here's another weird thing about transition metals — when they
become ions, they lose their 4s electrons before their 3d electrons.

> **Example**
>
> The electron configuration of an Fe atom is: $1s^2 \, 2s^2 \, 2p^6 \, 3s^2 \, 3p^6 \, 3d^6 \, 4s^2$
>
> To become an Fe^{3+} ion it loses three electrons — two 4s electrons
> and one 3d electron. So the electron configuration of an
> Fe^{3+} ion is : $1s^2 \, 2s^2 \, 2p^6 \, 3s^2 \, 3p^6 \, 3d^5$

Tip: Some people prefer
to write the 4s sub-shell
before the 3d subshell,
because it's lower in
energy. Either way is
fine — for example, you
could write the electron
configuration of copper
like this instead:

$1s^2 \, 2s^2 \, 2p^6 \, 3s^2 \, 3p^6 \, 4s^1 \, 3d^{10}$

Electronic structure and chemical properties

The number of outer shell electrons decides the chemical properties of an
element. You can use the periodic table to help you work them out.

- The s block elements (Groups 1 and 2) have 1 or 2 outer shell electrons.
  These are easily lost to form positive ions with an inert gas configuration.
  E.g. Na — $1s^2 \, 2s^2 \, 2p^6 \, 3s^1 \rightarrow$ Na$^+$ — $1s^2 \, 2s^2 \, 2p^6$ (the electron
  configuration of neon).

- The elements in Groups 5, 6 and 7 (in the p block) can gain 1, 2 or 3
  electrons to form negative ions with an inert gas configuration.
  E.g. O — $1s^2 \, 2s^2 \, 2p^4 \rightarrow$ O^{2-} — $1s^2 \, 2s^2 \, 2p^6$. Groups 4 to 7 can also
  share electrons when they form covalent bonds.

- Group 0 elements have completely filled s and p sub-shells and don't need
  to gain, lose or share electrons — their full sub-shells make them inert.

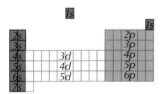

Figure 4: *Elements can
be classified as s block
elements, p block elements
or d block elements
depending on where they
are in the periodic table and
which sub-shell their outer
electrons are in.*

Tip: Group 0 elements
are know as the noble
gases (or the inert gases).

Practice Questions — Application

Q1 Give the full electron configuration of Cr^{2+} using sub-shell notation.

Q2 Give the full electron configuration of Ni^{2+} using sub-shell notation.

Q3 Give the full electron configuration of V^{3+} using sub-shell notation.

Practice Questions — Fact Recall

Q1 How many orbitals does a p sub-shell contain?

Q2 How many electrons can a p sub-shell hold?

Q3 How many electrons can the 3rd electron shell hold in total?

Q4 What does "electron configuration" mean?

Q5 The electron configuration shown here
is wrong. Explain why.

1s	2s	2p		
↑↓	↑↓	↑↓		

Q6 What is the electron configuration of a chromium atom?

Q7 The electron configuration of copper is $1s^2 \, 2s^2 \, 2p^6 \, 3s^2 \, 3p^6 \, 3d^{10} \, 4s^1$.
Why isn't it $1s^2 \, 2s^2 \, 2p^6 \, 3s^2 \, 3p^6 \, 3d^9 \, 4s^2$?

Q8 Describe the ions that Group 5, 6 and 7 elements form.

7. Ionisation Energies

Electrons might be tiny, but moving them around can be pretty hard work.

Ionisation

When electrons have been removed from an atom or molecule, it's been ionised. The energy you need to remove the first electron is called the **first ionisation energy**.

> The first ionisation energy is the energy needed to remove 1 electron from each atom in 1 mole of gaseous atoms to form 1 mole of gaseous 1+ ions.

You can write equations for this process — here's the equation for the first ionisation of oxygen:

$$O_{(g)} \rightarrow O^+_{(g)} + e^- \qquad \text{1st ionisation energy} = +1314 \text{ kJ mol}^{-1}$$

Here are a few rather important points about ionisation energies:

- You must use the gas state symbol, (g), because ionisation energies are measured for gaseous atoms.
- Always refer to 1 mole of atoms, as stated in the definition, rather than to a single atom.
- The lower the ionisation energy, the easier it is to form a positive ion.

Factors affecting ionisation energy

A high **ionisation energy** means there's a high attraction between the electron and the nucleus, so more energy is needed to remove the electron. There are three things that can affect ionisation energy:

1 Nuclear charge
The more protons there are in the nucleus, the more positively charged the nucleus is and the stronger the attraction for the electrons.

2 Distance from nucleus
Attraction falls off very rapidly with distance. An electron close to the nucleus will be much more strongly attracted than one further away.

3 Shielding
As the number of electrons between the outer electrons and the nucleus increases, the outer electrons feel less attraction to the nucleus. This lessening of the pull of the nucleus thanks to the inner electron shells is called shielding.

┌─ **Example** ──────────────────

There are only two electrons between the nucleus and the outer electron in a lithium atom.

There are ten electrons between the nucleus and the outer electron in a sodium atom — the shielding effect is greater.

The distance between the nucleus and the electron being removed is greater in the sodium atom.

Figure 1: *A lithium atom and a sodium atom.*

This means that lithium has a higher first ionisation energy (+519 kJ mol^{-1}) than sodium (+496 kJ mol^{-1}). (The shielding and distance from the nucleus have a bigger effect than the increased nuclear charge in this example.)

Learning Objectives:
- Know the meaning of the term ionisation energy.
- Be able to define first ionisation energy.
- Know how to write equations for first and successive ionisation energies.
- Explain how first and successive ionisation energies in Period 3 (Na–Ar) and in Group 2 (Be–Ba) give evidence for electron configuration in sub-shells and shells.

Specification Reference 3.1.1.3

Tip: You might see 'ionisation energy' referred to as 'ionisation enthalpy' instead.

Tip: You have to put energy in to remove an electron from an atom or molecule, so ionisation (in this sense) is always an endothermic process (see page 100).

Tip: You can only really see the effect of nuclear charge on ionisation energy if you compare atoms with outer electrons the same distance from the nucleus and with equal shielding effects. That only really happens with elements that are in the same period of the periodic table.

Second ionisation energy

The second ionisation energy is the energy needed to remove an electron from each ion in 1 mole of gaseous 1+ ions. For example:

$$O^+_{(g)} \rightarrow O^{2+}_{(g)} + e^-$$ 2nd ionisation energy = +3388 kJ mol^{-1}

Just like first ionisation energy, the value of second ionisation energy depends on nuclear charge, the distance of the electron from the nucleus and the shielding effect of inner electrons. Second ionisation energies are greater than first ionisation energies because the electron is being removed from a positive ion (and not an atom), which will require more energy. The electron configuration of the atom will also play a role in how much larger the second ionisation energy is than the first.

Example

The first electron removed from a lithium atom comes from the second shell ($2s^1$). The second electron removed comes from the first shell ($1s^2$). So the second electron to be removed is closer to the nucleus and experiences a stronger nuclear attraction than the first electron to be removed. The second electron will also not experience shielding from any inner electron shells, unlike the first electron. This means that the second ionisation energy of lithium is much higher than the first.

lithium atom   *Li$^+$ ion*

Figure 2: *The 2nd electron removed from lithium is closer to the nucleus than the 1st electron, so the attraction between it and the nucleus is greater.*

Successive ionisation energies

You can remove all the electrons from an atom, leaving only the nucleus. Each time you remove an electron, there's a successive ionisation energy.

You need to be able to write equations for any successive ionisation.

The general equation for the nth ionisation is:

$$X^{(n-1)+}_{(g)} \rightarrow X^{n+}_{(g)} + e^-$$

Example

The equation for the fifth ionisation of oxygen is: $O^{4+}_{(g)} \rightarrow O^{5+}_{(g)} + e^-$

Ionisation trends down Group 2

First ionisation energy decreases down Group 2.

Figure 3: *The first five Group 2 elements (left to right: beryllium, magnesium, calcium, strontium, barium).*

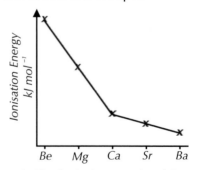

Figure 4: *First ionisation energies of Group 2.*

This provides evidence that electron shells really exist. If each element going down Group 2 has one more electron shell than the one above, the extra shell will shield the outer electrons from the attraction of the nucleus. Also, the extra shell means that the outer electrons will be further from the nucleus, so the nucleus's attraction will be reduced. It makes sense that both of these factors make it easier to remove outer electrons, resulting in lower ionisation energies.

Ionisation trends across periods

The graph below shows the first ionisation energies of the elements in Period 3.

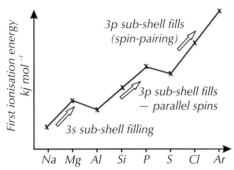

Figure 5: First ionisation energies of Period 3.

Exam Tip
You don't just need to be able to state the ionisation energy trends down Group 2 and across Period 3 — make sure you can explain them too. You could also be asked to explain why the ionisation energy for one element is higher or lower than it is for another element.

As you move across a period, the general trend is for the ionisation energies to increase — i.e. it gets harder to remove the outer electrons. This can be explained by the fact that the number of protons is increasing, which means a stronger nuclear attraction.

All the extra electrons are at roughly the same energy level, even if the outer electrons are in different orbital types. This means there's generally little extra shielding effect or extra distance to lessen the attraction from the nucleus. But, there are small drops between Groups 2 and 3, and 5 and 6. Tell me more I hear you cry. Well, alright then...

The drop between Groups 2 and 3 shows sub-shell structure.

> **Example**
>
> Mg $1s^2\,2s^2\,2p^6\,3s^2$ 1st ionisation energy = +738 kJ mol^{-1}
>
> Al $1s^2\,2s^2\,2p^6\,3s^2\,3p^1$ 1st ionisation energy = +578 kJ mol^{-1}
>
> - Aluminium's outer electron is in a 3p orbital rather than a 3s. The 3p orbital has a slightly higher energy than the 3s orbital, so the electron is, on average, to be found further from the nucleus.
>
> - The 3p orbital has additional shielding provided by the 3s electrons.
>
> These two factors together are strong enough to override the effect of the increased nuclear charge, resulting in the ionisation energy dropping slightly. This pattern in ionisation energies provides evidence for the theory of electron sub-shells.

The drop between Groups 5 and 6 is due to electron repulsion.

> **Example**
>
> P $1s^2\,2s^2\,2p^6\,3s^2\,3p^3$ 1st ionisation energy = +1012 kJ mol^{-1}
>
> S $1s^2\,2s^2\,2p^6\,3s^2\,3p^4$ 1st ionisation energy = +1000 kJ mol^{-1}
>
> The shielding is identical in the phosphorus and sulfur atoms, and the electron is being removed from an identical orbital.
>
> In phosphorus's case, the electron is being removed from a singly-occupied orbital. But in sulfur, the electron is being removed from an orbital containing two electrons.
>
> _Phosphorus:_ [Ne]   3s 3p   _Sulfur:_ [Ne]   3s 3p
>
> The repulsion between two electrons in an orbital means that electrons are easier to remove from shared orbitals. It's yet more evidence for the electronic structure model.

Tip: Writing out or drawing the electron configurations of elements can help you work out why their ionisation energies are what they are.
For example, drawing

will show you that the next electron being removed is paired, so there will be repulsion.

Ionisation energies and shell structure

If you know the successive ionisation energies of an element you can work out the number of electrons in each shell of the atom and which group the element is in. A graph of successive ionisation energies provides evidence for the shell structure of atoms (see Figure 6).

Tip: The *y*-axis of this graph has a log (logarithmic) scale. Log scales go up in powers of a number (e.g. 1, 10, 100, etc.) rather than in units (1, 2, 3, etc.). Log scales are often used for graphs like this because ionisation energy values have such a huge range.

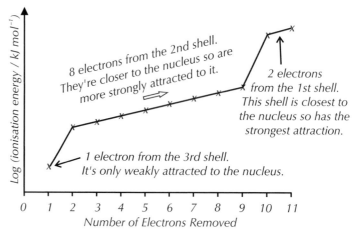

8 electrons from the 2nd shell. They're closer to the nucleus so are more strongly attracted to it.

2 electrons from the 1st shell. This shell is closest to the nucleus so has the strongest attraction.

1 electron from the 3rd shell. It's only weakly attracted to the nucleus.

Figure 6: *Successive ionisation energies of sodium.*

Within each shell, successive ionisation energies increase. This is because electrons are being removed from an increasingly positive ion — there's less repulsion amongst the remaining electrons, so they're held more strongly by the nucleus. The big jumps in ionisation energy happen when a new shell is broken into — an electron is being removed from a shell closer to the nucleus.

Graphs like the one in Figure 7 can tell you which group of the periodic table an element belongs to. Just count how many electrons are removed before the first big jump to find the group number.

> **Example**
>
> In Figure 6, one electron is removed before the first big jump — sodium is in Group 1.

These graphs can be used to predict the electronic structure of an element. Working from right to left, count how many points there are before each big jump to find how many electrons are in each shell, starting with the first.

> **Example**
>
> Working from right to left in Figure 6, the graph has 2 points on the right-hand side, then a jump, then 8 points, a jump, and 1 final point. Sodium has 2 electrons in the first shell, 8 in the second and 1 in the third.

Practice Questions — Application

Q1 a) Write an equation for the first ionisation of chlorine.

   b) Write an equation for the second ionisation of chlorine.

Q2 Sketch a graph showing the trend of the first ionisation energies of the elements in Period 2.

Q3 The first ionisation energy of nitrogen is +1402 kJ mol^{-1}.
    The first ionisation energy of oxygen is +1314 kJ mol^{-1}.
    Explain why oxygen has a lower first ionisation energy than nitrogen.

Q4 The first ionisation energy of beryllium is +900 kJ mol^{-1}.
    The first ionisation energy of boron is +801 kJ mol^{-1}.
    Explain why boron has a lower first ionisation energy than beryllium.

Q5 The first ionisation energy of lithium is +519 kJ mol^{-1}.
    The second ionisation energy is +7298 kJ mol^{-1} and the
    third ionisation energy is +11815 kJ mol^{-1}.

    Explain why the difference between the first and second ionisation
    energies is much greater than the difference between the second and
    third ionisation energies.

Q6 The graph below shows the successive ionisation energies
    of an element.

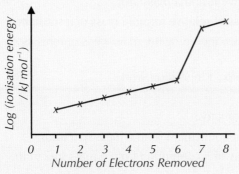

    a) Which group is this element in?

    b) State the number of electrons it has in each shell.

    c) Name the element.

Q7 a) Sketch a graph showing the pattern of the successive
        ionisation energies of magnesium.

    b) Explain the shape of the graph.

Exam Tip
If you get a question like this in the exam asking you to compare ionisation energies, make sure you remember the three factors that affect ionisation energy. Work out how the factors differ between each element, and you should have a very good idea of the answer.

Practice Questions — Fact Recall

Q1 Define first ionisation energy.

Q2 How does the number of protons in an atom affect its
    first ionisation energy?

Q3 Give two other factors that affect first ionisation energy.

Q4 Define second ionisation energy.

Q5 Explain why successive ionisation energies increase within
    each shell of an atom.

Q6 What happens to the first ionisation energy of elements in Group 2
    as you go down the group?

Q7 What is the general trend in first ionisation energy across a period?

Exam Tip
Make sure you learn the definition of first ionisation energy — if it comes up in an exam question it'll be a nice easy way to get marks.

Section Summary

Make sure you know...

- The structure of the atom — including the location, relative masses and relative charges of protons, neutrons and electrons.
- What nuclear symbols, mass numbers (A) and atomic (proton) numbers (Z) are.
- What atoms, ions and isotopes are.
- How to calculate the number of protons, neutrons and electrons in an atom or ion using its mass number, proton number and charge.
- How the accepted model of the structure of the atom has changed over time.
- What relative atomic mass (A_r) is.
- What relative isotopic mass is.
- How to calculate relative atomic mass.
- What relative molecular mass (M_r) and relative formula mass are.
- How to calculate the relative molecular mass or relative formula mass of a substance.
- How a time of flight mass spectrometer works, including the main steps of ionisation, acceleration, ion drift and detection.
- How electrospray ionisation and electron impact ionisation work.
- How to interpret a mass spectrum.
- How to identify elements using mass spectrometry.
- How to calculate the relative atomic mass of an element from a mass spectrum.
- How to calculate the relative molecular mass of a compound from a mass spectrum.
- How electrons are arranged in energy levels (shells) within an atom.
- That each electron shell is divided into sub-shells.
- That sub-shells can be s, p, d or f sub-shells.
- That each sub-shell is divided into orbitals.
- How many electrons each orbital and sub-shell can hold.
- How to show electron configurations using sub-shell notation, arrows in boxes and energy level diagrams.
- How to work out electron configurations of the first 36 elements of the periodic table and their ions (including the electron configurations of chromium and copper).
- What ionisation energy and first ionisation energy are.
- The factors that affect ionisation energy.
- How to write equations to show ionisation energies.
- The trend in ionisation energy down Group 2, and the reasons for this trend.
- How ionisation energy changes across Period 3, and the reasons for these changes.
- How the successive ionisation energies of an element are related to its electron shell structure.
- How ionisation energies give evidence for electron arrangement in shells and sub-shells.

Exam-style Questions

1   An element, Z, has the electron configuration $1s^2\ 2s^2\ 2p^6\ 3s^2\ 3p^2$.
A sample of element Z is passed through a mass spectrometer.

1.1   Identify element Z.

(1 mark)

1.2   State the block of the periodic table that element Z belongs to.

(1 mark)

1.3   Give the full electron configuration of the particle formed when a single electron is removed from an atom of element Z.

(1 mark)

The mass spectrum produced when element Z is passed through the mass spectrometer is shown below.

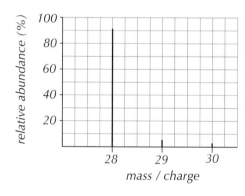

1.4   State how many different isotopes of element Z were present in the sample.

(1 mark)

1.5   Give the nuclear symbol of the isotope in the sample with the highest relative isotopic abundance.

(2 marks)

1.6   State whether you would expect the isotopes of element Z to have the same chemical properties or different chemical properties. Explain your answer.

(1 mark)

2   Compound Q is analysed in a time of flight mass spectrometer. A sample of compound Q in solution is injected into the mass spectrometer at high pressure. A high voltage is then applied to remove electrons from atoms of the sample.

2.1   Give the name of this process.

(1 mark)

2.2   Explain how a time of flight mass spectrometer separates charged particles with different mass/charge ratios.

(4 marks)

3   The table below shows the first ionisation energies of some of the elements in Period 3.

Element	Na	Mg	Al	Si	P	S	Cl
First ionisation energy / kJ mol^{-1}	+496	+738	+578		+1012	+1000	+1251

3.1   State the general trend in first ionisation energy across Period 3.

(1 mark)

3.2   Write an equation for the first ionisation of sodium.

(1 mark)

3.3   Explain why the first ionisation energy of aluminium is lower than the first ionisation energy of magnesium.

(3 marks)

3.4   In which of the following ranges would you expect to find the first ionisation energy of silicon?

A   +300 kJ mol^{-1} to +600 kJ mol^{-1}

B   +600 kJ mol^{-1} to +1000 kJ mol^{-1}

C   +1000 kJ mol^{-1} to +1200 kJ mol^{-1}

D   +1200 kJ mol^{-1} to +1600 kJ mol^{-1}

(1 mark)

3.5   Use your understanding of the electronic structures of aluminium, silicon and phosphorus to explain your answer to question 3.4.

(4 marks)

3.6   Explain why the first ionisation energy of sulfur is lower than the first ionisation energy of phosphorus.

(2 marks)

4   Vanadium and copper are both transition metals.

4.1   Give the full electron configuration of vanadium.

(1 mark)

4.2   When vanadium is ionised it can form V^{2+} and V^{3+} ions. Give the full electron configurations of both of these ions.

(2 marks)

4.3   Give the full electron configuration of copper and explain why it deviates from the normal rules of electron configuration.

(2 marks)

4.4   Identify the transition metal with the electron configuration $1s^2\ 2s^2\ 2p^6\ 3s^2\ 3p^6\ 3d^6\ 4s^2$.

(1 mark)

4.5   A transition metal is ionised to form a 2+ ion. The ion has the electron configuration $1s^2\ 2s^2\ 2p^6\ 3s^2\ 3p^6\ 3d^5$. Identify the transition metal.

(1 mark)

5 The relative isotopic masses and relative abundances of element X were identified using mass spectrometry. The isotopes and their relative abundances are shown in the table below.

Isotope	Relative abundance
^{20}X	90.48
^{21}X	0.27
^{22}X	9.25

5.1 Calculate the relative atomic mass of element X, and identify the element.

(3 marks)

5.2 State the number of protons, neutrons and electrons in an atom of each isotope of element X.

(3 marks)

Isotopes of an element, such as the isotopes of element X, have the same proton number but different mass numbers.

5.3 Define the term **mass number (A)**.

(1 mark)

5.4 Define the term **proton number (Z)**.

(1 mark)

The first ionisation energy of element X is +2080.7 kJ mol^{-1}. Atoms of another element, element A, contain 24 more electrons than atoms of element X.

5.5 Define the term **first ionisation energy**.

(2 marks)

5.6 Using your understanding of the factors that affect ionisation energy, state how you would expect the first ionisation energy of element A to be different from element X. Explain your answer.

(2 marks)

5.7 There is a large jump in the trend of the successive ionisation energies of element X between the removal of the eight and ninth electrons.

Use your understanding of the factors that affect ionisation energy to explain why this is the case.

(3 marks)

Unit 1 Section 2: Amount of Substance

Learning Objectives:

- Understand the concept of a mole as applied to electrons, atoms, molecules, ions, formulas and equations.
- Understand the concept of the Avogadro constant and use it to carry out calculations.
- Be able to carry out calculations using mass of substance, M_r and amount in moles.
- Understand the concentration of a substance in solution, measured in mol dm^{-3}.
- Be able to carry out calculations using concentration, volume and amount of substance in a solution.

Specification Reference 3.1.2.2

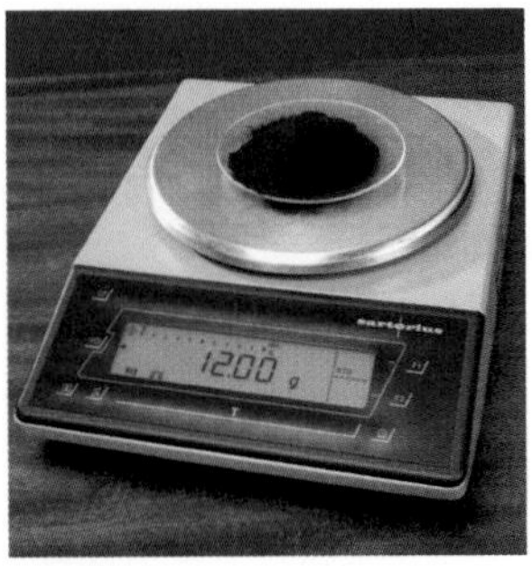

Figure 1: *1 mole of carbon.*

Tip: The Avogadro constant's a huge number so it's always written in standard form. There's more about standard form on pages 256-257.

1. The Mole

Amount of substance is a really important idea in chemistry. It's all about working out exactly how much of a chemical you have and what amount of it is reacting with other chemicals. Then you can use that information in all sorts of calculations to do with things like mass, concentration and volume.

What is a mole?

Amount of substance is measured using a unit called the **mole** (mol for short) and given the symbol n. One mole is roughly 6.02×10^{23} particles (the Avogadro constant). It doesn't matter what the particles are. They can be atoms, molecules, electrons, ions, penguins — anything.

Examples

1 mole of carbon (C) contains 6.02×10^{23} atoms.

1 mole of methane (CH_4) contains 6.02×10^{23} molecules.

1 mole of sodium ions (Na^+) contains 6.02×10^{23} ions.

1 mole of electrons contains 6.02×10^{23} electrons.

The Avogadro constant

You can use the **Avogadro constant** to convert between number of particles and number of moles. Just remember this formula:

Number of particles = Number of moles × Avogadro's constant

Examples — Maths Skills

How many atoms are in 0.450 moles of pure iron?

Number of atoms = $0.450 \times (6.02 \times 10^{23}) = 2.71 \times 10^{23}$

How many ions are in 0.724 moles of calcium ions?

Number of ions = $0.724 \times (6.02 \times 10^{23}) = 4.36 \times 10^{23}$

You can rearrange the formula and use it to work out the number of moles:

Example — Maths Skills

How many moles are in 1.14×10^{24} molecules of NH_3?

Rearrange the formula to find number of moles (divide both sides by the Avogadro constant):

number of moles = number of particles ÷ Avogadro's constant

Number of moles of NH_3 = $(1.14 \times 10^{24}) \div (6.02 \times 10^{23}) = 1.89$ moles

Calculations with moles

1 mole of any substance has a mass that's the same as its relative molecular mass (M_r) in grams.

> **Example**
>
> **What is the mass of 1 mole of water?**
>
> M_r of H_2O = (1.0 × 2) + 16.0 = 18.0, so 1 mole of water has a mass of 18.0 g.

This means that you can work out how many moles of a substance you have from the mass of the substance and its relative molecular mass (M_r). Here's the formula you need:

$$\text{Number of moles} = \frac{\text{mass of substance}}{M_r}$$

> **Examples** — **Maths Skills**
>
> **How many moles of aluminium oxide are present in 5.10 g of Al_2O_3?**
>
> M_r of Al_2O_3 = (2 × 27.0) + (3 × 16.0) = 102
>
> Number of moles of Al_2O_3 = $\frac{5.10}{102}$ = 0.0500 moles
>
> **How many moles of calcium bromide are present in 39.98 g of $CaBr_2$?**
>
> M_r of $CaBr_2$ = 40.1 + (2 × 79.9) = 199.9
>
> Number of moles of $CaBr_2$ = $\frac{39.98}{199.9}$ = 0.200 moles

You can also rearrange the formula and use it to work out either the mass of a substance or its relative molecular mass:

> **Examples** — **Maths Skills**
>
> **What is the mass of 2 moles of NaF?**
>
> Rearrange the formula to find mass (multiply both sides by relative molecular mass):
>
> $$\text{mass of substance} = \text{number of moles} \times M_r$$
>
> M_r of NaF = 23.0 + 19.0 = 42.0
>
> Mass of 2 moles of NaF = 2 × 42.0 = 84.0 g
>
> **0.0500 moles of a solid weighs 2.60 g. Find its relative molecular mass.**
>
> Rearrange the formula:
>
> $$M_r = \text{mass} \div \text{number of moles}$$
>
> So, relative molecular mass = 2.60 ÷ 0.0500 = 52.0.

Exam Tip
This formula crops up in all sorts of chemistry calculations — you'll need to know it off by heart for your exams. You might see it with 'molar mass' instead of M_r — molar mass just means 'the mass of 1 mole of a substance', so its value for a compound is the same as the M_r.

Exam Tip
Make sure you give your final answer to an appropriate number of significant figures. See page 257 for more about this.

Tip: If it helps you to remember how to rearrange the equation, you could use this formula triangle:

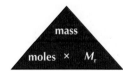

Just cover the thing you want to calculate to find the right formula.

(For example, if you cover mass it will tell you that to calculate mass you multiply moles by M_r.)

Practice Questions — Application

Q1 How many molecules are in 0.360 moles of H_2O?

Q2 How many ions are in 0.0550 moles of magnesium ions?

Q3 1.5 moles of a mystery compound weighs 66 g.
    Find its relative molecular mass.

Q4 How many moles of sodium nitrate are present in 212.5 g of $NaNO_3$?

Q5 How many moles of zinc chloride are present in 15.5 g of $ZnCl_2$?

Q6 What is the mass of 2 moles of NaCl?

Tip: 1 dm³ is the same as 1000 cm³ or 1 litre.

Exam Tip
You need to know all of the formulas in this section by heart — so look out for the formula boxes, and learn them.

Tip: This is another formula that you can stick in a formula triangle if it helps you:

Exam Tip
Remember to watch out for the units in this type of calculation. Double check whether the volume you've been given is in cm³ or dm³.

Moles and concentration

The concentration of a solution is how many moles are dissolved per 1 dm³ of solution. The units are mol dm⁻³.

Here's the formula to find the number of moles.

$$\text{Number of moles} = \frac{\text{Concentration} \times \text{Volume (in cm}^3)}{1000}$$

Or: Number of moles = Concentration × Volume (in dm³)

You need to be able to use these formulas to do calculations in the exam.

Examples — Maths Skills

How many moles of lithium chloride are present in 25 cm³ of a 1.2 mol dm⁻³ solution of LiCl?

$$\text{Number of moles} = \frac{\text{concentration} \times \text{volume (in cm}^3)}{1000}$$

$$= \frac{1.2 \times 25}{1000} = 0.030 \text{ moles}$$

A solution of $FeCl_3$ contains 0.2 moles of iron(III) chloride in 0.4 dm³. What is the concentration of the solution?

Rearrange the formula to find concentration (divide both sides by volume):

$$\text{concentration} = \frac{\text{number of moles}}{\text{volume (in dm}^3)}$$

$$= \frac{0.2}{0.4} = 0.5 \text{ mol dm}^{-3}$$

A 0.50 mol dm⁻³ solution of zinc sulfate contains 0.080 moles of $ZnSO_4$. What volume does the solution occupy?

Rearrange the formula to find volume (divide both sides by volume):

$$\text{volume (in dm}^3) = \frac{\text{number of moles}}{\text{concentration}}$$

$$= \frac{0.080}{0.50} = 0.16 \text{ dm}^3$$

You might be asked to combine a concentration calculation with a moles and mass calculation. This just means using both formulas, one after the other.

Example — Maths Skills

What mass of sodium hydroxide needs to be dissolved in water to give 50.0 cm³ of solution with a concentration of 2.00 mol dm⁻³?

First look at the question and see what information it gives you. You've got concentration and volume — so you can work out number of moles.

$$\text{Number of moles} = \frac{2.00 \times 50.0}{1000} = 0.100 \text{ moles of NaOH}$$

Then you can use this to work out the mass using the equation
number of moles = mass ÷ M_r

M_r of NaOH = 23.0 + 16.0 + 1.0 = 40.0

Mass = number of moles × M_r = 0.100 × 40.0 = 4.00 g

Q1 How many moles of potassium phosphate are present in 50 cm^3 of a 2 mol dm^{-3} solution?

Q2 How many moles of sodium chloride are present in 0.5 dm^3 of a 0.08 mol dm^{-3} solution?

Q3 How many moles of silver nitrate are present in 30 cm^3 of a 0.70 mol dm^{-3} solution?

Q4 A solution contains 0.25 moles of copper bromide in 0.50 dm^3. What is the concentration of the solution?

Q5 A solution contains 0.080 moles of lithium chloride in 0.75 dm^3. What is the concentration of the solution?

Q6 A solution contains 0.10 moles of magnesium sulfate in 36 cm^3. What is the concentration of the solution?

Q7 A solution of calcium chloride contains 0.46 moles of $CaCl_2$. The concentration of the solution is 1.8 mol dm^{-3}. What volume, in dm^3, does the solution occupy?

Q8 A solution of copper sulfate contains 0.010 moles of $CuSO_4$. The concentration of the solution is 0.55 mol dm^{-3}. What volume, in dm^3, does the solution occupy?

Q9 The molecular formula of sodium oxide is Na_2O. What mass of sodium oxide would you have to dissolve in 75 cm^3 of water to make a 0.80 mol dm^{-3} solution?

Q10 The molecular formula of cobalt(II) bromide is $CoBr_2$. What mass of cobalt(II) bromide would you have to dissolve in 30 cm^3 of water to make a 0.50 mol dm^{-3} solution?

Q11 A solution is made by dissolving 4.08 g of a compound in 100 cm^3 of pure water. The solution has a concentration of 1.20 mol dm^{-3}. What is the relative molecular mass of the compound?

Figure 2: *Preparing a solution of copper sulfate.*

Q1 a) How many particles are there in a mole?

   b) What's the name for this special number?

Q2 What's the formula that links number of particles and number of moles?

Q3 What's the formula that links relative molecular mass and number of moles?

Q4 How many cm^3 are there in one dm^3?

Q5 Give an example of the units that you could use to describe concentration.

Q6 What's the formula that links number of moles and concentration? (Write it out twice, once using each volume measurement.)

Learning Objectives:

- Be able to recall the ideal gas equation $pV = nRT$ with the variables in SI units.
- Be able to use the ideal gas equation in calculations.
  Specification Reference 3.1.2.3

2. Gases and the Mole

Lots of things in chemistry relate back to how many moles of a substance you have. And that includes how much volume a gas takes up.

The ideal gas equation

In the real world (and AQA exam questions), it's not always room temperature and pressure. The **ideal gas equation** lets you find the number of moles in a certain volume at any temperature and pressure:

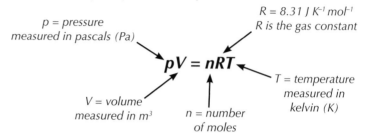

$$pV = nRT$$

p = pressure measured in pascals (Pa)

$R = 8.31 \, J \, K^{-1} \, mol^{-1}$
R is the gas constant

T = temperature measured in kelvin (K)

V = volume measured in m^3

n = number of moles

You could be asked to find any of the values in the equation. Its the same old idea — just rearrange the equation and put in the numbers you know.

Tip: All of these units are SI units. That means they're part of an agreed system of measurements used by scientists all over the world.

Exam Tip
Make sure you've learnt the ideal gas equation off by heart, because you <u>won't</u> be given it in the exam. You <u>will</u> be given the value of the gas constant if you need it though. (In fact, if you're given the value of the gas constant in a question, it's a good clue that you need to use the ideal gas equation.)

--- **Examples** — **Maths Skills** ---

How many moles are there in 0.0600 m^3 of hydrogen gas, at 283 K and 50 000 Pa?

Rearrange the equation to find number of moles (divide both sides by RT):

$$n = \frac{pV}{RT} = \frac{50000 \times 0.0600}{8.31 \times 283} = 1.28 \text{ moles (3 s.f.)}$$

At what pressure would 0.400 moles of argon gas occupy 0.0100 m^3 at 298 K?

Rearrange the equation to find pressure (divide both sides by V):

$$p = \frac{nRT}{V} = \frac{0.400 \times 8.31 \times 298}{0.0100} = 99\ 100 \text{ Pa (3 s.f.)}$$

Tip: There's more about converting units in the Maths Skills section on pages 261-262.

If you're given the values in different units from the ones used in the ideal gas equation you'll need to convert them to the right units first.

- You might be given pressure in kPa (kilopascals). To convert from kPa to Pa you multiply by 1000 (e.g. 2 kPa = 2000 Pa).
- You might be given temperature in °C. To convert from °C to K you add 273 (e.g. 25 °C = 298 K).
- You might be given volume in cm^3 or dm^3. To convert from cm^3 to m^3 you multiply by 10^{-6}. To convert from dm^3 to m^3 you multiply by 10^{-3}. (1 m^3 = 1 × 10^6 cm^3 = 1 × 10^3 dm^3)

Tip: There's no need to worry about units for number of moles (it doesn't have any units) or R (it always has the same units).

--- **Example** — **Maths Skills** ---

What volume does 2.00 moles of argon gas occupy at 27.0 °C and 100 kPa?

First put all the values you have into the right units:

T = 27.0 °C = (27.0 + 273) K = 300 K

p = 100 kPa = 100 000 Pa

Now rearrange the equation to find volume (divide both sides by pressure):

$$V = \frac{nRT}{p} = \frac{2.00 \times 8.31 \times 300}{100\ 000} = 0.0499 \text{ } m^3 \text{ (3 s.f.)}$$

You might be asked to combine an ideal gas equation calculation with another type of calculation.

Examples — Maths Skills

At a temperature of 60.0 °C and a pressure of 250 kPa, a gas occupied a volume of 1100 cm³ and had a mass of 1.60 g. Find its relative molecular mass.

You've been given temperature, pressure and volume, so you need to find the number of moles:

$$n = \frac{pV}{RT} = \frac{(2.50 \times 10^5) \times (1.1 \times 10^{-3})}{8.31 \times 333} = 0.993... \text{ moles}$$

Now you've got the number of moles, you can calculate relative molecular mass using the formula M_r = mass ÷ number of moles.

M_r = mass ÷ number of moles = 1.60 ÷ 0.993... = 16.1...

So the relative molecular mass is 16.1 (3 s.f.).

Tip: There's a 10^5 and a 10^{-3} in this formula because the numbers have been put into standard form. It's easier to write very big or very small numbers in standard form — see page 256 for more.

Tip: This is just the formula from page 39 again, but it's been rearranged to make M_r the subject. There's more about rearranging formulas on page 260.

Practice Questions — Application

Q1 How many moles are there in 0.040 m³ of oxygen gas at a temperature of 350 K and a pressure of 70 000 Pa?

Q2 What volume would 0.65 moles of carbon dioxide gas occupy at a temperature of 280 K and a pressure of 100 000 Pa?

Q3 How many moles are there in 0.55 dm³ of nitrogen gas at a temperature of 35 °C and a pressure of 90 000 Pa?

Q4 At a pressure of 110 000 Pa, 0.0500 moles of hydrogen gas occupied a volume of 1200 cm³. What was the temperature in °C?

Q5 What volume, in m³, would 0.75 moles of helium gas occupy at a temperature of 22 °C and a pressure of 75 kPa?

Q6 At a temperature of 300 K and a pressure of 80 kPa a gas had a volume of 1.5 dm³ and a mass of 2.6 g. Find its relative molecular mass.

Q7 A student had a sample of neon gas, Ne. They heated it to 44 °C. At this temperature the gas had a volume of 0.00300 m³. If the pressure was 100 kPa, what was the mass of the neon gas?

Practice Question — Fact Recall

Q1 Write out the ideal gas equation. Say what the terms mean and give the standard units that each is measured in.

Figure 1: *Neon gas lighting up restaurant signs.*

- Be able to balance equations for unfamiliar reactions when reactants and products are specified.
- Be able to write balanced full and ionic equations for reactions studied.

Specification Reference 3.1.2.5

3. Chemical Equations

Writing and balancing equations is one of those topics that gets everywhere in chemistry, so here's your chance to make sure you've got your head round it.

How to balance equations

Balanced equations have the same number of each atom on both sides. If you've got an equation that isn't balanced, you can add more atoms to balance it, but only by adding whole reactants or products. You do this by changing the number in front of a reactant or product — you never mess with formulas (e.g. you can change H_2O to $2H_2O$, but never to H_4O).

Exam Tip
Being able to balance equations is a key skill in Chemistry. Whenever you write an equation in an exam it should be balanced (whether the question specifically asks you to balance it or not).

Examples — Maths Skills

Balance the equation $H_2SO_4 + NaOH \rightarrow Na_2SO_4 + H_2O$.

First you need to count how many of each atom you have on each side.

$$H_2SO_4 + NaOH \rightarrow Na_2SO_4 + H_2O$$

| $H = 3$ | $Na = 1$ | $H = 2$ | $Na = 2$ |
| $O = 5$ | $S = 1$ | $O = 5$ | $S = 1$ |

The left side needs 2 Na's, so try changing NaOH to 2NaOH:

$$H_2SO_4 + 2NaOH \rightarrow Na_2SO_4 + H_2O$$

| $H = 4$ | $Na = 2$ | $H = 2$ | $Na = 2$ |
| $O = 6$ | $S = 1$ | $O = 5$ | $S = 1$ |

Now the right side needs 4 H's, so try changing H_2O to $2H_2O$:

$$H_2SO_4 + 2NaOH \rightarrow Na_2SO_4 + 2H_2O$$

| $H = 4$ | $Na = 2$ | $H = 4$ | $Na = 2$ |
| $O = 6$ | $S = 1$ | $O = 6$ | $S = 1$ |

Both sides have the same number of each atom — the equation is balanced.

Balance the equation $C_2H_6 + O_2 \rightarrow CO_2 + H_2O$.

First work out how many of each atom you have on each side.

$$C_2H_6 + O_2 \rightarrow CO_2 + H_2O$$

| $C = 2$ | $H = 6$ | $C = 1$ | $H = 2$ |
| | $O = 2$ | | $O = 3$ |

The right side needs 2 C's, so try $2CO_2$. It also needs 6 H's, so try $3H_2O$.

$$C_2H_6 + O_2 \rightarrow 2CO_2 + 3H_2O$$

| $C = 2$ | $H = 6$ | $C = 2$ | $H = 6$ |
| | $O = 2$ | | $O = 7$ |

The left side needs 7 O's, so try $3\frac{1}{2}O_2$

$$C_2H_6 + 3\frac{1}{2}O_2 \rightarrow 2CO_2 + 3H_2O$$

| $C = 2$ | $H = 6$ | $C = 2$ | $H = 6$ |
| | $O = 7$ | | $O = 7$ |

This balances the equation.

Tip: You can use ½ to balance equations, but you should only use it for diatomic molecules like O_2, H_2 or Cl_2. (For example, you can't really have $\frac{1}{2}H_2O$. That would mean splitting an oxygen atom.)

Tip: Always do a quick check to make sure your final equation balances.

Ionic equations

You can write an **ionic equation** for any reaction involving ions that happens in solution. In ionic equations, only the reacting particles (and the products they form) are included.

To write an ionic equation, you start by writing a full, balanced equation for the reaction. Then you split any dissolved ionic species up into ions. Finally, you take out any ions that appear on both sides of the equation.

Write an ionic equation for the reaction between sodium hydroxide and nitric acid: $HNO_{3\,(aq)} + NaOH_{(aq)} \rightarrow NaNO_{3\,(aq)} + H_2O_{(l)}$

First, check the full equation is balanced. This one is — there are the same numbers of each type of atom on each side of the equation.

The ionic substances from the equation will dissolve, breaking up into ions in solution. So you can rewrite the equation to show all the ions that are in the reaction mixture:

$$H^+ + NO_3^- + Na^+ + OH^- \rightarrow Na^+ + NO_3^- + H_2O$$

To get from this to the ionic equation, just cross out any ions that appear on both sides — in this case, that's the sodium ions and the nitrate ions.

$$H^+ + \cancel{NO_3^-} + \cancel{Na^+} + OH^- \rightarrow \cancel{Na^+} + \cancel{NO_3^-} + H_2O$$

So the ionic equation for this reaction is: $\mathbf{H^+ + OH^- \rightarrow H_2O}$

Once you've written the ionic equation, check that the charges are balanced. In this example, the net charge on the left-hand side is $+1 + (-1) = 0$, and the net charge on the right-hand side is 0 — so the charges balance.

Write an ionic equation for this reaction:
$$Na_3PO_{4\,(aq)} + CaCl_{2\,(aq)} \rightarrow NaCl_{(aq)} + Ca_3(PO_4)_{2\,(s)}$$

This time the full equation isn't balanced. So the first thing to do is to balance it. (Look back at the last page for more on how to do this.)

$$2Na_3PO_4 + 3CaCl_2 \rightarrow 6NaCl + Ca_3(PO_4)_2$$

Now split up everything that dissolves into its constituent ions. Remember to make sure you've included the correct number of atoms of each type from the full, balanced equation.

$$(2 \times 3)Na^+ + 2PO_4^{3-} + 3Ca^{2+} + (3 \times 2)Cl^- \rightarrow 6Na^+ + 6Cl^- + Ca_3(PO_4)_2$$
$$6Na^+ + 2PO_4^{3-} + 3Ca^{2+} + 6Cl^- \rightarrow 6Na^+ + 6Cl^- + Ca_3(PO_4)_2$$

Finally, cross out the ions that appear on both sides of the equation.

$$\cancel{6Na^+} + 2PO_4^{3-} + 3Ca^{2+} + \cancel{6Cl^-} \rightarrow \cancel{6Na^+} + \cancel{6Cl^-} + Ca_3(PO_4)_2$$

This leaves you with the ionic equation: $\mathbf{2PO_4^{3-} + 3Ca^{2+} \rightarrow Ca_3(PO_4)_2}$

Practice Questions — Application

Q1 Balance these equations:
   a) $Mg + HCl \rightarrow MgCl_2 + H_2$
   b) $S_8 + F_2 \rightarrow SF_6$
   c) $Ca(OH)_2 + H_2SO_4 \rightarrow CaSO_4 + H_2O$
   d) $Na_2CO_3 + HCl \rightarrow NaCl + CO_2 + H_2O$
   e) $C_4H_{10} + O_2 \rightarrow CO_2 + H_2O$

Q2 Write ionic equations for these reactions:
   a) $Fe_{(s)} + CuSO_{4\,(aq)} \rightarrow FeSO_{4(aq)} + Cu_{(s)}$
   b) $BaCl_{2\,(aq)} + Na_2SO_{4(aq)} \rightarrow NaCl_{(aq)} + BaSO_{4\,(s)}$
   c) $Na_2CO_{3\,(aq)} + HNO_{3\,(aq)} \rightarrow NaNO_{3\,(aq)} + H_2O_{(l)} + CO_{2\,(g)}$

Tip: The state symbols tell you that HNO_3, NaOH and $NaNO_3$ are in solution, but the water is a liquid. (There's more about state symbols on page 48.)

Tip: Leave anything that isn't an ion in solution (like the water) as it is.

Tip: An ion that's present in the reaction mixture but doesn't get involved in the reaction is called a spectator ion.

Tip: As long as you started off with a full, <u>balanced</u> equation, the charges should balance.

Tip: The state symbols in the full equation show that the $Ca_3(PO_4)_2$ is solid. You <u>don't</u> split it up into ions, because it isn't in solution.

Tip: The net charge on the left-hand side is $(2 \times -3) + (3 \times +2) = 0$. This is the same as the net charge on the right-hand side, so your equation balances.

Tip: If you're not sure what the charges on the ions of different elements are, or how to work them out, look at pages 68 to 69.

Learning Objectives:

- Be able to calculate masses from balanced equations.
- Be able to calculate volumes of gases from balanced equations.

Specification Reference 3.1.2.5

Tip: The ratio of the moles of each reactant and product in a balanced chemical equation is called the molar ratio. The big numbers in front of the species in a balanced equation tell you what the molar ratio is.

Tip: Look — it's that moles = mass ÷ M_r formula yet again...

Tip: Reactants are the chemicals you start with that get used up during a reaction. Products are the chemicals that are formed during a reaction.

4. Equations and Calculations

Once you've made sure that an equation is balanced, you can use it to calculate all sorts of things — like how much product a reaction will make...

Calculating masses

You can use the balanced equation for a reaction to work out how much product you will get from a certain mass of reactant.

Here are the steps to follow:

1. Write out the balanced equation for the reaction.
2. Work out how many moles of the reactant you have.
3. Use the **molar ratio** from the balanced equation to work out the number of moles of product that will be formed from this much reactant.
4. Calculate the mass of that many moles of product.

Here's a nice juicy example to help you get to grips with the method:

┌─ **Example** — **Maths Skills** ─────────────────────

Find the mass of iron(III) oxide produced when 28.0 g of iron is burnt in air.

1. Write out the balanced equation: $2Fe_{(s)} + 1\frac{1}{2}O_{2\,(g)} \rightarrow Fe_2O_{3\,(s)}$

2. Work out how many moles of iron you have:
   A_r of Fe = 55.8
   Moles = mass ÷ A_r = 28.0 ÷ 55.8 = 0.502... moles of iron

3. The molar ratio of Fe : Fe_2O_3 is 2 : 1. This means that for every 2 moles of Fe that you have, you will produce 1 mole of Fe_2O_3. But you only have 0.502... moles of Fe here.
   So you will produce: 0.502... ÷ 2 = 0.251... moles of Fe_2O_3

4. Now find the mass of 0.251... moles of Fe_2O_3:
   M_r of Fe_2O_3 = (2 × 55.8) + (3 × 16) = 159.6
   Mass = moles × M_r = 0.25 × 159.6 = 40.0 g of iron(III) oxide (3 s.f.)

└──

You can use similar steps to work out how much of a reactant you had at the start of a reaction when you're given a certain mass of product:

┌─ **Example** — **Maths Skills** ─────────────────────

Hydrogen gas can react with nitrogen gas to give ammonia (NH_3). Calculate the mass of hydrogen needed to produce 6.8 g of ammonia.

1. $N_{2\,(g)} + 3H_{2\,(g)} \rightarrow 2NH_{3\,(g)}$
2. M_r of NH_3 = 14.0 + (3 × 1.0) = 17.0
   Moles = mass ÷ M_r = 6.8 ÷ 17.0 = 0.4 moles of NH_3
3. From the equation: the molar ratio of NH_3 : H_2 is 2 : 3.
   So to make 0.4 moles of NH_3, you must need to start with (0.4 ÷ 2) × 3 = 0.6 moles of H_2
4. M_r of H_2 = 2 × 1.0 = 2.0
   Mass = moles × M_r = 0.6 × 2.0 = 1.2 g of hydrogen

└──

Q1 3.4 g of zinc is dissolved in hydrochloric acid, producing zinc chloride ($ZnCl_2$) and hydrogen gas.

   a) Write a balanced equation for this reaction.

   b) Calculate the number of moles of zinc in 3.4 g.

   c) How many moles of zinc chloride does the reaction produce?

   d) What mass of zinc chloride does the reaction produce?

Q2 A student burns some ethene gas (C_2H_4) in oxygen, producing carbon dioxide gas and 15 g of water.

   a) Write a balanced equation for this reaction.

   b) Calculate the number of moles of water in 15 g.

   c) How many moles of ethene did the student begin with?

   d) What mass of ethene did the student begin with?

Q3 Calculate the mass of barium carbonate ($BaCO_3$) produced if 4.58 g of barium chloride ($BaCl_2$) is reacted with sodium carbonate (Na_2CO_3).

Figure 1: *Zinc dissolving in hydrochloric acid.*

Calculating gas volumes

It's handy to be able to work out how much gas a reaction will produce, so that you can use large enough apparatus. Or else there might be a large bang. The first three steps of this method are the same as the method on the last page. Once you've found the number of moles of product, the final step is to put that number into the ideal gas equation (see page 42).

Examples — Maths Skills

What volume of hydrogen gas, in m³, is produced when 15.0 g of sodium is reacted with excess water at a temperature of 25.0 °C and a pressure of 100 kPa? The gas constant is 8.31 J K⁻¹ mol⁻¹.

1. $2Na_{(s)} + 2H_2O_{(l)} \rightarrow 2NaOH_{(aq)} + H_{2(g)}$

2. A_r of Na = 23.0
   number of moles = mass ÷ A_r
                = 15.0 ÷ 23.0 = 0.652... moles of sodium

3. From the equation: the molar ratio of Na : H_2 is 2 : 1.
   So 0.652... moles of Na produces (0.652... ÷ 2) = 0.326... moles of H_2.

4. Volume = $\dfrac{nRT}{p} = \dfrac{0.326... \times 8.31 \times 298}{100\ 000}$ = 0.00808 m³ (3 s.f.)

What volume of carbon dioxide, in dm³, is produced when 10.0 g of calcium carbonate reacts with excess hydrochloric acid at a temperature of 25.0 °C and a pressure of 100 kPa? The gas constant is 8.31 J K⁻¹ mol⁻¹.

1. $CaCO_{3(s)} + 2HCl_{(aq)} \rightarrow CaCl_{2(aq)} + CO_{2(g)} + H_2O_{(l)}$

2. M_r of $CaCO_3$ = 40.1 + 12.0 + (3 × 16.0) = 100.1
   number of moles = mass ÷ M_r
                = 10.0 ÷ 100.1 = 0.0999... moles of calcium carbonate

3. From the equation: the molar ratio of $CaCO_3$: CO_2 is 1 : 1.
   So 0.0999... moles of $CaCO_3$ produces 0.0999... moles of CO_2.

4. Volume = $\dfrac{nRT}{p} = \dfrac{0.0999... \times 8.31 \times 298}{100\ 000}$
                = 0.00247... m³ = 2.47 dm³ (3 s.f.)

Tip: 'Excess water' just means that all of the sodium will react.

Exam Tip
Sometimes, exam questions will tell you what units to give your answer in — if they do, make sure you follow those instructions, or you could lose marks.

State symbols

State symbols are put after each compound in an equation. They tell you what state of matter things are in:

$$s = \text{solid}, \quad l = \text{liquid}, \quad g = \text{gas}, \quad aq = \text{aqueous (solution in water)}.$$

Example

$$CaCO_{3\,(s)} + 2HCl_{(aq)} \rightarrow CaCl_{2\,(aq)} + H_2O_{(l)} + CO_{2\,(g)}$$

$$\text{solid} \qquad \text{aqueous} \qquad \text{aqueous} \quad \text{liquid} \quad \text{gas}$$

Practice Questions — Application

Q1 Give the state symbols that you would use in an equation to show the state of the following substances.
  a) a solution of magnesium chloride in water
  b) a piece of magnesium metal
  c) a measured amount of water at room temperature and pressure
  d) a solution of sodium nitrate in water
  e) ethane gas
  f) copper oxide powder

Q2 9.00 g of water is split apart to give hydrogen gas and oxygen gas.
  a) Write a balanced equation for this reaction.
  b) Calculate the number of moles of water in 9.00 g.
  c) How many moles of oxygen gas does the reaction produce?
  d) What volume of oxygen gas will the reaction produce at 298 K and 100 000 Pa?

Q3 7.0 g of zinc sulfide (ZnS) is burnt in oxygen. This produces solid zinc oxide (ZnO) and sulfur dioxide gas (SO_2).
  a) Write a balanced equation for this reaction.
  b) Calculate the number of moles of zinc sulfide in 7.0 g.
  c) How many moles of sulfur dioxide gas does the reaction produce?
  d) What volume of sulfur dioxide gas will the reaction produce at 298 K and 100 000 Pa?

Q4 A sample of hexane gas (C_6H_{14}) is cracked to give butane gas (C_4H_{10}) and ethene gas (C_2H_4). The mass of butane produced is 3.0 g.
  a) Write a balanced equation for this reaction.
  b) Calculate the number of moles of butane in 3.0 g.
  c) How many moles of hexane gas were present in the sample?
  d) What volume would this many moles of hexane gas occupy at a temperature of 308 K and a pressure of 100 000 Pa?

Q5 Magnesium metal will react with steam to produce solid magnesium oxide and hydrogen gas. Calculate the volume of steam needed to create 10 g of MgO at 100 °C and 101 325 Pa.

5. Titrations

You can do a titration to find the concentration of an acid or an alkali.
But first you'll have to prepare a standard solution to use in your titration...

Neutralisation

When an acid reacts with an alkali you get a salt and water. This is called
a neutralisation reaction.

> **Example**
>
> $$H_2SO_{4\,(aq)} + 2NaOH_{(aq)} \rightarrow Na_2SO_{4\,(aq)} + 2H_2O_{(l)}$$
>
> acid   alkali   salt   water

Titrations involve neutralisation reactions to work out the
concentration of an acidic or alkaline solution.

Making a standard solution

REQUIRED PRACTICAL **1**

Before you do a titration, you might have to make up a **standard solution**
to use. A standard solution is any solution that you know the exact
concentration of. Making a standard solution involves dissolving a known
amount of solid in a known amount of water to create a known concentration.

> **Example**
>
> **Make 250 cm³ of a 2.00 mol dm⁻³ solution of sodium hydroxide.**
>
> 1. First work out how many moles of sodium hydroxide you
>   need using the formula:
>   moles = concentration × volume
> $$= 2.00\ mol\ dm^{-3} \times 0.250\ dm^3 = 0.500\ moles$$
>
> 2. Now work out how many grams of sodium hydroxide
>   you need using the formula: mass = moles × M_r
> M_r of NaOH = 23.0 + 16.0 + 1.0 = 40.0
>   Mass = 0.500 × 40.0 = 20.0 g
>
> 3. Place a weighing bottle on a digital balance. Weigh out the
>   required mass of solid approximately and tip it into a beaker.
>
> 4. Weigh the weighing bottle (which may still contain traces of the solid).
>   Subtract the mass of the bottle from the mass of the bottle and the
>   solid together to find the precise mass of solid you have weighed out.
>
> 5. Add distilled water to the beaker and stir until all the
>   sodium hydroxide has dissolved.
>
> 6. Tip the solution into a 250 cm³ volumetric flask —
>   use a funnel to make sure it all goes in.
>
> 7. Rinse the beaker, stirring rod and funnel with distilled water and add
>   that to the flask too. This makes sure there's no solute clinging
>   to the beaker or rod.
>
> 8. Now top the flask up to the correct volume with more distilled water.
>   Make sure the bottom of the meniscus reaches the line (see Figure 1).
>   When you get close to the line add the water drop by drop — if you
>   go over the line you'll have to start all over again.
>
> 9. Stopper the flask and turn it upside down a few times to
>   make sure it's mixed well.
>
> 10. Now calculate the exact concentration of your standard solution.

Learning Objective:

- Be able to make up
  a volumetric solution
  and carry out a simple
  acid–base titration
  (Required Practical 1).

- Be able to use
  balanced equations
  to calculate
  concentrations and
  volumes for reactions
  in solutions.

**Specification
Reference 3.1.2.5**

Tip: Standard solutions
can also be called
volumetric solutions.

Tip: If you're doing
this experiment, make
sure you carry out a risk
assessment before you
start.

Figure 1: *The meniscus of a
liquid in a volumetric flask.*

Performing titrations

REQUIRED PRACTICAL 1

Titrations allow you to find out exactly how much acid is needed to neutralise a measured quantity of alkali (or the other way round). You can use this data to work out the concentration of the alkali.

Start off by using a pipette to measure out a set volume of the solution that you want to know the concentration of. Put it in a flask. Add a few drops of an appropriate indicator (see below) to the flask. Then fill a burette (see Figure 3) with a standard solution of the acid — remember, that means you know its exact concentration. Use a funnel to carefully pour the acid into the burette. Always do this below eye level to avoid any acid splashing on to your face or eyes. (You should wear safety glasses too.) Now you're ready to titrate.

Tip: Make sure you are aware of any safety issues involved in the experiment before carrying it out.

Figure 2: *A student doing a titration. She is adding acid from the burette to the alkali in the flask. The alkali looks pink because it contains phenolphthalein.*

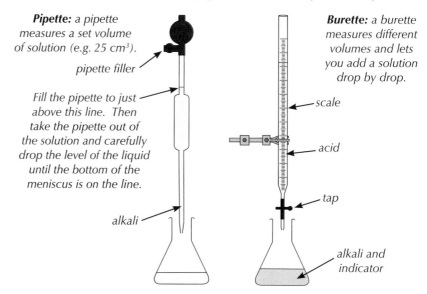

Pipette: *a pipette measures a set volume of solution (e.g. 25 cm³).*

pipette filler

Fill the pipette to just above this line. Then take the pipette out of the solution and carefully drop the level of the liquid until the bottom of the meniscus is on the line.

alkali

Burette: *a burette measures different volumes and lets you add a solution drop by drop.*

scale

acid

tap

alkali and indicator

Figure 3: *The apparatus needed for a titration.*

First do a rough titration to get an idea where the end point (the point where the alkali is neutralised and the indicator changes colour) is. Take an initial reading of how much acid is in the burette. Then gradually add the acid to the alkali, giving the flask a regular swirl. When the colour changes, take a final reading.

Then do an accurate titration. Take an initial reading, then run the acid in to within 2 cm³ of the end point. When you get to this stage, add it dropwise. If you don't see exactly when the colour changes you'll overshoot and your result won't be accurate. Find the amount of acid used to neutralise the alkali by subtracting the final reading from the initial reading. This is called the **titre.**

Repeat the titration a few times, until you have at least three results that are concordant (for titrations, this means three results within 0.1 cm³ of each other). Use the results from each repeat to calculate the mean volume of acid used. Remember to leave out any anomalous results when calculating your mean — anomalous results can distort your answer.

Tip: There's loads of stuff about how to handle the data you get from experiments like this on pages 4-11. Have a look if you want to know more about means, anomalous results and error.

Indicators

In titrations, **indicators** that change colour quickly over a very small pH range are used so you know exactly when the reaction has ended. The main two indicators used for acid/alkali titrations are methyl orange, which is red in acids and yellow in alkalis, and phenolphthalein, which is colourless in acids and pink in alkalis. It's a good idea to stand your flask on a white tile when you're titrating — it'll make it easier to see exactly when the end point is.

Tip: Universal indicator is no good here — its colour change is too gradual.

Calculating concentrations

You need to be able to use the results of a titration to calculate the concentration of acids and alkalis. There's more on concentration calculations on page 40.

Examples — Maths Skills

In a titration experiment, 25.0 cm³ of 0.500 mol dm⁻³ HCl neutralised 35.0 cm³ of NaOH solution. Calculate the concentration of the sodium hydroxide solution in mol dm⁻³.

First write a balanced equation and decide what you know and what you need to know:

$$HCl \quad + \quad NaOH \rightarrow NaCl + H_2O$$

Volume:	*25.0 cm³*	*35.0 cm³*
Concentration:	*0.500 mol dm⁻³*	*?*

You know the volume and concentration of the HCl, so first work out how many moles of HCl you have:

$$\text{Number of moles HCl} = \frac{\text{concentration} \times \text{volume}(cm^3)}{1000}$$

$$= \frac{0.500 \times 25.0}{1000} = 0.0125 \text{ moles}$$

From the equation, you know 1 mole of HCl neutralises 1 mole of NaOH.

So 0.0125 moles of HCl must neutralise 0.0125 moles of NaOH.

Now it's a doddle to work out the concentration of NaOH.

$$\text{Concentration of NaOH} = \frac{\text{moles of NaOH} \times 1000}{\text{volume }(cm^3)}$$

$$= \frac{0.0125 \times 1000}{35.0} = 0.357 \text{ mol dm⁻³ (3 s.f)}$$

Here's an example where it's an alkali being added to an acid instead.

40.0 cm³ of 0.250 mol dm⁻³ KOH was used to neutralise 22.0 cm³ of HNO₃ solution. Calculate the concentration of the nitric acid in mol dm⁻³.

Write out the balanced equation and the information that you have:

$$HNO_3 + KOH \rightarrow KNO_3 + H_2O$$

Volume:	*22.0 cm³*	*40.0 cm³*
Concentration:	*?*	*0.250 mol dm⁻³*

You know the volume and concentration of the KOH, so now work out how many moles of KOH you have:

$$\text{Number of moles KOH} = \frac{\text{concentration} \times \text{volume}(cm^3)}{1000}$$

$$= \frac{0.250 \times 40.0}{1000} = 0.0100 \text{ moles}$$

From the equation, you know 1 mole of KOH neutralises 1 mole of HNO₃.

So 0.0100 moles of KOH must neutralise 0.0100 moles of HNO₃.

$$\text{Concentration of HNO}_3 = \frac{\text{moles of HNO}_3 \times 1000}{\text{volume }(cm^3)}$$

$$= \frac{0.0100 \times 1000}{22.0} = 0.455 \text{ mol dm⁻³ (3 s.f)}$$

Exam Tip
Keep a close eye on the units in questions like these. You don't want to lose marks just because you didn't check whether you needed the formula for dm³ or cm³ before you started.

Q1 28 cm³ of 0.75 mol dm⁻³ hydrochloric acid (HCl) was used to neutralise 40 cm³ of potassium hydroxide (KOH) solution.
    a) Write a balanced equation for this reaction.
    b) Calculate the number of moles of HCl used to neutralise the solution.
    c) How many moles of KOH were neutralised by the HCl?
    d) What was the concentration of the KOH solution?

Q2 15.3 cm³ of 1.5 mol dm⁻³ sodium hydroxide (NaOH) was used to neutralise 35 cm³ of nitric acid (HNO_3).
    a) Write a balanced equation for this reaction.
    b) Calculate the number of moles of NaOH used to neutralise the nitric acid.
    c) How many moles of HNO_3 were neutralised by the NaOH?
    d) What was the concentration of the HNO_3 solution?

Q3 12 cm³ of 0.50 mol dm⁻³ HCl solution was used to neutralise 24 cm³ of KOH solution. What was the concentration of the KOH solution?

Exam Tip
Don't forget to think about numbers of significant figures when doing any calculations. See page 257 for more on this.

Calculating volumes

You can use a similar method to find the volume of acid or alkali that you need to neutralise a solution. You'll need to use this formula again:
number of moles = (concentration × volume (cm³)) ÷ 1000
but this time rearrange it to find the volume:

$$\text{volume (cm}^3) = \frac{\text{number of moles} \times 1000}{\text{concentration}}$$

Examples — Maths Skills

20.4 cm³ of a 0.500 mol dm⁻³ solution of sodium carbonate reacts with 1.50 mol dm⁻³ nitric acid. Calculate the volume of nitric acid required to neutralise the sodium carbonate.

Like before, first write a balanced equation for the reaction and decide what you know and what you want to know:

$$Na_2CO_3 \ + \ 2HNO_3 \rightarrow 2NaNO_3 + H_2O + CO_2$$

Volume: 20.4 cm³   ?
Concentration: 0.500 mol dm⁻³   1.50 mol dm⁻³

Now work out how many moles of Na_2CO_3 you've got:

$$\text{Number of moles } Na_2CO_3 = \frac{\text{concentration} \times \text{volume (cm}^3)}{1000}$$

$$= \frac{0.500 \times 20.4}{1000} = 0.0102 \text{ moles}$$

1 mole of Na_2CO_3 neutralises 2 moles of HNO_3, so 0.0102 moles of Na_2CO_3 neutralises 0.0204 moles of HNO_3.

Now you know the number of moles of HNO_3 and the concentration, you can work out the volume:

$$\text{Volume of } HNO_3 = \frac{\text{number of moles} \times 1000}{\text{concentration}}$$

$$= \frac{0.0204 \times 1000}{1.50} = 13.6 \text{ cm}^3$$

And here's an example where you're finding the volume of alkali used.

Examples — Maths Skills

18.2 cm³ of a 0.800 mol dm⁻³ solution HCl reacts with 0.300 mol dm⁻³ KOH. Calculate the volume of KOH required to neutralise the HCl.

Write out the balanced equation and the information that you have:

$$HCl \quad + \quad KOH \rightarrow KCl + H_2O$$

Volume: 18.2 cm³   ?

Concentration: 0.800 mol dm⁻³   0.300 mol dm⁻³

Now work out how many moles of HCl you've got:

$$\text{Number of moles HCl} = \frac{\text{concentration} \times \text{volume (cm}^3)}{1000}$$

$$= \frac{0.800 \times 18.2}{1000} = 0.0145... \text{ moles}$$

1 mole of HCl neutralises 1 moles of KOH, so 0.0145... moles of HCl neutralises 0.0145... moles of KOH.

Now use this to work out the volume:

$$\text{Volume of KOH} = \frac{\text{number of moles} \times 1000}{\text{concentration}}$$

$$= \frac{0.0145... \times 1000}{0.300} = 48.53... = 48.5 \text{ cm}^3 \text{ (to 3 s.f.)}$$

Figure 4: *A titration where an alkali is being added to an acid. The indicator in the flask is phenolphthalein, so the solution starts clear and turns pink at the endpoint.*

Practice Questions — Application

Q1   18.8 cm³ of a 0.20 mol dm⁻³ solution of nitric acid (HNO_3) reacts with 0.45 mol dm⁻³ potassium hydroxide (KOH) solution.
   a)   Write a balanced equation for this reaction.
   b)   Calculate the number of moles of HNO_3 present in the acid added.
   c)   How many moles of KOH were in the sample of the alkali?
   d)   What volume of KOH was required to neutralise the HNO_3 solution?

Q2   37.3 cm³ of a 0.420 mol dm⁻³ solution of potassium hydroxide (KOH) reacts with 1.10 mol dm⁻³ ethanoic acid (CH_3COOH) solution.
   a)   Write a balanced equation for this reaction.
   b)   Calculate the number of moles of KOH present in the alkali added.
   c)   How many moles of CH_3COOH were in the sample of the acid?
   d)   What volume of CH_3COOH was required to neutralise the KOH solution?

Q3   14 cm³ of a 1.5 mol dm⁻³ NaOH solution reacts with 0.60 mol dm⁻³ H_2SO_4 solution. What volume of H_2SO_4 was required to neutralise the NaOH solution?

Practice Questions — Fact Recall

Q1   What is a standard solution?
Q2   Name the piece of equipment that you would use to measure out a set volume of alkali or acid for a titration.
Q3   Name the piece of equipment that you would use to add liquid drop by drop to the flask during a titration.
Q4   What is the 'end point' of a titration?

- Know that the
empirical formula is
the simplest whole
number ratio of atoms
of each element in a
compound.
- Know that the
molecular formula is
the actual number of
atoms of each element
in a compound.
- Understand the
relationship between
empirical and
molecular formulas.
- Be able to calculate
a molecular formula
from the empirical
formula and relative
molecular mass.
- Be able to calculate
empirical formulas
from data giving
percentage by mass or
composition by mass.
**Specification
Reference 3.1.2.4**

Tip: There's more
about the molecular
an empirical formulas
of organic compounds
on pages 172-173.

6. Formulas

*Now for a few pages about chemical formulas. A formula tells you what
atoms are in a compound. Useful, I think you'll agree.*

Empirical and molecular formulas

You need to know what's what with empirical and molecular formulas.
The **empirical formula** gives the smallest whole number ratio of atoms of
each element present in a compound. The **molecular formula** gives the
actual numbers of atoms in a molecule. The molecular formula is made up
of a whole number of empirical units.

Example

This molecule is butane:

$$H-\overset{\displaystyle \overset{|}{H}}{\underset{\displaystyle \underset{|}{H}}{C}}-\overset{\displaystyle \overset{|}{H}}{\underset{\displaystyle \underset{|}{H}}{C}}-\overset{\displaystyle \overset{|}{H}}{\underset{\displaystyle \underset{|}{H}}{C}}-\overset{\displaystyle \overset{|}{H}}{\underset{\displaystyle \underset{|}{H}}{C}}-H$$

A butane molecule contains 4 carbon (C) atoms and 10 hydrogen (H) atoms.
So its molecular formula is C_4H_{10}.

Butane's empirical formula is C_2H_5. This means that the ratio of carbon
atoms to hydrogen atoms in the molecule is 2:5. That's as much as you
can simplify it.

If you know the empirical formula and the relative molecular mass of a
compound, you can calculate its molecular formula. Just follow these steps:

1. Find the empirical mass (that's just the relative mass of the
   empirical formula).

2. Divide the relative molecular mass by the empirical mass. This tells you how
   many multiples of the empirical formula are in the molecular formula.

3. Multiply the empirical formula by that number to find the
   molecular formula.

Here are a couple of examples to show you how it works.

Example — Maths Skills

**A molecule has an empirical formula of $C_4H_3O_2$, and a relative molecular
mass of 166. Work out its molecular formula.**

1. Find the empirical mass — add up by the relative atomic mass values
   of all the atoms in the empirical formula.

   3 H atoms *A_r of H*

   empirical mass $= (4 \times 12.0) + (3 \times 1.0) + (2 \times 16.0) = 83.0$

   4 C atoms *A_r of C* *2 O atoms* *A_r of O*

2. Divide the relative molecular mass by the empirical mass. The relative
   molecular mass is 166, so there are $(166 \div 83.0) = 2$ empirical units in
   the molecule.

3. The molecular formula is the empirical formula × 2,
   so the molecular formula $= C_8H_6O_4$.

Example ── **Maths Skills**

The empirical formula of glucose is CH_2O. Its relative molecular mass is 180. Find its molecular formula.

1. Find the empirical mass of glucose.
   empirical mass = $(1 \times 12.0) + (2 \times 1.0) + (1 \times 16.0) = 30.0$

2. Divide the relative molecular mass by the empirical mass. The relative molecular mass is 180, so there are $(180 \div 30.0) = 6$ empirical units in the molecule.

3. Molecular formula = $C_6H_{12}O_6$

Practice Questions — Application

Q1 A molecule has the empirical formula C_4H_9, and a relative molecular mass of 171. Find its molecular formula.

Q2 A molecule has the empirical formula $C_3H_5O_2$, and a relative molecular mass of 146. Find its molecular formula.

Q3 A molecule has the empirical formula C_2H_6O, and a relative molecular mass of 46. Find its molecular formula.

Q4 A molecule has the empirical formula $C_4H_6Cl_2O$, and a relative molecular mass of 423. Find its molecular formula.

Calculating empirical formulas

You need to know how to work out empirical formulas from the percentages of the different elements. Follow these steps each time:

1. Assume you've got 100 g of the compound — you can turn the percentages straight into masses. Then you can work out how many moles of each element are in 100 g of the compound.

2. Divide each number of moles by the smallest number of moles you found in step 1. This gives you the ratio of the elements in the compound.

3. Apply the numbers from the ratio to the formula.

Example ── **Maths Skills**

A compound is found to have percentage composition 56.5% potassium, 8.70% carbon and 34.8% oxygen by mass.
Calculate its empirical formula.

1. If you had 100 g of the compound you would have 56.5 g of potassium, 8.70 g of carbon and 34.8 g of oxygen. Use the formula moles = mass $\div A_r$ to work out how many moles of each element that is.

   K: $\frac{56.5}{39.1} = 1.45$ moles   C: $\frac{8.70}{12.0} = 0.725$ moles   O: $\frac{34.8}{16.0} = 2.18$ moles

2. Divide each number of moles by the smallest number (0.725 here).

   K: $\frac{1.45}{0.725} = 2.0$ C: $\frac{0.725}{0.725} = 1.0$ O: $\frac{2.18}{0.725} = 3.0$

   This tells you that the ratio of K : C : O in the molecule is 2 : 1 : 3.

3. So you know the empirical formula's got to be K_2CO_3.

Tip: The formula for the number of moles is a bit different here — when you're dealing with elements, you need to use A_r instead of M_r.

Exam Tip
Make sure you write down all your working for calculation questions. You'll be more likely to spot any mistakes and if you do go wrong you might get some marks for the working.

Sometimes you might only be given the percentage of some of the elements in the compound. Then you'll have to work out the percentages of the others.

Examples Maths Skills

An oxide of nitrogen contains 26.0% by mass of nitrogen. Calculate its empirical formula.

1. The compound only contains nitrogen and oxygen, so if it is 26.0% N it must be $100 - 26.0 = 74.0\%$ O. So if you had 100 g of the compound you would have 26.0 g of nitrogen and 74.0 g of oxygen.

   N: $\dfrac{26.0}{14.0} = 1.86$ moles   O: $\dfrac{74.0}{16.0} = 4.63$ moles

2. Divide each number of moles by 1.86.

   N: $\dfrac{1.86}{1.86} = 1.0$ O: $\dfrac{4.63}{1.86} = 2.5$

   This tells you that the ratio of N : O in the molecule is 1 : 2.5.

3. All the numbers in an empirical formula have to be whole numbers, so you need to multiply the ratio by 2 to put it into its simplest whole number form: $2 \times (1 : 2.5) = 2 : 5$.
   So the empirical formula is N_2O_5.

You need to be able to work out empirical formulas from experimental results too. In a way this is easier than by percentages, as you already know the masses, however you have to think a bit more about what is actually happening in the experiment.

Examples Maths Skills

When a hydrocarbon is burnt in excess oxygen, 4.40 g of carbon dioxide and 1.80 g of water are made. What is the empirical formula of the hydrocarbon?

1. First work out how many moles of the products you have:

   No. of moles of $CO_2 = \dfrac{mass}{M_r} = \dfrac{4.40}{12.0 + (16.0 \times 2)} = \dfrac{4.40}{44.0} = 0.100$ moles

   No. of moles of $H_2O = \dfrac{mass}{M_r} = \dfrac{1.80}{(2 \times 1.0) + 16.0} = \dfrac{1.80}{18.0} = 0.100$ moles

2. All the hydrogen and carbon in the carbon dioxide and water must have come from the hydrocarbon. This means we can use the number of moles of carbon dioxide and water to work out how many moles of hydrogen and carbon atoms were in the hydrocarbon:

   1 mole of CO_2 contains 1 mole of carbon atoms, so the original hydrocarbon must have contained 0.100 moles of carbon atoms.

   1 mole of H_2O contains 2 moles of hydrogen atoms, so the original hydrocarbon must have contained 0.200 moles of hydrogen atoms.

3. Divide each number of moles by the smallest number (0.100).

   C: $\dfrac{0.100}{0.100} = 1$ H: $\dfrac{0.200}{0.100} = 2$

   This tells you that the ratio of C : H in the hydrocarbon is 1 : 2.

4. So the empirical formula must be CH_2.

Tip: When hydrocarbons undergo complete combustion, the only products are carbon dioxide and water. If they undergo incomplete combustion (combustion in limited oxygen) then other products such as carbon monoxide and soot may form. See page 198 for more on this.

Example — Maths Skills

2.50 g of copper is heated to form 3.13 g of copper oxide.
What is the empirical formula of the oxide?

1. First work out the mass of oxygen which reacted with the copper to form the copper oxide: $3.13 - 2.50 = 0.630$ g of oxygen.

2. Then work out the number of moles of each reactant:

   No. of moles of Cu $= \dfrac{mass}{A_r} = \dfrac{2.50}{63.5} = 0.0394$ moles

   No. of moles of O $= \dfrac{mass}{A_r} = \dfrac{0.630}{16.0} = 0.0394$ moles

3. Divide each number of moles by the smallest number (0.0394).

   Cu: $\dfrac{0.0394}{0.0394} = 1$ O: $\dfrac{0.0394}{0.0394} = 1$

   This tells use that the ratio of Cu : O in the oxide is 1 : 1.

4. So the empirical formula must be CuO.

Tip: Here you don't really need to divide each number of moles by the smallest number — you can tell the ratio will be 1 : 1 as the number of moles of copper is the same as the number of moles of oxygen.

Practice Questions — Application

Q1 A compound is found to have percentage composition 5.9% hydrogen and 94.1% oxygen by mass. Find its empirical formula.

Q2 A compound is found to have percentage composition 20.2% aluminium and 79.8% chlorine by mass. Find its empirical formula.

Q3 A compound is found to have percentage composition 8.5% carbon, 1.4% hydrogen and 90.1% iodine by mass. Find its empirical formula.

Q4 A compound is found to have percentage composition 50.1% copper, 16.3% phosphorus and 33.6% oxygen by mass. Find its empirical formula.

Q5 A compound containing only vanadium and chlorine is found to be 32.3% vanadium by mass. Find its empirical formula.

Q6 An oxide of chromium contains 31.58% by mass of oxygen. Find its empirical formula.

Q7 2.00 g of phosphorus was burnt to form 4.58 g of phosphorus oxide. Find the empirical formula of the phosphorus oxide.

Q8 0.503 g of silver reacts with chlorine to form 0.669 g of silver chloride. Find the empirical formula of the silver chloride.

Q9 A hydrocarbon is burnt to form 9.70 g of CO_2 and 7.92 g of H_2O. Find the empirical formula of the hydrocarbon.

Tip: You should add up the percentages each time there's a question like this to make sure they add up to 100% and you haven't missed out any elements.

Practice Questions — Fact Recall

Q1 What information does the empirical formula of a compound give you?

Q2 What information does the molecular formula of a compound give you?

Learning Objective:
- Be able to calculate percentage yields from balanced equations.

Specification Reference 3.1.2.5

7. Chemical Yield

If you're making a chemical (in a lab or a factory), it helps to know how much of it you can expect to get. In real life you'll never manage to make exactly that much — but percentage yield can give you an idea of how close you got.

Calculating theoretical yield

The **theoretical yield** is the mass of product that should be formed in a chemical reaction. It assumes no chemicals are 'lost' in the process. You can use the masses of reactants and a balanced equation to calculate the theoretical yield for a reaction. It's a bit like calculating reacting masses (see page 46) — here are the steps you have to go through:

1. Work out how many moles of the reactant you have.

2. Use the equation to work out how many moles of product you would expect that much reactant to make.

3. Calculate the mass of that many moles of product — and that's the theoretical yield.

Tip: 'Hydrated' means that the crystals have a bit of water left in them. That's what the dot in $(NH_4)_2Fe(SO_4)_2 \cdot 6H_2O$ means — for every mole of $(NH_4)_2Fe(SO_4)_2$ that the salt contains, it also contains 6 moles of water.

--- **Example** — **Maths Skills** -------------------------------

1.40 g of iron filings react with ammonia and sulfuric acid to make hydrated ammonium iron(II) sulfate. The balanced equation for the reaction is:

$$Fe_{(s)} + 2NH_{3\,(aq)} + 2H_2SO_{4\,(aq)} + 6H_2O_{(l)} \rightarrow (NH_4)_2Fe(SO_4)_2 \cdot 6H_2O_{(s)} + H_{2\,(g)}$$

Calculate the theoretical yield of this reaction.

1. Work out how many moles of iron you have:
   M_r of Fe = 55.8
   Number of moles Fe = mass ÷ M_r = 1.40 ÷ 55.8 = 0.0251

2. Work out how many moles of product you would expect to make:
   From the equation, you know that 1 mole of Fe produces 1 mole of $(NH_4)_2Fe(SO_4)_2 \cdot 6H_2O$ so 0.0251 moles of Fe will produce 0.0251 moles of $(NH_4)_2Fe(SO_4)_2 \cdot 6H_2O$.

3. Now calculate the mass of that many moles of product:
   M_r of $(NH_4)_2Fe(SO_4)_2 \cdot 6H_2O$ = [2 × (14.0 + (4 × 1.0))] + 55.8
   + [2 × (32.1 + (4 × 16.0))] + [6 × ((2 × 1.00) + 16.0)]
   = 392.0
   Theoretical yield = number of moles × M_r = 0.0251 × 392.0 = 9.84 g.

Figure 1: *A student pouring and filtering a solution. Some chemicals will be left on the glassware and some will be left on the filter paper.*

Calculating percentage yield

For any reaction, the actual mass of product (the actual yield) will always be less than the theoretical yield. There are many reasons for this. For example, sometimes not all the starting chemicals react fully. And some chemicals are always 'lost', e.g. some solution gets left on filter paper, is lost during transfers between containers, or forms other products you don't want in side reactions.

Once you've found the theoretical yield and the actual yield, you can work out the **percentage yield**.

$$\text{Percentage Yield} = \frac{\text{Actual Yield}}{\text{Theoretical Yield}} \times 100$$

Examples — Maths Skills

In the ammonium iron(II) sulfate example on the previous page, the theoretical yield was 9.84 g. Say you weighed the hydrated ammonium iron(II) sulfate crystals produced and found the actual yield was 5.2 g. Calculate the percentage yield of this reaction.

Then you just have to plug the numbers into the formula:

$$\text{Percentage yield} = \frac{\text{actual yield}}{\text{theoretical yield}} \times 100$$

$$= (5.2 \div 9.84) \times 100 = 53\%$$

Here's another example:

In an experiment 5.00 g of copper was heated in air to produce copper oxide. The theoretical yield of this reaction was 6.26 g. When the copper oxide was weighed it was found to have a mass of 5.23 g.

Calculate the percentage yield of this reaction.

All you need to do here is put the right numbers into the formula:

$$\text{Percentage yield} = \frac{\text{actual yield}}{\text{theoretical yield}} \times 100$$

$$= (5.23 \div 6.26) \times 100 = 83.5\%$$

Exam Tip
This is a percentage yield, so it can never be more than 100%.
If your answer is bigger than 100%, check the working for mistakes.

If you're not given the theoretical yield, you need to work this out first before you can calculate the percentage yield.

Example — Maths Skills

0.475 g of CH_3Br reacts with excess NaOH in the following reaction:

$CH_3Br + NaOH \rightarrow CH_3OH + NaBr$

0.153 g of CH_3OH is produced. What is the percentage yield?

1. Work out how many moles of CH_3Br you have:
   M_r of $CH_3Br = 12.0 + (3 \times 1.0) + 79.9 = 94.9$
   Number of moles CH_3Br = mass $\div M_r$
   $\qquad\qquad = 0.475 \div 94.9 = 0.00501...$ moles.

2. Work out how many moles of product you would expect to make:
   From the equation, you know that 1 mole of CH_3Br produces 1 mole of CH_3OH so 0.00501... moles of CH_3Br will produce 0.00501... moles of CH_3OH.

3. Now calculate the mass of that many moles of product:
   M_r of $CH_3OH = 12.0 + (4 \times 1.0) + 16.0 = 32.0$
   Theoretical yield = number of moles $\times M_r$
   $\qquad\qquad = 0.00501... \times 32.0 = 0.160...$ g.

4. Now put these numbers into the percentage yield formula:
   $$\text{Percentage yield} = \frac{\text{actual yield}}{\text{theoretical yield}} \times 100$$
   $$= (0.153... \div 0.160...) \times 100 = 95.5\%$$

Practice Questions — Application

Q1 The theoretical yield of a reaction used in an experiment was 3.24 g. The actual yield was 1.76 g. Calculate the percentage yield of the reaction.

Q2 In an experiment sodium metal was reacted with chlorine gas to produce sodium chloride. The theoretical yield of this reaction was 6.1 g. The sodium chloride produced had a mass of 3.7 g. Calculate the percentage yield of this reaction.

Q3 Hydrogen reacts with oxygen to produce 138 g of water. The theoretical yield of this reaction was 143 g. Calculate the percentage yield of this reaction.

Q4 3.0 g of iron filings are burnt in air to give iron oxide (Fe_2O_3):

$$4Fe_{(s)} + 3O_{2\,(g)} \rightarrow 2Fe_2O_{3\,(s)}$$

a) How many moles of iron are there in 3.0 g of metal?

b) Calculate the theoretical yield of iron oxide for this reaction.

c) Calculate the percentage yield if 3.6 g of Fe_2O_3 is made.

Q5 Aluminium metal can be extracted from aluminium oxide by electrolysis. The balanced equation for this reaction is:

$$2Al_2O_{3\,(l)} \rightarrow 4Al_{(l)} + 3O_{2\,(g)}$$

What mass of aluminium would you expect to get from 1000 g of Al_2O_3?

Q6 4.70 g of sodium hydroxide is dissolved in water. This solution is reacted with an excess of sulfuric acid to make sodium sulfate:

$$2NaOH_{(aq)} + H_2SO_{4\,(g)} \rightarrow Na_2SO_{4\,(aq)} + H_2O_{(l)}$$

The sodium sulfate is allowed to crystallise. The dry crystals have a mass of 6.04 g. Calculate the percentage yield of this reaction.

Q7 In an experiment 40.0 g of magnesium was reacted with an excess of nitric acid. The balanced equation for this reaction is:

$$Mg_{(s)} + 2HNO_{3\,(aq)} \rightarrow Mg(NO_3)_{2\,(aq)} + H_{2\,(g)}$$

If 1.70 g of hydrogen was produced, what was the percentage yield of the reaction?

Practice Questions — Fact Recall

Q1 What is meant by the 'theoretical yield' of a reaction?

Q2 Write down the formula for percentage yield.

Exam Tip
If you're asked to calculate yields in an exam, make sure you've written down a balanced equation to work from.

8. Atom Economy

Atom economy is one way to work out how efficient a reaction is. Efficient reactions are better for the environment and save the chemical industry money.

What is atom economy?

In the previous topic you met the idea of percentage yield. Percentage yield can give you useful information about how wasteful a process is. It's based on how much of the product is lost because of things like reactions not completing or losses during collection and purification.

But percentage yield doesn't measure how wasteful the reaction itself is. A reaction that has a 100% yield could still be very wasteful if a lot of the atoms from the reactants wind up in by-products rather than the desired product. **Atom economy** is a measure of the proportion of reactant atoms that become part of the desired product (rather than by-products) in the balanced chemical equation.

Advantages of high atom economy

Companies in the chemical industry will often choose to use reactions with high atom economies. Reactions with high atom economies have environmental, economic and ethical benefits.

Economic advantages

A company using a process that has a high atom economy will make more efficient use of its raw materials. A process with low atom economy will involve using large quantities of raw materials to make relatively small amounts of the desired product and lots of by-products. It's a waste of money if a high proportion of the reactant chemicals they buy end up as useless by-products.

Using a process with a high atom economy also means that the company will have less waste to deal with. This means they will spend less on separating the desired product from the waste products. Any waste products that are produced need to be disposed of safely, which increases costs further.

Environmental and ethical advantages

Processes that use fewer raw materials and produce less waste are better for the environment as well as for business. Many raw materials are in limited supply, so it makes sense to use them efficiently so they last as long as possible. Producing less waste is better for the environment as waste chemicals are often harmful to the environment. It can be difficult to dispose of them in a way that minimises their harmful effects.

Using high atom economy processes tends to be more **sustainable** than using low atom economy processes. Doing something sustainably means using up as little of the Earth's resources as you can and not putting loads of damaging chemicals into the environment — in other words not messing things up for the future.

It can also be good for society if chemical companies can find easier, cheaper ways to mass produce medicines and other useful chemicals, as this may mean the products can be sold for lower prices and be made available to more people.

Learning Objectives:

- Know the economic, ethical and environmental advantages for society and for industry of developing chemical processes with a high atom economy.
- Know the formula for calculating percentage atom economy.
- Be able to calculate percentage atom economies from balanced equations.

Specification Reference 3.1.2.5

Figure 1: *Tablets of the painkiller ibuprofen. Ibuprofen was originally made using a reaction with a 40% atom economy. Now a new way of making it with a 77% atom economy is used. This produces much less waste.*

Calculating atom economy

Atom economy is calculated using this formula:

$$\% \text{ atom economy} = \frac{\text{molecular mass of desired product}}{\text{sum of molecular masses of all reactants}} \times 100$$

Tip: Any reaction where there's only one product will have a 100% atom economy.

To calculate the atom economy for a reaction, you just need to add up the molecular masses of the reactants, find the molecular mass of the product you're interested in and put them both into the formula.

Example — Maths Skills

Bromomethane is reacted with sodium hydroxide to make methanol:

$$CH_3Br + NaOH \rightarrow CH_3OH + NaBr$$

Calculate the percentage atom economy for this reaction.

First, calculate the total mass of the reactants — add up the relative molecular masses of everything on the left side of the balanced equation:

Total mass = $(12.0 + (3 \times 1.0) + 79.9) + (23.0 + 16.0 + 1.0) = 134.9$

Then find the mass of the desired product — that's the methanol:

Mass of desired product = $12.0 + (3 \times 1.0) + 16.0 + 1.0 = 32.0$

Now you can find the % atom economy:

$$\% \text{ atom economy} = \frac{\text{molecular mass of desired product}}{\text{sum of molecular masses of all reactants}} \times 100$$

$$= \frac{32.0}{134.9} \times 100 = 23.7\%$$

Exam Tip
You should always calculate atom economy from a balanced equation, so the first thing you do when you start a question like this is to make sure you've got one written down.

When you calculate the masses, you should use the number of moles of each compound that is in the balanced equation (e.g. the mass of '$2H_2$' should be $2 \times (2 \times 1.0) = 4.0$). Here's a quick example:

Example — Maths Skills

Ethanol can be produced by fermenting glucose, $C_6H_{12}O_6$:

$$C_6H_{12}O_6 \rightarrow 2C_2H_5OH + 2CO_2$$

Calculate the percentage atom economy for this reaction.

Calculate the total mass of the reactants (1 mole of glucose):

Total mass of reactants = $(6 \times 12.0) + (12 \times 1.0) + (6 \times 16.0) = 180.0$

Then find the mass of the desired product (2 moles of ethanol):

Mass of desired product = $2 \times ((12.0 \times 2) + (5 \times 1.0) + 16.0 + 1.0) = 92.0$

So, $\% \text{ atom economy} = \dfrac{\text{molecular mass of desired product}}{\text{sum of molecular masses of all reactants}} \times 100$

$$= \frac{92.0}{180.0} \times 100 = 51.1\%$$

Practice Questions — Application

Q1 Chlorine gas can react with excess methane to make chloromethane:
$$CH_4 + Cl_2 \rightarrow CH_3Cl + HCl$$
   a) Find the total molecular mass of the reactants in this reaction.
   b) Find the molecular mass of the chloromethane produced.
   c) Calculate the percentage atom economy of this reaction.
   d) A company wants to use this reaction to make chloromethane, despite its low atom economy. Suggest one way that they could increase their profit and reduce the waste they produce.

Q2 Aluminium chloride can be produced using this reaction:
$$2Al + 3Cl_2 \rightarrow 2AlCl_3$$
   Calculate the percentage atom economy of this reaction.

Q3 Pure iron can be produced from iron oxide in the blast furnace:
$$2Fe_2O_3 + 3C \rightarrow 4Fe + 3CO_2$$
   Calculate the percentage atom economy of this reaction.

Q4 In industry, ammonia (NH_3) is usually produced using this reaction:
   Reaction 1: $N_2 + 3H_2 \rightarrow 2NH_3$
   It can also be made using this reaction:
   Reaction 2: $2NH_4Cl + Ca(OH)_2 \rightarrow CaCl_2 + 2NH_3 + 2H_2O$
   a) Calculate the percentage atom economy of both reactions.
   b) Give one reason why reaction 1 is used to produce ammonia industrially rather than reaction 2.

Exam Tip
To save time on calculations, make sure you check how many products there are in the reaction first. If there's only one, you already know the atom economy will be 100%.

Practice Questions — Fact Recall

Q1 What is meant by the 'atom economy' of a reaction?

Q2 What are the economic and environmental advantages of using a process with a high atom economy?

Q3 Write down the formula for calculating % atom economy.

Section Summary

Make sure you know...

- What a mole is and how many particles there are in one.
- What the Avogadro constant represents.
- How to calculate the number of particles in a substance using the Avogadro constant.
- How to find the number of moles, mass or relative molecular mass of a substance using the equation 'number of moles = mass of substance $\div M_r$'.
- How to find the number of moles of a substance in a solution, or its concentration or volume, using the concentration equation.
- What the ideal gas equation is.
- The standard units of all the values in the ideal gas equation.
- How to convert units of temperature, pressure and volume into the correct units for the ideal gas equation.
- How to use the ideal gas equation to calculate the pressure, volume, number of moles or temperature of a gas.
- How to write and balance full and ionic equations for reactions.
- How to calculate the mass of a reactant or a product from a balanced equation.
- How to calculate the volume of gas produced by a reaction from a balance equation.
- The four state symbols used in equations.
- How to make up a standard solution.
- How to perform an accurate titration.
- How to calculate the concentration of an acid or alkali from the results of a titration.
- How to calculate the volume of acid needed to neutralise an alkali (and vice versa).
- What an empirical formula and a molecular formula are.
- How to find the molecular formula of a compound from its empirical formula and molecular mass.
- How to find the empirical formula of a compound from its percentage or composition by mass.
- What the ethical, economic and environmental advantages of high atom economy processes are.
- How to calculate the percentage yield of a reaction.
- How to calculate the atom economy of a reaction.

Exam-style Questions

1   Which of these contains the largest number of particles?

    A   1 mole of C_2H_6

    B   3 moles of N

    C   2 moles of CO_2

    D   2 moles of Ag^+ *(1 mark)*

2   5.00 g of CO reacts with excess O_2 to produce 6.40 g of CO_2.
What is the percentage yield of CO_2?

$$2CO_{(g)} + O_{2\,(g)} \rightarrow 2CO_{2\,(g)}$$

    A   72.3%

    B   79.4%

    C   81.5%

    D   83.5%   *(1 mark)*

3   Chlorine gas (Cl_2) is used in water treatment and in the production of plastics.
It is usually produced by the electrolysis of sodium chloride solution:

$$2NaCl_{(aq)} + 2H_2O_{(l)} \rightarrow Cl_{2\,(g)} + H_{2\,(g)} + 2NaOH_{(aq)}$$

3.1   20.0 g of NaCl was dissolved in an excess of water,
and the resulting solution was electrolysed.
Calculate the amount, in moles, of NaCl in 20.0 g.

        (2 marks)

3.2   Calculate the amount, in moles, of Cl_2 gas that would be
produced from a 20.0 g sample of NaCl.

        (1 mark)

3.3   In another experiment a different sample of sodium chloride
solution was electrolysed to produce 0.65 moles of chlorine gas.
Calculate the volume in m^3 that this gas would occupy at 330 K and 98 kPa.
(The gas constant, R = 8.31 J K^{-1} mol^{-1}.)

        (3 marks)

3.4   Calculate the percentage atom economy for the formation
of Cl_2 gas from the electrolysis of NaCl solution.

        (2 marks)

3.5   This reaction has a low atom economy. There are other ways of producing
chlorine that have a higher atom economy. Given that this is the case, suggest
why most chemical companies still use this reaction to produce chlorine.

        (1 mark)

4   Phosphoric acid (H_3PO_4) is made by dissolving oxides of phosphorus in water.

4.1   An oxide of phosphorus contains 43.6% oxygen by mass.
Find the empirical formula of this oxide.

(3 marks)

4.2   Given that the molecular mass of the oxide in **4.1** is 220,
find its molecular formula.

(2 marks)

4.3   Diammonium phosphate $(NH_4)_2HPO_4$ can be used as a fertiliser.
It can be made from ammonia and phosphoric acid according to this equation:

$$2NH_{3\,(g)} + H_3PO_{4\,(aq)} \rightarrow (NH_4)_2HPO_{4\,(s)}$$

Calculate the amount, in moles, of NH_3 in 2.50 g of ammonia gas.

(2 marks)

4.4   Calculate the amount, in moles, of $(NH_4)_2HPO_4$ that would be produced from
2.50 g of ammonia gas. (Assume the phosphoric acid was present in excess.)

(1 mark)

4.5   Calculate the mass of $(NH_4)_2HPO_4$ that would be
produced from 2.50 g of ammonia gas.

(2 marks)

5   A 3.40 g piece of calcium metal was burned in air to make calcium oxide.
Here is the balanced equation for this reaction:

$$2Ca_{(s)} + O_{2\,(g)} \rightarrow 2CaO_{(s)}$$

5.1   State the atom economy of this reaction.
Explain your answer.

(2 marks)

5.2   Calculate the amount, in moles, of Ca in 3.40 g of calcium metal.

(2 marks)

5.3   Calculate the maximum amount, in moles, of CaO that could
be produced by burning the piece of calcium metal.

(1 mark)

5.4   Calculate the maximum mass of CaO that could be produced
by burning this piece of calcium metal.

(2 marks)

5.5   The actual mass of CaO produced was 3.70 g.
Calculate the percentage yield of CaO.

(1 mark)

6   Octane is a hydrocarbon with the molecular formula C_8H_{18}.
It can be used as a fuel in cars, and is a liquid at room temperature.

6.1   Octane burns completely in air to give water and carbon dioxide.
Write a balanced equation for this reaction, including state symbols.

(2 marks)

6.2   A sample of octane is burnt in air. The amount of carbon dioxide
produced occupies a volume of $0.020 \ m^3$ at 308 K and 101 000 Pa.

Calculate the number of moles of CO_2 present in $0.020 \ m^3$ of carbon dioxide
at this temperature and pressure. (The gas constant, $R = 8.31 \ J \ K^{-1} \ mol^{-1}$)

(2 marks)

6.3   How many moles of octane were burnt to produce the amount of CO_2 in **6.2**?

(1 mark)

6.4   A different hydrocarbon contains 85.7% carbon by mass.
Find the empirical formula of this hydrocarbon.

(3 marks)

7   A $20 \ cm^3$ sample of hydrochloric acid was titrated with $0.50 \ mol \ dm^{-3}$
potassium hydroxide in order to determine its concentration.

The acid and the base reacted according to the following equation:

$$HCl_{(aq)} + KOH_{(aq)} \rightarrow KCl_{(aq)} + H_2O_{(l)}$$

7.1   Calculate the mass of pure solid potassium hydroxide that you would
need to dissolve in $150 \ cm^3$ of water to make a $0.50 \ mol \ dm^{-3}$ solution.
Give your answer to two significant figures.

(3 marks)

7.2   The results of the titration experiment are shown in the table below.

Titration	1	2	3	4
Volume of KOH solution added (cm^3)	26.00	26.05	28.30	26.00

Use this data to calculate the concentration of the
hydrochloric acid solution that was used in the titration.

(4 marks)

7.3   Hydrogen chloride gas ($HCl_{(g)}$) is a hydrogen halide.
Hydrochloric acid ($HCl_{(aq)}$) can be made by dissolving this gas in water.

A different acid was made by dissolving 3.07 g of a mystery hydrogen
halide, HX, in pure water. This produced a $0.20 \ dm^3$ sample of the acid.

This sample of acid was then titrated with KOH and found to have a
concentration of $0.12 \ mol \ dm^{-3}$.
Find the relative atomic mass of the halogen, X, and suggest its identity.

(6 marks)

Learning Objectives:

- Be able to predict the charge on a simple ion using the position of the element in the Periodic Table.
- Know the formulas of compound ions, e.g. sulfate, hydroxide, nitrate, carbonate and ammonium.
- Know that ionic bonding involves electrostatic attraction between oppositely charged ions in a lattice.
- Be able to construct formulas for ionic compounds.
- Know that the ionic structure is one of the four types of crystal structure.
- Know that the structure of sodium chloride is an example of an ionic crystal structure.
- Be able to draw diagrams to represent the structure of giant ionic lattices.
- Be able to relate the melting point and conductivity of ionic compounds to their structure and bonding.

**Specification Reference
3.1.3.1, 3.1.3.4**

Tip: The notation, e.g. '2, 8, 7' shows the electron configuration of chlorine. There's more about how to work out electron configurations on page 26.

1. Ionic Bonding

When atoms join together, you get a compound. There are two main types of bonding in compounds — ionic and covalent. First up is ionic bonding.

Ions

Ions are formed when electrons are transferred from one atom to another. The simplest ions are single atoms which have either lost or gained 1, 2 or 3 electrons so that they've got a full outer shell.

Examples

The sodium ion

A sodium atom (Na) loses 1 electron to form a sodium ion (Na^+) — see Figure 1.

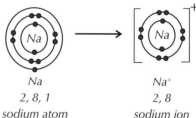

Na
2, 8, 1
sodium atom

Na^+
2, 8
sodium ion

Figure 1: *Formation of a sodium ion.*

This can be shown by the equation: $Na \rightarrow Na^+ + e^-$.

The chloride ion

A chlorine atom (Cl) gains 1 electron to form a chloride ion (Cl^-) — see Figure 2.

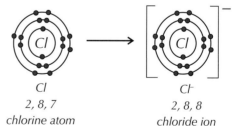

Cl
2, 8, 7
chlorine atom

Cl^-
2, 8, 8
chloride ion

Figure 2: *Formation of a chloride ion.*

This can be shown by the equation: $Cl + e^- \rightarrow Cl^-$.

Other examples:

A magnesium atom (Mg) loses 2 electrons to form a magnesium ion (Mg^{2+}), shown by the equation: $Mg \rightarrow Mg^{2+} + 2e^-$.

An oxygen atom (O) gains 2 electrons to form an oxide ion (O^{2-}), shown by the equation: $O + 2e^- \rightarrow O^{2-}$.

You don't have to remember what ion each element forms — nope, for many of them you just look at the periodic table. Elements in the same group all have the same number of outer electrons. So they have to lose or gain the same number to get the full outer shell that they're aiming for. And this means that they form ions with the same charges. Figure 3 shows the ions formed by the elements in different groups.

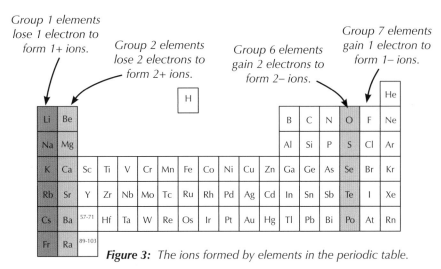

Group 1 elements lose 1 electron to form 1+ ions.

Group 2 elements lose 2 electrons to form 2+ ions.

Group 6 elements gain 2 electrons to form 2– ions.

Group 7 elements gain 1 electron to form 1– ions.

Figure 3: *The ions formed by elements in the periodic table.*

There are lots of ions that are made up of groups of atoms with an overall charge. These are called **compound ions**. Figure 4 gives the formulas of some common compound ions that you need to know for your exam.

Compound ion	Ionic formula
Ammonium	NH_4^+
Carbonate	CO_3^{2-}
Hydroxide	OH^-
Nitrate	NO_3^-
Sulfate	SO_4^{2-}

Figure 4: *The names and formulas of some common compound ions.*

Ionic compounds

Electrostatic attraction holds positive and negative ions together — it's very strong. When atoms are held together in a lattice like this, it's called ionic bonding. When oppositely charged ions come together and form ionic bonds you get an ionic compound.

Examples

Sodium chloride

The formula of sodium chloride is NaCl. Each sodium atom loses an electron to form an Na^+ ion, and each chlorine atom gains an electron to form a Cl^- ion — see Figure 6.

So sodium chloride is made up of Na^+ ions and Cl^- ions held together by electrostatic attraction in a 1:1 ratio. The single positive charge on the Na^+ ion balances the single negative charge on the Cl^- ion so the compound is neutral overall.

Figure 5: *The reaction between sodium and chlorine to form sodium chloride.*

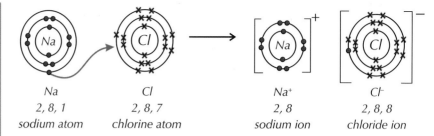

Figure 6: *Formation of sodium chloride from a sodium atom and a chlorine atom.*

Magnesium oxide

Magnesium oxide, MgO, is another example of an ionic compound. The formation of magnesium oxide involves the transfer of two electrons — each magnesium atom loses two electrons to form an Mg^{2+} ion, whilst each oxygen atom gains two electrons to form an O^{2-} ion — see Figure 7.

So as you can see from the formula, magnesium oxide is made up of Mg^{2+} ions and O^{2-} ions in a 1:1 ratio.

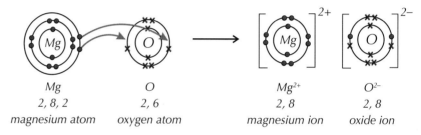

Figure 7: *Formation of magnesium oxide from a magnesium atom and an oxygen atom.*

Magnesium chloride

Magnesium chloride, $MgCl_2$, is yet another ionic compound. When it forms, each magnesium atom loses two electrons to form an Mg^{2+} ion, whilst each chlorine atom gains one electron to form a Cl^- ion — see Figure 8.

So each magnesium atom donates its two outer electrons to two chlorine atoms, resulting in the formula being $MgCl_2$.

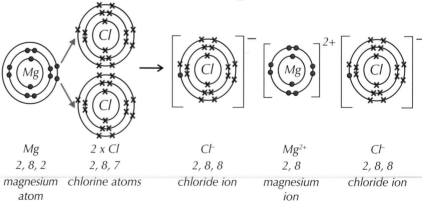

Figure 8: *Formation of magnesium chloride from a magnesium atom and two chlorine atoms.*

Tip: The diagram on the right is a 'dot-and-cross' diagram of sodium chloride. The dots represent the electrons from sodium, and the crosses show the electrons that come from chlorine. Dot-and-cross diagrams are a great way of showing how ions form, as they clearly show where the electrons move from and to.

Tip: The numbers outside the brackets tells you the charge on each ion in the compound.

Tip: These diagrams only show the ions given in the ionic formula, but don't forget that ionic compounds are actually made up of loads of these basic units.

The formula of a compound tells you what ions the compound has in it. The positive charges in the compound balance the negative charges exactly — so the total overall charge is zero. This is a dead handy way of working out the formula of an ionic compound, if you know what ions it contains.

Examples

Sodium nitrate

Sodium nitrate contains Na^+ (+1) and NO_3^- (–1) ions.

The charges are balanced with one of each ion, so the formula of sodium nitrate is $NaNO_3$.

Calcium chloride

Calcium chloride contains Ca^{2+} (+2) and Cl^- (–1) ions.

Chloride ions only have a –1 charge so two of them are needed to balance out the +2 charge of a calcium ion. This gives the formula $CaCl_2$.

Exam Tip
If you're trying to work out the formula of an ionic compound in the exam, always make sure your charges balance.

Giant ionic lattices

Ionic crystals are **giant lattices** of ions. A lattice is just a regular structure. The structure's called 'giant' because it's made up of the same basic unit repeated over and over again. In sodium chloride, the Na^+ and Cl^- ions are packed together. Sodium chloride is an example of a compound with an ionic crystal structure. The sodium chloride lattice is cube shaped (see Figure 10).

Figure 9: Crystals of table salt (sodium chloride).

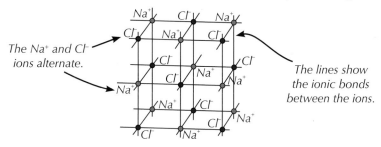

The Na^+ and Cl^- ions alternate.

The lines show the ionic bonds between the ions.

Figure 10: The structure of sodium chloride.

Different ionic compounds have different shaped structures, but they're all still giant lattices.

Tip: Ionic lattices are a type of crystal structure — a regular arrangement of atoms in a solid (or liquid) lattice.

Behaviour of ionic compounds

The structure of ionic compounds decides their physical properties — things like their electrical conductivity, melting point and solubility.

Electrical conductivity

Ionic compounds conduct electricity when they're molten or dissolved — but not when they're solid. The ions in a liquid are free to move (and they carry a charge). In a solid they're fixed in position by the strong ionic bonds.

Melting point

Ionic compounds have high melting points. The giant ionic lattices are held together by strong electrostatic forces. It takes loads of energy to overcome these forces, so melting points are very high (801 °C for sodium chloride).

Solubility

Ionic compounds tend to dissolve in water. Water molecules are polar — part of the molecule has a small negative charge, and the other bits have small positive charges (see pages 84-85). The water molecules pull the ions away from the lattice and cause it to dissolve.

Exam Tip
Make sure you learn these — you might get asked in the exam what properties you'd expect a specific ionic compound to have. It doesn't matter if you've never heard of the compound before — if you know it's an ionic compound you know it'll have these properties.

Practice Questions — Application

Q1 Use the periodic table to give the charge on the following ions:
   a) bromide   b) potassium   c) beryllium

Q2 Calcium reacts with iodine to form an ionic compound.
   a) What is the charge on a calcium ion?
   b) What is the charge on an iodide ion?
   c) Give the formula of calcium iodide.

Q3 Fluorine forms ionic bonds with lithium.
   a) Give the formula of the compound formed.
   b) Describe the formation of an ionic bond between fluorine and lithium atoms.

Q4 Magnesium sulfate is an ionic compound. With reference to its bonding, explain whether you would expect magnesium sulfate to have a high or a low melting point.

Practice Questions — Fact Recall

Q1 Give the formulas of the following compound ions:
   a) sulfate
   b) ammonium

Q2 What effect does electrostatic attraction have on oppositely charged ions?

Q3 Explain what an ionic lattice is.

Q4 Draw the structure of sodium chloride, showing at least 12 ions.

Q5 Explain why ionic compounds conduct electricity when molten.

Q6 Magnesium oxide is an ionic compound. Apart from electrical conductivity when molten or dissolved, describe two physical properties you would expect magnesium oxide to have.

2. Covalent Bonding

Ionic bonding done — now it's on to covalent bonding.

Molecules

Molecules form when two or more atoms bond together — it doesn't matter if the atoms are the same or different. Chlorine gas (Cl_2), carbon monoxide (CO), water (H_2O) and ethanol (C_2H_5OH) are all molecules. Molecules are held together by strong covalent bonds. Covalent bonds can be single, double or triple bonds. In Chemistry, you'll often see covalent bonds represented as lines.

Single bonds

In covalent bonding, two atoms share electrons, so they've both got full outer shells of electrons. A single covalent bond contains a shared pair of electrons. Both the positive nuclei are attracted electrostatically to the shared electrons.

┌─ Examples ───────────────────────────────

Two iodine atoms (I) bond covalently to form a molecule of iodine (I_2) — see Figure 1. These diagrams just show the electrons in the outer shells. (The electrons are really all the same, but dots and crosses are used to make it obvious which atoms the electrons originally came from.)

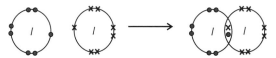

An iodine molecule can also be drawn as:

I—I

Figure 1: *Formation of a molecule of iodine.*

The diagrams below show other examples of covalent molecules.

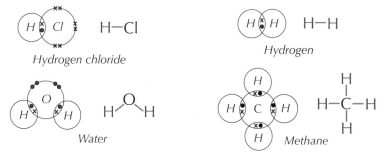

Hydrogen chloride   H—Cl

Hydrogen   H—H

Water   Methane

└──

Double and triple bonds

Atoms in covalent molecules don't just form single bonds — double or even triple covalent bonds can form too. These are shown using multiple lines.

┌─ Examples ───────────────────────────────

Double bonds
One carbon atom (C) can bond to two oxygen atoms (O). Each oxygen atom shares two pairs of electrons with the carbon atom. So, each molecule of carbon dioxide (CO_2) contains two double bonds.

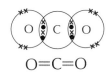

O=C=O

Triple bonds
When a molecule of nitrogen (N_2) forms, the nitrogen atoms share three pairs of electrons. So, each molecule of nitrogen contains one triple bond.

N≡N

Tip: The molecules shown on the previous page are all simple covalent compounds.

Simple covalent compounds

Compounds that are made up of lots of individual molecules are called **simple covalent compounds**. The atoms in the molecules are held together by strong covalent bonds, but the molecules within the simple covalent compound are held together by much weaker forces called **intermolecular forces** (see page 86). It's the intermolecular forces, rather than the covalent bonds within the molecules, that determine the properties of simple covalent compounds. In general, they have low melting and boiling points and are electrical insulators (see page 90).

Giant covalent structures

Giant covalent structures are type of crystal structure. They have a huge network of covalently bonded atoms. (They're sometimes called **macromolecular** structures.)

Carbon atoms can form this type of structure because they can each form four strong, covalent bonds. There are two types of giant covalent carbon structure you need to know about — graphite and diamond.

Tip: 'Delocalised' means an electron isn't attached to a particular atom — it can move around between atoms.

Graphite

The carbon atoms in graphite are arranged in sheets of flat hexagons covalently bonded with three bonds each (see Figure 2). The fourth outer electron of each carbon atom is delocalised. The sheets of hexagons are bonded together by weak van der Waals forces (see page 86).

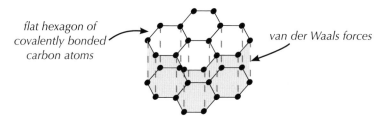

flat hexagon of covalently bonded carbon atoms

van der Waals forces

Figure 2: *The structure of graphite.*

Graphite's structure means it has certain properties:

- The weak bonds between the layers in graphite are easily broken, so the sheets can slide over each other — graphite feels slippery and is used as a dry lubricant and in pencils.
- The delocalised electrons in graphite are free to move along the sheets, so an electric current can flow.
- The layers are quite far apart compared to the length of the covalent bonds, so graphite has a low density and is used to make strong, lightweight sports equipment.

Tip: 'Sublimes' means it changes straight from a solid to a gas, skipping out the liquid stage.

- Because of the strong covalent bonds in the hexagon sheets, graphite has a very high melting point (it sublimes at over 3900 K).
- Graphite is insoluble in any solvent.
  The covalent bonds in the sheets are too difficult to break.

Tip: Tetrahedral is a molecular shape — see pages 78-82 for more on the shapes of molecules.

Diamond

Diamond is also made up of carbon atoms. Each carbon atom is covalently bonded to four other carbon atoms (see Figure 3). The atoms arrange themselves in a tetrahedral shape — its crystal lattice structure.

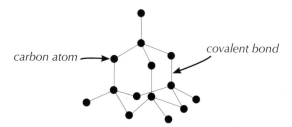

Figure 3: The structure of diamond.

Because of its strong covalent bonds:

- Diamond has a very high melting point — it actually sublimes at over 3800 K.

- Diamond is extremely hard — it's used in diamond-tipped drills and saws.

- Vibrations travel easily through the stiff lattice, so it's a good thermal conductor.

- It can't conduct electricity — all the outer electrons are held in localised bonds.

- Like graphite, diamond won't dissolve in any solvent.

Figure 4: A cut and polished diamond.

Co-ordinate (dative covalent) bonds

In a normal single covalent bond, atoms share a pair of electrons — with one electron coming from each atom. In a **co-ordinate bond**, also known as a **dative covalent bond**, one of the atoms provides both of the shared electrons.

Example

The ammonium ion

The ammonium ion (NH_4^+) is formed by co-ordinate bonding. It forms when the nitrogen atom in an ammonia molecule donates a pair of electrons to a proton (H^+) — see Figure 5.

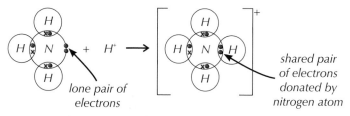

lone pair of electrons

shared pair of electrons donated by nitrogen atom

Figure 5: Co-ordinate bonding in NH_4^+.

Co-ordinate bonding can also be shown in diagrams by an arrow, pointing away from the 'donor' atom (see Figure 6).

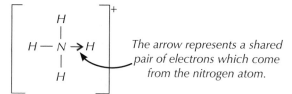

The arrow represents a shared pair of electrons which come from the nitrogen atom.

Figure 6: An alternative way of showing co-ordinate bonding in NH_4^+.

Co-ordinate bonds form when one of the atoms in the bond has a lone pair of electrons, and the other doesn't have any electrons available to share.

The hydroxonium ion

Tip: There's more about working out how many electrons surround an atom on page 78.

The hydroxonium ion (H_3O^+), is formed when H_2O reacts with H^+. Hydrogen ions have no electrons so can only receive electrons, not donate them. However, a water molecule contains an oxygen atom and two hydrogen atoms. Oxygen has six electrons in its outer shell, which is then filled by sharing one electron from each hydrogen atom. This makes eight electrons in total. Only four of these electrons take part in covalent bonding with H atoms so the oxygen is left with two lone pairs of electrons.

So, oxygen donates one lone pair of electrons to the hydrogen ion, forming a dative bond (see Figure 7).

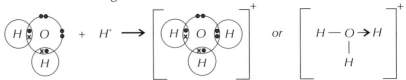

Figure 7: *Dative bonding in H_3O^+.*

Practice Questions — Application

Q1 PH_3 is a covalent compound that reacts with H^+ to form PH_4^+.
   a) How many electrons are in the outer shell of a phosphorus atom?
   b) How many electrons are in the outer shell of phosphorus in a PH_3 molecule?
   c) Name the donor atom in PH_4^+.
   d) Draw a diagram to show the formation of PH_4^+.

Q2 SiO_2 is a giant covalent compound with a structure similar to diamond. Use your knowledge of structure and bonding to predict and explain the properties of SiO_2, limited to its melting point, electrical conductivity and solubility.

Practice Questions — Fact Recall

Q1 How is a covalent bond formed?

Q2 Draw a 'dot-and-cross' diagram to show two iodine atoms coming together to form an iodine molecule.

Q3 Explain what a triple covalent bond is.

Q4 Explain why graphite is used as a lubricant.

Q5 Describe the structure of diamond.

Q6 What is a co-ordinate bond?

Q7 In a diagram showing the bonding in a molecule, what does an arrow show?

3. Charge Clouds

Electrons can be found whizzing around nuclei in charge clouds.

Charge clouds

Molecules and molecular ions come in loads of different shapes. The shape depends on the number of pairs of electrons in the outer shell of the central atom. Pairs of electrons can be shared in a covalent bond or can be unshared. Shared electrons are called bonding pairs, unshared electrons are called **lone pairs** or non-bonding pairs.

Bonding pairs and lone pairs of electrons exist as charge clouds. A charge cloud is an area where you have a big chance of finding an electron. The electrons don't stay still — they whizz around inside the charge cloud.

> **Example**
>
> In ammonia, the outer shell of nitrogen has four pairs of electrons. These electrons can be shown in a 'dot-and-cross' diagram or as charge clouds:
>
>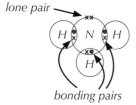
>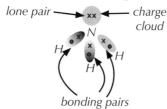
>
> **Figure 1:** 'Dot-and-cross' diagram.   **Figure 2:** Ammonia's charge clouds.

Electron pair repulsion

Electrons are all negatively charged, so charge clouds repel each other until they're as far apart as possible. This sounds simple, but the shape of a charge cloud affects how much it repels other charge clouds. Lone-pair charge clouds repel more than bonding-pair charge clouds, so bond angles are often reduced because bonding pairs are pushed together by lone-pair repulsion. This is known by the snappy name '**Valence Shell Electron Pair Repulsion Theory**'.

> **Example**
>
> The central atom in methane, ammonia and water each has four pairs of electrons in its outer shell, but their bond angles are different:
>
> *The lone pair repels the bonding pairs.*   *2 lone pairs reduce the bond angle even more.*
>
>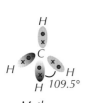
>
>
>
> Methane   Ammonia   Water —
> — no lone pairs   — 1 lone pair   2 lone pairs

So lone pair/lone pair angles are the biggest, lone pair/bonding pair angles the second biggest and bonding pair/bonding pair angles are the smallest.

Practice Questions — Fact Recall

Q1 What is a lone pair of electrons?

Q2 Briefly describe a charge cloud.

Q3 Describe valence shell electron pair repulsion theory.

Learning Objectives:

- Be able to describe bonding pairs and lone (non-bonding) pairs of electrons as charge clouds that repel each other.

- Know that pairs of electrons in the outer shell of atoms arrange themselves as far apart as possible to minimise repulsion.

- Know that lone pair-lone pair repulsion is greater than lone pair-bond pair repulsion, which is greater than bond pair-bond pair repulsion.

- Understand the effect of electron pair repulsion on the bond angles in molecules.

Specification Reference 3.1.3.5

Tip: There's lots more coming up about bond angles and shapes of molecules in the next few pages.

- Be able to explain the shapes of, and bond angles in, simple molecules and ions with up to six electron pairs (including lone pairs of electrons) surrounding the central atom.

- Understand the effect of electron pair repulsion on the bond angles in molecules.

Specification Reference 3.1.3.5

4. Shapes of Molecules

There's a lot of variation in molecular shape and you need to understand how to work out the shape of any molecule or molecular ion. Don't worry though, the next few pages have lots of advice to help you along.

Drawing shapes of molecules

It can be tricky to draw molecules showing their shapes, because you're trying to show a 3D shape on a 2D page. Usually you do it is by using different types of lines to show which way the bonds are pointing. In a molecule diagram, use wedges to show a bond pointing towards you, and a broken (or dotted) line to show a bond pointing away from you (see Figure 1).

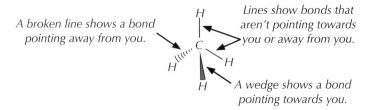

A broken line shows a bond pointing away from you.

Lines show bonds that aren't pointing towards you or away from you.

A wedge shows a bond pointing towards you.

Figure 1: *A molecular diagram showing the shape of methane.*

Tip: It might help you to think of wedges as bonds that stick out of the page, broken lines as bonds that point behind the page and straight lines as bonds that are flat against the page.

Finding the number of electron pairs

To work out the shape of a molecule or an ion you need to know how many lone pairs and how many bonding pairs of electrons are on the central atom. To find that out, you just follow these steps:

1. Find the central atom — it's the one all the other atoms are bonded to.

2. Work out how many electrons are in the outer shell of the central atom. This will be the same as its group number in the periodic table.

3. Add 1 electron for every atom that the central atom is bonded to. (You can work this out from the formula of the molecule or ion.)

4. If you're looking at an ion, you need to take its charge into account — add 1 electron for each negative charge or subtract 1 for each positive charge.

5. Add up all the electrons. Divide by 2 to find the number of electron pairs.

6. Compare the number of electron pairs to the number of bonds to find the number of lone pairs and the number of bonding pairs on the central atom.

Figure 2: *A molecular model of a molecule of methane.*

Tip: The exception to the rule that the number of electrons in the outer shell of an atom being the same as its group number is group 0. Group 0 elements have 8 electrons in their outer shells (apart from helium, which has 2).

┌─ **Example** ─────────────────

Carbon tetrafluoride, CF_4

1. The central atom in this molecule is carbon.

2. Carbon's in group 4. It has 4 electrons in its outer shell.

3. The carbon atom is bonded to 4 fluorine atoms.

4. CF_4 isn't an ion.

5. There are $4 + 4 = 8$ electrons in the outer shell of the carbon atom, which is $8 \div 2 = 4$ electron pairs.

6. 4 pairs of electrons are involved in bonding the fluorine atoms to the carbon so there must be 4 bonding pairs of electrons. That's all the electrons, so there are no lone pairs.

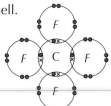

Figure 3: *Dot-and-cross diagram for CF_4.*

Example

Phosphorus trihydride, PH_3

1. The central atom in this molecule is phosphorus.
2. Phosphorus is in group 5, so it has five electrons in its outer shell.
3. Phosphorus has formed 3 bonds with hydrogen atoms.
4. PH_3 isn't an ion.
5. There are $5 + 3 = 8$ electrons in the outer shell of the phosphorus atom, so there are $8 \div 2 = 4$ electron pairs.
6. 3 electron pairs are involved in bonding with the hydrogen atoms (bonding pairs), so there must also be 1 lone pair of electrons on the phosphorus atom.

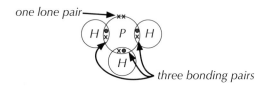

Figure 4: Dot-and-cross diagram for PH_3.

Tip: A hydrogen atom will form one covalent bond with another atom to complete its outer shell.

Molecular shapes

Once you know how many bonding pairs and how many lone pairs are on the central atom, you can work out the shape of the molecule. Here's a run down of the different shapes that you might come across (and their bond angles).

Tip: You need to know how to calculate the number of electron pairs before you try and learn this bit. Make sure you've got the previous page firmly in your head before you go any further.

Central atoms with two electron pairs

Molecules with two electron pairs have a bond angle of 180° and have a **linear** shape. This is because the pairs of bonding electrons want to be as far away from each other as possible.

Example ─ Maths Skills

Beryllium chloride, $BeCl_2$

In $BeCl_2$, the central beryllium atom has two bonding pairs of electrons and no lone pairs. So the bond angle in $BeCl_2$ is 180° and it has a linear shape.

$$Cl-Be-Cl \quad 180°$$

Exam Tip
You'll be expected to know the bond angles for different shapes of molecules in your exam — so make sure you learn them.

Central atoms with three electron pairs

Molecules that have three electron pairs around the central atom don't always have the same shape — the shape depends on the combination of bonding pairs and lone pairs of electrons.

If there are three bonding pairs of electrons the repulsion of the charge clouds is the same between each pair and so the bond angles are all 120°. The shape of the molecule is called **trigonal planar**.

Example ─ Maths Skills

Boron trifluoride, BF_3

The central boron atom has three bonding pairs and no lone pairs, so the bond angle in BF_3 is 120° and it has a **trigonal planar** shape.

If you have a molecule with two bonding pairs of electrons and one lone pair of electrons, you'll get a non-linear or 'bent' molecule (see below for more on bent molecules). The bond angle will be a bit less than 120°.

Central atoms with four electron pairs

If there are four pairs of bonding electrons and no lone pairs on a central atom, all the bond angles are 109.5° — the charge clouds all repel each other equally. The shape of the molecule is **tetrahedral**.

Example — Maths Skills

Ammonium ion, NH_4^+

In NH_4^+, the central nitrogen atom has four bonding pairs of electrons and no lone pairs, so the shape of NH_4^+ is **tetrahedral**.

If there are three bonding pairs of electrons and one lone pair, the lone-pair/bonding-pair repulsion will be greater than the bonding-pair/bonding-pair repulsion and so the angles between the atoms will change. There'll be smaller bond angles between the bonding pairs of electrons and larger bond angles between the lone pair and the bonding pairs. The bond angle is 107° and the shape of the molecules is **trigonal pyramidal**.

Example — Maths Skills

Ammonia, NH_3

In NH_3, the central nitrogen atom has three bonding pairs of electrons and a lone pair so the shape of NH_3 is **trigonal pyramidal**.

If there are two bonding pairs of electrons and two lone pairs of electrons the lone-pair/lone-pair repulsion will squish the bond angle even further. The bond angle will be around 104.5° and the shape of the molecules is **bent** (or **non-linear**).

Example — Maths Skills

Water, H_2O

In H_2O, the central oxygen atom has two bonding pairs shared with hydrogen atoms and two lone pairs so the shape of H_2O is **bent** (or **non-linear**).

Figure 5: *A molecular model of water, showing it to have a bent (non-linear) shape.*

Central atoms with five electron pairs

Some central atoms can 'expand the octet' — which just means that they can have more than eight bonding electrons in their outer shells.

A molecule with five bonding pairs will be **trigonal bipyramidal**. Repulsion between the bonding pairs means that three of the atoms will form a trigonal planar shape with bond angles of 120° and the other two atoms will be at 90° to them.

Example — **Maths Skills**

Phosphorus pentachloride, PCl$_5$

In PCl$_5$, the central phosphorus atom has five bonding pairs and no lone pairs, so it has a **trigonal bipyramidal** shape.

If there are four bonding pairs and one lone pair of electrons, the molecule forms a **seesaw** shape. The lone pair is always positioned where one of the trigonal planar atoms would be in a trigonal bipyramidal molecule.

Example — **Maths Skills**

Sulfur tetrafluoride, SF$_4$

In SF^4, the cental sulfur atom has four bonding pairs and one lone pair so it has a **seesaw** shape.

If there are three bonding pairs and two lone pairs of electrons, the molecule will be **T-shaped**.

Example — **Maths Skills**

Chlorine trifluoride, ClF$_3$

In ClF$_3$, the central chlorine atom has three bonding pairs and two lone pairs so it has a **T-shape**.

Tip: If you look at the shapes of the molecules where five pairs of electrons surround the central atom, you can see how they're all based on a trigonal bipyramidal shape. Some just have the bonds replaced by lone pairs of electrons. Similarly, molecules with six pairs of electrons are based on an octahedral shape, and molecules with four pairs of electrons are based on a tetrahedral shape.

Central atoms with six electron pairs

A molecule with six bonding pairs will be **octahedral**. All of the bond angles in the molecule will be 90°.

Example — **Maths Skills**

Sulfur hexafluoride, SF$_6$

In SF6, the central sulfur atom has six bonding pairs and no lone pairs, making its shape **octahedral**.

If there are five bonding pairs and one lone pair, the molecule forms a **square pyramidal** structure. (Molecules with this shape are very rare.)

Figure 6: *A molecular model of sulfur hexafluoride.*

Example — **Maths Skills**

Chlorine pentafluoride, ClF$_5$

In ClF$_5$, the central chlorine has five bonding pairs and one lone pair of electrons, making its shape **square pyramidal**.

If there are four bonding pairs and two lone pairs of electrons, the molecule will be **square planar**.

Example — **Maths Skills**

Xenon tetrafluoride, XeF$_4$

In XeF$_4$, the central xenon atom has four bonding pairs and two lone pairs of electrons — its shape is **square planar**.

Finding the shape of an unfamiliar molecule

In the exam you could be asked to draw the shape of a molecule you've never met before. Don't panic, just take it step by step. Work out how many electron pairs the molecule has, then work out how many of those are lone pairs. Decide what the bond angles are in the molecule, then draw and label it neatly.

--- Example ---

Predict the shape of the BF_4^- ion.

First, follow the steps on page 78 to find the number of electron pairs:

1. The central atom is boron.
2. Boron is in Group 3, so it has 3 electrons in its outer shell.
3. The boron atom is bonded to 4 fluorine atoms.
4. BF_3 is an ion with a 1– charge, so you need to add one extra electron to account for that.
5. That means there are $3 + 4 + 1 = 8$ electrons in the outer shell of the central boron atom. That's $8 \div 2 = 4$ pairs.
6. The boron atom has 4 electron pairs around it, and has made 4 bonds. So it has 4 bonding pairs and no lone pairs.

A molecule with 4 bonding pairs and no lone pairs will have a tetrahedral shape, with bond angles of 109.5°. Now all you have to do is draw it.

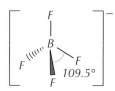

Figure 7: The shape of the BF_4^- ion.

Awkward molecules

There are some special cases where molecules don't follow the normal rules. If a molecule has multiple bonds, you treat each multiple bond as if it was one single bond when you're working out the shape (even though there's usually slightly more repulsion between double bonds).

Figure 8: A molecular model of carbon dioxide, showing it to be a linear molecule with a bond angle of 180°.

Tip: If the central atom forms multiple bonds (i.e. double or triple bonds), then treat each multiple bond as a single electron pair when you're working out the shape.

--- Examples ---

Carbon dioxide, CO_2

Carbon has four bonding pairs of electrons (found in two carbon-oxygen double bonds) and no lone pairs. Double bonds can be treated as one bond, so you can say that there are two bonds and no lone pairs — CO_2 will be **linear**.

$$O{=}C{=}O$$
180°

Sulfur dioxide, SO_2

120°

The extra electron density in the double bonds cancels out the extra repulsion from the lone pair, so you get 120° angles.

Sulfur has four bonding pairs of electrons (found in two sulfur-oxygen double bonds) and one lone pair. Double bonds can be treated as one bond so you can say there that there are two bonds and one lone pair — SO_2 will be **bent** (non-linear).

Practice Questions — Application

Q1 a) How many electron pairs are on the central atom of an H_2S molecule?

   b) How many lone pairs does a molecule of H_2S have?

   c) Draw the shape of an H_2S molecule.

   d) Name the shape of an H_2S molecule.

   e) Give the bond angle between bonding pairs in H_2S.

Q2 a) How many electron pairs are on the central atom of an H_3O^+ molecule?

   b) How many lone pairs does a molecule of H_3O^+ have?

   c) Draw and name the shape of H_3O^+.

   d) Give the bond angle between bonding pairs in H_3O^+.

Q3 a) Draw and name the shape of a molecule of AsH_3.

   b) Give the bonding pair/bonding pair bond angle in AsH_3.

Q4 Draw and name the shape of a molecule of CCl_2F_2.

Exam Tip
Make sure you practise drawing the different shapes that molecules can have — it'll make it easier if you have to in the exam.

Practice Questions — Fact Recall

Q1 What is the bond angle between electron pairs in a trigonal planar molecule?

Q2 How many electron pairs are on the central atom in a tetrahedral molecule?

Q3 Name the shape that a molecule will have if it has four bonding pairs and one lone pair on its central atom.

Learning Objectives:

- Know that electronegativity is the power of an atom to attract the pair of electrons in a covalent bond.
- Know that the electron distribution in a covalent bond between elements with different electronegativities will be unsymmetrical and that this produces a polar covalent bond and may cause a molecule to have a permanent dipole.
- Be able to use partial charges to show that a bond is polar.
- Be able to explain why some molecules with polar bonds do not have a permanent dipole.

Specification Reference 3.1.3.6

Exam Tip
You don't need to learn the electronegativity values — if you need them you'll be given them in the exam.

Tip: The atoms in polar bonds generally have an electronegativity difference that is greater than 0.4.

5. Polarisation

Polarisation of bonds occurs because of the nature of different atomic nuclei — some are just more attractive than others.

Electronegativity

The ability to attract the bonding electrons in a covalent bond is called **electronegativity**. Electronegativity is measured on the Pauling Scale. A higher number means an element is better able to attract the bonding electrons. Fluorine is the most electronegative element. Oxygen, nitrogen and chlorine are also very strongly electronegative — see Figure 1.

Element	H	C	N	Cl	O	F
Electronegativity (Pauling Scale)	2.20	2.55	3.04	3.16	3.44	3.98

Figure 1: The electronegativity of different elements.

Polar and non-polar bonds

The covalent bonds in diatomic gases (e.g. H_2, Cl_2) are non-polar because the atoms have equal electronegativities and so the electrons are equally attracted to both nuclei (see Figure 2). Some elements, like carbon and hydrogen, have pretty similar electronegativities, so bonds between them are essentially non-polar.

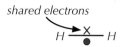

Figure 2: A non-polar covalent bond in a hydrogen molecule.

In a covalent bond between two atoms of different electronegativities, the bonding electrons are pulled towards the more electronegative atom. This makes the bond polar (see Figure 3). The greater the difference in electronegativity, the more polar the bond.

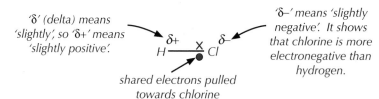

Figure 3: A polar covalent bond in a hydrogen chloride molecule.

In a polar bond, the difference in electronegativity between the two atoms causes a **dipole**. A dipole is a difference in charge between the two atoms caused by a shift in electron density in the bond.

Polar molecules

If charge is distributed unevenly over a whole molecule, then the molecule will have a **permanent dipole**. Molecules that have a permanent dipole are called **polar molecules**. Whether or not a molecule is polar depends on whether it has any polar bonds, and its overall shape.

In simple molecules, such as hydrogen chloride, the one polar bond means charge is distributed unevenly across the whole molecule, so it has a permanent dipole (see Figure 4).

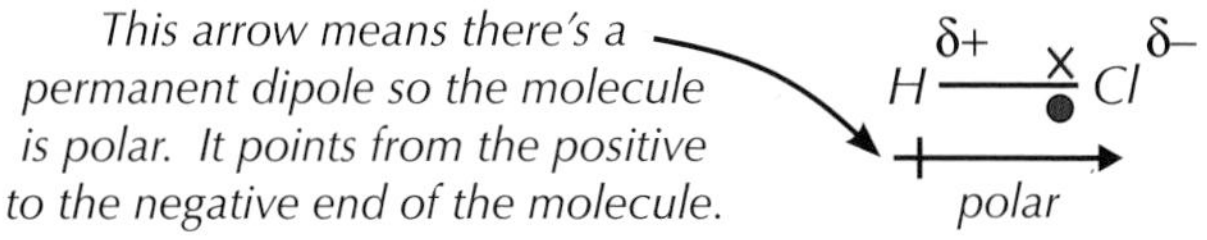

This arrow means there's a permanent dipole so the molecule is polar. It points from the positive to the negative end of the molecule.

$\delta+$ $\underset{\bullet}{\times}$ $\delta-$
$H —— Cl$
polar

Figure 4: *The permanent dipole in a molecule of hydrogen chloride.*

More complicated molecules might have several polar bonds. The shape of the molecule will decide whether or not it has an overall permanent dipole. If the polar bonds are arranged symmetrically so that the dipoles cancel each other out, such as in carbon dioxide, then the molecule has no permanent dipole and is non-polar — see Figure 5.

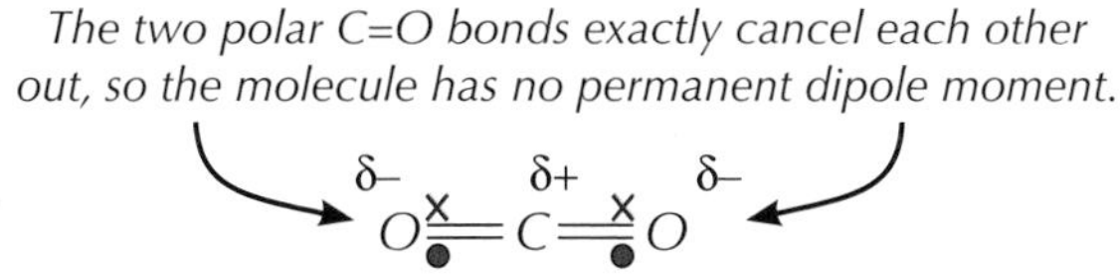

The two polar C=O bonds exactly cancel each other out, so the molecule has no permanent dipole moment.

$O\overset{\times}{\underset{\bullet}{=}}C\overset{\times}{\underset{\bullet}{=}}O$
$\delta-$ $\delta+$ $\delta-$

Figure 5: *A molecule of carbon dioxide has no permanent dipole moment.*

If the polar bonds are arranged so that they all point in roughly the same direction, and they don't cancel each other out, then charge will be arranged unevenly across the whole molecule. This results in a polar molecule — the molecule has a permanent dipole (see Figure 6).

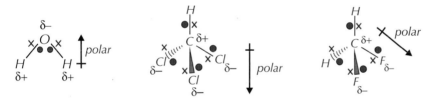

Figure 6: *The permanent dipoles in some polar molecules.*

Tip: It's really, really important that you get your head around the relationship between electronegativity, polarisation and dipoles. Differences in the <u>electronegativity</u> of atoms <u>cause</u> bonds to become <u>polarised</u>, which results in a <u>dipole</u> — a <u>difference in charge</u> between the two atoms. If these dipoles don't cancel out then the molecule will be <u>polar</u> (it will have a <u>permanent dipole</u>).

Practice Questions — Application

Q1 Draw the shapes of the following molecules.
Then predict whether or not they have a permanent dipole:

a) BCl_3 (The B–Cl bonds are polar.)

b) CH_2Cl_2

c) PF_3 (The P–F bonds are polar.)

Q2 Given that the Pauling electronegativities of silicon and chlorine are 1.90 and 3.16 respectively, explain whether silicon tetrachloride ($SiCl_4$) will possess polar bonds and/or have a permanent dipole.

Tip: Have a look back at pages 78-82 for the rules on predicting the shapes of molecules.

Practice Questions — Fact Recall

Q1 Chlorine is more electronegative than hydrogen.
Explain what this means.

Q2 Explain why the H–F bond is polarised.

Q3 What is a dipole?

- Know that
  intermolecular
  forces exist between
  molecules, including
  induced dipole–dipole
  forces (van der Waals
  forces), permanent
  dipole–dipole forces
  and hydrogen bonds.

- Be able to draw
  diagrams of molecular
  crystal structures.

- Be able to explain
  how the melting and
  boiling points of
  molecular substances
  are influenced by
  the strength of these
  intermolecular forces.

- Explain the
  importance of
  hydrogen bonds in the
  low density of ice and
  the anomalous boiling
  points of compounds.

- Be able to explain
  the existence of
  intermolecular forces
  between familiar and
  unfamiliar molecules.

- Know that the
  molecular lattice
  structure is one of the
  four types of crystal
  structure.

- Know that the
  structures found in
  iodine and ice are
  examples of molecular
  crystal structures.

- Be able to relate
  the melting point
  and conductivity of
  molecular compounds
  to their structure and
  bonding.

**Specification Reference
3.1.3.4, 3.1.3.7**

6. Intermolecular Forces

Molecules don't just exist independently — they can interact with each other. And you need to know how they interact.

What are intermolecular forces?

Intermolecular forces are forces between molecules. They're much weaker than covalent, ionic or metallic bonds. There are three types you need to know about: induced dipole-dipole (or van der Waals) forces, permanent dipole-dipole forces and hydrogen bonding (this is the strongest type).

Van der Waals forces

Van der Waals forces cause all atoms and molecules to be attracted to each other. Electrons in charge clouds are always moving really quickly. At any particular moment, the electrons in an atom are likely to be more to one side than the other. At this moment, the atom would have a temporary dipole. This dipole can cause another temporary dipole in the opposite direction on a neighbouring atom (see Figure 1). The two dipoles are then attracted to each other. The second dipole can cause yet another dipole in a third atom. It's kind of like the domino effect. Because the electrons are constantly moving, the dipoles are being created and destroyed all the time. Even though the dipoles keep changing, the overall effect is for the atoms to be attracted to each other.

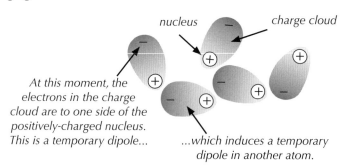

At this moment, the electrons in the charge cloud are to one side of the positively-charged nucleus. This is a temporary dipole...

...which induces a temporary dipole in another atom.

Figure 1: *Temporary dipoles in a liquid resulting in van der Waals forces.*

--- Example ---

Van der Waals forces are responsible for holding iodine molecules together in a lattice. Iodine atoms are held together in pairs by strong covalent bonds to form molecules of I_2 (see Figure 2). But the molecules are then held together in a molecular lattice arrangement by weak van der Waals forces (see Figure 3). Molecular lattices are a type of crystal structure.

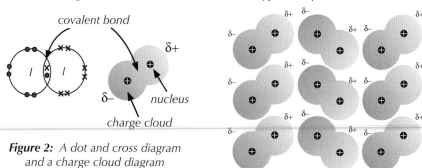

Figure 2: *A dot and cross diagram and a charge cloud diagram showing a molecule of iodine.*

Figure 3: *Lattice of iodine molecules held together by van der Waals forces.*

Not all van der Waals forces are the same strength — larger molecules have larger electron clouds, meaning stronger van der Waals forces.

The shape of molecules also affects the strength of van der Waals forces. Long, straight molecules can lie closer together than branched ones — the closer together two molecules are, the stronger the forces between them.

When you boil a liquid, you need to overcome the intermolecular forces, so that the particles can escape from the liquid surface. It stands to reason that you need more energy to overcome stronger intermolecular forces, so liquids with stronger Van der Waals forces will have higher boiling points. Van der Waals forces affect other physical properties, such as melting point and viscosity too.

Tip: As well as induced dipole-dipole forces, van der Waals forces can also be called London forces or dispersion forces.

Tip: Remember — there are van der Waals forces between the molecules in every chemical.

┌ **Examples** ─────────────────────

As you go down the group of noble gases, the number of electrons increases. So the van der Waals forces increase, and so do the boiling points (see Figure 4).

Tip: The noble gases are all in Group 0 in the periodic table.

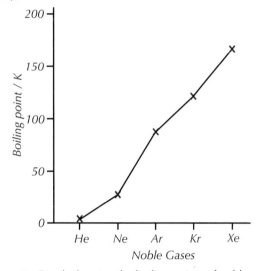

Figure 4: Graph showing the boiling points of noble gases.

As the alkane chains get longer, the number of electrons in the molecules increases. The area over which the van der Waals forces can act also increases. This means the van der Waals forces are stronger, and so the boiling points increase (see Figure 5).

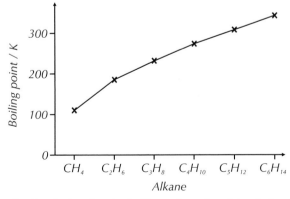

Figure 5: Graph showing the boiling points of straight-chain alkanes

Permanent dipole-dipole forces

In a substance made up of molecules that have permanent dipoles, there will be weak electrostatic forces of attraction between the δ+ and δ– charges on neighbouring molecules. These are called permanent dipole-dipole forces.

Example

Hydrogen chloride gas has polar molecules due to the difference in electronegativity of hydrogen and chlorine.

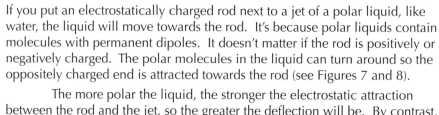

The molecules have weak electrostatic forces between them because of the shift in electron density.

Figure 6: *Permanent dipole-dipole forces in hydrogen chloride gas.*

Exam Tip
When you're drawing dipoles in the exam, make sure you include the δ+ and δ– symbols to show the charges.

If you put an electrostatically charged rod next to a jet of a polar liquid, like water, the liquid will move towards the rod. It's because polar liquids contain molecules with permanent dipoles. It doesn't matter if the rod is positively or negatively charged. The polar molecules in the liquid can turn around so the oppositely charged end is attracted towards the rod (see Figures 7 and 8).

The more polar the liquid, the stronger the electrostatic attraction between the rod and the jet, so the greater the deflection will be. By contrast, liquids made up of non-polar molecules, such as hexane, will not be affected at all when placed near a charged rod.

Figure 7: *A charged glass rod bends water.*

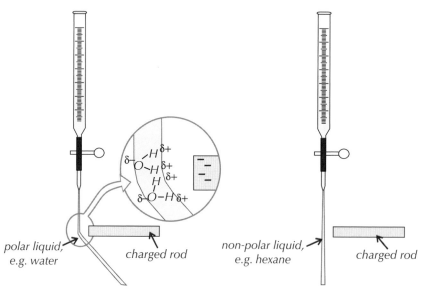

polar liquid, e.g. water — charged rod

non-polar liquid, e.g. hexane — charged rod

Figure 8: *A charged glass rod bends polar liquids such as water but has no effect on non-polar liquids such as hexane.*

Hydrogen bonding

Hydrogen bonding is the strongest intermolecular force. It only happens when hydrogen is covalently bonded to fluorine, nitrogen or oxygen. Fluorine, nitrogen and oxygen are very electronegative, so they draw the bonding electrons away from the hydrogen atom.

Exam Tip
Hydrogen bonding is a special case scenario — it only happen in specific molecules. In the exam, you could be asked to compare intermolecular forces in different substances, so you'll need to know the different intermolecular forces and their relative strengths. Don't forget that not <u>every</u> molecule with hydrogen in it makes hydrogen bonds.

The bond is so polarised, and hydrogen has such a high charge density because it's so small, that the hydrogen atoms form weak bonds with lone pairs of electrons on the fluorine, nitrogen or oxygen atoms of other molecules. Molecules which have hydrogen bonding are usually organic, containing -OH or -NH groups.

Examples

Water and ammonia both have hydrogen bonding (see Figures 9 and 10).

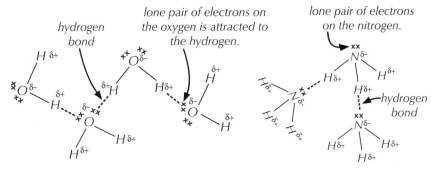

hydrogen bond

lone pair of electrons on the oxygen is attracted to the hydrogen.

lone pair of electrons on the nitrogen.

hydrogen bond

Figure 9: *Hydrogen bonding in water.*   **Figure 10:** *Hydrogen bonding in ammonia.*

Hydrogen bonding has a huge effect on the properties of substances. Substances with hydrogen bonds have higher boiling and melting points than other similar molecules because of the extra energy needed to break the hydrogen bonds. This is the case with water which has a much higher boiling point than the other group 6 hydrides — see Figure 11.

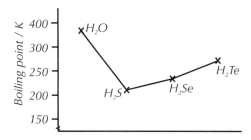

Figure 11: *Graph showing the boiling points of group 6 hydrides.*

The effects of hydrogen bonding are very apparent in other physical properties of water as well. As liquid water cools to form ice, the molecules make more hydrogen bonds and arrange themselves into a regular lattice structure. Since hydrogen bonds are relatively long, the average distance between H_2O molecules is greater in ice than in liquid water — so ice is less dense than liquid water (see Figures 12 and 13). This is unusual — most substances are more dense as solids than they are as liquids.

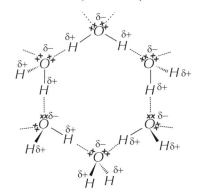

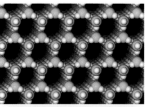

Figure 13: *Lattice of water molecules in ice held together by hydrogen bonds.*

Figure 12: *The structures of ice (top) and liquid water (bottom).*

Behaviour of simple covalent compounds

Simple covalent compounds have strong covalent bonds within molecules (see pages 73-74), but weak forces between the molecules. Their physical properties, such as electrical conductivity, melting point and solubility are determined by the bonding in the compound.

Electrical conductivity

Simple covalent compounds don't conduct electricity because there are no free ions or electrons to carry the charge.

Melting point

Simple covalent compounds have low melting points because the weak forces between molecules are easily broken.

Solubility

Some simple covalent compounds dissolve in water depending on how polarised the molecules are (see pages 84-85 for more on polarisation).

Tip: When you melt or boil a simple covalent compound, the weak intermolecular forces are broken. The strong covalent bonds between the atoms in a molecule stay the same.

Trends in melting and boiling points

In general, the main factor that determines the melting or boiling point of a substance will be the strength of the induced dipole-dipole forces (unless the molecule can form hydrogen bonds).

┌─ **Example** ─────────────────────────────────

As you go down the Group 7 hydrides from HCl to HI, there are two competing factors that could affect the overall strength of the intermolecular bonds, and so the boiling points:

- The polarity of the molecules decreases, so the strength of the permanent dipole-dipole interactions decreases.

- The number of electrons in the molecules increases, so the strength of the induced dipole-dipole interactions increases.

As you can see from Figure 14, the boiling points of the Group 7 hydrides increase from HCl to HI. So the increasing strength of the induced dipole-dipole interactions has a greater effect on the boiling point than the decreasing strength of the permanent dipole-dipole interactions.

Tip: The boiling points of the Group 7 hydrides are still very low — except for HF, they're all gases at room temperature.

Tip: HF has the highest boiling point of the Group 7 hydrides because it can form hydrogen bonds.

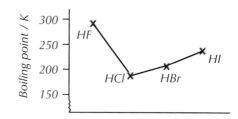

Figure 14: *Boiling points of the Group 7 hydrides.*

If you have two molecules with a similar number of electrons, then the strength of their induced dipole-dipole interactions will be similar. So if one of the substances has molecules that are more polar than the other, it will have stronger permanent dipole-dipole interactions and so a higher boiling point.

Practice Questions — Application

Q1 What intermolecular force(s) exist(s) in H_2?

Q2 Chlorine (Cl_2) is a simple covalent molecule.

    a) Explain why chlorine has a very low melting point.

    b) Would you expect chlorine to conduct electricity? Explain your answer.

Q3 Look at the information in the table below.

Compound	Melting point / °C
Decane, $C_{10}H_{22}$	−30.5
Methane, CH_4	−182

Explain why the melting point of decane is higher than the melting point of methane.

Q4 The table below shows the electronegativity values of some elements

Element	H	C	Cl	O	F
Electronegativity (Pauling Scale)	2.20	2.55	3.16	3.44	3.98

    a) Use the table above to explain why there are hydrogen bonds between H_2O molecules but not between HCl molecules.

    b) Identify one other element from the table that would form hydrogen bonds when covalently bonded to hydrogen.

    c) Name one other element from the table that would not form hydrogen bonds when covalently bonded to hydrogen.

Q5 Hydrogen has an electronegativity value of 2.20 on the Pauling scale, nitrogen has a value of 3.04 and phosphorous has a value of 2.19.

    a) The boiling point of NH_3 is −33 °C and the boiling point of PH_3 is −88 °C. Explain why the boiling point of PH_3 is lower.

    b) Arsenic (As) has an electronegativity value of 2.18. Would you expect the boiling point of AsH_3 to be higher or lower than that of NH_3?

Exam Tip

It's pretty common to be asked to identify and compare the intermolecular forces in different substances in the exam. You'll also need to know the effects that the intermolecular forces have on the properties of the substances, so make sure you know all this stuff inside out.

Practice Questions — Fact Recall

Q1 Describe the bonding within and between iodine molecules.

Q2 What are permanent dipole-dipole forces?

Q3 Name the strongest type of intermolecular force in water.

Q4 a) What is the strongest intermolecular force in ammonia?

    b) Draw a diagram to show this intermolecular force between two ammonia molecules.

Q5 Explain why ice is less dense than liquid water.

Exam Tip

If you're asked to draw a diagram to show hydrogen bonding you'll need to include the lone pairs of electrons on the electronegative atom (O, N or F). You may also have to show the partial charges — the δ+ goes on the H atom and the δ− goes on the electronegative atom.

7. Metallic Bonding

You might remember metallic bonding from GCSE, but there's more to know...

Metallic bonding

Metal elements exist as **giant metallic lattice structures**. The outermost shell of electrons of a metal atom is delocalised — the electrons are free to move about the metal. This leaves a positive metal ion, e.g. Na^+, Mg^{2+}, Al^{3+}. The positive metal ions are attracted to the delocalised negative electrons. They form a lattice of closely packed positive ions in a sea of delocalised electrons — this is **metallic bonding** (see Figure 1).

- Know that metallic bonding involves attraction between delocalised electrons and positive ions arranged in a lattice.

- Know that metallic lattices are one of the four types of crystal structure.

- Know that the structure found in magnesium is an example of a metallic lattice.

- Be able to draw diagrams to represent the structure of metallic lattices.

- Be able to relate the melting point and conductivity of metallic compounds to their structure and bonding.

Specification Reference 3.1.3.3, 3.1.3.4

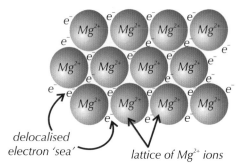

delocalised electron 'sea'   *lattice of Mg^{2+} ions*

Figure 1: *Metallic bonding in magnesium.*

Metallic bonding explains the properties of metals.

Melting point

Metals have high melting points because of the strong electrostatic attraction between the positive metal ions and the delocalised sea of electrons. The number of delocalised electrons per atom affects the melting point. The more there are, the stronger the bonding will be and the higher the melting point. Mg^{2+} has two delocalised electrons per atom, so it's got a higher melting point than Na^+, which only has one. The size of the metal ion and the lattice structure also affect the melting point.

Ability to be shaped

As there are no bonds holding specific ions together, the metal ions can slide over each other when the structure is pulled, so metals are malleable (can be shaped) and ductile (can be drawn into a wire, see Figure 2).

Conductivity

The delocalised electrons can pass kinetic energy to each other, making metals good thermal conductors. Metals are good electrical conductors because the delocalised electrons can move and carry a current.

Figure 2: *Copper drawn into a wire.*

Solubility

Metals are insoluble, except in liquid metals, because of the strength of the metallic bonds.

Practice Questions — Fact Recall

Q1 Describe the structure of magnesium.

Q2 What type of bonding can be found in magnesium?

Q3 Explain the following:

a) Copper can be drawn into wires.

b) Copper is a good thermal conductor.

8. Properties of Materials

You've covered loads of different types of bonds and intermolecular forces. Here are the last few bits to compare how these bonds and forces affect the properties of materials.

Learning Objectives:

- Be able to explain the energy changes associated with changes of state.
- Be able to relate the melting point and conductivity of materials to the type of structure and the bonding present.

Specification Reference 3.1.3.4

Solids, liquids and gases

A typical solid has its particles very close together. This gives it a high density and makes it incompressible. The particles vibrate about a fixed point and can't move about freely. A typical liquid has a similar density to a solid and is virtually incompressible. The particles move about freely and randomly within the liquid, allowing it to flow. In gases, the particles have loads more energy and are much further apart. So the density is generally pretty low and it's very compressible. The particles move about freely, with not a lot of attraction between them, so they'll quickly diffuse to fill a container (see Figures 1 and 2).

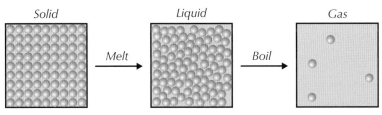

Solid   *Liquid*   *Gas*

Melt → *Boil* →

Figure 1: *The arrangement of particles in solids, liquids and gases.*

In order to change from a solid to a liquid or a liquid to a gas, you need to break the forces that are holding the particles together. To do this you need to give the particles more energy, e.g. by heating them.

Melting and boiling covalent substances

In simple covalent substances, the covalent bonds don't break during melting and boiling. To melt or boil simple covalent substances you only have to overcome the weak intermolecular forces that hold the molecules together. You don't need to break the strong covalent bonds that hold the atoms together within the molecules. That's why simple covalent compounds have relatively low melting and boiling points.

By contrast, to melt or boil a giant covalent substance you do need to break the covalent bonds holding the atoms together. That's why giant covalent compounds have very high melting and boiling points.

Figure 2: *Bromine liquid changing state to become a gas and diffusing to fill the container.*

--- Examples ---

Chlorine, Cl_2, is a simple covalent substance. To melt or boil chlorine, all you have to do is break the weak Van der Waals forces that hold the molecules together. Because of this, chlorine has a melting point of –101 °C and a boiling point of –34 °C — it's a gas at room temperature and pressure.

Bromine, Br_2, is also a simple covalent substance with low melting and boiling points. But bromine has slightly larger molecules than chlorine, which gives it slightly stronger Van der Waals forces. So bromine has a melting point of –7 °C and a boiling point of 59 °C — it's a liquid at room temperature and pressure.

Diamond is a giant covalent substance. To turn it into a liquid or a gas, you have to break the covalent bonds between carbon atoms. Diamond never really melts, but sublimes (goes straight from solid to gas) at over 3600 °C.

Figure 4: Chlorine (top) is a simple covalent compound and a gas at room temperature. Cobalt chloride (bottom) is an ionic compound and is a solid at room temperature.

Tip: A solvent is a liquid that a solid will dissolve in to form a solution.

Exam Tip
In the exam, make sure you can explain why each material has these properties, as well as what the properties are.

Tip: Make sure you do a risk assessment before you carry out any experiments in class.

Physical properties of materials

The particles that make up a substance, and the type of bonding that exists between them, will affect the physical properties of a material.

Melting and boiling points

The melting and boiling points of a substance are determined by the strength of the attraction between its particles. For example, ionic compounds have much higher boiling and melting points than simple covalent substances — the strong electrostatic attraction between the ions requires a lot more energy to break than the weak intermolecular forces between molecules (see Figure 4).

Electrical conductivity

A substance will only conduct electricity if it contains charged particles that are free to move, such as the delocalised electrons in a metal.

Solubility

How soluble a substance is in water depends on the type of particles that it contains. Water is a polar solvent, so substances that are polar or charged will dissolve in it well, whereas non-polar or uncharged substances won't.

Summary of typical properties

The table in Figure 5 is a summary of the typical physical properties of the types of materials you've met in this section. You should make sure you know it like the back of your hand.

Bonding	Melting/ boiling points	Typical state under standard conditions	Does it conduct electricity?	Is it soluble in water?
Ionic	High	Solid	Not as a solid (ions are held in place), but it will when molten or dissolved (ions are free to move).	Yes
Simple covalent (molecular)	Low	May be solid (e.g. I_2) but usually liquid or gas.	No	Depends on how polar the molecules are.
Giant covalent	High	Solid	No (except graphite)	No
Metallic	High	Solid	Yes (delocalised electrons)	No

Figure 5: A summary of the physical properties of different types of compound.

If you have an unknown compound and you want to predict the type of structure it has, you can carry out experiments to work out its physical properties. For example, you could test its electrical conductivity as a solid and a liquid, or investigate whether it has a high or low boiling point. From its physical properties, you can use the table above to predict what structure the compound is likely to have.

Example

A student is trying to predict the structure of an unknown compound called substance X, which is a solid at room temperature. He carries out the following tests:

- First, he tests the conductivity of the compound when it is solid and finds that, when solid, it is an electrical insulator.

- Next, he tries to dissolve a sample of the compound in water and finds that it is soluble.

- Finally, he tests the conductivity of the solution of substance X and finds that it now conducts electricity.

From this information the student predicts that substance X is an ionic compound. This is because it doesn't conduct electricity when it's solid, but does conduct electricity once dissolved. It's also soluble in water.

It's also clear that substance X isn't metallic because it doesn't conduct electricity when it's solid, and it definitely isn't giant covalent or simple covalent because it does conduct electricity when dissolved.

Figure 6: An experiment to test the conductivity of a solution.

Tip: If you're trying to work out the structure of a compound, you have to plan your experiment carefully to prove that it must be one structure and can't be any of the others. If the student in the example had just tested the electrical conductivity of the solid compound and then the solubility, he couldn't have ruled out the possibility of it being a polar, simple covalent compound.

Practice Questions — Application

Q1 The melting point of silicon dioxide is 1610 °C. It is insoluble in water and doesn't conduct electricity.

a) Suggest what type of structure silicon dioxide has.

b) Explain why silicon dioxide has a high melting point.

Q2 A student has a sample of a solid substance. She performs a series of tests on the sample and determines that it will not conduct electricity when solid, will not dissolve in water and has a low melting point.

Predict the structure of the substance.

Practice Questions — Fact Recall

Q1 Describe what happens to the particles in a substance when a solid changes to a liquid.

Q2 Explain why simple covalent substances have lower melting points than giant covalent substances.

Q3 Give three typical physical properties of metallic compounds.

Section Summary

Make sure you know...

- That ions form when electrons are transferred from one atom to another.
- How to predict the charge of a simple ion based on the Group of the Periodic Table that it is in.
- That compound ions are made up of groups of two or more atoms.
- The formulas of the compound ions sulfate, hydroxide, nitrate, carbonate and ammonium.
- That electrostatic attraction holds ions together and that this is called ionic bonding.
- How to work out the formulas of neutral ionic compounds.
- That ions form crystals that are giant ionic lattices.
- The structure of sodium chloride.
- How the structure of ionic compounds decides their physical properties — their electrical conductivity, melting point and solubility.
- That covalent bonds form when atoms share pairs of electrons.
- How single and multiple (double and triple) covalent bonds form between atoms.
- What a giant covalent (macromolecular) structure is.
- The structures of graphite and diamond and how the structures determine their properties.
- That co-ordinate (dative covalent) bonds form when one atom donates both shared electrons in a bond.
- That covalent bonds can be represented using a line and co-ordinate bonds can be represented using an arrow that points away from the donor atom.
- That charge clouds represent the areas where bonding pairs and lone pairs of electrons are most likely to be found.
- That charge clouds repel each other and arrange so that they are as far apart as possible.
- That Valence Shell Electron Pair Repulsion Theory states that lone-pair/lone-pair bond angles are the biggest, lone-pair/bonding-pair bond angles are the second biggest and bonding-pair/bonding-pair bond angles are the smallest.
- How to predict the shapes of molecules with up to six pairs of electrons surrounding the central atom, including their bond angles and shape names.
- That electronegativity is the ability to attract the bonding electrons in a covalent bond.
- How differences in electronegativities between bonding atoms causes polarisation.
- The difference between polar and non-polar bonds.
- That a molecule with polar bonds may have a permanent dipole, depending on its shape.
- What van der Waals forces and permanent dipole-dipole forces are, and what causes them.
- That simple covalent molecules can form molecular lattices.
- The structure of solid iodine.
- How hydrogen bonds form and their effect on the properties of compounds.
- The structure of ice, and how the formation of hydrogen bonds explains its unusually low density.
- How the structure of simple covalent compounds decides their physical properties — their electrical conductivity, melting point and solubility.
- What metallic bonding is and how to recognise giant metallic lattice structures.
- The structure of magnesium.
- How the structure of metals decides their physical properties — their conductivity, melting point, ability to be shaped and solubility.
- The energy changes that take place when a substance changes state.
- How to predict the structure of a compound based on its physical properties.

Exam-style Questions

1   Solid aluminium is an electrical conductor, used in overhead cables.
    It has a melting point of 660 °C and is insoluble in water.
    Predict the structure of aluminium.

    A   giant covalent

    B   giant ionic lattice

    C   metallic

    D   simple covalent

(1 mark)

2   Which of the following statements about hydrogen selenide, H_2Se, is correct?

    A   Hydrogen selenide is a linear molecule.

    B   Hydrogen selenide has a higher boiling point than hydrogen sulfide (H_2S).

    C   There is one lone pair and two bonding pairs around the central Se atom in H_2Se.

    D   Hydrogen selenide is able to form hydrogen bonds.

(1 mark)

3   Germanium is in the same group of the periodic table as carbon.
    Germanium reacts with hydrogen to form the compound germane, GeH_4.

3.1   Name the type of bonding between germanium and hydrogen in germane,
       and describe how the bonds are formed.

(2 marks)

3.2   Draw the shape of a molecule of GeH_4, labelling the bond angles,
       and name the shape.

(3 marks)

3.3   State whether or not you would expect germane to conduct electricity.
       Explain your answer.

(2 marks)

3.4   Germanium also combines with chlorine to form germanium dichloride,
       $GeCl_2$. Draw and name the shape of a molecule of $GeCl_2$.

(2 marks)

3.5   Suggest a value for the bond angle in $GeCl_2$ and explain your answer.

(2 marks)

4   The Group 5 elements include nitrogen, phosphorus, arsenic and antimony.
They can form covalent bonds with hydrogen.

The graph below shows the boiling points of some Group 5 hydrides.

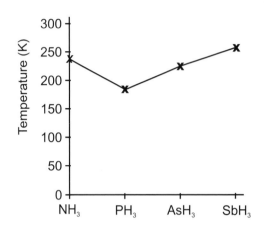

4.1   Explain the trend in boiling points shown by the graph for PH_3, AsH_3 and SbH_3.

(2 marks)

4.2   Name the strongest type of intermolecular force found in NH_3.

(1 mark)

4.3 NH_3 reacts with H^+ to form an NH_4^+ ion. Name the type of bond that forms
in this reaction and explain how it is formed.

(3 marks)

4.4   Explain why the bond angle in NH_3 is smaller than in NH_4^+.

(3 marks)

5   Sodium chloride (NaCl) is an ionic compound formed from sodium metal
and chlorine gas (Cl_2).

5.1   Name and describe the structure and bonding in sodium metal.

(3 marks)

5.2   Explain how this bonding structure allows sodium to be easily shaped.

(1 mark)

5.3   State what is meant by the term ionic bond.

(1 mark)

5.4   Describe the structure of sodium chloride.

(2 marks)

6 The table below shows the electronegativities of some elements.

Element	C	H	Cl	O	F
Electronegativity (Pauling Scale)	2.55	2.20	3.16	3.44	3.98

6.1 Define the term electronegativity and explain how electronegativity can give rise to permanent dipole-dipole interactions.

(4 marks)

6.2 Use the information in the table to name all the intermolecular forces present in each of the following compounds:

HCl

CH_4

H_2O

(3 marks)

6.3 Draw a diagram to show the strongest intermolecular forces between HF molecules. Include partial charges and all lone pairs.

(3 marks)

6.4 Explain why the only forces between Cl_2 molecules are van der Waals forces.

(1 mark)

7 Carbon can form lots of different structures and can combine with other elements to form lots of different compounds.

7.1 Graphite and diamond contain only carbon atoms. Both substances have the same type of structure. Name this structure.

(1 mark)

7.2 Describe the structures and bonding of graphite and diamond

(4 marks)

7.3 Explain why graphite can conduct electricity but diamond cannot.

(1 mark)

7.4 State the type of intermolecular forces found between molecules of methane, CH_4.

Compare the strength of the intermolecular forces between molecules of CH_4 to the intermolecular forces between molecules of C_3H_8.

(2 marks)

7.5 Explain why the boiling point of diamond is much higher than the boiling point of methane.

(2 marks)

Learning Objectives:

- Understand that enthalpy change (ΔH) is the heat energy change measured under conditions of constant pressure.

- Know that standard enthalpy changes refer to standard conditions, i.e. 100 kPa and a stated temperature (e.g. $\Delta H_{298}^{\ominus}$).

- Know that reactions can be endothermic or exothermic.

Specification Reference 3.1.4.1

1. Enthalpy

When chemical reactions happen, there'll be a change in energy. The souped-up chemistry term for this is enthalpy change.

Enthalpy notation

Enthalpy change, ΔH (delta H), is the heat energy transferred in a reaction at constant pressure. The units of ΔH are kJ mol^{-1}. You write $\Delta H^{\ominus}$ to show that the reactants and products were in their standard states and that the measurements were made under **standard conditions**. Standard conditions are 100 kPa (about 1 atm) pressure and a stated temperature (e.g. $\Delta H_{298}^{\ominus}$). In this book, all the enthalpy changes are measured at 298 K (25 °C). Sometimes the notation will also include a letter to signify whether the enthalpy change is for a reaction (r), combustion (c), or the formation of a new compound (f). See page 103 for more on this notation.

Exothermic reactions

Exothermic reactions give out energy to their surroundings, so the temperature in the reaction usually goes up. The products of the reaction end up with less energy than the reactants. This means that the enthalpy change for the reaction, ΔH, will be negative.

Tip: $\Delta_c H_{298}^{\ominus}$ is the notation for the enthalpy change of a combustion under standard conditions (a pressure of 100 kPa with all substances in their standard states) and at a temperature of 298 K.

Examples

Oxidation is usually exothermic. Here are two examples:

The combustion of a fuel like methane:

$$CH_{4(g)} + 2O_{2(g)} \rightarrow CO_{2(g)} + 2H_2O_{(l)} \qquad \Delta_c H_{298}^{\ominus} = -890 \text{ kJ mol}^{-1}$$

ΔH is negative so the reaction is **exothermic**.

The oxidation of carbohydrates, like glucose, in respiration is exothermic.

Endothermic reactions

Endothermic reactions take in energy from their surroundings, so the temperature in the reaction usually falls. This means that the products of the reaction have more energy than the reactants, so the enthalpy change for the reaction, ΔH, is positive.

Examples

The thermal decomposition of calcium carbonate is endothermic.

$$CaCO_{3(s)} \rightarrow CaO_{(s)} + CO_{2(g)} \qquad \Delta_r H_{298}^{\ominus} = +178 \text{ kJ mol}^{-1}$$

ΔH is positive so the reaction is **endothermic**.

The main reactions of photosynthesis are also endothermic — sunlight supplies the energy.

Figure 1: *Photosynthesis in plants is endothermic.*

Practice Questions — Fact Recall

Q1 Give the notation for an enthalpy change under standard conditions, at a temperature of 298 K.

Q2 Describe the difference between exothermic and endothermic reactions.

2. Bond Enthalpies

Reactions involve breaking and making bonds. The enthalpy change for a reaction depends on which bonds are broken and which are made.

What are bond enthalpies?

Atoms in molecules are held together by strong covalent bonds. It takes energy to break bonds and energy is given out when new bonds form. **Bond enthalpy** is the energy needed to break a bond. Bond enthalpies have specific values that differ depending on which atoms are attached on either side of the bond.

Breaking and making bonds

When reactions happen, reactant bonds are broken and product bonds are formed. You need energy to break bonds, so bond breaking is endothermic (ΔH is positive). Stronger bonds take more energy to break. Energy is released when bonds are formed, so this is exothermic (ΔH is negative). Stronger bonds release more energy when they form. The enthalpy change for a reaction is the overall effect of these two changes. If you need more energy to break bonds than is released when bonds are made, ΔH is positive. If it's less, ΔH is negative.

> **Example —** **Maths Skills**
>
> Nitrogen reacts with hydrogen to form ammonia (NH_3) in this reaction:
>
> $$N_2 + 3H_2 \rightarrow 2NH_3$$
>
> The energy needed to break all the bonds in N_2 and H_2 = 2253 kJ mol^{-1}.
>
> The energy released when forming the bonds in NH_3 = 2346 kJ mol^{-1}.
>
> The amount of energy released is bigger than the amount needed, so the reaction is exothermic, and ΔH is negative.

Mean bond enthalpies

Bond enthalpy is the energy needed to break a bond. The energy required to break a certain type of bond can change depending on where it is, e.g. it takes different amounts of energy to break the C-C bond in methane, ethane, ethene, etc. So in calculations, you use **mean bond enthalpy** — that's the average energy needed to break a certain type of bond, over a range of compounds. It is often given in data tables and used in calculations.

> **Example —** **Maths Skills**
>
> Water (H_2O) has got two O–H bonds (see Figure 1). You'd think it'd take the same amount of energy to break them both, but it doesn't.
>
> The first bond, H–OH$_{(g)}$: E(H–OH) = +492 kJ mol^{-1}
>
> The second bond, H–O$_{(g)}$: E(H–O) = +428 kJ mol^{-1}
>
> (OH$^-$ is a bit easier to break apart because of the extra electron repulsion.)
>
> So, the mean bond enthalpy for O–H bonds in water is:
>
> $$\frac{492 + 428}{2} = +460 \text{ kJ mol}^{-1}.$$
>
> The data book says the bond enthalpy for O–H is +464 kJ mol^{-1}. It's a bit different than the one calculated above because it's the average for a much bigger range of molecules, not just water. For example, it includes the O–H bonds in alcohols and carboxylic acids too.

Learning Objectives:

- Define, understand and use the terms bond enthalpy and mean bond enthalpy.
- Be able to use mean bond enthalpies to calculate an approximate value of ΔH for reactions in the gaseous phase.
- Be able to explain why values from mean bond enthalpy calculations differ from those determined using Hess's Law.
- Be able to recall the definition of standard enthalpies of combustion ($\Delta_c H^\ominus$) and formation ($\Delta_f H^\ominus$).

Specification Reference 3.1.4.1, 3.1.4.4

Tip: You can look up the mean (average) bond enthalpies for different bonds in a data book, or calculate the mean bond enthalpies from given data. In an exam you'll be given any bond enthalpies you need.

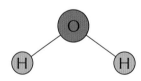

Figure 1: *The bonds in a water molecule.*

Tip: Breaking bonds is always an endothermic process, so mean bond enthalpies are always positive.

Calculating enthalpy changes

In any chemical reaction, energy is absorbed to break bonds and given out during bond formation. The difference between the energy absorbed and released is the overall enthalpy change of reaction:

Enthalpy change of reaction = Total energy absorbed − Total energy released

- To calculate the overall enthalpy change for a reaction, first calculate the total energy needed to break the bonds in the reactants. You'll usually be given the average bond enthalpies for each type of bond, so just multiply each value by the number of each bond present. This total will be the total energy absorbed in the reaction.

- To find the total energy released by the reaction, calculate the total energy needed to form all the new bonds in the products. Use the average bond enthalpies to do this.

- The overall enthalpy change for the reaction can then be found by subtracting the total energy released from the total energy absorbed.

Examples — Maths Skills

Calculate the overall enthalpy change for the following reaction:

$$N_{2(g)} + 3H_{2(g)} \rightarrow 2NH_{3(g)}$$

Use the mean bond enthalpy values shown in Figure 2.

You might find it helpful to draw a sketch of the molecules in the reaction (it doesn't have to be 3D, it's just to help you to see all the bonds):

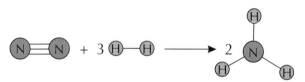

Bonds broken: $1 \times N\equiv N$ bond broken $= 1 \times 945 = 945$ kJ mol⁻¹
            $3 \times H-H$ bonds broken $= 3 \times 436 = 1308$ kJ mol⁻¹
Total Energy Absorbed $= 945 + 1308 = 2253$ kJ mol⁻¹

Bonds formed: $6 \times N-H$ bonds formed $= 6 \times 391 = 2346$ kJ mol⁻¹
Total Energy Released $= 2346$ kJ mol⁻¹

Now you just subtract 'total energy released' from 'total energy absorbed':
Enthalpy change of reaction $= 2253 - 2346 = -93$ kJ mol⁻¹.

Calculate the overall enthalpy change for the following reaction:

$$H_{2(g)} + \tfrac{1}{2}O_{2(g)} \rightarrow H_2O_{(g)}$$

Use the mean bond enthalpy values shown in Figure 2.

The molecules present are shown below:

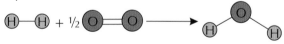

Bonds broken: $1 \times H-H$ bond broken $= 1 \times 436 = 436$ kJ mol⁻¹
            $\tfrac{1}{2} \times O=O$ bonds broken $= \tfrac{1}{2} \times 498 = 249$ kJ mol⁻¹
Total Energy Absorbed $= 436 + 249 = 685$ kJ mol⁻¹

Bonds formed: $2 \times O-H$ bonds formed $= 2 \times 464 = 928$ kJ mol⁻¹
Total Energy Released $= 928$ kJ mol⁻¹

Enthalpy change of reaction $= 685 - 928 = -243$ kJ mol⁻¹.

Tip: Draw sketches to show the bonds present in the reactants and products to make sure you include them all in your calculations.

	Bond Enthalpy
Bond	(Mean value except where stated)
N≡N	945 kJ mol⁻¹
H–H	436 kJ mol⁻¹
N–H	391 kJ mol⁻¹
O=O	498 kJ mol⁻¹
O–H	464 kJ mol⁻¹

Figure 2: *Table of bond enthalpies.*

Tip: Calculating this enthalpy change using Hess's Law gives a value of −92.4 kJ mol⁻¹. This is slightly different because Hess's Law uses precise data, whilst this calculation uses mean bond enthalpy values. See pages 108-110 for more on Hess's Law.

Tip: If you can't remember which value to subtract from which, just take the smaller number from the bigger one then add the sign at the end — positive if 'bonds broken' was the bigger number (endothermic), negative if 'bonds formed' was bigger (exothermic).

The different types of ΔH

Standard enthalpy change of formation

Standard enthalpy change of formation, $\Delta_f H^\ominus$, is the enthalpy change when 1 mole of a compound is formed from its elements in their standard states under standard conditions, e.g $2C_{(s)} + 3H_{2(g)} + \frac{1}{2}O_{2(g)} \rightarrow C_2H_5OH_{(l)}$

Standard enthalpy change of combustion

Standard enthalpy change of combustion, $\Delta_c H^\ominus$, is the enthalpy change when 1 mole of a substance is completely burned in oxygen under standard conditions with all reactants and products in their standard states.

Standard enthalpy change of reaction

Standard enthalpy change of reaction, $\Delta_r H^\ominus$, is the enthalpy change when a reaction occurs in the molar quantities shown in the chemical equation, under standard conditions with all reactants and products in their standard states.

Exam Tip
There's quite a bit of maths in this section but you need to learn all these definitions too — you can be asked to write them down in an exam, and it's often the thing that people forget or get wrong.

Tip: $\Delta_c H^\ominus$ is sometimes written as $\Delta H_c^\ominus$ — the same goes for $\Delta_f H^\ominus$ and $\Delta_r H^\ominus$.

Practice Questions — Application

Q1 Use the mean bond enthalpies shown in Figure 3 to calculate the enthalpy changes for the following reactions:

a)
$$\begin{array}{c}H\\H\end{array}\!\!\!\!C=C\!\!\!\!\begin{array}{c}H\\H\end{array} + H-H \rightarrow H-\!\!\!\begin{array}{c}H\ \ H\\ \overset{|}{C}-\overset{|}{C}\\ H\ \ H\end{array}\!\!\!-H$$

b)
$$H-\overset{\overset{\displaystyle H}{|}}{\underset{\underset{\displaystyle H}{|}}{C}}-OH + H-Cl \rightarrow H-\overset{\overset{\displaystyle H}{|}}{\underset{\underset{\displaystyle H}{|}}{C}}-Cl + H\!\!\diagdown\!\!O\!\!\diagup\!\!H$$

c) $C_3H_8 + 5O_2 \rightarrow 3CO_2 + 4H_2O$

d) $C_2H_5Cl + NH_3 \rightarrow C_2H_5NH_2 + HCl$

Q2 Calculate the enthalpy change for the complete combustion of ethene (C_2H_4) using the bond enthalpies given in Figure 3.
(The products of complete combustion are CO_2 and H_2O.)

Q3 Calculate the enthalpy change for the formation of hydrogen chloride ($HCl_{(g)}$) from hydrogen ($H_{2(g)}$) and chlorine ($Cl_{2(g)}$) using the bond enthalpies given in Figure 3.

Q4 The enthalpy change for the following reaction is -181 kJ mol^{-1}:
$$2NO_{(g)} \rightarrow N_{2(g)} + O_{2(g)}$$
Use this value for $\Delta_f H$, along with the data in Figure 3, to estimate a value for the mean bond enthalpy for the bond between nitrogen and oxygen in NO.

Tip: You can ignore any bonds that don't actually change during the reaction. Just work out which bonds actually break and which new bonds form.

Bond Enthalpy	
Bond	(Mean value except where stated)
N≡N	945 kJ mol^{-1}
H–H	436 kJ mol^{-1}
N–H	391 kJ mol^{-1}
O=O	498 kJ mol^{-1}
O–H	464 kJ mol^{-1}
C–H	413 kJ mol^{-1}
C=C	612 kJ mol^{-1}
C–C	347 kJ mol^{-1}
C–O	358 kJ mol^{-1}
C–Cl	346 kJ mol^{-1}
C=O (in CO_2)	805 kJ mol^{-1}
C–N	286 kJ mol^{-1}
H–Cl	432 kJ mol^{-1}
Cl–Cl	243 kJ mol^{-1}

Figure 3: *Table of bond enthalpies.*

Practice Questions — Fact Recall

Q1 What notation is used for the standard enthalpy change of:

a) formation?

b) combustion?

Q2 Define the 'standard enthalpy change of formation'.

- Know how to measure an enthalpy change (Required Practical 2).

- Know that the heat change, q, in a reaction is given by the equation $q = mc\Delta T$, where m is the mass of the substance that has a specific heat capacity, c, and ΔT is the change in temperature.

- Be able to use the equation $q = mc\Delta T$ in related calculations, including calculating the molar enthalpy change for a reaction.

Specification Reference 3.1.4.2

Tip: Always carry out a risk assessment and put in place any safety precautions that you might need before starting an experiment.

3. Measuring Enthalpy Changes

A lot of the data we have on enthalpy changes has come from someone, somewhere, measuring the enthalpy change of a reaction in a lab.

Measuring an enthalpy change in the lab

To find the enthalpy change for a reaction, you only need to know three things — the number of moles of the stuff that's reacting, the change in temperature, and how much stuff you're heating. Experiments that measure the heat given out by reactions are called **calorimetry** experiments. How you go about doing an experiment like this depends on what type of reaction it is.

For reactions that happen in solution (see page 106), you just put the reactants in a container and use a thermometer to measure the temperature of the mixture at regular intervals (see Figure 1). It's best to use a polystyrene beaker to reduce the amount of heat lost or gained through the sides.

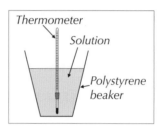

Figure 1: *Simple equipment used to measure the enthalpy change of reaction.*

Calorimetry and combustion reactions

You can find out how much energy is given out by a combustion reaction by measuring the temperature change it causes as it burns. To find the enthalpy of combustion of a flammable liquid, you burn it in a calorimeter (see Figure 2).

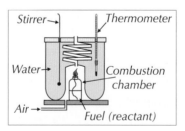

Figure 2: *A calorimeter used to measure the enthalpy change of combustion.*

Figure 3: *A bomb calorimeter. This is a very accurate piece of equipment that works on the same principle as the one shown in the diagram in Figure 2.*

As the fuel burns, it heats the water. You can work out the heat energy that has been absorbed by the water if you know the mass of the water, the temperature change (ΔT), and the specific heat capacity of water (= 4.18 J g^{-1} K^{-1}) — see the next page for the details of how to do this.

Ideally, all the heat given out by the burning fuel would be absorbed by the water, allowing you to work out the enthalpy change of combustion exactly. In practice you always lose some heat to the surroundings, however well your calorimeter is insulated. This makes it hard to get an accurate result.

Also, when you burn a fuel, some of the combustion that takes place may be incomplete, meaning that less energy is given out. Flammable liquids are often quite volatile too, so you may lose some of the fuel to evaporation.

Calculating an accurate temperature change

The most obvious way of finding the temperature change in a calorimetry experiment is to subtract the starting temperature from the highest temperature you recorded. But that won't give you a very accurate value, because of the heat lost from the calorimeter to the surroundings. Instead, you can use a graph of your results to find a more accurate value. Here's what you do:

1. During the experiment, record the temperature at regular intervals, beginning a couple of minutes before you start the reaction.

2. Plot a graph of your results.

3. Draw two lines of best fit: one going through the points from before the reaction started and one going through the points from after it started.

4. Extend both lines so that they both pass the time when the reaction started.

5. The distance between the two lines at the time the reaction started (before any heat was lost) is the accurate temperature change (ΔT) for the reaction.

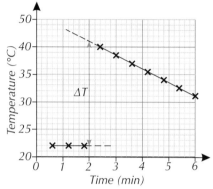

Figure 4: A graph being used to find the temperature change for a reaction beginning at time = 2 minutes.

Using the equation $q = mc\Delta T$

The equation used to calculate the enthalpy change of a reaction is:

q = heat lost or gained (in J). This is the same as the enthalpy change if the pressure is constant. ⟶ $q = mc\Delta T$ ⟵ ΔT = the change in temperature of the solution / water (in Kelvin).

m = mass (in g) of solution in the polystyrene beaker (or mass of water in the calorimeter).

c = specific heat capacity of the solution / water (4.18 J g^{-1}K^{-1}).

> **Tip:** The specific heat capacity of a solution is the amount of heat energy it takes to raise the temperature of 1 g of the solution by 1 K.

Calculating the standard enthalpy change of combustion

To calculate the standard enthalpy change of combustion, $\Delta_c H^\circ$, using data from a laboratory experiment, follow these steps:

Step 1: Calculate the amount of heat lost or gained during the combustion using $q = mc\Delta T$ and your measured or given values of m and ΔT. You'll then need to change the units of q from joules to kilojoules, because standard enthalpies of combustion are always given in units of kJ mol^{-1}.

Step 2: Calculate the number of moles of fuel that caused this enthalpy change, from the mass that reacted. Use the equation:

$n = \dfrac{mass}{M_r}$ n is the number of moles of fuel burned. M is the fuel's relative molecular mass.

Step 3: Calculate the standard enthalpy change of combustion, $\Delta_c H^\circ$ (in kJ mol^{-1}), using the actual heat change for the reaction, q (in kJ), and the number of moles of fuel that burned, n. Use the equation:

$$\Delta_c H^\circ = \frac{q}{n}$$

> **Tip:** ΔH° is the standard enthalpy change of a reaction carried out at 100 kPa with all reactants and products in their standard states (see page 100). If the experiment was carried out under different conditions, this method wouldn't give you the value for ΔH°.

In a laboratory experiment, 1.16 g of an organic liquid fuel was completely burned in oxygen. The heat formed during this combustion raised the temperature of 100 g of water from 295.3 K to 357.8 K. Calculate the standard enthalpy of combustion, $\Delta_c H^\circ$, of the fuel. Its M_r is 58.

Step 1: Calculate the amount of heat given out by the fuel using $q = mc\Delta T$. Remember that m is the mass of water, not the mass of fuel.

$q = mc\Delta T$

$q = 100 \times 4.18 \times (357.8 - 295.3) = 26\ 125$ J

Change the amount of heat from J to kJ: $q = 26.125$ kJ.

Step 2: Find out how many moles of fuel produced this heat:

$$n = \frac{mass}{M_r} = \frac{1.16\,g}{58\,g\,mol^{-1}} = 0.0200 \text{ moles of fuel.}$$

Step 3: The standard enthalpy of combustion involves 1 mole of fuel.

So $\Delta_c H^\circ = \dfrac{q}{n} = \dfrac{-26.125\,kJ}{0.0200\,mol} \approx$ **−1310 kJ mol⁻¹** (to 3 s.f.)

(q is negative here because combustion is an exothermic reaction.)

Tip: −26.125 kJ is the <u>enthalpy change</u> of this reaction. That's the amount of energy given out when this mass of this fuel is burned. −1310 kJ mol⁻¹ is the <u>molar enthalpy change</u> of this reaction. That's the amount of energy that would be given out when 1 mole of this fuel was burned.

Measuring enthalpy changes in solution

The same formula can also be used to calculate the enthalpy change for a reaction that happens in solution, such as neutralisation, dissolution (dissolving) or displacement. Here's an example:

Measuring an enthalpy of neutralisation

REQUIRED PRACTICAL **2**

The enthalpy of neutralisation is the energy change when one mole of water is formed by the reaction of an acid and an alkali.

Tip: Make sure that you carry out all necessary safety precautions whilst doing any experiment.

To find the enthalpy change for a neutralisation reaction, add a known volume of acid to an insulated container (e.g. a polystyrene cup) and measure the temperature. Then add a known volume of alkali and record the temperature at regular intervals. Stir the solution to make sure it's evenly heated. When you've worked out the temperature change (using the method from page 105), you can work out the heat energy given out by the reaction using the formula from the previous page.

─ Example ─

50 cm³ of 1.0 mol dm⁻³ sodium hydroxide was added to 50 cm³ of 1.0 mol dm⁻³ hydrochloric acid. The temperature rose by 6.9 °C. Calculate the enthalpy change of neutralisation for this reaction. The equation for the reaction is: HCl + NaOH → NaCl + H₂O

First calculate the heat energy given out by the reaction:

- You can assume that all solutions have the same density as water. Since 1 cm³ of water has a mass of 1 g, each cm³ of solution you use will have a mass of 1g. So $m = 50 + 50 = 100$ g.

- You can also usually assume that all solutions have the same specific heat capacity as water (4.18 kJ g⁻¹ K⁻¹).

- ΔT is the change in temperature in K, which is equal to the change in temperature in °C — so $\Delta T = 6.9$.

Tip: Don't forget that if you're mixing two solutions you need to include the masses of both when you're finding m.

$q = mc\Delta T = 100 \times 4.18 \times 6.9 = 2884.2$ J $= 2.8842$ kJ.

Now calculate the enthalpy change of neutralisation — to do this you need to divide the heat energy change by the number of moles of H_2O produced.

- First work out how many moles of acid you started off with
  moles = concentration (mol dm^{-3}) × volume (dm^3)
  $= 1.0 \times (50 \div 1000) = 1.0 \times 0.050 = 0.05$

Tip: You could work out how many moles of alkali you started with here instead — it's fine to use either.

- From the balanced equation, the ratio between HCl and H_2O is 1:1 — so if 0.050 moles of HCl reacted, 0.050 moles of H_2O was produced.

- So enthalpy of neutralisation = = $\frac{q}{n} = \frac{-2.8842}{0.050} = $ **−58 kJ mol^{-1}** (to 2 s.f.)

(q is negative because this is an exothermic reaction.)

Measuring the enthalpy change of a dissolution reaction works in a very similar way. You just add a known mass of the solid that you're dissolving to a known volume of water in the polystyrene cup and stir, recording the temperature regularly. Once you've found the temperature change, you can use it to work out the energy change for the reaction.

If you're asked to find the molar enthalpy change for this type of reaction, you need to find the enthalpy change per mole of solute dissolved (this is the **enthalpy of solution**). This means that you need to divide the heat energy change for the reaction by the number of moles of solid that you started off with.

Tip: Dissolution can be exothermic or endothermic, so make sure that the sign of your final answer is right. If the temperature increases, your answer should be negative. If it decreases, your answer should be positive.

Displacement reactions often mean mixing a solid (such as a metal) with a salt solution. Some displacement reactions involve mixing two solutions though, so you can just use whichever method fits your reactants.

Tip: If you're finding the molar enthalpy change for a displacement reaction, you might be told which substance to find the number of moles of and divide by. (For example "Find the enthalpy change per mole of copper sulfate used".) If you're not told, use the number of moles of the reactant that isn't present in excess.

Practice Questions — Application

Q1 0.0500 mol of a compound dissolves in water, causing the temperature of the solution to increase from 298 K to 301 K. The total mass of the solution is 220 g. Calculate the enthalpy change for the reaction in kJ mol^{-1}. Assume $c = 4.18$ J g^{-1} K^{-1}.

Q2 A calorimeter, containing 200 g of water ($c = 4.18$ J g^{-1} K^{-1}), was used to measure the enthalpy change of combustion of pentane ($C_5H_{12(l)}$, $M_r = 72$). 0.500 g of pentane was burnt. The temperature of the water increased by 29.0 K.

  a) Calculate the enthalpy change of combustion of pentane. Give your answer in kJ mol^{-1}.

  b) Suggest one reason why this value may be different to the standard enthalpy change of combustion of pentane given in a data book.

Q3 The standard enthalpy of combustion of octane ($C_8H_{18(l)}$, $M_r = 114$) is −5470 kJ mol^{-1}. Some octane was burnt in a calorimeter containing 300 g of water ($c = 4.18$ J g^{-1} K^{-1}). The temperature of the water went up by 55 K. Calculate an estimate of the mass of octane burnt.

Practice Questions — Fact Recall

Q1 What three things need to be measured in order to calculate the enthalpy change for a reaction in a laboratory?

Q2 Sketch and label a calorimeter that could be used in the lab to measure the enthalpy change of a combustion.

4. Hess's Law

For some reactions, there is no easy way to measure enthalpy changes in the lab. For these, we can use Hess's Law.

What is Hess's Law?

Hess's Law says that:

> The total enthalpy change for a reaction is independent of the route taken.

This law is handy for working out enthalpy changes that you can't find directly by doing an experiment — for example, the enthalpy change of the reaction that breaks down NO_2 into N_2 and O_2. We can call this reaction 'route 1'. But we can also think of the reaction as NO_2 breaking down into NO and O_2, and then reacting further to form N_2 and O_2. This longer route, with an intermediate step, can be called 'route 2' (see Figure 1).

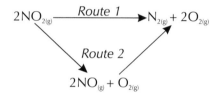

Figure 1: *Two possible routes for the formation of nitrogen and oxygen from nitrogen dioxide.*

Hess's Law says that the total enthalpy change for route 1 is the same as for route 2. So if you know the enthalpy changes for the stages of route 2, you can calculate the enthalpy change for route 1, as shown in the example below.

Example ⸺ Maths Skills

Use Hess's Law to calculate the enthalpy change, $\Delta_r H^\circ$, for route 1 of the reaction shown below.

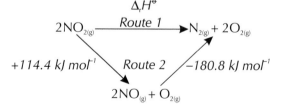

The total enthalpy change for route 1 is the same as the total enthalpy change for route 2. So the enthalpy change for route 1 is the sum of the steps in route 2:

$\Delta_r H^\circ = 114.4$ kJ mol^{-1} + (-180.8 kJ mol^{-1}) = -66.4 kJ mol^{-1}.

Using enthalpies of formation

Enthalpy changes of formation are useful for calculating enthalpy changes you can't find directly. You need to know $\Delta_f H^\circ$ for all the reactants and products that are compounds. The value of $\Delta_f H^\circ$ for elements is zero — the element's being formed from the element, so there's no change in enthalpy.
The standard enthalpy changes are all measured at 298 K.

Exam Tip
You'll be given all the information you need in your exam — you don't need to memorise any enthalpy values.

Example — Maths Skills

Calculate $\Delta_r H^\circ$ for this reaction using the enthalpies of formation in Figure 2:

$$SO_{2(g)} + 2H_2S_{(g)} \rightarrow 3S_{(s)} + 2H_2O_{(l)}$$

- Write under the reaction a list of all the elements present in the reaction, balanced in their correct molar quantities, as shown below:

Reactants   Products
$$SO_{2(g)} + 2H_2S_{(g)} \longrightarrow 3S_{(s)} + 2H_2O_{(l)}$$

$$3S_{(s)} + 2H_{2(g)} + O_{2(g)}$$
Elements

Compound	$\Delta_f H^\circ$
$SO_{2(g)}$	-297 kJ mol^{-1}
$H_2S_{(g)}$	-20.6 kJ mol^{-1}
$H_2O_{(l)}$	-286 kJ mol^{-1}

Figure 2: *Table of enthalpies of formation for three compounds.*

- Enthalpies of formation ($\Delta_f H^\circ$) tell you the enthalpy change going from the elements to the compounds. The enthalpy change of reaction ($\Delta_r H^\circ$) is the enthalpy change going from the reactants to the products.
Draw and label arrows to show this on your diagram:

Reactants ΔH_r° Products
$$SO_{2(g)} + 2H_2S_{(g)} \longrightarrow 3S_{(s)} + 2H_2O_{(l)}$$

$\Delta_f H^\circ_{(reactants)}$ $\Delta_f H^\circ_{(products)}$

$$3S_{(s)} + 2H_{2(g)} + O_{2(g)}$$
Elements

- The calculation is often simpler if you keep the arrows end to end, so make both routes go from the elements to the products. Route 1 gets there via the reactants (and includes $\Delta_r H^\circ$), whilst route 2 gets there directly. Label the enthalpy changes along each arrow, as shown below. There are 2 moles of H_2O and 2 moles of H_2S, so their enthalpies of formation will need to be multiplied by 2. $\Delta_f H^\circ$ of sulfur is zero because it's an element, but you can still label it on the diagram.

Tip: You don't have to pick a route that follows the direction of the arrows. If your route goes against an arrow you can just change the signs (so negative enthalpies become positive and positive enthalpies become negative).

Reactants $\Delta_r H^\circ$ Products
$$SO_{2(g)} + 2H_2S_{(g)} \longrightarrow 3S_{(s)} + 2H_2O_{(l)}$$
Route 1   Route 2

$\Delta_f H^\circ_{[reactants]} = \Delta_f H^\circ_{[SO_2]} + 2 \times \Delta_f H^\circ_{[H_2S]}$ $\Delta_f H^\circ_{[products]} = 3 \times \Delta_f H^\circ_{[S]} + 2 \times \Delta_f H^\circ_{[H_2O]}$

$$3S_{(s)} + 2H_{2(g)} + O_{2(g)}$$
Elements

- Use Hess's Law, Route 1 = Route 2, and plug the numbers from Figure 2 into the equation:

$$\Delta_f H^\circ[SO_2] + 2\Delta_f H^\circ[H_2S] + \Delta_r H^\circ = 3\Delta_f H^\circ[S] + 2\Delta_f H^\circ[H_2O]$$
$$-297 + (2 \times -20.6) + \Delta_r H^\circ = (3 \times 0) + (2 \times -286)$$
$$\Delta_r H^\circ = (3 \times 0) + (2 \times -286) - [-297 + (2 \times -20.6)] = -233.8 \text{ kJ mol}^{-1}.$$

Using enthalpies of combustion

You can use a similar method to find an enthalpy change from enthalpy changes of combustion, instead of using enthalpy changes of formation.

Example — **Maths Skills**

Calculate $\Delta_f H^\circ$ of ethanol using the enthalpies of combustion in Figure 3.

- The desired reaction in this case is the formation of ethanol from its elements, so write out the balanced equation:

Reactants   Product

$$2C_{(s)} + 3H_{2(g)} + \tfrac{1}{2}O_{2(g)} \longrightarrow C_2H_5OH_{(l)}$$

Substance	$\Delta_c H^\circ$
$C_{(s)}$	−394 kJ mol^{-1}
$H_{2(g)}$	−286 kJ mol^{-1}
$C_2H_5OH_{(l)}$	−1367 kJ mol^{-1}

Figure 3: *Table of enthalpies of combustion for three substances.*

- Figure 3 tells you the enthalpy change when each of the 'reactants' and 'products' is burned in oxygen. Add these combustion reactions to your diagram, making sure they are balanced, as shown below:

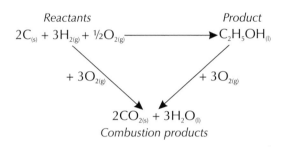

Tip: The products of a complete combustion are carbon dioxide (CO_2) and water (H_2O).

- Choose which reactions will form which route. Label the diagram with the enthalpy changes along each arrow as before (taking into account molar quantities):

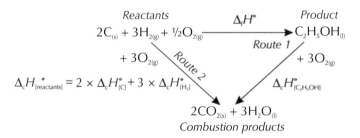

Tip: You can ignore the enthalpy change of combustion of oxygen in these calculations. Oxygen <u>doesn't have</u> an enthalpy change of combustion — you <u>can't</u> burn 1 mole of oxygen in oxygen.

- Use Hess's Law as follows: Route 1 = Route 2

$\Delta_f H^\circ[\text{ethanol}] + \Delta_c H^\circ[C_2H_5OH] = 2\Delta_c H^\circ[C] + 3\Delta_c H^\circ[H_2]$

$\Delta_f H^\circ[\text{ethanol}] + (-1367) = (2 \times -394) + (3 \times -286)$

$\Delta_f H^\circ[\text{ethanol}] = -788 + -858 - (-1367)$

$\Delta_f H^\circ[\text{ethanol}] = -279$ kJ mol^{-1}.

Practice Questions — Application

Q1 Calculate $\Delta_r H^{\circ}$ for the following reactions using Hess's Law, and the enthalpies of formation given in Figure 4:

a) $CaCO_{3(s)} \rightarrow CaO_{(s)} + CO_{2(g)}$

b) $N_2O_{5(s)} \rightarrow 4NO_{2(g)} + O_{2(g)}$

Q2 Calculate $\Delta_f H^{\circ}$ for the following organic compounds using Hess's Law, and the enthalpies of combustion given in Figure 5 and below:

a) propan-1-ol ($CH_3CH_2CH_2OH$): $\Delta_c H^{\circ} = -2021$ kJ mol⁻¹.

b) ethane-1,2-diol (CH_2OHCH_2OH): $\Delta_c H^{\circ} = -1180$ kJ mol⁻¹.

c) butan-2-one ($CH_3COCH_2CH_3$): $\Delta_c H^{\circ} = -2442$ kJ mol⁻¹.

Compound	$\Delta_f H^{\circ}$
$CO_{2(g)}$	-394 kJ mol⁻¹
$CaO_{(s)}$	-635 kJ mol⁻¹
$CaCO_{3(s)}$	-1207 kJ mol⁻¹
$N_2O_{5(s)}$	-41 kJ mol⁻¹
$NO_{2(g)}$	33 kJ mol⁻¹

Figure 4: Table of enthalpies of formation for five compounds.

Element	$\Delta_c H^{\circ}$
$C_{(s)}$	-394 kJ mol⁻¹
$H_{2(g)}$	-286 kJ mol⁻¹

Figure 5: Enthalpies of combustion for carbon and hydrogen.

Section Summary

Make sure you know...

- That enthalpy change, ΔH (in kJ mol⁻¹), is the heat energy transferred in a reaction at constant pressure.
- That ΔH° is the enthalpy change for a reaction where the reactants and products are in their standard states and the measurements are made at 100 kPa pressure and a stated temperature (usually 298 K).
- That exothermic reactions give out energy, so ΔH is negative.
- That endothermic reactions absorb energy, so ΔH is positive.
- That mean bond enthalpies tell us the average energy (per mole) required to break the bond between two atoms.
- How to use mean bond enthalpies to calculate enthalpy changes for reactions, using the equation: Enthalpy change of reaction = Total energy absorbed – Total energy released.
- That $\Delta_r H^{\circ}$ is the enthalpy change when a reaction occurs in the molar quantities shown in the chemical equation, under standard conditions with all reactants and products in their standard states.
- That $\Delta_f H^{\circ}$ is the enthalpy change when 1 mole of a compound is formed from its elements in their standard states under standard conditions.
- That $\Delta_c H^{\circ}$ is the enthalpy change when 1 mole of a substance is completely burned in oxygen under standard conditions.
- How to measure an enthalpy change.
- How to calculate the heat lost or gained (q) by a reaction using the equation $q = mc\Delta T$, where m is the mass of the reaction mixture, c is its specific heat capacity, and ΔT is the temperature change due to the reaction.
- How to calculate the enthalpy change of combustion and the enthalpy change of reaction given values for q and n, the number of moles reacted.
- That Hess's Law states that:
  The total enthalpy change for a reaction is independent of the route taken.
- How to use Hess's Law to calculate enthalpy changes for reactions from enthalpies of formation.
- How to use Hess's Law to calculate enthalpy changes for reactions from enthalpies of combustion.

Exam-style Questions

1   A scientist is conducting the following reaction:

$$CH_3COOH_{(l)} + C_2H_5OH_{(l)} \rightarrow CH_3COOC_2H_{5(l)} + H_2O_{(l)}$$

   ethanoic acid   *ethanol*   *ethyl ethanoate*   *water*

She adds 0.0500 mol of ethanoic acid to an excess of ethanol in a polystyrene beaker. She records the temperature of the mixture at regular intervals and uses her data to find the temperature change associated with the reaction.

The solution in the beaker has a total mass of 50.0 g, and a specific heat capacity of 2.46 J g^{-1} K^{-1}.

1.1   The temperature rises by 1.00 °C.
Calculate the enthalpy change due to the reaction.

(3 marks)

1.2   State two conditions necessary for the enthalpy change calculated in part 1.1 to be the standard enthalpy change of reaction.

(2 marks)

2   The table below shows the standard enthalpy change of combustion, $\Delta_c H^\circ$, for carbon, hydrogen and octane ($C_8H_{18(l)}$). The standard enthalpy of formation of octane can be calculated from this data using Hess's Law.

	$\Delta_c H^\circ$
$C_{(s)}$	−394 kJ mol^{-1}
$H_{2(g)}$	−286 kJ mol^{-1}
$C_8H_{18(l)}$	−5470 kJ mol^{-1}

2.1   State Hess's Law.

(1 mark)

2.2   Write out a balanced chemical equation for the complete combustion of octane.

(1 mark)

2.3   Use your answers to **2.1** and **2.2**, and the data in the table above, to calculate the standard enthalpy change of formation of octane, $\Delta_f H^\circ$.

(3 marks)

2.4   State whether the formation of octane is exothermic or endothermic.
Explain your answer.

(2 marks)

3 The structure of but-1-ene is shown below.

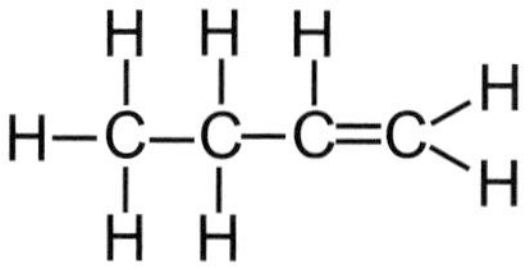

But-1-ene will burn completely in oxygen to produce CO_2 and H_2O.

The table below shows bond enthalpies for the bonds present in the reactants and products of this combustion reaction.

Bond	Bond Enthalpy (Mean value except where stated)
C–H	413 kJ mol^{-1}
C=C	612 kJ mol^{-1}
C–C	347 kJ mol^{-1}
O=O	498 kJ mol^{-1}
C=O (in CO_2)	805 kJ mol^{-1}
O–H	464 kJ mol^{-1}

These bond enthalpies can be used to calculate the standard enthalpy change of combustion for but-1-ene.

3.1 Define the term 'standard enthalpy of combustion'.

(3 marks)

3.2 Use the data in the table to calculate a value for the standard enthalpy change of combustion for but-1-ene.

(3 marks)

3.3 The standard enthalpy change of combustion for but-1-ene calculated from the mean bond enthalpies is different to the value given in the data book. Explain why.

(1 mark)

4 Potassium hydroxide reacts with sulfuric acid in the following way:

$$2KOH_{(s)} + H_2SO_{4(l)} \rightarrow K_2SO_{4(s)} + 2H_2O_{(l)}$$

The table below shows the standard enthalpies of formation of each of the reactants and products in this reaction.

	$\Delta_f H^\circ$
$KOH_{(s)}$	−425 kJ mol^{-1}
$H_2SO_{4(l)}$	−814 kJ mol^{-1}
$K_2SO_{4(s)}$	−1438 kJ mol^{-1}
$H_2O_{(l)}$	−286 kJ mol^{-1}

4.1 Define the term 'standard enthalpy of formation'.

(3 marks)

4.2 Use the data in the table to calculate a value for the standard enthalpy change of the reaction, $\Delta_r H^\circ$.

(3 marks)

1. Reaction Rates

Learning Objectives:

- Understand that reactions can only occur when collisions take place between particles having sufficient energy and that this is called the activation energy.
- Be able to define the term activation energy.
- Be able to explain why most collisions do not lead to a reaction.
- Understand the Maxwell–Boltzmann distribution of molecular energies in gases.
- Be able to draw and interpret distribution curves for different temperatures.
- Understand the qualitative effect of temperature changes on the rate of reaction.
- Use the Maxwell-Boltzmann distribution to explain why a small temperature increase can lead to a large increase in rate.
- Understand the qualitative effect of changes in concentration, or a change in the pressure of a gas, on collision frequency.
- Be able to explain how a change in concentration or pressure influences the rate of a reaction.

Specification Reference 3.1.5.1, 3.1.5.2, 3.1.5.3, 3.1.5.4

The rate of a reaction is the change in the amount of a reactant or product over time — it describes how fast a reaction's happening. But if particles are going to react, they have to meet first. That's where collision theory comes in...

Collision theory and activation energy

Particles in liquids and gases are always moving and colliding with each other. They don't react every time though — only when the conditions are right. **Collision theory** says that a reaction won't take place between two particles unless they collide in the right direction (they need to be facing each other the right way) and they collide with at least a certain minimum amount of kinetic (movement) energy.

The minimum amount of kinetic energy particles need to react is called the **activation energy**. This much energy is needed to break the bonds within reactant particles to start the reaction. Reactions with low activation energies often happen pretty easily. But reactions with high activation energies don't. You need to give the particles extra energy by heating them. You can show the activation energy of a reaction on an enthalpy profile diagram like the one shown below in Figure 1.

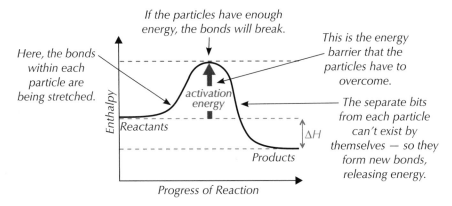

Figure 1: *An enthalpy profile diagram.*

Maxwell-Boltzmann distributions

Imagine looking down on Oxford Street when it's teeming with people. You'll see some people ambling along slowly, some hurrying quickly, but most of them will be walking with a moderate speed. It's the same with the molecules in a gas. Some don't have much kinetic energy and move slowly. Others have loads of kinetic energy and whizz along. But most molecules are somewhere in between.

If you plot a graph of the numbers of molecules in a gas with different kinetic energies you get a **Maxwell-Boltzmann distribution**. The Maxwell-Boltzmann distribution is a theoretical model that has been developed to explain scientific observations. It looks like this:

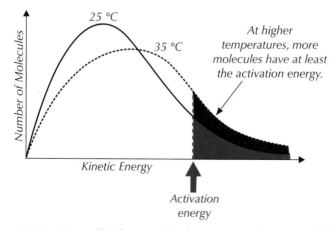

The peak of the curve represents the most likely energy of any single molecule.

The mean (average) energy of all the molecules is a bit to the right of the peak.

Most molecules are moving at a moderate speed so their energies are in the middle.

number of molecules

kinetic energy

The curve starts at (0, 0) because no molecules have zero energy.

A few molecules are moving slowly.

activation energy

Some molecules have more than the activation energy. These are the only ones that can react.

Figure 2: *A Maxwell-Boltzmann distribution curve showing the different kinetic energies of molecules in a gas.*

Figure 3: *James Clerk Maxwell, the Scottish physicist who studied the motion of gas molecules.*

The area under a Maxwell-Boltzmann distribution curve is equal to the total number of molecules.

The effect of temperature on reaction rate

If you increase the temperature of a gas, the molecules will on average have more kinetic energy and will move faster. So, a greater proportion of molecules will have at least the activation energy and be able to react. This changes the shape of the Maxwell-Boltzmann distribution curve — it pushes it over to the right (see Figure 5). The total number of molecules is still the same, which means the area under each curve must be the same.

Figure 4: *Ludwig Boltzmann, the Austrian physicist who developed Maxwell's ideas on the energy distribution of gas molecules.*

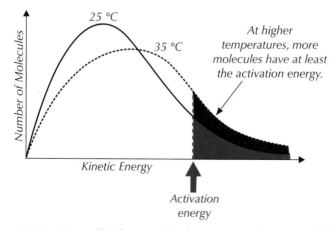

Number of Molecules

25 °C

35 °C

At higher temperatures, more molecules have at least the activation energy.

Kinetic Energy

Activation energy

Figure 5: *Two Maxwell-Boltzmann distribution curves for a gas at different temperatures. Increasing the temperature of the gas shifts the distribution of the kinetic energies of the molecules.*

Exam Tip
You need to be able to draw distribution curves for different temperatures so remember — if the temperature **i**ncreases the curve moves to the **r**ight, if it d**e**creases the curve moves to the **l**eft.

Because the molecules are flying about faster, they'll collide more often. This is another reason why increasing the temperature makes a reaction faster. So, small temperature increases can lead to large increases in reaction rate.

The effect of concentration on reaction rate

If you increase the concentration of reactants in a solution, the particles will on average be closer together. If they're closer, collisions are more frequent. If collisions are more frequent, they'll be more chances for particles to react.

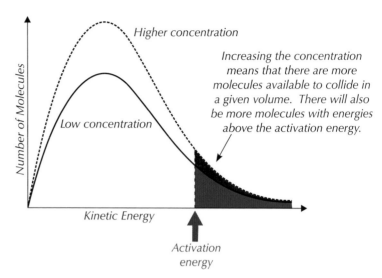

Increasing the concentration means that there are more molecules available to collide in a given volume. There will also be more molecules with energies above the activation energy.

Figure 6: *Two Maxwell-Boltzmann distribution curves for a solution at different concentrations.*

If the reaction involves gases, increasing the pressure of the gases works in just the same way. Raising the pressure pushes all of the gas particles closer together, increasing the number in a given volume. This increases the frequency of collisions, which increases the reaction rate.

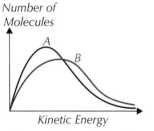

Figure 7: *Two Maxwell-Boltzmann distribution curves for a volume of gas at different temperatures.*

Practice Question — Application

Q1 The two Maxwell-Boltzmann distribution curves shown in Figure 7 are for the same volume of the same gas. Which curve, A or B, is for the gas at a higher temperature? Explain your answer.

Practice Questions — Fact Recall

Q1 What conditions are required for a collision between two particles to result in a reaction?

Q2 What does the term 'activation energy' mean?

Q3 Explain why a small increase in temperature can lead to a large increase in reaction rate.

Q4 Describe and explain the effect that increasing the concentration of a solution has on the rate of a reaction involving that solution.

2. Catalysts

Sometimes you need to speed up a reaction, but you can't (or don't want to) increase the temperature, concentration or pressure any further. That's where catalysts come in.

What is a catalyst?

You can use **catalysts** to make chemical reactions happen faster. A catalyst increases the rate of a reaction by providing an alternative reaction pathway with a lower activation energy. The catalyst is chemically unchanged at the end of the reaction.

Catalysts are great. They don't get used up in reactions, so you only need a tiny bit of catalyst to catalyse a huge amount of stuff. They do take part in reactions, but they're remade at the end. Catalysts are very fussy about which reactions they catalyse. Many will usually only work on a single reaction. Catalysts save heaps of money in industrial processes.

Example

The Haber-Bosch process uses an iron catalyst to increase the rate of forming ammonia from nitrogen and hydrogen in the following reaction:

$$N_{2(g)} + 3H_{2(g)} \rightleftharpoons 2NH_{3(g)}$$

This reaction has a very high activation energy, due to a very strong $N{\equiv}N$ bond in N_2. For the reaction rate to be high enough to make ammonia in any great quantity, the temperature and pressure would have to be extremely high — too high to be practical or profitable.

In reality, the reaction is performed with the use of an iron catalyst, which increases the reaction rate at a workable temperature and pressure (around 400-500 °C and 20 MPa).

The nitrogen and hydrogen molecules bind to the surface of the catalyst. This makes it easier to break the bonds at lower energies, and so the activation energy of the reaction decreases. The broken nitrogen and hydrogen molecules then form ammonia molecules, and break away from the surface of the catalyst.

How do catalysts work?

If you look at an enthalpy profile (see Figure 2) alongside a Maxwell-Boltzmann distribution (Figure 3, on the next page), you can see why catalysts work.

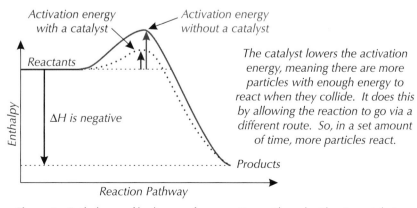

Activation energy with a catalyst

Activation energy without a catalyst

Reactants

ΔH is negative

Products

Enthalpy

Reaction Pathway

The catalyst lowers the activation energy, meaning there are more particles with enough energy to react when they collide. It does this by allowing the reaction to go via a different route. So, in a set amount of time, more particles react.

Figure 2: *Enthalpy profile diagram for a reaction with and without a catalyst.*

Learning Objectives:

- Understand that a catalyst is a substance that increases the rate of a chemical reaction without being changed in chemical composition or amount.

- Understand that catalysts work by providing an alternative reaction route of lower activation energy.

- Explain, using a Maxwell-Boltzmann distribution, how a catalyst increases the rate of a reaction involving a gas.

Specification Reference 3.1.5.5

Figure 1: *Fritz Haber, the German chemist who developed the process of ammonia production with Carl Bosch.*

Tip: The reaction used to make ammonia is a reversible reaction — there's more on reversible reactions on pages 125-128.

With a catalyst present, the molecules still have the same amount of energy, so the Maxwell-Boltzmann distribution curve is unchanged. But because the catalyst lowers the activation energy, more of the molecules have energies above this threshold and are able to react, as shown in Figure 3.

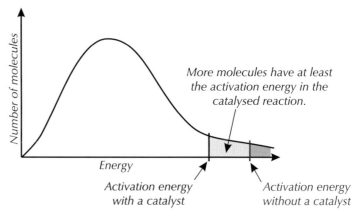

Figure 3: *A Maxwell-Boltzmann distribution curve for a reaction with and without a catalyst.*

Practice Question — Application

Q1 The Maxwell-Boltzmann distribution curve shown below is for an uncatalysed chemical reaction to produce 'Product X'.

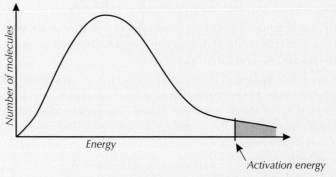

A company wants to produce 'Product X' on a large scale. They are considering using a catalyst.

a) Draw a sketch to show how the addition of a catalyst would affect the Maxwell-Boltzmann distribution curve for the reaction.

b) The uncatalysed reaction will only take place at temperatures above 1000 °C. Suggest how adding a catalyst would improve the industrial process.

Practice Questions — Fact Recall

Q1 What is a catalyst?

Q2 Explain how a catalyst can speed up the rate of a reaction.

3. Measuring Reaction Rates

Understanding all about the rates of chemical reactions is a really important part of chemistry. You need to know how to measure reaction rate as well.

Learning Objectives:
- Understand the meaning of the term rate of reaction.
- Investigate how the rate of a reaction changes with temperature (Required Practical 3).

Specification Reference 3.1.5.3

Calculating reaction rates

Rate of reaction is the change in the amount of a reactant or product over time. The units of reaction rate will be 'change you're measuring ÷ unit of time' (e.g. $g\ s^{-1}$ or $cm^3\ s^{-1}$). Here's a simple formula for finding the rate of a reaction:

$$\text{rate of reaction} = \frac{\text{amount of reactant used or product formed}}{\text{time}}$$

Measuring the rate of a reaction

If you want to find the rate of a reaction, you need to be able to follow the reaction as it's occurring. Although there are quite a few ways to follow reactions, not every method works for every reaction. You've got to pick a property that changes as the reaction goes on. Here are a few examples:

REQUIRED PRACTICAL **3**

Tip: Carrying out experiments can be hazardous so you should always do a risk assessment before beginning.

Time taken for a precipitate to form

You can use this method when the product's a precipitate that clouds a solution.

--- **Example** ---

When you mix colourless sodium thiosulfate solution and colourless hydrochloric acid solution, a yellow precipitate of sulfur is formed:

$$Na_2S_2O_{3(aq)} + 2HCl_{(aq)} \rightarrow 2NaCl_{(aq)} + SO_{2(g)} + S_{(s)}$$

You can stand a conical flask on top of a white tile with a black mark on it. Then you add fixed volumes of the reactant solutions to the flask and start a stopwatch. Look through the solutions to observe the mark on the tile. As the precipitate forms, the mark will become harder to see clearly. Stop the timer when the mark is no longer visible. The reading on the timer is recorded as the time taken for the precipitate to form.

Tip: If the same person uses the same mark each time you can compare the reaction rate, because roughly the same amount of precipitate will have been formed when the mark is obscured. But this method is subjective — different people might not agree on exactly when the mark has 'disappeared'.

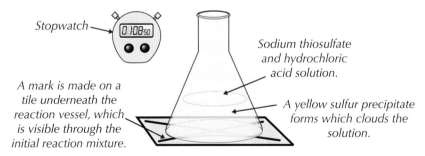

Stopwatch

Sodium thiosulfate and hydrochloric acid solution.

A mark is made on a tile underneath the reaction vessel, which is visible through the initial reaction mixture.

A yellow sulfur precipitate forms which clouds the solution.

Figure 1: *Experimental setup for measuring reaction rate by monitoring the time taken for a precipitate to form.*

You can repeat this reaction for solutions at different temperatures to investigate how temperature affects reaction rate. Use a water bath to gently heat both solutions to the desired temperature before mixing them. The volumes and concentrations of the solutions must be kept the same each time. The results should show that the higher the temperature, the less time it takes for the mark to disappear and the faster the rate of the reaction gets.

Tip: In this experiment, temperature is the independent variable because you're changing it to see what happens. Time is the dependent variable because that's what you're measuring. See page 1 for more about this.

Change in mass

When the product is a gas, its rate of formation can be measured using a mass balance.

Example

This would work for the reaction between hydrochloric acid and calcium carbonate in which carbon dioxide gas is given off.

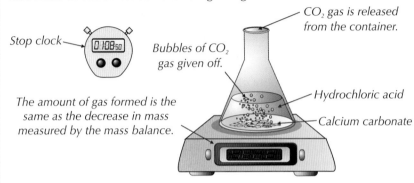

CO₂ gas is released from the container.

Stop clock

Bubbles of CO₂ gas given off.

Hydrochloric acid

The amount of gas formed is the same as the decrease in mass measured by the mass balance.

Calcium carbonate

Figure 2: *Experimental setup for measuring the reaction rate by monitoring the change in mass of a reaction mixture.*

Time (s)	Mass (g)
0	280.0
30	279.3
60	278.7
90	278.2
120	278.0
150	277.9
180	277.8
210	277.7
240	277.7
270	277.7

Figure 3: *Example results for the experiment carried out in Figure 2.*

Tip: These methods are known as continuous monitoring methods because you can monitor the reaction rate from the beginning of the reaction to the end.

When the reaction starts, start a stop clock or timer, then read off the mass at regular time intervals. Make a table with a column for 'time' and a column for 'mass' and fill it in as the reaction goes on (see Figure 3). You'll know the reaction is finished when the reading on the mass balance stops decreasing. This method is very accurate and easy to use but does release gas into the room, which could be dangerous if the gas is toxic or flammable. So it's best to carry out the experiment in a fume cupboard.

You can repeat this reaction for acids at different temperatures to investigate how temperature affects reaction rate. All other experimental variables must be kept the same. The results should show that the higher the temperature, the faster the mass decreases and the faster the reaction rate gets.

Gas volume

If a gas is given off during a reaction, you can measure reaction rate by collecting it in a gas syringe and recording how much you've got at regular time intervals.

Example

This would work for the reaction between magnesium and an acid in which hydrogen gas is given off.

Airtight seal so all the gas produced goes into the syringe.

The gas collects in the syringe and its production can be measured over time.

Bubbles of H₂ gas given off.

Acid

Magnesium

Stop clock

Figure 4: *Experimental setup for measuring the reaction rate by monitoring the volume of gas given off by a reaction mixture.*

Again, start a stop clock or timer when the reaction starts, then read off the volume of gas in the gas syringe at regular time intervals (see Figure 5 for a sample results table). You know that the reaction has finished when the gas volume stops increasing.

This method is accurate because gas syringes usually give volumes to the nearest 0.1 cm³. Because no gas escapes, you can use this method for reactions that produce toxic or flammable gases (although you should still do reactions like these in a fume cupboard to be safe). Vigorous reactions can blow the plunger out of the syringe, so you should do a rough calculation of how much gas you expect the reaction to produce before you begin. Then you can use an appropriate size of gas syringe.

The reaction can be repeated with the acid at different temperatures to investigate the effect on reaction rate. The results should show that the higher the temperature, the faster the gas is produced, and therefore the faster the rate of reaction.

Time (s)	Volume (cm³)
0	0.0
30	6.1
60	10.9
90	15.2
120	17.7
150	20.0
180	21.1
210	21.9
240	22.0
270	22.0

Figure 5: *Example results for the experiment carried out in Figure 4.*

Practice Question — Application

Q1 A student is asked to measure the rate of the reaction below.

$$A_{(aq)} \rightarrow B_{(l)} + C_{(g)}$$

a) Suggest an experimental method the student could use to measure the rate of reaction.

b) How would the student know when the reaction has finished, using the method in your answer to part a)?

c) The student carries out the reaction at eight different temperatures and measures how long it takes the reaction to finish. The results are presented in the table in Figure 6. Make an estimate of how long it takes the reaction to finish at 45 °C.

Temp (°C)	Time (s)
20	230
25	228
30	225
35	219
40	208
45	
50	160
55	117

Figure 6: *Results of the experiment carried out in Q1 c).*

Practice Questions — Fact Recall

Q1 What is meant by the term 'rate of reaction'?

Q2 Outline a method which could be used to measure the rate of a reaction in which one of the products is a precipitate.

Section Summary

Make sure you know...

- That most collisions between particles don't result in a reaction.
- That collision theory says that a collision will only result in a reaction if it's in the right direction and has at least a certain minimum amount of kinetic energy.
- That the minimum amount of kinetic energy required for a reaction is called the activation energy.
- That the Maxwell-Boltzmann distribution describes the spread of energies of the molecules in a gas.
- How to draw and interpret Maxwell-Boltzmann distribution curves for gases at different temperatures.
- That even a small increase in temperature can increase the reaction rate, by increasing the number of molecules with energies above the activation energy. This will increase the frequency of collisions and also mean that more particles will react when they collide.
- That increasing the concentration of reactants (or the pressure if they're gases) will increase the reaction rate, because the molecules will be closer together and so collisions will be more frequent.
- That a catalyst is a substance that increases the rate of a reaction by providing an alternative pathway with a lower activation energy, and is chemically unchanged at the end of the reaction.
- That the shape of the Maxwell-Boltzmann distribution curve doesn't change for a catalysed reaction, only the position of the activation energy on the curve.
- That the rate of a reaction is the change in the amount of reactants or products per unit time.
- That various experimental methods can be used to investigate how the rate of a reaction changes with temperature.

Exam-style Questions

Questions 1 and 2 are about the two Maxwell-Boltzmann energy distributions for molecules of a gas shown below.

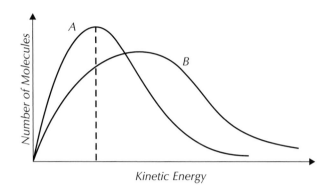

1 What does the dotted line on curve A represent?

   A The total number of molecules in the distribution.

   B The most likely energy of molecules in the distribution.

   C The enthalpy change of the reaction.

   D The mean energy of the molecules in the distribution. *(1 mark)*

2 Distributions A and B are for the same volume of the same gas.
     Which of these could distribution B represent?

   A Distribution A at lower concentration.

   B Distribution A at lower temperature.

   C Distribution A at higher temperature.

   D Distribution A at higher concentration. *(1 mark)*

3 1.5 g of magnesium is added to a flask containing 40 cm³ 1.0 mol dm³ hydrochloric acid and the volume of hydrogen gas given off over time is measured using a gas syringe. The experiment is then repeated at different temperatures, using an identical set-up, to see what effect this has on the rate of reaction.
     Which of the following variables is the independent variable in the experiment?

   A Temperature of the hydrochloric acid.

   B Volume of hydrochloric acid.

   C Mass of magnesium added.

   D Volume of hydrogen gas produced. *(1 mark)*

4   Which of the following is a unit that could be used to show the rate of a reaction?

   A $g\ l^{-1}$

   B $kJ\ mol^{-1}$

   C $mol\ dm^{-3}$

   D $g\ s^{-1}$

(1 mark)

5   The Maxwell-Boltzmann distribution curve for a gas is shown below.

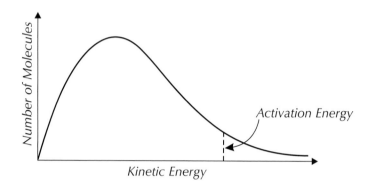

   5.1   What is meant by the term 'activation energy'?

(1 mark)

   5.2   Draw another curve on the axes above that would show the same
             volume of the same gas at a higher temperature.

(1 mark)

   5.3   Define the term catalyst.

(1 mark)

   5.4   How does the addition of a catalyst to a reaction affect the shape
             of a Maxwell-Boltzmann distribution curve?
             Explain your answer.

(2 marks)

   5.5   The reactants in a particular reaction are heated.
             Explain the effect that this will have on the rate of the reaction.

(3 marks)

   5.6   For a particular reaction, the best yield is obtained
             by keeping the pressure as low as possible.
             Explain the effect that lowering the pressure will have
             on the rate of the reaction.

(3 marks)

1. Reversible Reactions

We usually think of a reaction as a one-way process to make products from reactants. In reality though, many reactions are reversible.

Dynamic equilibrium

Lots of chemical reactions are reversible — they go both ways.
To show a reaction's reversible, you stick in a $\rightleftharpoons$.

--- Example ---

Hydrogen reacts with iodine to give hydrogen iodide: $H_{2(g)} + I_{2(g)} \rightleftharpoons 2HI_{(g)}$

This reaction can go in either direction,
forwards: $H_{2(g)} + I_{2(g)} \rightarrow 2HI_{(g)}$ ...or backwards: $2HI_{(g)} \rightarrow H_{2(g)} + I_{2(g)}$

As the reactants get used up, the forward reaction slows down — and as more product is formed, the reverse reaction speeds up. After a while, the forward reaction will be going at exactly the same rate as the backward reaction. The concentration of reactants and products won't be changing any more, so it'll seem like nothing's happening. It's a bit like you're digging a hole, while someone else is filling it in at exactly the same speed. This is called a **dynamic equilibrium**. A dynamic equilibrium can only happen in a **closed system** (this just means nothing can get in or out) which is at a constant temperature.

Le Chatelier's principle

If you change the concentration, pressure or temperature of a reversible reaction, you're going to alter the position of equilibrium. This just means you'll end up with different amounts of reactants and products at equilibrium. If the position of equilibrium moves to the left, the backwards reaction is faster than the forwards reaction, and so you'll get more reactants.

--- Example ---

If the position of equilibrium in the reaction $H_{2(g)} + I_{2(g)} \rightleftharpoons 2HI_{(g)}$ shifts to the left, the backwards reaction is fastest, so more H_2 and I_2 are produced:

$$2HI_{(g)} \rightarrow H_{2(g)} + I_{2(g)}$$

If the position of equilibrium moves to the right, the forwards reaction is faster than the backwards reaction, and so you'll get more products.

--- Example ---

If the position of equilibrium in the reaction $H_{2(g)} + I_{2(g)} \rightleftharpoons 2HI_{(g)}$ shifts to the right, the forwards reaction is fastest, so more HI is produced:

$$H_{2(g)} + I_{2(g)} \rightarrow 2HI_{(g)}$$

Le Chatelier's principle tells you how the position of equilibrium will change if a condition changes:

> If a reaction at equilibrium is subjected to a change in concentration, pressure or temperature, the position of equilibrium will move to counteract the change.

Learning Objectives:

- Know that many chemical reactions are reversible.
- Know that in a reversible reaction at equilibrium, forward and reverse reactions proceed at equal rates.
- Know that in a reversible reaction at equilibrium, the concentrations of reactants and products remain constant.
- Know and be able to use Le Chatelier's principle to predict qualitatively the effects of changes in temperature, pressure and concentration on the position of equilibrium in homogeneous reactions.
- Know that a catalyst does not affect the position of equilibrium.

Specification Reference 3.1.6.1

Tip: $H_{2(g)} + I_{2(g)} \rightarrow 2HI_{(g)}$ is an example of a homogeneous reaction — the reactants and products are all in the same state (in this case they're all gases).

So, basically, if you raise the temperature, the position of equilibrium will shift to try to cool things down. And, if you raise the pressure or concentration, the position of equilibrium will shift to try to reduce it again. Catalysts have no effect on the position of equilibrium. They can't increase yield — but they do mean equilibrium is reached faster.

Using Le Chatelier's principle

Changing concentration

If you increase the concentration of a reactant, the equilibrium tries to get rid of the extra reactant. It does this by making more product. So the equilibrium's shifted to the right. If you increase the concentration of the product, the equilibrium tries to remove the extra product. This makes the reverse reaction go faster — so the equilibrium shifts to the left. Decreasing the concentrations has the opposite effect.

> **Examples**
>
> Sulfur dioxide reacts with oxygen to produce sulfur trioxide:
> $$2SO_{2(g)} + O_{2(g)} \rightleftharpoons 2SO_{3(g)}$$
> If you increase the concentration of SO_2 or O_2, the equilibrium tries to get rid of it by making more SO_3, so the equilibrium shifts to the right. If you increase the concentration of SO_3, the equilibrium shifts to the left to make the backwards reaction faster to get rid of the extra SO_3.
>
> In the Haber process, nitrogen reacts with hydrogen to produce ammonia:
> $$N_{2(g)} + 3H_{2(g)} \rightleftharpoons 2NH_{3(g)}$$
> If you increase the concentration of N_2 or H_2, the equilibrium shifts to the right and you'll make more NH_3. If you increase the concentration of NH_3, the equilibrium shifts to the left and you'll make more N_2 and H_2.

Changing pressure

Changing the pressure only affects equilibria involving gases. Increasing the pressure shifts the equilibrium to the side with fewer gas molecules. This reduces the pressure. Decreasing the pressure shifts the equilibrium to the side with more gas molecules. This raises the pressure again.

> **Examples**
>
> When sulfur dioxide reacts with oxygen you get sulfur trioxide:
> $$2SO_{2(g)} + O_{2(g)} \rightleftharpoons 2SO_{3(g)}$$
> There are 3 moles on the left, but only 2 on the right. So, an increase in pressure shifts the equilibrium to the right, making more SO_3 and reducing the pressure. Decreasing the pressure favours the backwards reaction, so the equilibrium shifts to the left and more SO_2 and O_2 will be made to increase the pressure.
>
> Methane reacts with water to produce carbon monoxide and hydrogen:
> $$CH_{4(g)} + H_2O_{(g)} \rightleftharpoons CO_{(g)} + 3H_{2(g)}$$
> There are 2 moles on the left and 4 on the right. So for this reaction, an increase in pressure shifts the equilibrium to the left, making more CH_4 and H_2O. Decreasing the pressure shifts the equilibrium to the right to make more CO and H_2. This reaction is used in industry to produce hydrogen. It is best performed at a low pressure to favour the forwards reaction so that more H_2 is produced.

Tip: Le Chatelier's principle only applies to homogeneous equilibria — i.e. when every species in the reaction is in the same physical state (e.g. all liquid or all gas).

Figure 1a: *Equilibrium between $NO_{2(g)}$ (brown) and $N_2O_{4(l)}$ (colourless).*

Figure 1b: *When pressure is applied the colour changes because the equilibrium shifts in favour of $N_2O_{4(l)}$.*

Changing temperature

Increasing the temperature means adding heat. The equilibrium shifts in the endothermic (positive ΔH) direction to absorb this heat. Decreasing the temperature removes heat. The equilibrium shifts in the exothermic (negative ΔH) direction to try to replace the heat. If the forward reaction's endothermic, the reverse reaction will be exothermic, and vice versa.

Tip: An enthalpy change given with a reversible reaction always refers to the forwards reaction, unless you're told otherwise.

┌─ **Examples** ─────────────────────────────

This reaction's exothermic in the forward direction, which means it is endothermic in the backward direction.

Exothermic $\longrightarrow$

$$2SO_{2(g)} + O_{2(g)} \rightleftharpoons 2SO_{3(g)} \qquad \Delta H = -197 \text{ kJ mol}^{-1}$$

$\longleftarrow$ *Endothermic*

If you increase the temperature, the equilibrium shifts to the left (the endothermic direction) to absorb the extra heat. This means more SO_2 and O_2 are produced.

If you decrease the temperature, the equilibrium shifts to the right (the exothermic direction) to produce more heat. This means more SO_3 is produced.

This reaction's endothermic in the forward direction (and so exothermic in the backward direction).

Endothermic $\longrightarrow$

$$N_2O_{4(g)} \rightleftharpoons 2NO_{2(g)} \qquad \Delta H = +57.2 \text{ kJ mol}^{-1}$$

$\longleftarrow$ *Exothermic*

Increasing the temperature will shift the equilibrium to the right, producing more NO_2.

Decreasing the temperature shifts the equilibrium to the left, producing more N_2O_4.

Exam Tip
In an exam question, make it clear exactly how the equilibrium shift opposes a temperature change — i.e. by removing or producing heat.

Tip: A lot of questions in this section ask about the effect of increasing temperature, pressure and concentration on the position of equilibrium. These questions can look quite similar to the ones on reaction rate from the last section, so make sure you're really clear what you're being asked about.

Following equilibrium reactions

There are some reactions you can do in the lab to follow equilibrium shifts. The reaction of $[Cu(H_2O)_6]^{2+}$ with concentrated hydrochloric acid (HCl) is one of these reactions.

When $[Cu(H_2O)_6]^{2+}$ reacts with hydrochloric acid, a copper chloride complex, $[CuCl_4]^{2-}$, forms (see Figure 2). This reaction is a reversible reaction, so at any point there will be a mixture of $[Cu(H_2O)_6]^{2+}$ and $[CuCl_4]^{2-}$ present in the reaction container.

$[Cu(H_2O)_6]^{2+}$ is a light blue colour, while $[CuCl_4]^{2-}$ is a greeny-yellow. You can therefore monitor the equilibrium position of this reaction by noting what colour the solution is. If the solution is blue, then the position of equilibrium must lie to the left and there'll be more reactants than products. But, if the solution's greeny-yellow, the equilibrium position must lie to the right and there'll be more of the products.

Tip: Before carrying out any reactions in the lab, you should do a thorough risk assessment and take any relevant safety precautions.

$$[Cu(H_2O)_6]^{2+}{}_{(aq)} + 4Cl^-{}_{(aq)} \rightleftharpoons [CuCl_4]^{2-}{}_{(aq)} + 6H_2O_{(l)}$$

blue copper aqua complex

greeny-yellow copper chloride complex

Figure 2: *The reaction between $[Cu(H_2O)_6]^{2+}$ and concentrated HCl.*

Figure 3: *A solution of $[Cu(H_2O)_6]^{2+}$ (left). Upon addition of an excess of HCl, the $[CuCl_4]^{2-}$ complex forms which turns the solution green (right).*

Changing the concentration

If you have a test tube containing $[Cu(H_2O)_6]^{2+}$, you'll see it's a light blue colour. If you slowly add concentrated HCl, you'll notice the solution turn from light blue to a bluey-green as the equilibrium in Figure 2 is established. The more HCl you add, the more green the solution goes as more and more of the $[CuCl_4]^{2-}$ complex forms — this is because, by adding HCl, you're increasing the concentration of Cl⁻ in the solution. The equilibrium shifts to the right to try and remove the excess Cl⁻ ions from the solution, and more greeny-yellow $[CuCl_4]^{2-}$ forms (see Figure 3).

You can push the equilibrium back to the right by adding distilled water to the reaction container. The equilibrium position moves to try and mop up all the extra H_2O molecules you're adding to the solution by forming more $[Cu(H_2O)_6]^{2+}$, which turns the solution blue again.

Changing the temperature

The forward reaction of the equilibrium is endothermic (it takes in heat). So, if you heat a sample containing an equilibrium mixture of $[Cu(H_2O)_6]^{2+}$ and $[Cu(Cl)_4]^{2-}$, the equilibrium will move to the right to try and absorb the extra heat. This means more of the product forms, and you'll see the solution turn green as more $[CuCl_4]^{2-}$ is made.

The opposite happens if you cool the mixture down. Since the reverse reaction is exothermic, the equilibrium will move to the left to favour the reverse reaction to try and make up for the loss of heat. This means more of the $[Cu(H_2O)_6]^{2+}$ complex will form, and the solution will turn more blue.

Practice Questions — Application

Q1 An industrial process uses the following reversible reaction:

$$A_{(g)} + 2B_{(g)} \rightleftharpoons C_{(g)} + D_{(g)} \qquad \Delta H = -189 \text{ kJ mol}^{-1}$$

a) Explain the effect of increasing the concentration of A on the position of equilibrium.

b) Explain the effect of increasing the pressure on the position of equilibrium.

c) Explain the effect of increasing the temperature on the position of equilibrium.

d) Briefly outline the best reaction conditions (in terms of high or low concentration, pressure and temperature) to maximise the production of product D.

Q2 What will be the effect of increasing the pressure on the position of equilibrium of the following reaction? Explain your answer.

$$H_{2(g)} + I_{2(g)} \rightleftharpoons 2HI_{(g)}$$

Exam Tip
If you're asked to define something like 'dynamic equilibrium' in an exam, look at the number of marks allocated for the answer. If there's more than one, you'll need more than one point in your definition.

Practice Questions — Fact Recall

Q1 What does it mean if a reaction is at dynamic equilibrium?

Q2 What conditions are needed for dynamic equilibrium to be established?

Q3 What is Le Chatelier's Principle?

Q4 How does the addition of a catalyst affect the position of equilibrium in a reversible reaction?

2. Industrial Processes

Le Chatelier's principle can be applied to lots of industrial processes — like the production of ethanol and methanol.

Compromise conditions in industry

Companies have to think about how much it costs to run a reaction and how much money they can make from it. This means they have a few factors to think about when they're choosing the best conditions for a reaction.

Learning Objective:
- Be able to explain why, for a reversible reaction used in an industrial process, a compromise of temperature and pressure may be used.

Specification Reference 3.1.6.1

--- Example ---

Ethanol can be made via a reversible reaction between ethene and steam:

$$C_2H_{4(g)} + H_2O_{(g)} \rightleftharpoons C_2H_5OH_{(g)} \qquad \Delta H = -46 \text{ kJ mol}^{-1}$$

The industrial conditions for the reaction are:
- a pressure of 60-70 atmospheres,
- a temperature of 300 °C,
- a phosphoric acid catalyst.

Because it's an exothermic reaction, lower temperatures favour the forward reaction. This means that at lower temperatures more ethene and steam are converted to ethanol — you get a better **yield**. But lower temperatures mean a slower rate of reaction. You'd be daft to try to get a really high yield of ethanol if it's going to take you 10 years. So the 300 °C is a compromise between maximum yield and a faster reaction.

Higher pressure favours the forward reaction, since it moves the reaction to the side with fewer molecules of gas, so a pressure of 60-70 atmospheres is used. Increasing the pressure also increases the rate of reaction. Cranking up the pressure as high as you can sounds like a great idea, but high pressures are expensive to produce. You need stronger pipes and containers to withstand high pressure. So the 60-70 atmospheres is a compromise between maximum yield and minimum expense.

Only a small proportion of the ethene reacts each time the gases pass through the reactor. To save money and raw materials, the unreacted ethene is separated from the ethanol and recycled back into the reactor. Thanks to this, around 95% of the ethene is eventually converted to ethanol.

Tip: The yield is the amount of product you get from a reaction. Increasing the reaction rate will give you a higher yield in a given time, but you need to shift the equilibrium to increase the maximum yield.

--- Example ---

Methanol is also made industrially in a reversible reaction:

$$2H_{2(g)} + CO_{(g)} \rightleftharpoons CH_3OH_{(g)} \qquad \Delta H = -90 \text{ kJ mol}^{-1}$$

Just like ethanol production, the conditions are a compromise between keeping costs low and yield high. The conditions for this reaction are:
- a pressure of 50-100 atmospheres,
- a temperature of 250 °C,
- a catalyst of a mixture of copper, zinc oxide and aluminium oxide.

***Figure 1:** Methanol has many uses. For example, it is widely used as a solvent.*

Tip: As with ethanol production, low temperatures favour the forward (exothermic) reaction, so the temperature is kept as low as possible without reducing the reaction rate too much.

Practice Question — Fact Recall

Q1 In the production of ethanol from ethene and steam, using a low temperature and a high pressure favours the forward reaction and gives a better yield. Given that this is the case, explain why a moderate temperature and pressure are used when making ethanol industrially.

3. The Equilibrium Constant

You don't just need to know what dynamic equilibrium means — you'll also need to be able to describe it, using some mathsy bits...

K_c, the equilibrium constant

If you know the molar concentration of each substance at equilibrium, you can work out the **equilibrium constant**, K_c. This is a ratio worked out from the concentrations of the products and reactants after equilibrium is reached. Your value of K_c will only be true for that particular temperature. Before you can calculate K_c, you have to write an expression for it. Here's how:

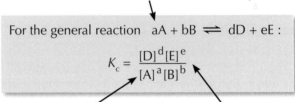

The lower-case letters a, b, d and e are the number of moles of each substance in the equation.

For the general reaction $aA + bB \rightleftharpoons dD + eE$:

$$K_c = \frac{[D]^d[E]^e}{[A]^a[B]^b}$$

The square brackets, [ ], mean concentration in mol dm^{-3}.

The products go on the top line and the reactants go on the bottom line.

Example

For the reaction $H_{2(g)} + I_{2(g)} \rightleftharpoons 2HI_{(g)}$ there are two reactants (H_2 and I_2) and one product (HI). There's one mole of each of the reactants and two moles of the product. So the expression for K_c is:

$$K_c = \frac{[HI]^2}{[H_2]^1[I_2]^1} = \frac{[HI]^2}{[H_2][I_2]}$$

Calculating K_c

If you know the equilibrium concentrations, just bung them in your expression. Then with a bit of help from the old calculator, you can work out the value for K_c. The units are a bit trickier though — they vary, so you have to work them out after each calculation.

Example — Maths Skills

For the hydrogen iodide example above, the equilibrium concentrations are: [HI] = 0.80 mol dm^{-3}, [H$_2$] = 0.10 mol dm^{-3} and [I$_2$] = 0.10 mol dm^{-3} at 640 K. What is the equilibrium constant for this reaction at 640 K?

Just stick the concentrations into the expression for K_c:

$$K_c = \frac{[HI]^2}{[H_2][I_2]} = \frac{0.80^2}{0.10 \times 0.10} = 64$$

To work out the units of K_c, put the units in the expression instead of the numbers:

$$\text{Units of } K_c = \frac{(\text{mol dm}^{-3})^2}{(\text{mol dm}^{-3})(\text{mol dm}^{-3})} = \frac{(\text{mol dm}^{-3})(\text{mol dm}^{-3})}{(\text{mol dm}^{-3})(\text{mol dm}^{-3})}$$

The concentration units cancel, so there are no units and K_c is just **64**.

You might have to figure out some of the equilibrium concentrations before you can find K_c. To do this follow these steps:

Step 1: Find out how many moles of each reactant and product there are at equilibrium. You'll usually be given the number of moles at equilibrium for one of the reactants. You can then use the balanced reaction equation to work out the number of moles of all the others.

Step 2: Calculate the molar concentrations of each reactant and product by dividing each number of moles by the volume of the reaction. You'll be told the volume in the question but you may have to convert it into different units. To work out molar concentrations you need the volume to be in dm^3.

Tip: The molar concentration is just the concentration in $mol\,dm^{-3}$.

Once you've done this you're ready to substitute your values into the expression for K_c and calculate it.

Exam Tip
With long wordy questions like this it can help to circle important bits of information before you start — e.g. any concentrations or volumes you're likely to need for the calculation.

Example — Maths Skills

0.20 moles of phosphorus(V) chloride decomposes at 600 K in a vessel of 5.0 dm^3. The equilibrium mixture is found to contain 0.080 moles of chlorine. Write the expression for K_c and calculate its value, including units.

$$PCl_{5(g)} \rightleftharpoons PCl_{3(g)} + Cl_{2(g)}$$

1. Find out how many moles of PCl_5 and PCl_3 there are at equilibrium:

   - The equation tells you that when 1 mole of PCl_5 decomposes, 1 mole of PCl_3 and 1 mole of Cl_2 are formed.

   - So if 0.080 moles of chlorine are produced at equilibrium, then there will be 0.080 moles of PCl_3 as well.

   - 0.080 mol of PCl_5 must have decomposed, so there will be 0.12 moles left (0.20 − 0.080 = 0.12).

Exam Tip
You may be asked to calculate the molar amounts of some substances in an earlier part of the question — if this happens you can reuse your answers to find K_c. Handy.

2. Divide each number of moles by the volume of the flask to give the molar concentrations:

$$[PCl_3] = [Cl_2] = \frac{0.080}{5.0} = 0.016 \text{ mol dm}^{-3}$$

$$[PCl_5] = \frac{0.12}{5.0} = 0.024 \text{ mol dm}^{-3}$$

3. Put the concentrations in the expression for K_c and calculate it:

$$K_c = \frac{[PCl_3]\,[Cl_2]}{[PCl_5]} = \frac{[0.016]\,[0.016]}{[0.024]} = 0.011$$

Exam Tip
When you're writing expressions for K_c make sure you use [square brackets]. If you use (rounded brackets) you won't get the marks.

4. Now find the units of K_c:

$$\text{Units of } K_c = \frac{(\text{mol dm}^{-3})(\text{mol dm}^{-3})}{\text{mol dm}^{-3}} = \frac{(\text{mol dm}^{-3})(\cancel{\text{mol dm}^{-3}})}{\cancel{\text{mol dm}^{-3}}} = \text{mol dm}^{-3}$$

So K_c = 0.011 mol dm^{-3}

Tip: If you're finding the units of K_c and you end up with units left on their own on the bottom of the fraction, you can simplify them by swapping the signs of the powers. For example:
$$\frac{\cancel{\text{mol dm}^{-3}}}{(\cancel{\text{mol dm}^{-3}})(\text{mol dm}^{-3})}$$
= mol^{-1} dm^3.

Using K_c

If you know the value of K_c you can use it to find unknown equilibrium concentrations. Here's how you do it:

Step 1: Put all the values you know into the expression for K_c.

Step 2: Rearrange the equation and solve it to find the unknown values.

When ethanoic acid was allowed to reach equilibrium with ethanol at 25 °C, it was found that the equilibrium mixture contained 2.0 mol dm^{-3} ethanoic acid and 3.5 mol dm^{-3} ethanol. The K_c of the equilibrium is 4.0 at 25 °C. What are the concentrations of the other components?

$$CH_3COOH_{(l)} + C_2H_5OH_{(l)} \rightleftharpoons CH_3COOC_2H_{5(l)} + H_2O_{(l)}$$

1. Put all the values you know in the K_c expression:

$$K_c = \frac{[CH_3COOC_2H_5]\,[H_2O]}{[CH_3COOH]\,[C_2H_5OH]} \quad \text{so} \quad 4.0 = \frac{[CH_3COOC_2H_5]\,[H_2O]}{2.0 \times 3.5}$$

Tip: The units of concentration should always be mol dm^{-3}. If your answer doesn't give you this then go back and check your calculation to see where you've gone wrong.

2. Rearranging this gives:
$$[CH_3COOC_2H_5][H_2O] = 4.0 \times 2.0 \times 3.5 = 28$$

3. From the equation, you know that $[CH_3COOC_2H_5] = [H_2O]$, so:
$$[CH_3COOC_2H_5] = [H_2O] = \sqrt{28} = 5.3 \text{ mol dm}^{-3}$$

The concentration of $CH_3COOC_2H_5$ and H_2O is 5.3 mol dm^{-3}.

Practice Questions — Application

Q1 The following equilibrium exists under certain conditions:

$$C_2H_4 + H_2O \rightleftharpoons C_2H_5OH$$

a) Write out the expression for K_c for this reaction.

5.00 moles of C_2H_5OH was placed in a container and allowed to reach equilibrium. At a certain temperature and pressure the equilibrium mixture was found to contain 1.85 moles of C_2H_4, and have a total volume of 15.0 dm^3.

b) Determine the number of moles of each substance at equilibrium.

c) Calculate the molar concentrations (in mol dm^{-3}) of all the reagents at equilibrium.

d) Calculate K_c for this equilibrium.

Tip: Don't forget — you need to work out the units of K_c too.

e) At a different temperature and pressure the equilibrium constant (K_c) for this reaction is 3.8 and the equilibrium mixture contained 0.80 mol dm^{-3} C_2H_5OH. Determine the equilibrium concentrations of C_2H_4 and H_2O under these conditions.

Q2 Under certain conditions the following equilibrium is established:

$$2SO_2 + O_2 \rightleftharpoons 2SO_3$$

a) Write out an expression for K_c for this reaction.

At a certain temperature the equilibrium concentrations for the three reagents were found to be:

$SO_2 = 0.250$ mol dm^{-3}, $O_2 = 0.180$ mol dm^{-3}, $SO_3 = 0.360$ mol dm^{-3}

b) Calculate K_c for this equilibrium.

c) If all other conditions (including the concentrations of O_2 and SO_3) were to stay the same, what would the equilibrium concentration of SO_2 have to be for K_c to be 15?

4. Factors Affecting the Equilibrium Constant

By tweaking some of the conditions of a system, you can change the position of the equilibrium. However, not all conditions have an effect...

Changing the temperature

If you increase the temperature, you add heat. The equilibrium shifts in the **endothermic** (positive ΔH) direction to absorb the heat. Decreasing the temperature removes heat energy. The equilibrium shifts in the **exothermic** (negative ΔH) direction to try to replace the heat. If the forward reaction's endothermic, the reverse reaction will be exothermic, and vice versa. If the change means more product is formed, K_c will rise. If it means less product is formed, then K_c will decrease.

Learning Objectives:
- Be able to predict the qualitative effects of changes of temperature on the value of K_c.
- Know that the value of the equilibrium constant is not affected either by changes in concentration or addition of a catalyst.

Specification Reference 3.1.6.2

--- Examples ---

The reaction below is exothermic in the forward direction:

$$\text{Exothermic} \longrightarrow$$
$$2SO_{2(g)} + O_{2(g)} \rightleftharpoons 2SO_{3(g)} \qquad \Delta H = -197 \text{ kJ mol}^{-1}$$
$$\longleftarrow \text{Endothermic}$$

Tip: The ΔH values given for reversible reactions show the ΔH of the forward reaction.

If you increase the temperature, the equilibrium shifts to the left (in the endothermic direction) to absorb some of the extra heat energy. This means that less product's formed so the concentration of product ($[SO_3]$) will be less.

$$K_c = \frac{[SO_3]^2}{[SO_2]^2[O_2]}$$
As $[SO_3]$ will be a smaller value, and $[SO_2]$ and $[O_2]$ will have higher values, K_c will be lower.

The reaction below is endothermic in the forward direction:

$$\text{Endothermic} \longrightarrow$$
$$2CH_{4(g)} \rightleftharpoons 3H_{2(g)} + C_2H_{2(g)} \qquad \Delta H = +377 \text{ kJ mol}^{-1}$$
$$\longleftarrow \text{Exothermic}$$

This time increasing the temperature shifts the equilibrium to the right. This means more product's formed, so K_c increases.

$$K_c = \frac{[H_2]^3[C_2H_2]}{[CH_4]^2}$$
As $[H_2]$ and $[C_2H_2]$ will have higher values and $[CH_4]$ will have a smaller value, K_c will be higher.

Tip: If the temperature decreases the opposite will happen — for reactions that are exothermic in the forward direction K_c will increase and for reactions that are endothermic in the forward direction K_c will decrease.

Changing the concentration

The value of the equilibrium constant, K_c, is fixed at a given temperature. So if the concentration of one thing in the equilibrium mixture changes then the concentrations of the others must change to keep the value of K_c the same.

--- Example ---

$$CH_3COOH_{(l)} + C_2H_5OH_{(l)} \rightleftharpoons CH_3COOC_2H_{5(l)} + H_2O_{(l)}$$

If you increase the concentration of CH_3COOH then the equilibrium will move to the right to get rid of some of the extra CH_3COOH — so more $CH_3COOC_2H_5$ and H_2O are produced. This keeps the equilibrium constant the same.

Tip: Remember — saying that the equilibrium moves to the right is just another way of saying more of the products form. If the equilibrium moves to the left, the opposite happens — more products are converted into reactants.

Adding a catalyst

Catalysts have no effect on the position of equilibrium or on the value of K_c. This is because a catalyst will increase the rate of both the forward and backward reactions by the same amount. As a result, the equilibrium position will be the same as the uncatalysed reaction, but equilibrium will be reached faster. So catalysts can't increase yield (the amount of product produced) — but they do decrease the time taken to reach equilibrium.

Exam Tip
Don't be thrown if a reaction you're given in an exam question about K_c has a catalyst. Catalysts don't affect K_c.

Exam Tip
Writing out the expression for K_c can really help solve questions like these. Remember — if the numbers on the top of the expression for K_c increase, then K_c will generally increase. If the numbers on the bottom of the expression for K_c increase, then K_c will generally decrease.

Practice Questions — Application

Q1 The following equilibrium is established under certain conditions:

$$2CHClF_{2(g)} \rightleftharpoons C_2F_{4(g)} + 2HCl_{(g)} \qquad \Delta H = +128 \text{ kJ mol}^{-1}$$

State and explain how you would expect the following to affect the value of K_c for this equilibrium:

a) Increasing the concentration of C_2F_4.

b) Increasing the temperature.

c) Adding a catalyst

Q2 The value of K_c for the following equilibrium increases if the temperature is decreased:

$$2SO_{2(g)} + O_{2(g)} \rightleftharpoons 2SO_{3(g)}$$

Is the forward reaction endothermic or exothermic? Explain your answer.

Practice Questions — Fact Recall

Q1 How will increasing the temperature affect K_c if:

a) the forward reaction is endothermic?

b) the forward reaction is exothermic?

Q2 Explain why changing the concentration of a reagent does not affect K_c.

Q3 How does adding a catalyst affect the equilibrium constant?

5. Redox Reactions

This'll probably ring a bell from GCSE, but don't go thinking you know it all already — there's plenty to learn about redox reactions.

What are redox reactions?

A loss of electrons is called **oxidation**. A gain in electrons is called **reduction**. Reduction and oxidation happen simultaneously — hence the term "redox" reaction. An **oxidising agent** accepts electrons and gets reduced. A **reducing agent** donates electrons and gets oxidised (see Figure 1).

Example

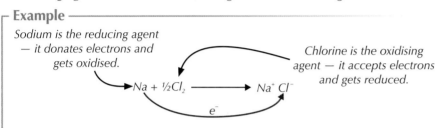

Sodium is the reducing agent — it donates electrons and gets oxidised.

Chlorine is the oxidising agent — it accepts electrons and gets reduced.

$Na + \frac{1}{2}Cl_2 \longrightarrow Na^+ Cl^-$

e^-

Figure 1: *A redox reaction between sodium and chlorine to form sodium chloride.*

Oxidation states

The **oxidation state** of an element tells you the total number of electrons it has donated or accepted. Oxidation states are also called oxidation numbers. There are lots of rules for working out oxidation states. Take a deep breath...

Uncombined elements have an oxidation state of 0. Elements just bonded to identical atoms also have an oxidation state of 0.

Examples

Uncombined elements — oxidation state = 0

Elements bonded to identical elements — oxidation state = 0

Figure 2: *Oxidation states of uncombined atoms and elements bonded to identical elements.*

The oxidation state of a simple monatomic ion is the same as its charge.

Examples

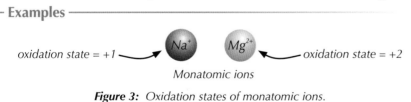

oxidation state = +1

oxidation state = +2

Monatomic ions

Figure 3: *Oxidation states of monatomic ions.*

In compounds or compound ions, each of the constituent atoms has an oxidation state of its own and the sum of the oxidation states equals the overall oxidation state (see Figure 4). This overall oxidation state is equal to the overall charge on the ion.

Within a compound ion, the most electronegative element has a negative oxidation state (equal to its ionic charge). Other elements have more positive oxidation states.

Tip: Now's your chance to learn the most famous memory aid thingy in the world...
<u>OIL RIG</u>
<u>O</u>xidation <u>I</u>s <u>L</u>oss
<u>R</u>eduction <u>I</u>s <u>G</u>ain
(of electrons)

Tip: Take a look back at page 84 for more about electronegativity.

Example

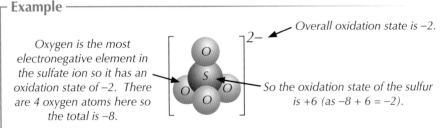

Oxygen is the most electronegative element in the sulfate ion so it has an oxidation state of –2. There are 4 oxygen atoms here so the total is –8.

Overall oxidation state is –2.

So the oxidation state of the sulfur is +6 (as –8 + 6 = –2).

***Figure 4:** Oxidation states of elements in the SO_4^{2-} ion.*

The sum of the oxidation states for a neutral compound is 0 (see Figure 5). If the compound is made up of more than one element, each element will have its own oxidation number.

Example

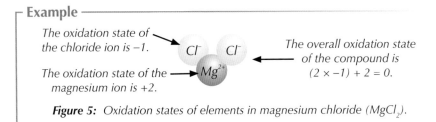

The oxidation state of the chloride ion is –1.

The oxidation state of the magnesium ion is +2.

The overall oxidation state of the compound is $(2 \times -1) + 2 = 0$.

***Figure 5:** Oxidation states of elements in magnesium chloride ($MgCl_2$).*

Combined oxygen is nearly always –2, except in peroxides, where it's –1 (see Figure 6). Combined hydrogen is +1, except in metal hydrides where it is –1 (see Figure 7) and H_2, where it's 0.

Examples

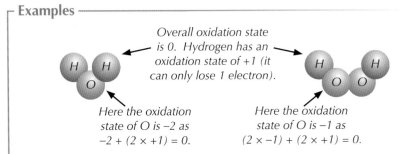

Overall oxidation state is 0. Hydrogen has an oxidation state of +1 (it can only lose 1 electron).

Here the oxidation state of O is –2 as $-2 + (2 \times +1) = 0$.

Here the oxidation state of O is –1 as $(2 \times -1) + (2 \times +1) = 0$.

***Figure 6:** Oxidation states of hydrogen and oxygen in water (H_2O) and hydrogen peroxide (H_2O_2).*

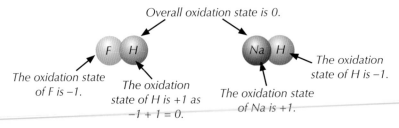

Overall oxidation state is 0.

The oxidation state of F is –1.

The oxidation state of H is +1 as $-1 + 1 = 0$.

The oxidation state of Na is +1.

The oxidation state of H is –1.

***Figure 7:** Oxidation states of hydrogen in hydrogen fluoride (HF) and sodium hydride (NaH).*

Finding oxidation states

You can work out oxidation states from formulas or systematic names.

Finding oxidation states from formulas

In your exam, you may get a question asking you to work out the oxidation state of one element in a compound. To do this you just have to follow all the rules on the previous two pages and you'll be fine.

Examples

Find the oxidation state of Zn in $Zn(OH)_2$.

- $Zn(OH)_2$ is neutral (it has no charge), so its overall oxidation state is 0.
- Oxygen's oxidation state is usually −2, and hydrogen's is usually +1.
- So the oxidation state of the $(OH)_2$ bit of the molecule is $2 \times (-2 + 1) = -2$.
- So the oxidation state of Zn in $Zn(OH)_2$ is $0 - (-2) = +2$.

Finding oxidation states from systematic names

If an element can have multiple oxidation states (or isn't in its 'normal' oxidation state) its oxidation state is sometimes shown using Roman numerals, e.g. (I) = +1, (II) = +2, (III) = +3 and so on. The Roman numerals are written after the name of the element they correspond to.

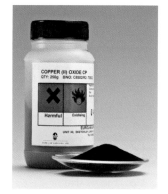

Figure 8: A bottle of copper(II) oxide. The Roman numerals show that the copper has an oxidation number of +2.

Examples

In iron(II) sulfate, iron has an oxidation state of +2. Formula = $FeSO_4$
In iron(III) sulfate, iron has an oxidation state of +3. Formula = $Fe_2(SO_4)_3$

This is particularly useful when looking at -ate ions. Ions with names ending in -ate (e.g. sulfate, nitrate, carbonate) contain oxygen, as well as another element. For example, sulfates contain sulfur and oxygen, nitrates contain nitrogen and oxygen... and so on. But sometimes the 'other' element in the ion can exist with different oxidation states, and so form different '-ate ions'. You can use the systematic name to work out the formula of the ion.

Examples

In sulfate(VI) ions the sulfur has oxidation state +6. This is the SO_4^{2-} ion.
In sulfate(IV) ions, the sulfur has oxidation state +4. This is the SO_3^{2-} ion.
In nitrate(III), nitrogen has an oxidation state of +3. This is the NO_2^- ion.

Tip: The oxidation state in sulfate ions applies to the sulfur, not the oxygen, because oxygen always has an oxidation state of −2 in -ate ions.

Practice Questions — Application

Q1 Give the oxidation states of the following ions.

    a) Na^+

    b) F^-

    c) Ca^{2+}

Q2 Give the overall oxidation states of the following ions.

    a) OH^-

    b) CO_3^{2-}

    c) NO_3^-

Tip: Several ions have widely used common names that are different from their correct systematic names. E.g. the sulfate(IV) ion (SO_3^{2-}) is often called the sulfite ion.

Exam Tip
It's really important to remember the basic rules for working out oxidation states, as well as the exceptions — it's the kind of thing that could easily trip you up in exam questions.

Q3 Work out the oxidation states of all the elements in the following compounds and compound ions.

a) HCl
b) SO_2
c) CO_3^{2-}
d) ClO_4^-
e) Cu_2O
f) HSO_4^-

Q4 Work out the oxidation states of carbon in the following.

a) CO
b) CO_2
c) CCl_4
d) C
e) $CaCO_3$

Q5 Work out the oxidation states of phosphorus in the following.

a) P_4
b) PH_3
c) PO_4^{3-}
d) P_2F_4
e) PBr_5
f) P_2H_4

Q6 Look at the reaction below.

$$Cu_{(s)} + H_2SO_{4(aq)} \rightarrow CuSO_{4(aq)} + H_{2(g)}$$

Give the oxidation states at the beginning and end of the reaction for the following elements:

a) Cu
b) S
c) H
d) O

Tip: The oxidation state of an atom doesn't always change when it reacts, so don't be alarmed if your answer is the same for the beginning and end of the reaction.

Practice Questions — Fact Recall

Q1 What is oxidation?
Q2 What is reduction?
Q3 Describe the role of an oxidising agent in a redox reaction.
Q4 Describe the role of a reducing agent in a redox reaction.
Q5 Give the oxidation state of an element bonded to an identical atom.
Q6 What is the sum of the oxidation states for a neutral compound?
Q7 What is the oxidation state of oxygen in a peroxide?
Q8 Give the oxidation state of hydrogen in a metal hydride.

6. Redox Equations

In redox reactions, oxidation and reduction go on simultaneously. You can write separate equations to show the two things happening, or you can package them up into one nice, neat redox equation.

Half-equations and redox equations

Ionic **half-equations** show oxidation or reduction (see Figure 1). The electrons are shown in a half-equation so that the charges balance.

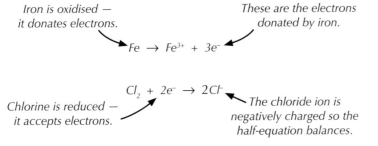

Iron is oxidised —
it donates electrons.

These are the electrons
donated by iron.

$$Fe \rightarrow Fe^{3+} + 3e^-$$

Chlorine is reduced —
it accepts electrons.

$$Cl_2 + 2e^- \rightarrow 2Cl^-$$

The chloride ion is
negatively charged so the
half-equation balances.

Figure 1: Half-equations showing the oxidation
of iron and the reduction of chlorine.

Learning Objectives:

- Be able to write half-equations identifying the oxidation and reduction processes in redox reactions.

- Be able to combine half-equations to give an overall redox equation.

Specification Reference 3.1.7

You can combine half-equations for oxidising and reducing agents to make full equations for redox reactions. Just make sure both half-equations have the same number of electrons in, stick them together and cancel out the electrons.

Tip: Remember — the charges as well as the number of atoms must be balanced in a balanced equation. See pages 44-45 for more on balancing equations.

Example

Iron reacts with chlorine to form iron(III) chloride ($FeCl_3$).

You can see the half-equations for the oxidation of iron and the reduction of chlorine in Figure 1. Oxidising iron produces three electrons — but to reduce chlorine you only need two.

If you multiply the iron equation by two and the chlorine equation by three then they'll both have six electrons in:

$$Fe \rightarrow Fe^{3+} + 3e^- \xrightarrow{\times 2} 2Fe \rightarrow 2Fe^{3+} + 6e^-$$

$$Cl_2 + 2e^- \rightarrow 2Cl^- \xrightarrow{\times 3} 3Cl_2 + 6e^- \rightarrow 6Cl^-$$

Now you can combine them. If you stick them together you get:

$$2Fe + 3Cl_2 + 6e^- \rightarrow 2Fe^{3+} + 6e^- + 6Cl^-$$

But the electrons on each side cancel out:

$$2Fe + 3Cl_2 + \cancel{6e^-} \rightarrow 2Fe^{3+} + \cancel{6e^-} + 3Cl^-$$

So the full redox equation for this reaction is:

$$2Fe + 3Cl_2 \rightarrow 2FeCl_3$$

Tip: In any <u>redox reaction</u> the number of electrons released by the oxidation reaction must be <u>the same</u> as the number used up by the reduction reaction.

You can also work out the half-equations for a given equation — just make sure the atoms and charges balance.

Example

Magnesium burns in oxygen to form magnesium oxide:

$$2Mg + O_2 \rightarrow 2MgO$$

Write half-equations for the oxidation and reduction reactions that are part of this process.

Tip: Take your time balancing half-equations and always double check them — it's easy to get confused and end up with electrons all over the place.

Tip: The only things you're allowed to <u>add</u> to half-equations to balance them are electrons, H^+ ions and water.

Exam Tip
If you're told that it's an acid solution, that's a really big hint that you need to have H^+ ions in the equation somewhere.

Tip: If you come across other reactions like this with complicated oxidising or reducing agents, just follow the same steps and you'll be fine.

Start with the half-equation of oxygen being reduced to O^{2-}: $O_2 \rightarrow 2O^{2-}$
Now balance the charges by adding some electrons in: $\mathbf{O_2 + 4e^- \rightarrow 2O^{2-}}$

Then do the same for the half-equation of magnesium being oxidised to Mg^{2+}: $2Mg \rightarrow 2Mg^{2+}$.
Balance it by adding in the electrons: $\mathbf{2Mg \rightarrow 2Mg^{2+} + 4e^-}$

You can check your answer by making sure all the electrons cancel out:
$$2Mg + O_2 + \cancel{4e^-} \rightarrow 2MgO + \cancel{4e^-}$$

Sometimes you might have to write half-equations for a more complicated reaction where the oxidising or reducing agent contains oxygen or hydrogen. If so, you might need to add in H_2O and H^+ ions to balance the equation.

── **Example** ──────────

Write a half-equation for the conversion of manganate(VIII) ions (MnO_4^-) in acid solution into Mn^{2+} ions.

Start by writing out the basic reaction:
$$MnO_4^- \rightarrow Mn^{2+}$$

Add some H_2O to the right side to balance the oxygen in MnO_4^-:
$$MnO_4^- \rightarrow Mn^{2+} + 4H_2O$$

Next, add H^+ ions to the left side to balance the hydrogen:
$$MnO_4^- + 8H^+ \rightarrow Mn^{2+} + 4H_2O$$

Finally, add electrons in to balance the charges:
$$MnO_4^- + 8H^+ + 5e^- \rightarrow Mn^{2+} + 4H_2O$$

Practice Questions — Application

Q1 Combine the 2 half-equations below to give the full redox equation for the displacement of silver by zinc:
$$Zn \rightarrow Zn^{2+} + 2e^- \qquad \text{and} \qquad Ag^+ + e^- \rightarrow Ag$$

Q2 Write the oxidation and reduction half-equations for this reaction:
$$Ca + Cl_2 \rightarrow CaCl_2$$

Q3 Balance this half-equation: $NO_3^- + H^+ + e^- \rightarrow N_2 + H_2O$

Q4 Write a half-equation for the reduction of $Cr_2O_7^{2-}$ ions in acid solution to Cr^{3+} ions.

Q5 H_2SO_4 can act as an oxidising agent. Give the half-equation for the reduction of H_2SO_4 to H_2S and water.

Practice Questions — Fact Recall

Q1 What does an ionic half-equation show?

Q2 Which of these (**A**, **B** or **C**) is a half-equation?
    A $2Mg + O_2 \rightarrow 2MgO$
    B $Fe \rightarrow Fe^{3+} + 3e^-$
    C $2Mg + O_2 + 4e^- \rightarrow 2MgO + 4e^-$

Section Summary

Make sure you know...

- That reversible reactions have both a forwards and a backwards reaction.
- That reversible reactions can reach dynamic equilibrium when the concentrations of reactants and products stay constant and the forwards and backwards reactions have the same reaction rate.
- That dynamic equilibrium can only be reached in a closed system which is at a constant temperature.
- That Le Chatelier's principle states that "if a reaction at equilibrium is subjected to a change in concentration, pressure or temperature, the equilibrium will move to help counteract the change."
- That a catalyst does not affect the position of equilibrium in a reversible reaction.
- That increasing the concentration of a reactant shifts the equilibrium to remove the extra reactant.
- That increasing the pressure shifts the equilibrium in favour of the reaction that produces the fewest moles of gas, in order to reduce the pressure.
- That increasing the temperature shifts the equilibrium in favour of the endothermic reaction, to remove the excess heat. (Low temperatures favour exothermic reactions.)
- Why, in industrial processes, there is a compromise in the temperatures and pressures used, in terms of rate, equilibrium and production costs.
- That K_c is the equilibrium constant.
- How to derive expressions for the equilibrium constant, K_c.
- How to calculate K_c and its units from the equilibrium concentrations and molar ratios for a reaction.
- How to use K_c to find unknown equilibrium concentrations for a reaction.
- That increasing the temperature of exothermic reactions will decrease K_c.
- That increasing the temperature of endothermic reactions will increase K_c.
- That changing the concentrations of reactants or adding a catalyst has no effect on the value of K_c.
- That loss of electrons is called oxidation and gain of electrons is called reduction.
- That oxidising agents are electron acceptors and reducing agents are electron donors.
- What redox reactions are.
- The rules for assigning the oxidation states of common atoms and ions.
- How to work out the oxidation state of an element in a compound or ion.
- How to write half-equations for the oxidation and reduction parts of a redox reaction.
- How to combine half-equations to make a full redox equation.

Exam-style Questions

1 Which of the following statements about redox is true?

    A   An oxidising agent loses electrons.

    B   Hydrogen always has an oxidation state of +1.

    C   Reduction is gain of electrons.

    D   The manganese in a manganate(VI) ion has an oxidation state of –6.

(1 mark)

2 Four different units are listed below.

    1 $mol^2\ dm^{-6}$ **2** $mol^2\ dm^{-1}$ **3** $mol^3\ dm^{-1}$ **4** $mol\ dm^{-3}$

    Which of the units listed above could be the units for the equilibrium constant, K_c?

    A   4 only

    B   1, 2 and 4 only

    C   1, 2, 3 and 4

    D   1 and 4 only

(1 mark)

3 Silver nitrate reacts with copper to form copper nitrate and silver.
The reaction is shown below.

$$2AgNO_3 + Cu \rightarrow Cu(NO_3)_2 + 2Ag$$

    Which of the following options shows the correct half-equations for this reaction?

    A $2Ag^+ + 2e^- \rightarrow 2Ag$ and $Cu \rightarrow Cu^{2+} + 2e^-$

    B $Ag^{6+} + 6e^- \rightarrow 2Ag$ and $Cu \rightarrow Cu^{6+} + 6e^-$

    C $Ag^+ \rightarrow Ag + e^-$ and $NO_3^- + e^- \rightarrow NO_3^{2-}$

    D $2Ag^+ + e^- \rightarrow 2Ag$ and $Cu \rightarrow Cu^{2+} + e^-$

(1 mark)

4 What is the oxidation state of N in N_2O_5?

    A   +2

    B   +5

    C   –2

    D   –10

(1 mark)

5 A chemical factory produces ethanol (C_2H_5OH) from ethene (C_2H_4) and steam (H_2O) using the following reversible reaction:

$$C_2H_{4(g)} + H_2O_{(g)} \rightleftharpoons C_2H_5OH_{(g)} \qquad \Delta H = -46 \text{ kJ mol}^{-1}$$

The reaction is carried out under the following conditions:

Pressure = 60 atm
Temperature = 300 °C
Catalyst = phosphoric acid

5.1 Without the phosphoric acid catalyst the rate of reaction is so slow that dynamic equilibrium takes a very long time to occur. Describe what it means for a reaction to be at dynamic equilibrium.

(2 marks)

5.2 The process conditions for the reaction were chosen with consideration of Le Chatelier's principle. State Le Chatelier's principle.

(1 mark)

5.3 Explain why the pressure chosen for the process is a compromise.

(3 marks)

5.4 A leak in one of the pipes reduces the amount of H_2O in the reaction mixture. Explain the effect this has on the maximum yield of ethanol.

(3 marks)

6 Ammonia (NH_3) is produced industrially using the Haber-Bosch process. It uses the following reaction between nitrogen and hydrogen:

$$N_{2(g)} + 3H_{2(g)} \rightleftharpoons 2NH_{3(g)} \qquad \Delta H = -92 \text{ kJ mol}^{-1}$$

The reaction is usually carried out under the following conditions:

Pressure = 200 atm
Temperature = 400 °C – 500 °C
Catalyst = iron

6.1 What effect does the iron catalyst have on the position of equilibrium?

(1 mark)

The reaction needs to be carried out at a reasonably high temperature in order to keep the reaction rate high. As well as affecting the rate, increasing the temperature also affects the position of equilibrium for the reaction.

6.2 State whether this reaction is endothermic or exothermic.

(1 mark)

6.3 Explain the effect of increasing the temperature on the position of equilibrium.

(3 marks)

6.4 Other than changing the temperature, suggest two ways to shift the position of equilibrium in order to get an increased yield of ammonia from the reaction.

(2 marks)

7 The following equilibrium establishes at temperature X:

$$CH_{4(g)} + 2H_2O_{(g)} \rightleftharpoons CO_{2(g)} + 4H_{2(g)} \qquad \Delta H = +165 \text{ kJ mol}^{-1}$$

At equilibrium the mixture was found to contain 0.0800 mol dm^{-3} CH_4, 0.320 mol dm^{-3} H_2O, 0.200 mol dm^{-3} CO_2 and 0.280 mol dm^{-3} H_2.

7.1 Write an expression for K_c for this equilibrium.

(1 mark)

7.2 Calculate the value of K_c at temperature X, and give its units.

(3 marks)

At a different temperature, Y, the value of K_c was found to be 0.0800 and the equilibrium concentrations were as follows:

Gas	CH_4	H_2O	CO_2	H_2
Concentration (mol dm^{-3})	?	0.560	0.420	0.480

7.3 Calculate the equilibrium concentration of CH_4 at this temperature.

(2 marks)

7.4 At another temperature, Z, the value of K_c was found to be 1.2×10^{-3}. Suggest whether temperature Z is higher or lower than temperature Y. Explain your answer.

(3 marks)

7.5 State how the value of K_c would change if a catalyst was added to the reaction. Explain your answer.

(2 marks)

8 Aluminium chloride, ($AlCl_3$), is a useful ionic substance, used as a catalyst in Friedel-Crafts reactions. It is synthesised in industry by reacting aluminium with chlorine (Cl_2) at high temperatures.

8.1 Write the ionic half-equations for this reaction.

(2 marks)

8.2 Identify the oxidising agent in the reaction between chlorine and aluminium.

(1 mark)

8.3 Aluminium is also used to form the ionic compound, $Al_2(SO_4)_3$. What is the oxidation state of sulfur in $Al_2(SO_4)_3$?

(1 mark)

1. The Periodic Table

You'll remember from GCSE that the periodic table isn't just arranged how it is by chance. There are well-thought-out reasons behind it, and you can find out lots of stuff from it, not least about the numbers of electron shells and electrons each element has. Read on...

Learning Objective:

- Know that an element is classified as s, p, d or f block according to its position in the periodic table, which is determined by its proton number.

Specification Reference 3.2.1.1

How is the periodic table arranged?

Dmitri Mendeleev developed the modern periodic table in the 1800s. Although there have been changes since then, the basic idea is still the same. The periodic table is arranged into periods (rows) and groups (columns), by atomic (proton) number.

Figure 1: Dmitri Mendeleev (1834-1907) was a Russian chemist who developed the periodic table.

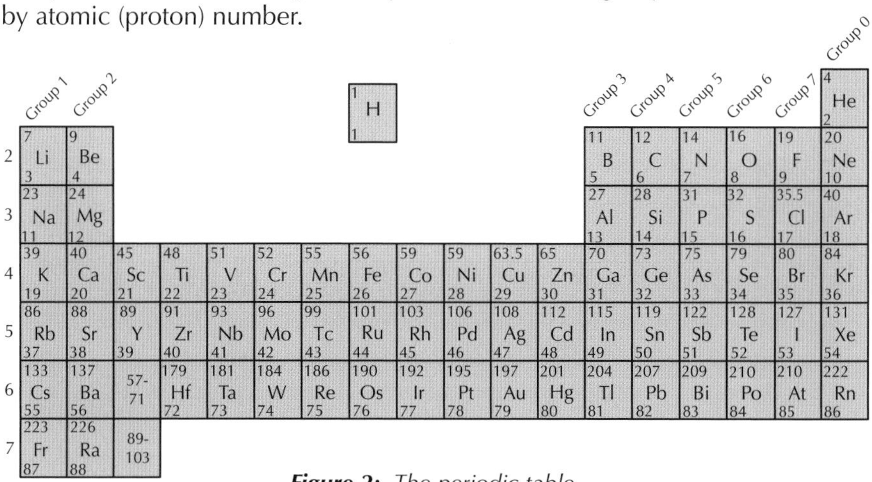

Figure 2: The periodic table.

The period and group of an element gives you information about the number of electrons and electron shells that an element has.

Elements and periods

All the elements within a period have the same number of electron shells (if you don't worry about s and p sub-shells).

Exam Tip
You'll be given a periodic table in your exam, so you'll always have a copy to refer to to answer exam questions. It's a good idea to be familiar with how it works before you go into the exam though.

> **Example**
>
> The elements in Period 2 have 2 electron shells.
>
>
>
> *Figure 3: Atoms of the first three elements in Period 2.*

Elements and groups

All the elements within a group have the same number of electrons in their outer shell — so they have similar properties (see Figure 5). The group number tells you the number of electrons in the outer shell.

Figure 5: *The Group 1 elements potassium, sodium and lithium all react strongly with water.*

Exam Tip
You won't get a periodic table split up like this in the exam, so you need to remember where the different blocks are.

Tip: If you can't remember what sub-shells are, don't know what the electron configuration of an element shows, or can't quite get your head around what all this $1s^2\ 2s^2\ 2p^6$ business is, then have a look back at pages 25-27 — it's all explained in lots of lovely detail there.

Examples

Group 1 elements have 1 electron in their outer shell (see Figure 4), Group 4 elements have 4 electrons and so on.

Figure 4: *Atoms of elements in Group 1.*

The exception to this rule is Group 0. All Group 0 elements have eight electrons in their outer shell (apart from helium, which has two), giving them full outer shells.

Electron configurations

The periodic table can be split into an s block, d block, p block and f block (see Figure 6). Doing this shows you which sub-shells all the electrons go into.

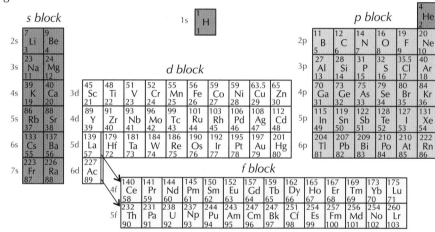

Figure 6: *The periodic table showing the s block, p block, d block and f block.*

When you've got the periodic table labelled with the shells and sub-shells, it's pretty easy to read off the electron structure of any element by starting at the top and working your way across and down until you get to your element.

Example

To work out the electron configuration of phosphorus (P), you can use the periodic table to see that it's in Group 5 and Period 3. Starting with Period 1, the electron configuration of a full shell is $1s^2$. For Period 2 it's $2s^2\ 2p^6$. However, phosphorus' outer shell is only partially filled — it's got 5 outer electrons in the configuration $3s^2\ 3p^3$.

So: Period 1 — $1s^2$

         Period 2 — $2s^2\ 2p^6$

         Period 3 — $3s^2\ 3p^3$

The full electron structure of phosphorus is: $1s^2\ 2s^2\ 2p^6\ 3s^2\ 3p^3$.

Practice Questions — Application

Q1 Give the number of electron shells that atoms of the following elements have:

a) Sulfur, S

b) Beryllium, Be

c) Bromine, Br

d) Neon, Ne

e) Rubidium, Rb

Q2 How many electrons are in the outer shell of atoms of the following elements?

a) Selenium, Se

b) Potassium, K

c) Fluorine, F

d) Aluminium, Al

e) Strontium, Sr

Q3 Work out the electron configurations of the following elements:

a) Sodium, Na

b) Calcium, Ca

c) Chlorine, Cl

d) Arsenic, As

e) Vanadium, V

f) Scandium, Sc

Tip: It doesn't really matter how you work out the electron configurations of elements, whether you use the rules on pages 25-27 or whether you read them off the periodic table like on these pages. The important thing is that you get them right — so find a method you're happy with and stick with it.

Tip: Don't forget that for d-block elements, the sub-shells aren't written in the order that they're filled.

Practice Questions — Fact Recall

Q1 How is the periodic table arranged?

Q2 Look at the diagram below.

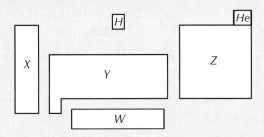

a) Which letter(s) (W, X, Y or Z) represent(s) the p block of the periodic table?

b) Which letter(s) (W, X, Y or Z) represent(s) the d block of the periodic table?

c) Which letter(s) (W X, Y or Z) represent(s) the s block of the periodic table?

Learning Objectives:

- Know the trends in atomic radius, first ionisation energy and melting point of the elements Na–Ar.
- Understand and explain the reasons for these trends in terms of the structure of and bonding in the elements.

Specification Reference 3.2.1.2

2. Periodicity

Periodicity is an important idea in chemistry. It's all to do with the trends in physical and chemical properties of elements across the periodic table — things like atomic radius, melting point, boiling point, and ionisation energy.

Atomic radius

Atomic radius decreases across a period (see Figure 1). As the number of protons increases, the positive charge of the nucleus increases. This means electrons are pulled closer to the nucleus, making the atomic radius smaller (see Figure 2). The extra electrons that the elements gain across a period are added to the outer energy level, so they don't really provide any extra shielding effect (shielding is mainly provided by the electrons in the inner shells).

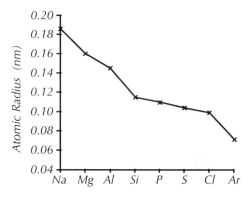

Figure 1: The atomic radii of the Period 3 elements.

Tip: Shielding is when the inner electrons effectively 'screen' the outer electrons from the pull of the nucleus. Look back at page 29 for more on shielding.

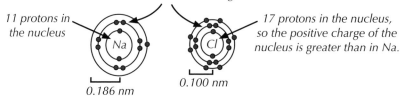

Na and Cl have the same number of electrons in the first and second shells, so the shielding is the same.

11 protons in the nucleus

17 protons in the nucleus, so the positive charge of the nucleus is greater than in Na.

0.186 nm

0.100 nm

Figure 2: The atomic radii of sodium and chlorine.

Melting points

If you look at how the melting points change across Period 3, the trend isn't immediately obvious. The melting points increase from sodium to silicon, but then generally decrease from silicon to argon (see Figure 4).

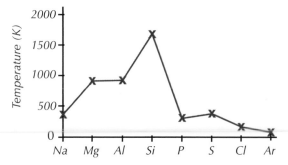

Figure 4: Melting points of Period 3 elements.

Figure 3: Chlorine (top) has lower melting and boiling points than silicon (bottom). So chlorine is a gas at r.t.p., whilst silicon is a solid.

Sodium, magnesium and aluminium

Sodium, magnesium and aluminium are metals. Their melting points increase across the period because the metal-metal bonds get stronger. The bonds get stronger because, as you go across the period, the metal ions have an increasing positive charge, an increasing number of delocalised electrons and a decreasing radius.

Figure 5: Magnesium (top) and aluminium (bottom).

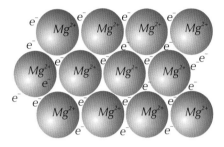
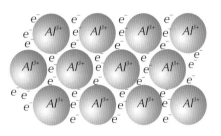

The magnesium ions have a larger radius and a charge of 2+, so there are two delocalised electrons for each ion...

...whereas the aluminium ions have a smaller radius and a charge of 3+, so there are three delocalised electrons for each ion.

Figure 6: The structures of magnesium and aluminium.

Silicon

Silicon is **macromolecular**, with a tetrahedral structure — strong covalent bonds link all its atoms together (see Figure 7). A lot of energy is needed to break these bonds, so silicon has a high melting point.

Tip: The structure of silicon should look familiar — it's similar to diamond (page 75). There's a good reason for this — carbon and silicon are both in Group 4, so have the same number of electrons in their outer shell.

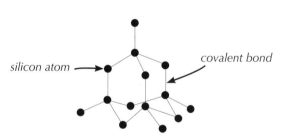

silicon atom

covalent bond

Figure 7: The structure of silicon.

Phosphorus, sulfur, chlorine and argon

Phosphorus (P_4), sulfur (S_8) and chlorine (Cl_2) are all molecular substances. Their melting points depend upon the strength of the van der Waals forces (see pages 86-87) between the molecules. Van der Waals forces are weak and easily overcome, so these elements have low melting points. More atoms in a molecule mean stronger van der Waals forces. Sulfur is the biggest molecule (S_8 — see Figure 9), so it's got a higher melting point than phosphorus or chlorine. Argon has a very low melting point because it exists as individual atoms (it's monatomic), resulting in very weak van der Waals forces.

Figure 8: Sulfur (yellow powder) and phosphorus (stored under water) are solids at room temperature, whereas chlorine is a gas (see Figure 4).

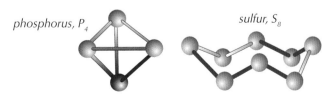

phosphorus, P_4

sulfur, S_8

Figure 9: The structures of phosphorus and sulfur.

Exam Tip
There's no need to
memorise the graphs
on these pages, but you
do need to know their
shapes and be able to
explain them.

First ionisation energy

The first ionisation energy is the energy needed to remove 1 electron from
each atom in 1 mole of gaseous atoms to form 1 mole of gaseous 1+ ions.
There's a general increase in the first ionisation energy as you go across
Period 3 (see Figure 10). This is because of the increasing attraction between
the outer shell electrons and the nucleus, due to the number of protons
increasing.

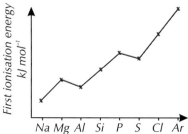

Figure 10: The first ionisation energies of the Period 3 elements.

Tip: There are a few
blips in the trend for
first ionisation energy —
check back to page 31
for more details.

Practice Questions — Application

Q1 a) Explain why the atomic radius of aluminium is larger
than the atomic radius of sulfur.

 b) Name a Period 3 element with a larger atomic radius
than aluminium.

Q2 Explain why the first ionisation energy of sulfur is higher
than the first ionisation energy of aluminium.

Q3 The melting point of silicon is 1414 °C and the melting point
of phosphorus is 44 °C.

 a) Explain why the melting point of phosphorus is lower
than the melting point of silicon.

 b) Name a Period 3 element with a lower melting point
than phosphorus.

Exam Tip
If you're asked about a
specific trend, it might
help you to roughly
sketch out the shape of
the relevant graph. That
way you'll easily be able
to see how the values for
the elements compare to
each other.

Practice Questions — Fact Recall

Q1 Describe the trend in atomic radius across Period 3
of the periodic table.

Q2 Describe the trend in melting points across Period 3
of the periodic table.

Q3 Describe the general trend in first ionisation energy
across Period 3 of the periodic table.

Section Summary

Make sure you know...

- That elements are classed as s block, p block, d block or f block depending on their position in the
  periodic table, which is determined by their proton number.
- The trends in atomic radius, melting point and first ionisation energy across Period 3.
- The reasons for the trends in atomic radius, melting point and first ionisation energy across Period 3.

Exam-style Questions

1   Which of the following determines the order that elements are arranged in in the periodic table?

    A   atomic mass

    B   proton number

    C   number of electrons in outer shell

    D   atomic radius

(1 mark)

2   Which of the following statements about sulfur is **not** correct?

    A   Its atomic radius is smaller than that of magnesium.

    B   Its electron configuration is $1s^2 2s^2 2p^6 3s^2 3p^4$.

    C   It's in the s block of the periodic table.

    D   Its first ionisation energy is higher than that of sodium.

(1 mark)

3   Which of the following elements has the lowest first ionisation energy?

    A   Cl

    B   Si

    C   P

    D   Ar

(1 mark)

4   Sodium, magnesium and aluminium are all metals in Period 3 of the periodic table.

   4.1   Explain why the atomic radius of aluminium is smaller than that of sodium.

(2 marks)

   4.2   Explain why the melting point of magnesium is greater than that of sodium.

(3 marks)

   4.3   Argon is another element in Period 3. Explain why the melting point of argon is lower than the melting points of sodium, magnesium and aluminium.

(2 marks)

Learning Objective:

- Know the trends in atomic radius, first ionisation energy and melting point of the elements Mg – Ba.

- Be able to explain the trends in atomic radius and first ionisation energy.

- Be able to explain the melting point of the elements in terms of their structure and bonding.

Specification Reference 3.2.2

1. Group 2 — The Alkaline Earth Metals

The alkaline earth metals are in the s block of the periodic table. You have to know the trends in their properties as you go down Group 2 — in atomic radius, ionisation energy and melting points.

Atomic radius

As you go down a group in the periodic table, the atomic radius gets larger. This is because extra electron shells are added as you go down the group (see Figures 2 and 3).

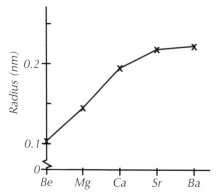

Figure 2: Atomic radii of the first five elements in Group 2.

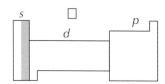

Figure 1: The s, p and d blocks of the periodic table (see page 28 for more on this). Group 2 is highlighted in grey.

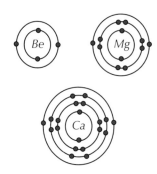

Figure 3: Electron configurations of the first three elements in Group 2.

First ionisation energy

Group 2 elements all have two electrons in their outer shell (s^2). They can lose their two outer electrons to form 2+ ions. Their ions then have every atom's dream electronic structure — that of a noble gas (see Figure 4).

Element	Atom	Ion
Be	$1s^2\,2s^2$	$1s^2$
Mg	$1s^2\,2s^2\,2p^6\,3s^2$	$1s^2\,2s^2\,2p^6$
Ca	$1s^2\,2s^2\,2p^6\,3s^2\,3p^6\,4s^2$	$1s^2\,2s^2\,2p^6\,3s^2\,3p^6$

Figure 4: Electronic structures of Group 2 atoms and ions.

Tip: See pages 29-32 for more on ionisation energies.

Group 2 element	1st ionisation energy / kJ mol⁻¹
Be	900
Mg	738
Ca	590
Sr	550
Ba	503

Figure 5: First ionisation energies of Group 2 elements.

First ionisation energy decreases down the group (see Figure 5). This is because each element down Group 2 has an extra electron shell compared to the one above. The extra inner shells shield the outer electrons from the attraction of the nucleus. Also, the extra shell means that the outer electrons are further away from the nucleus, which greatly reduces the nucleus's attraction. Both of these factors make it easier to remove outer electrons, resulting in a lower first ionisation energy. The positive charge of the nucleus does increase as you go down a group (due to the extra protons), but this effect is overridden by the effect of the extra shells.

Example

The first ionisation energy of calcium is lower than the first ionisation energy of magnesium (see Figure 6).

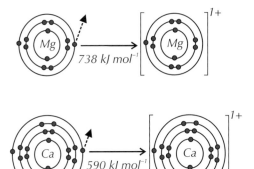

Figure 6: *First ionisation energy of magnesium and calcium.*

A magnesium atom has three electron shells, whereas a calcium atom has four electron shells. This means that the outer shell electrons are further from the nucleus in calcium than in magnesium. Also, a calcium atom has 18 electrons in inner shells, compared to only 10 in a magnesium atom. This means that shielding is greater in calcium atoms. So, less energy is needed to remove an electron from calcium than from magnesium.

Figure 7: *Magnesium ribbon reacting with hydrochloric acid.*

Reactivity

When Group 2 elements react they lose electrons, forming positive ions. The easier it is to lose electrons (i.e. the lower the first ionisation energy), the more reactive the element, so reactivity increases down the group (see Figures 7 and 8).

Melting point

Melting points generally decrease down the group (see Figure 9). The Group 2 elements have typical metallic structures, with positive ions in a crystal structure surrounded by delocalised electrons from the outer electron shells. Going down the group the metal ions get bigger. But the number of delocalised electrons per atom doesn't change (it's always 2) and neither does the charge on the ion (it's always +2). The larger the ionic radius, the further away the delocalised electrons are from the positive nuclei. So it takes less energy to break the bonds, which means the melting points generally decrease as you go down the group. However, there's a big 'blip' at magnesium, because the crystal structure (the arrangement of the metallic ions) changes.

Figure 8: *Calcium reacting with hydrochloric acid.*

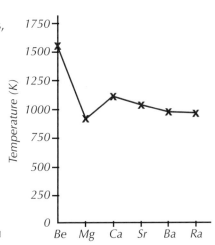

Figure 9: *Melting points of Group 2 elements.*

Exam Tip
There's no need to memorise the exact values on this graph, or the one on page 152, but you do need to know their shapes and be able to explain them.

Example

The atomic radii increase from calcium to strontium to barium,
but there are still only two delocalised electrons per ion (see Figure 10).
So melting point decreases.

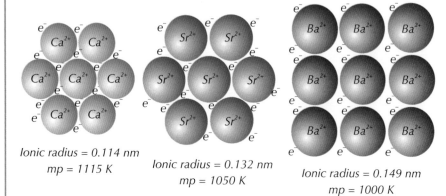

Ionic radius = 0.114 nm
mp = 1115 K

Ionic radius = 0.132 nm
mp = 1050 K

Ionic radius = 0.149 nm
mp = 1000 K

Figure 10: *Comparison of calcium, strontium and barium crystals.*
('mp' means melting point.)

Practice Questions — Application

Q1 The higher the ionisation energy of a group 2 element, the less readily
it will react. Calcium and strontium react with dilute hydrochloric
acid. Which reaction you would expect to occur more rapidly?

Q2 The table below shows the atomic radii of three elements from
Group 2.

Element	Atomic radius/nm
X	0.105
Y	0.200
Z	0.145

a) Which element you would expect to have the highest
first ionisation energy?

b) Which element you would expect to
have the lowest melting point?

Practice Questions — Fact Recall

Q1 Describe the trend in atomic radius in Group 2.

Q2 Explain the trend in first ionisation energy in Group 2.

Q3 a) Why is the melting point of barium higher than
the melting point of radium?

b) At which element in Period 2 is there an anomaly
in the trend of melting points? Explain why.

2. Group 2 Compounds

Here's a bit more about the alkaline earth metals and their compounds to follow on from what you learned in the previous topic. It's a Group 2 bonus...

Learning Objectives:

- Know the reactions of the elements Mg – Ba with water.
- Know the relative solubilities of the hydroxides of the elements Mg – Ba in water and that $Mg(OH)_2$ is sparingly soluble.
- Know the relative solubilities of the sulfates of the elements Mg – Ba in water and that $BaSO_4$ is insoluble.
- Be able to explain why $BaCl_2$ solution is used to test for sulfate ions and why it is acidified.
- Know the use of $BaSO_4$ in medicine.
- Know the use of magnesium in the extraction of titanium from $TiCl_4$.
- Know the use of CaO or $CaCO_3$ to remove SO_2 from flue gases.
- Know the use of $Mg(OH)_2$ in medicine and of $Ca(OH)_2$ in agriculture.
- Be able to carry out a simple test-tube reaction to identify SO_4^{2-} ions (Required Practical 4).

Specification Reference 3.2.2

Reactions with water

When Group 2 elements react, they are oxidised from a state of 0 to +2, forming M^{2+} ions.

$$M \rightarrow M^{2+} + 2e^-$$

Oxidation state: $0 \rightarrow +2$

Example

$$\mathbf{Ca \rightarrow Ca^{2+} + 2e^-}$$

Oxidation state: $0 \rightarrow +2$

The Group 2 metals react with water to give a metal hydroxide and hydrogen.

$$M_{(s)} + 2H_2O_{(l)} \rightarrow M(OH)_{2\,(aq)} + H_{2\,(g)}$$

Oxidation state: $0 \rightarrow +2$

Example

Calcium reacts with water to form calcium hydroxide and hydrogen.

$$\mathbf{Ca_{(s)} + 2H_2O_{(l)} \rightarrow Ca(OH)_{2\,(aq)} + H_{2\,(g)}}$$

Oxidation state: $0 \rightarrow +2$

The elements react more readily down the group because the ionisation energies decrease (see Figure 1).

Group 2 element	1st ionisation energy / kJ mol^{-1}	Rate of reactivity with water
Be	900	doesn't react
Mg	738	VERY slow
Ca	590	steady
Sr	550	fairly quick
Ba	503	rapid

Figure 1: *Comparison of first ionisation energies and reactivity with water for Group 2 elements.*

Solubility of compounds

The solubility of Group 2 compounds depends on the anion (negative ion) in the compound. Generally, compounds of Group 2 elements that contain singly charged negative ions (e.g. OH^-) increase in solubility down the group, whereas compounds that contain doubly charged negative ions (e.g. SO_4^{2-}) decrease in solubility down the group (see Figures 2 and 3).

Group 2 element	hydroxide (OH^-)	sulfate (SO_4^{2-})
magnesium	least soluble ↓	most soluble ↑
calcium		
strontium		
barium	most soluble	least soluble

Figure 2: *Solubility of Group 2 anions.*

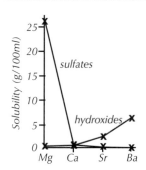

Figure 3: *Solubilities of Group 2 compounds at room temperature and pressure.*

Compounds like magnesium hydroxide, $Mg(OH)_2$, which have very low solubilities are said to be sparingly soluble.

Most sulfates are soluble in water, but barium sulfate ($BaSO_4$) is insoluble. The test for sulfate ions makes use of this property. If you add dilute hydrochloric acid and then barium chloride ($BaCl_2$) solution to a solution containing sulfate ions, then a white precipitate of barium sulfate is formed (see Figure 4).

REQUIRED PRACTICAL **4**

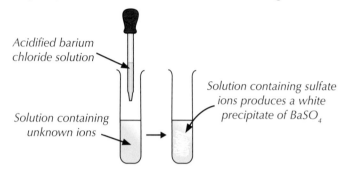

Acidified barium chloride solution

Solution containing unknown ions

Solution containing sulfate ions produces a white precipitate of $BaSO_4$

Figure 4: *The test for identifying sulfate ions in solution.*

Barium meals

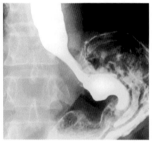

Figure 5: *X-ray showing the oesophagus and stomach following a barium meal.*

The fact that barium sulfate is insoluble is also useful in medicine. X-rays are great for finding broken bones, but they pass straight through soft tissue — so soft tissues, like the digestive system, don't show up on conventional X-ray pictures. Barium sulfate is opaque to X-rays — they won't pass through it. It's used in 'barium meals' to help diagnose problems with the oesophagus, stomach or intestines. A patient swallows the barium meal, which is a suspension of barium sulfate. The barium sulfate coats the tissues, making them show up on the X-rays, showing the structure of the organs (see Figure 5). You couldn't use other barium compounds for this because solutions containing barium ions are poisonous — barium sulfate is insoluble so forms a suspension rather than a solution.

Extraction of titanium

Magnesium is used as part of the process of extracting titanium from its ore. The main titanium ore, titanium(IV) oxide (TiO_2), is first converted to titanium(IV) chloride ($TiCl_4$) by heating it with carbon in a stream of chlorine gas. The titanium chloride is then purified by fractional distillation, before being reduced by magnesium in a furnace at almost 1000 °C.

$$TiCl_{4(g)} + 2Mg_{(l)} \rightarrow Ti_{(s)} + 2MgCl_{2(l)}$$

Removal of sulfur dioxide from flue gases

Burning fossil fuels to produce electricity also produces sulfur dioxide, which pollutes the atmosphere. The acidic sulfur dioxide can be removed from flue gases by reacting with an alkali — this process is called wet scrubbing. Calcium oxide (lime, CaO) and calcium carbonate (limestone, $CaCO_3$) can both be used for this. A slurry is made by mixing the calcium oxide or calcium carbonate with water. It's then sprayed onto the flue gases. The sulfur dioxide reacts with the alkaline slurry and produces a solid waste product, calcium sulfite.

$$CaO_{(s)} + 2H_2O_{(l)} + SO_{2(g)} \rightarrow CaSO_{3(s)} + 2H_2O_{(l)}$$

$$CaCO_{3(s)} + 2H_2O_{(l)} + SO_{2(g)} \rightarrow CaSO_{3(s)} + 2H_2O_{(l)} + CO_{2(g)}$$

Other uses of Group 2 compounds

Group 2 elements are known as the alkaline earth metals, and many of their common compounds are used for neutralising acids. Calcium hydroxide (slaked lime, $Ca(OH)_2$) is used in agriculture to neutralise acidic soils. Magnesium hydroxide ($Mg(OH)_2$) is used in some indigestion tablets as an antacid (a substance that neutralises excess stomach acid).

Figure 6: *A tractor spreading slaked lime on a field with acidic soil.*

Practice Questions — Application

Q1 One Group 2 element has a first ionisation energy of 550 kJ mol^{-1} and another has a first ionisation energy of 738 kJ mol^{-1}. Explain which element you would expect to react most rapidly with water.

Q2 Acidified barium chloride is added to a solution. No precipitate forms. What does this result show?

Tip: Remember that for Group 2 elements, a lower ionisation energy means they are more reactive. See page 153 for more.

Practice Questions — Fact Recall

Q1 Describe the trend in reactivity of Group 2 elements with water.

Q2 How does the solubility of hydroxides change down Group 2?

Q3 How does the solubility of sulfates change down Group 2?

Q4 Why is barium chloride solution acidified before it is used to test for sulfate ions?

Q5 What is a 'barium meal'?

Q6 Describe how magnesium is used in the extraction of titanium from TiO_2.

Q7 Suggest two Group 2 compounds are used to remove sulfur dioxide from flue gases?

Q8 Give the chemical name of a Group 2 hydroxide that is used in agriculture and say what it's used for.

- Be able to explain the trend in electronegativity of the halogens.

- Be able to explain the trend in the boiling point of the halogens in terms of their structure and bonding.

- Know the trend in oxidising ability of the halogens down the group, including displacement reactions of halide ions in aqueous solution.

- Know the reaction of chlorine with cold, dilute, aqueous NaOH and uses of the solution formed.

- Know the reaction of chlorine with water to form chloride ions and chlorate(I) ions.

- Know the reaction of chlorine with water to form chloride ions and oxygen.

- Understand the use of chlorine in water treatment.

- Appreciate that the benefits to health of water treatment by chlorine outweigh its toxic effects.

- Appreciate that society assesses the advantages and disadvantages when deciding if chemicals should be added to water supplies.

Specification Reference
3.2.3.1, 3.2.3.2

Tip: 'Halogen' is used to describe the atom (X) or molecule (X_2), but 'halide' describes the negative ion (X^-).

3. Group 7 — The Halogens

The halogens are highly-reactive non-metals found in Group 7 of the periodic table. You need to know about their properties and trends — oh, and just how much we rely on chlorine to give us nice clean water.

Properties of halogens

The table below gives some of the main properties of the first four halogens, at room temperature.

Halogen	Formula	Colour	Physical state	Electron configuration of atom
fluorine	F_2	pale yellow	gas	$1s^2\,2s^2\,2p^5$
chlorine	Cl_2	green	gas	$1s^2\,2s^2\,2p^6\,3s^2\,3p^5$
bromine	Br_2	red-brown	liquid	$1s^2\,2s^2\,2p^6\,3s^2\,3p^6\,3d^{10}\,4s^2\,4p^5$
iodine	I_2	grey	solid	$1s^2\,2s^2\,2p^6\,3s^2\,3p^6\,3d^{10}\,4s^2\,4p^6\,4d^{10}\,5s^2\,5p^5$

Boiling points

The boiling points of the halogens increase down the group. This is due to the increasing strength of the van der Waals forces as the size and relative mass of the molecules increases. This trend is shown in the changes of physical state from fluorine (gas) to iodine (solid).

Electronegativity

Electronegativity decreases down the group. Electronegativity, remember, is the tendency of an atom to attract a bonding pair of electrons. The halogens are all highly electronegative elements. But larger atoms attract electrons less than smaller ones. This is because their outer electrons are further from the nucleus and are more shielded, because they have more inner electrons.

Displacement reactions

When the halogens react, they gain an electron. This means they are oxidising agents. They get less reactive down the group, because the atoms become larger and the outer shell gets further from the nucleus. So the halogens become less oxidising down the group.

The relative oxidising strengths of the halogens can be seen in their displacement reactions with the halide ions. A halogen will displace a halide from solution if the halide is below it in the periodic table (e.g. chlorine can displace bromide ions, but chloride ions are displaced by fluorine). You can see this if you add a few drops of an aqueous halogen to a solution containing halide ions. A colour change is seen if there's a reaction:

	Potassium chloride solution $KCl_{(aq)}$ (colourless)	Potassium bromide solution $KBr_{(aq)}$ (colourless)	Potassium iodide solution $KI_{(aq)}$ (colourless)
Chlorine water $Cl_{2(aq)}$ (colourless)	no reaction	orange solution (Br_2) formed	brown solution (I_2) formed
Bromine water $Br_{2(aq)}$ (orange)	no reaction	no reaction	brown solution (I_2) formed
Iodine solution $I_{2(aq)}$ (brown)	no reaction	no reaction	no reaction

These displacement reactions can be used to help identify which halogen (or halide) is present in a solution. Halide ions are colourless in solution, but when the halogen is displaced it shows a distinctive colour, e.g. when bromide ions come out of solution to form bromine the colour changes from colourless to orange.

Tip: You don't need to know about fluorine here (because it will oxidise the water instead of forming a solution).

Examples

Chlorine

If you add chlorine to a solution containing bromide ions (e.g. potassium bromide), it will displace the bromide ions — and there will be a colour change.

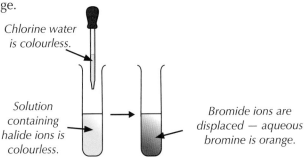

Chlorine water is colourless.

Solution containing halide ions is colourless.

Bromide ions are displaced — aqueous bromine is orange.

Figure 1: Green chlorine gas.

The equation for this reaction is: $Cl_{2(aq)} + 2KBr_{(aq)} \rightarrow 2KCl_{(aq)} + Br_{2(aq)}$

It can also be written as an ionic equation: $Cl_{2(aq)} + 2Br^-_{(aq)} \rightarrow 2Cl^-_{(aq)} + Br_{2(aq)}$

Tip: Carry out any safety precautions before doing these tests.

If you add chlorine to a solution of potassium iodide ions, it will displace the iodide ions. This time the colour change will be from colourless to brown.

The equation for this reaction is: $Cl_{2(aq)} + 2KI_{(aq)} \rightarrow 2KCl_{(aq)} + I_{2(aq)}$

The ionic equation is: $Cl_{2(aq)} + 2I^-_{(aq)} \rightarrow 2Cl^-_{(aq)} + I_{2(aq)}$

Bromine

If you add bromine to a solution of potassium iodide, it will displace the iodide ions — and there will be a colour change.

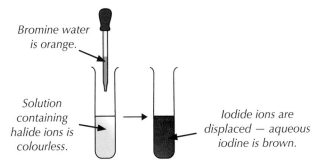

Bromine water is orange.

Solution containing halide ions is colourless.

Iodide ions are displaced — aqueous iodine is brown.

Figure 2: Red-brown bromine liquid.

The equation for this reaction is: $Br_{2(aq)} + 2KI_{(aq)} \rightarrow 2KBr_{(aq)} + I_{2(aq)}$

The ionic equation is: $Br_{2(aq)} + 2I^-_{(aq)} \rightarrow 2Br^-_{(aq)} + I_{2(aq)}$

There's no reaction if you add bromine water to a solution of chloride ions. Chlorine is above bromine in Group 7 so is more reactive and can't be displaced by it.

Iodine

Iodine is below chlorine and bromine in Group 7, so it's less reactive than them and won't displace either halide.

Figure 3: Grey iodine crystals.

Tip: Take a look at pages 135-137 for more on oxidation states and how to work them out.

Making bleach

If you mix chlorine gas with cold, dilute sodium hydroxide solution at room temperature, you get sodium chlorate(I) solution($NaClO_{(aq)}$). This just happens to be common household bleach (which kills bacteria). In this reaction chlorine is both oxidised and reduced. This is called **disproportionation**.

$$2NaOH_{(aq)} + Cl_{2\,(g)} \rightarrow NaClO_{(aq)} + NaCl_{(aq)} + H_2O_{(l)}$$

Chlorine is bonded to chlorine so its oxidation state is 0.

ClO^- is the chlorate(I) ion. Chlorine's oxidation state is +1 in this ion.

Here, chlorine's oxidation state is −1.

The sodium chlorate(I) solution (bleach) has loads of uses — it's used in water treatment, to bleach paper and textiles... and it's good for cleaning toilets, too. Handy...

Chlorine and water

When you mix chlorine with water, it undergoes disproportionation. You end up with a mixture of chloride ions and chlorate(I) ions.

$$Cl_{2(g)} + H_2O_{(l)} \rightleftharpoons 2H^+_{(aq)} + Cl^-_{(aq)} + ClO^-_{(aq)}$$

Chlorine's oxidation state is 0.

Chloride's oxidation state is −1.

In chlorate(I) ions chlorine's oxidation state is +1.

In sunlight, chlorine can also decompose water to form chloride ions and oxygen.

$$Cl_{2(g)} + H_2O_{(l)} \rightleftharpoons 2H^+_{(aq)} + 2Cl^-_{(aq)} + \tfrac{1}{2}O_{2(g)}$$

Figure 4: *Chlorine is used to treat tap water in the UK.*

Water treatment

Chlorate(I) ions kill bacteria. So, adding chlorine (or a compound containing chlorate(I) ions) to water can make it safe to drink or swim in. On the downside, chlorine is toxic.

In the UK our drinking water is treated to make it safe. Chlorine is an important part of water treatment. It kills disease-causing microorganisms (and some chlorine persists in the water and prevents reinfection further down the supply). It also prevents the growth of algae, eliminating bad tastes and smells, and removes discolouration caused by organic compounds.

However, there are risks from using chlorine to treat water. Chlorine gas is very harmful if it's breathed in — it irritates the respiratory system. Liquid chlorine on the skin or eyes causes severe chemical burns. Accidents involving chlorine could be really serious, even fatal.

Water contains a variety of organic compounds, e.g. from the decomposition of plants. Chlorine reacts with these compounds to form chlorinated hydrocarbons, e.g. chloromethane (CH_3Cl), and many of these chlorinated hydrocarbons are carcinogenic (cancer-causing). However, this increased cancer risk is small compared to the risks from untreated water — a cholera epidemic, say, could kill thousands of people. We have to weigh up these risks and benefits when making decisions about whether we should add chemicals to drinking water supplies.

Practice Questions — Application

Q1 Three test tubes, A, B and C, contain different halide solutions. Several drops of chlorine water are added to each test tube and the following colour changes are observed.

    Tube A — colourless to orange

    Tube B — no colour change

    Tube C — colourless to brown

  a) Suggest the halide ion present in each solution.

  b) The test is repeated, but iodine solution ($I_{2(aq)}$) is added to the test tubes instead of chlorine water. Explain how the results would be different.

Q2 Chlorine gas is mixed with sodium hydroxide solution. The solution is tested with litmus paper, which turns white. Explain why.

Practice Questions — Fact Recall

Q1 Describe the trend in the boiling points of the halogens.

Q2 Name the most electronegative halogen.

Q3 Which halide ions are displaced by reaction with chlorine water?

Q4 a) Describe the colour change when bromine water is added to potassium iodide solution.

  b) Give the full equation for this reaction.

  c) Give the ionic equation for this reaction.

Q5 a) Name three products of the reaction between sodium hydroxide and chlorine.

  b) Give the balanced equation for this reaction.

Q6 Describe the reactions that occur when chlorine is mixed with water, in and out of sunlight.

Q7 a) Explain why chlorine is used to treat water.

  b) Describe the disadvantages of using chlorine to treat water.

Figure 5: *The distinctive 'swimming pool smell' is due to the chlorine in the water.*

Learning Objectives:

- Know the trend in reducing ability of the halide ions, including the reactions of solid sodium halides with concentrated sulfuric acid.

- Understand the use of acidified silver nitrate solution to identify and distinguish between halide ions.

- Be able to explain why silver nitrate solution is used to identify halide ions, why the silver nitrate solution is acidified and why ammonia solution is added.

- Know the trend in solubility of the silver halides in ammonia.

- Be able to carry out simple test-tube reactions to identify halide ions (Required Practical 4).

Specification Reference 3.2.3.1

Tip: You already know one good example of halide ions as reducing agents — it's the good old halogen / halide displacement reaction (see pages 158-159). For example:
$Cl_2 + 2Br^- \rightarrow 2Cl^- + Br_2$

Tip: In chemistry, X is often used to stand for 'any halogen'.

Exam Tip
In an exam, you might have to construct half-equations, given the main reactants and products.

4. Halide Ions

Halides ions are the 1− ions formed by the halogens. The different halide ions react slightly differently, so telling them apart is easier than you might think.

Halide ion formation and oxidation

You'll remember from your chemistry basics that the elements in Group 7 form ions by gaining one electron. They end up as 1− ions with a full outer shell. For example:

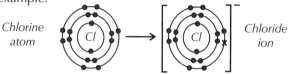

Chlorine atom → *Chloride ion*

Figure 1: *Chlorine gains an electron to form an ion.*

When a halide ion takes part in a **redox reaction**, it reduces something and is oxidised itself. To reduce something, the halide ion needs to lose an electron from its outer shell — think OIL RIG (see page 135).

The reducing power of halides

How easy it is for a halide ion to lose an electron depends on the attraction between the nucleus and the outer electrons. As you go down the group, the attraction gets weaker because the ions get bigger, so the electrons are further away from the positive nucleus. There are extra inner electron shells too, so there's a greater shielding effect (see Figure 2). Therefore, the reducing power of the halides increases down the group.

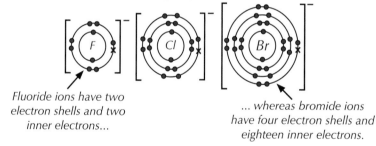

Fluoride ions have two electron shells and two inner electrons...

... whereas bromide ions have four electron shells and eighteen inner electrons.

Figure 2: *Electron shells and shielding in ions of the first three halogens.*

Reactions with sulfuric acid

All the halides react with concentrated sulfuric acid to give a hydrogen halide as a product to start with.

$$NaX + H_2SO_4 \rightarrow NaHSO_4 + HX$$

A sodium halide with the halogen labelled as 'X'.   *A hydrogen halide is produced.*

But what happens next depends on which halide you've got. Some halide ions are strong enough reducing agents that they can reduce the sulfuric acid to water and sulfur dioxide. Overall the reaction is:

$$2HX + H_2SO_4 \rightarrow X_2 + SO_2 + 2H_2O$$

The half equations are:

$$2X^-_{(g)} \rightarrow X_{2(s)} + 2e^- \quad \longleftarrow \text{ The halide is oxidised.}$$

$$H_2SO_4 + 2H^+ + 2e^- \rightarrow SO_2 + 2H_2O \longleftarrow \text{ The sulfuric acid is reduced.}$$

Iodide is such a strong reducing agent that it can reduce the SO_2 to H_2S or S.

Reaction of NaF or NaCl with H_2SO_4

$$NaF_{(s)} + H_2SO_{4(l)} \rightarrow NaHSO_{4(s)} + HF_{(g)}$$

$$NaCl_{(s)} + H_2SO_{4(l)} \rightarrow NaHSO_{4(s)} + HCl_{(g)}$$

Hydrogen fluoride (HF) or hydrogen chloride gas (HCl) is formed. You'll see misty fumes as the gas comes into contact with moisture in the air. But HF and HCl aren't strong enough reducing agents to reduce the sulfuric acid, so the reaction stops there. It's not a redox reaction — the oxidation states of the halide and sulfur stay the same (–1 and +6).

Reaction of NaBr with H_2SO_4

$$NaBr_{(s)} + H_2SO_{4(l)} \rightarrow NaHSO_{4(s)} + HBr_{(g)}$$

The first reaction gives misty fumes of hydrogen bromide gas (HBr). But the HBr is a stronger reducing agent than HCl and reacts with the H_2SO_4 in a redox reaction.

$$2HBr_{(aq)} + H_2SO_{4(l)} \rightarrow Br_{2(g)} + SO_{2(g)} + 2H_2O_{(l)}$$

Oxidation state of S: +6 $\rightarrow$ +4   *reduction*
Oxidation state of Br: –1 $\rightarrow$ 0   *oxidation*

The reaction produces choking fumes of SO_2 and orange fumes of Br_2.

Reaction of NaI with H_2SO_4

$$NaI_{(s)} + H_2SO_{4(l)} \rightarrow NaHSO_{4(s)} + HI_{(g)}$$

Same initial reaction giving HI gas. The HI then reduces H_2SO_4, as above.

$$2HI_{(g)} + H_2SO_{4(l)} \rightarrow I_{2(s)} + SO_{2(g)} + 2H_2O_{(l)}$$

Oxidation state of S: +6 $\rightarrow$ +4   *reduction*
Oxidation state of I: –1 $\rightarrow$ 0   *oxidation*

But HI (being the strongest reducing agent) keeps going and reduces the SO_2 to H_2S.

$$6HI_{(g)} + SO_{2(g)} \rightarrow H_2S_{(g)} + 3I_{2(s)} + 2H_2O_{(l)}$$

Oxidation state of S: +4 $\rightarrow$ –2   *reduction*
Oxidation state of I: –1 $\rightarrow$ 0   *oxidation*

The reaction produces fumes of H_2S and solid iodine.

Tip: This may seem like an awful lot of information at first glance. Don't worry though — just learn the principles and keep referring back to the equations on the previous page. It will really help if you can learn the general pattern of the reactions — you can always work out oxidation states if you need to (see pages 135-137).

Tip: Make sure that you have taken all necessary safety precautions if you're carrying out these experiments.

Tip: When iodine is produced, you'll see a grey solid and/or a purple gas.

Tip: This is no one's favourite reaction — H_2S is toxic and smells of bad eggs.

Testing for halides

The halogens are pretty distinctive to look at (see pages 158 and 159). Unfortunately, the same can't be said of halide solutions, which are colourless. You can test for halides using the **silver nitrate test** — it's easy. First you add dilute nitric acid to remove ions which might interfere with the test. Then you just add a few drops of silver nitrate solution ($AgNO_{3(aq)}$). A precipitate is formed (of the silver halide).

REQUIRED PRACTICAL **4**

$$Ag^+_{(aq)} + X^-_{(aq)} \rightarrow AgX_{(s)} \quad ...where\ X\ is\ Cl,\ Br\ or\ I$$

Tip: You can't use hydrochloric acid instead of nitric acid because the silver nitrate would just react with the chloride ions from the HCl — and that would mess up your results completely.

The colour of the precipitate identifies the halide (see Figures 3 and 4).

Figure 3: Results of silver nitrate tests for solutions containing (L-R) fluoride, chloride, bromide and iodide ions.

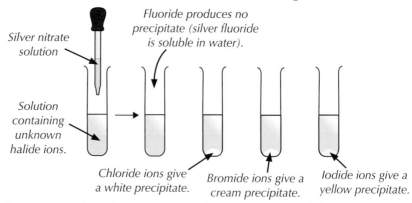

Silver nitrate solution

Fluoride produces no precipitate (silver fluoride is soluble in water).

Solution containing unknown halide ions.

Chloride ions give a white precipitate.

Bromide ions give a cream precipitate.

Iodide ions give a yellow precipitate.

Figure 4: The silver nitrate test for identifying an unknown halide ion in solution.

Then to be extra sure, you can test your results by adding ammonia solution. Each silver halide has a different solubility in ammonia (see Figures 5 and 6).

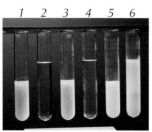

Figure 6: The chloride, bromide and iodide test tubes from Figure 3 (1, 3 and 5), and the same tubes with dilute $NH_{3(aq)}$ (2) or concentrated $NH_{3(aq)}$ (4 and 5) added.

Halide	Result	
Chloride Cl^-	precipitate dissolves in dilute $NH_{3(aq)}$	most soluble
Bromide Br^-	precipitate dissolves in conc. $NH_{3(aq)}$	
Iodide I^-	precipitate insoluble in conc. $NH_{3(aq)}$	least soluble

Figure 5: Solubility of silver halide precipitates in ammonia.

Practice Questions — Application

Q1 Sunil carries out a reaction between solid sodium bromide and concentrated sulfuric acid. Then he does the same reaction, replacing sodium bromide with sodium chloride. He predicts that the only gaseous product of both reactions will be a hydrogen halide. Explain whether Sunil's prediction is correct.

Q2 An experiment is carried out to identify the halide ions in three different solutions. The results are shown in the table below.

Sample	Colour of precipitate following addition of silver nitrate	Effect of adding concentrated NH_3 solution to the precipitate
A	yellow	no change
B	no precipitate	no change
C	cream	precipitate dissolves

Identify the halide ion in each sample.

Practice Questions — Fact Recall

Q1 Explain why the reducing power of the halide ions increases as you go down the group.

Q2 Write the equation(s) for the reactions that occur when sulfuric acid is mixed with:
    a) sodium fluoride,   b) sodium iodide.

Q3 a) Describe a test that could be used to distinguish between solutions of fluoride ions and chloride ions.

    b) Describe how you could use ammonia solution to confirm the result for the chloride ion.

5. Tests for Ions

REQUIRED PRACTICAL 4

You have to be able to carry out tests to find out which ions are in a solution. Luckily you've met some of these before...

Identifying positive ions

Positive ions (or cations) include things like the ions of Group 2 metals and ammonium ions. Here are the chemical tests that you need to know to help you identify them:

Flame tests

Compounds of some Group 2 metals burn with characteristic colours. You can identify them using a flame test. First you dip a nichrome wire loop in concentrated hydrochloric acid (to clean it) and then dip it into the unknown compound. Hold the loop in the clear blue part of a Bunsen burner flame and observe the colour change in the flame (see Figures 1 and 2).

Metal ion	Flame colour
Calcium, Ca^{2+}	brick red
Strontium, Sr^{2+}	red
Barium, Ba^{2+}	pale green

Figure 1: *The colours of the flames when different metal ions are burnt.*

Test for ammonium ions

Ammonia gas (NH_3) is alkaline — so you can test for it using a damp piece of red litmus paper. The litmus paper needs to be damp so the ammonia gas can dissolve. If there's ammonia present, the paper will turn blue. If you add hydroxide ions to (OH^-) a solution containing ammonium ions (NH_4^+), they will react to produce ammonia gas and water, like this:

$$NH_{4\ (aq)}^+ + OH_{\ (aq)}^- \rightarrow NH_{3(g)} + H_2O_{(l)}$$

You can use this reaction to test whether a substance contains ammonium ions (NH_4^+). Add some dilute sodium hydroxide solution to your mystery substance in a test tube and gently heat the mixture. If there's ammonia given off, ammonium ions must be present (see Figure 3).

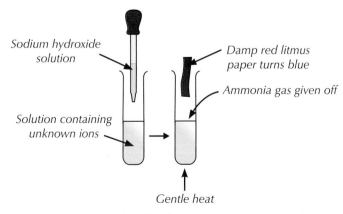

Sodium hydroxide solution

Damp red litmus paper turns blue

Ammonia gas given off

Solution containing unknown ions

Gentle heat

Figure 3: *The test for identifying ammonium ions in solution.*

Learning Objective:

- Be able to carry out simple test-tube reactions to identify cations (Group 2, NH_4^+) and anions (Group 7 (halide ions), OH^-, CO_3^{2-}, SO_4^{2-}) (Required Practical 4).

Specification Reference 3.2.3.2

Figure 2: *Results of flame tests for solutions containing calcium (top), strontium (bottom left) and barium (bottom right).*

Tip: Before carrying out any of the tests on these pages, you need to think about any safety issues that might be involved.

Identifying negative ions

Negative ions (or anions) include things like sulfate ions, hydroxide ions, halides and carbonate ions. Here are the chemical tests for these ions:

Test for sulfate ions

You've already met this test back on page 156, but here's a quick reminder in case you've forgotten. To identify a sulfate ion (SO_4^{2-}), you add a little dilute hydrochloric acid, followed by barium chloride solution, $BaCl_{2(aq)}$. If a white precipitate of barium sulfate forms, it means the original compound contained a sulfate.

$$Ba^{2+}_{(aq)} + SO_4^{2-}_{(aq)} \rightarrow BaSO_{4(s)}$$

Tip: The hydrochloric acid is added to get rid of any traces of carbonate and sulfite ions before you do the test. (These would also produce a precipitate, so they'd confuse the results.) You can't use sulfuric acid, because you don't want to add any sulfate ions.

Test for hydroxide ions

Hydroxide ions make solutions alkaline. So if you think a solution might contain hydroxide ions, you can use a pH indicator to test it. For example, if you dip a piece of red litmus paper into the solution and hydroxide ions are present, the paper will turn blue.

Test for halide ions

To test for chloride (Cl^-), bromide (Br^-) or iodide (I^-) ions, you just add dilute nitric acid (HNO_3), followed by silver nitrate solution ($AgNO_3$).

- A chloride gives a white precipitate of silver chloride.
- A bromide gives a cream precipitate of silver bromide.
- An iodide gives a yellow precipitate of silver iodide.

Tip: There's more info about this test on pages 163-164.

These precipitates can look a bit similar, so you might have to add ammonia solution to tell them apart. Silver chloride will dissolve in dilute ammonia solution. Silver bromide will only dissolve in concentrated ammonia solution. Silver iodide won't dissolve in either.

Test for carbonate ions

You can test to see if a solution contains carbonate ions (CO_3^{2-}) by adding an acid. When you add dilute hydrochloric acid, a solution containing carbonate ions will fizz. This is because the carbonate ions react with the hydrogen ions in the acid to give carbon dioxide:

$$CO_3^{2-}_{(aq)} + 2H^+_{(aq)} \rightarrow CO_{2(g)} + H_2O_{(l)}$$

You can test for carbon dioxide using limewater. Carbon dioxide turns limewater cloudy — just bubble the gas through a test tube of limewater and watch what happens. If the limewater goes cloudy, your solution contains carbonate ions (see Figures 4 and 5).

Figure 4: Testing for carbonate ions with hydrochloric acid and limewater.

Tip: You need to put a bung on the flask so that the carbon dioxide gas doesn't escape.

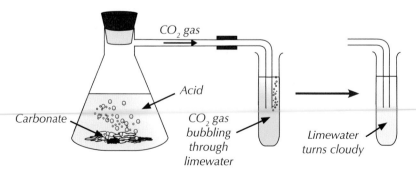

Figure 5: The test for identifying carbonate ions in solution.

Q1 Write the colour that a blue Bunsen burner flame would turn in the presence of:
a) barium ions,   b) calcium ions,   c) strontium ions.

Q2 What solution do you need to add to an unknown substance when testing for ammonium ions?

Q3 Describe a test that could be used to determine the presence of sulfate ions in a solution.

Q4 Describe a test you could do to confirm whether hydroxide ions are present in a solution.

Q5 Which two solutions do you need to add when testing for halide ions in an unknown solution?

Q6 Describe how you can use limewater to test for carbonate ions.

Exam Tip
Make sure you've absolutely definitely memorised which test is for which kind of ion — you don't want to mix them up if they come up in your exams.

Section Summary

Make sure you know...

- Why atomic radius increases as you go down Group 2.
- Why first ionisation energy decreases as you go down Group 2.
- How and why melting point changes as you go down Group 2.
- The reactions of Group 2 metals with water.
- How the solubilities of Group 2 hydroxides and sulfates vary.
- What the barium chloride test for sulfate ions is and what a positive test result is.
- How barium sulfate and magnesium hydroxide are used in medicine.
- How magnesium is used in the extraction of titanium from its ore.
- How calcium oxide and calcium carbonate are used to remove sulfur dioxide from flue gases.
- How calcium hydroxide is used in agriculture.
- Why the electronegativity of the halogens decreases as you go down the group.
- Why the boiling points of the halogens increase as you go down the group.
- That the oxidising ability of the halogens decreases down the group, and how this can be demonstrated by halide ion displacement reactions.
- The products of the reaction between chlorine and cold dilute sodium hydroxide and the uses of the solution formed.
- How chlorine reacts with water.
- Why chlorine is used in water treatment, even though it can be toxic.
- Why the reducing ability of the halide ions increases down the group.
- The reactions between concentrated sulfuric acid and the sodium halides.
- What the silver nitrate test for halides is and why the silver nitrate solution is acidified.
- The results of the silver nitrate test for solutions containing fluoride, chloride, bromide and iodide ions.
- The trend in the solubility of silver halides in ammonia and why this is useful.
- How to carry out tests to identify certain positive and negative ions in an unknown solution.

Exam-style Questions

1   To an unknown solution, X, a few drops of hydrochloric acid are added, followed by some barium chloride solution. A white precipitate forms. When a drop of solution X on a nichrome wire loop was placed in a blue Bunsen burner flame, the flame turned brick red. What is the identity of solution X?

    A   Strontium sulfate

    B   Calcium chloride

    C   Barium hydroxide

    D   Calcium sulfate

(1 mark)

2   Which of the following describes a simple test for ammonium ions?

    A   Add dilute nitric acid to the solution, followed by silver nitrate solution.

    B   Add some dilute sodium hydroxide solution, gently heat the mixture and test any gas that's released with damp red litmus paper.

    C   Add dilute hydrochloric acid and test any gas formed with limewater.

    D   Dip a piece of red litmus paper into the solution.

(1 mark)

3   After the 2010 earthquake in Haiti, there was an outbreak of cholera which has since killed thousands of people. The spread of the disease has partly been blamed on a lack of water treatment. It is possible to use chlorine to treat water.

  3.1   Write an equation for the reaction between chlorine and water.

(1 mark)

  3.2   Why does adding chlorine to water help to stop the spread of diseases such as cholera?

(2 marks)

  3.3   Explain why some people do not support the addition of chlorine to water supplies.

(1 mark)

  3.4   Using chlorine has some disadvantages.
         Suggest why we continue to treat water with it.

(1 mark)

4 Chlorine and bromine are halogens.

4.1 The halogens have different boiling points.

State whether chlorine has a higher or lower boiling point than bromine and explain why.

(3 marks)

4.2 Chlorine water and bromine water are added to solutions **A** and **B**.
Each solution contains a potassium halide. The table below shows the results.

	Solution A	Solution B
Chlorine water	solution turns orange	solution turns brown
Bromine water	no change	solution turns brown

Identify solution **A** and explain your reasoning.

(3 marks)

4.3 Identify solution **B** and write an ionic equation for its reaction with chlorine water.

(2 marks)

4.4 Chlorine can undergo the following reaction:

$$2NaOH_{(aq)} + Cl_{2\,(g)} \rightarrow NaClO_{(aq)} + NaCl_{(aq)} + H_2O_{(l)}$$

Give one use for the NaClO formed.

(1 mark)

4.5 Silver nitrate can be used to identify halide ions in solution.

Explain why dilute nitric acid (HNO_3) is added to the solution.

(1 mark)

4.6 State what you would observe if bromide ions are present in the solution being tested in **4.5**.

(1 mark)

4.7 Explain how ammonia solution can be used to confirm the result that you gave in **4.6**.

(1 mark)

5 Samples of three of the alkaline earth metals, strontium, calcium and magnesium, are placed in jars labelled **D**, **E** and **F**. Some information about the three metals is shown in the table below.

	D	E	F
Atomic radius	0.16 nm	0.19 nm	0.215 nm
1st ionisation energy	738 kJ mol^{-1}	590 kJ mol^{-1}	550 kJ mol^{-1}
Melting point	923 K	1115 K	1050 K

5.1 Which of the elements in the table is magnesium?

(1 mark)

5.2 Explain why the first ionisation energy of **D** is higher than the first ionisation energy of **E**.

(3 marks)

5.3 Using the information in the table, explain how the reactivity of metal **F** with water will compare with **E**.

(2 marks)

5.4 Barium has a lower melting point than metal **F**. Explain why this is the case.

(3 marks)

5.5 State the solubility of magnesium hydroxide in water.

(1 mark)

5.6 Describe how magnesium hydroxide is used in medicine.

(2 marks)

5.7 Magnesium can be used to reduce titanium(IV) chloride to pure titanium.

Write the equation for this reaction.

(1 mark)

Organic Chemistry

Organic chemistry is just the study of carbon-containing compounds.

The basics

There are a few basic concepts in organic chemistry that you'll need to get your head around before you study organic chemistry in more detail.

Formulas

Picturing molecules can be pretty difficult when you can't see them all around you. We can use the elemental symbols from the periodic table to help visualise molecules. For example, a molecule of methane is one carbon atom attached to four hydrogen atoms. You could show this by giving its molecular formula, CH_4, or you could draw its displayed formula (see Figure 1). There's more on formulas on pages 172-174.

$$H-\overset{\displaystyle H}{\underset{\displaystyle H}{C}}-H$$

Figure 1: *The displayed formula of methane.*

This isn't exactly what methane looks like, but visualising it like this lets us compare it to other molecules and means we can predict its properties and how it might react with other molecules. Molecular models can also be used to represent molecules (see Figure 2).

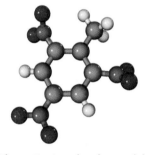

Figure 2: *A molecular model of a TNT molecule. Each grey sphere represents a carbon atom, each white sphere represents a hydrogen atom, the purple ones represent nitrogen atoms and the red ones oxygen atoms.*

Functional groups

The functional group of a molecule is the group of atoms that's responsible for its characteristic reactions — it's where all the interesting stuff happens. They're usually pretty easy to spot because they're the bits which aren't just hydrogen and carbon atoms (e.g. bromine atoms, oxygen atoms, etc.). You'll come across a few different functional groups in this course — here are a few examples...

$-OH$	$-\overset{\displaystyle O}{\underset{}{C}}-OH$	$\diagdown C=C \diagup$
Functional groups of... alcohols	carboxylic acids	alkenes

For now, remember that carbon atoms have four bonds, hydrogen atoms have one bond and oxygen atoms have two bonds joining them to other atoms.

Nomenclature

There are thousands, if not millions, of known organic compounds and it would be pretty silly if we didn't have an easy way to describe them. That's where **nomenclature** comes in. Don't be put off by the long name — all it means is naming molecules using specific rules. These rules (known as the IUPAC system for naming organic compounds) allow scientists to discuss organic chemistry safe in the knowledge that they're all talking about the same molecules. It means that some molecules end up with really long and complicated looking names (e.g. 1,2-dichloro-3-methylbutane), but once you know the rules it's easy to work out what they all mean. There's more about nomenclature on pages 180-183.

So there you go. That's pretty much all you need to know to get started. You'd better get on — next up is formulas...

■ Know that organic
compounds can be
represented by:
an empirical formula,
a molecular formula,
a general formula,
a structural formula,
a displayed formula
and a skeletal formula.

■ Know the
characteristics of a
homologous series.

■ Be able to draw
structural, displayed
and skeletal formulas
for given organic
compounds.

**Specification
Reference 3.3.1.1**

1. Formulas

*Organic compounds can be represented in lots of different ways, using
different types of formulas. You need to be familiar with what these formulas
show and how to switch between them.*

Types of formula

Molecular formulas

A molecular formula gives the actual number of atoms of each element
in a molecule.

┌─ **Examples** ────────────────

Ethane has the molecular formula C_2H_6 — each molecule is made up
of 2 carbon atoms and 6 hydrogen atoms.

Pentene has the molecular formula C_5H_{10} — each molecule is made up
of 5 carbon atoms and 10 hydrogen atoms.

1,4-dibromobutane has the molecular formula $C_4H_8Br_2$ — each molecule
is made up of 4 carbon atoms, 8 hydrogen atoms and 2 bromine atoms.

1,3-dichloropropane has the molecular formula $C_3H_6Cl_2$ — each molecule
is made up of 3 carbon atoms, 6 hydrogen atoms and 2 chlorine atoms.

Structural formulas

A structural formula shows the atoms carbon by carbon,
with the attached hydrogens and functional groups.

┌─ **Examples** ────────────────

Ethane has the structural formula CH_3CH_3.

Pent-1-ene has the structural formula $CH_3CH_2CH_2CHCH_2$.

1,4-dibromobutane has the structural formula $BrCH_2CH_2CH_2CH_2Br$.

1,3-dichloropropane has the structural formula $ClCH_2CH_2CH_2Cl$.

Displayed formulas

A displayed formula shows how all the atoms are arranged, and all the bonds
between them.

┌─ **Examples** ────────────────

Displayed formula of ethane:

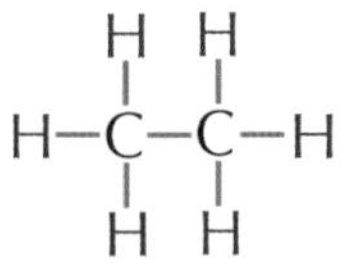

Displayed formula of pent-1-ene:

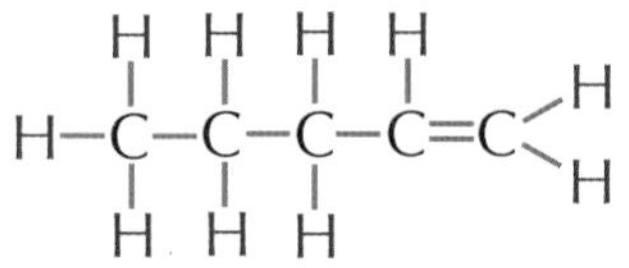

Displayed formula of
1,4-dibromobutane:

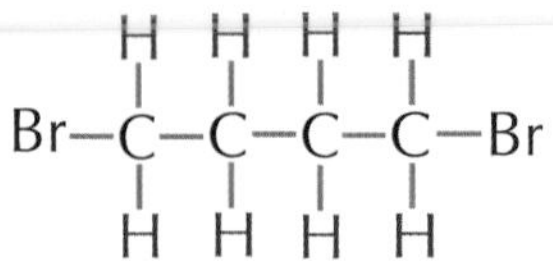

Displayed formula of
1,3-dichloropropane:

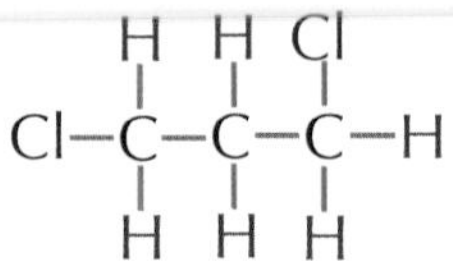

Tip: Don't worry for
now if you're not sure
exactly how all the
molecules in this topic
get their names. The
system for naming
organic molecules is
covered in full over the
next couple of topics.

Empirical formulas

An empirical formula gives the simplest whole number ratio of atoms of each element in a compound. To find the empirical formula you have to find the highest number that will go into each number in the molecular formula, then divide by it. For example, if the molecular formula is $C_6H_8Cl_4$, the highest number that goes into each number is 2, so divide the molecular formula by 2 and get the empirical formula $C_3H_4Cl_2$. Sometimes the empirical formula will be the same as the molecular formula. This happens when you can't divide all the numbers in the molecular formula by the same number and still end up with whole numbers of atoms.

Tip: If there's just one atom of something in a formula then you know you've got an empirical formula — it can't be simplified any further.

$C_4H_{10}O$ is an empirical formula — there's only 1 oxygen atom.

Examples

Name	Molecular Formula	Divide by...	Empirical Formula
Ethane	C_2H_6	2	CH_3
Pentene	C_5H_{10}	5	CH_2
1,4-dichlorobutane	$C_4H_8Cl_2$	2	C_2H_4Cl
1,3-dichloropropane	$C_3H_6Cl_2$		$C_3H_6Cl_2$
1,2,3-trichloroheptane	$C_7H_{13}Cl_3$		$C_7H_{13}Cl_3$

In the last two examples in the table, the molecular formula is the same as the empirical formula — there's nothing you can divide all the numbers in the molecular formula by and still get whole numbers.

Exam Tip
You need to make sure you know which type of formula is which. You won't get any marks for writing a structural formula when the examiner wants a molecular one.

General formulas and homologous series

A **general formula** is an algebraic formula that can describe any member of a family of compounds. Organic chemistry is more about groups of similar chemicals than individual compounds. These groups are called **homologous series**. A homologous series is a family of compounds that have the same functional group and general formula. Consecutive members of a homologous series differ by $-CH_2-$.

Tip: There's a lot more about the homologous series you need to know on pages 176-179.

Example

The simplest homologous series is the alkanes. They're straight-chain molecules that contain only carbon and hydrogen atoms. There are always twice as many hydrogen atoms as carbon atoms, plus two more. So the general formula for alkanes is C_nH_{2n+2}. You can use this formula to work out how many hydrogen atoms there are in any alkane if you know the number of carbon atoms. For example...

If an alkane has 1 carbon atom, n = 1.
This means the alkane will have $(2 \times 1) + 2 = 4$ hydrogen atoms.
So the molecular formula of this alkane would be CH_4 (you don't need to write the 1 in C_1).

If an alkane has 5 carbon atoms, n = 5.
This means the alkane will have $(2 \times 5) + 2 = 12$ hydrogen atoms.
So its molecular formula would be C_5H_{12}.

If an alkane has 15 carbon atoms, n = 15.
This means the alkane will have $(2 \times 15) + 2 = 32$ hydrogen atoms.
So its molecular formula is $C_{15}H_{32}$.

Figure 1: *Molecular model of methane — the alkane where n = 1.*

Skeletal formulas

A skeletal formula shows the bonds of the carbon skeleton only, with any functional groups. The hydrogen and carbon atoms that are part of the main carbon chain aren't shown. This is handy for drawing large complicated structures, like cyclic hydrocarbons. The carbon atoms are found at each junction between bonds and at the end of bonds (unless there's already a functional group there). Each carbon atom has enough hydrogen atoms attached to make the total number of bonds from the carbon up to four.

Exam Tip
Skeletal formulas are notoriously tricky to draw, so make sure that you get plenty of practice using them. Then if they come up in an exam question it'll be a breeze (relatively speaking).

Tip: You have to draw skeletal formulas as zig-zag lines, otherwise you can't tell where one bond ends and the next begins.

Tip: Drawing a displayed formula from a structural formula is dead easy — just draw it out exactly as it's written:

CH$_3$CH$_2$CH$_2$CH$_2$Cl

H H H H
| | | |
H–C–C–C–C–Cl
| | | |
H H H H

--- Examples ---

Displayed and skeletal formulas of 1,5-difluoropentane:

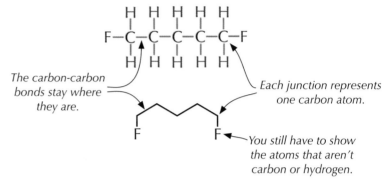

The carbon-carbon bonds stay where they are.

Each junction represents one carbon atom.

You still have to show the atoms that aren't carbon or hydrogen.

Skeletal formula of hex-1-ene:

A double line represents a carbon-carbon double bond.

This carbon atom only has one carbon-carbon bond drawn on the molecule. This means that it has three hydrogen atoms attached to make the number of bonds up to four.

This carbon atom has two carbon-carbon bonds, so it must have two hydrogen atoms attached to make the number of bonds up to four.

Practice Questions — Application

Q1 2-bromopropane has the structural formula CH$_3$CHBrCH$_3$. Draw the displayed formula of 2-bromopropane.

Q2 Here is the structure of 3-ethyl-2-methylpentane.

H H H CH$_3$H
|5 |4 |3 |2 |1
H–C–C–C–C–C–H
| | | | |
H H CH$_2$H H
|
CH$_3$

Write down the molecular formula for 3-ethyl-2-methylpentane.

Q3 Write down the empirical formula of the following compounds:
   a) C$_2$H$_4$
   b) C$_8$H$_{14}$Br$_2$
   c) C$_9$H$_{17}$Cl$_3$

Q4 Alkenes have the general formula C_nH_{2n}.

   a) Butene is an alkene with 4 carbon atoms.
      Write the molecular formula of butene.

   b) Heptene is an alkene with 7 carbon atoms.
      How many hydrogen atoms does it contain?

Q5 1,2-dibromopropane has the structural formula $CH_3CHBrCH_2Br$.

   a) Write down the molecular formula of 1,2-dibromopropane.

   b) Draw the displayed formula of 1,2-dibromopropane.

   c) Write the empirical formula of 1,2-dibromopropane.

Q6 Here is the displayed formula of pent-1-ene.

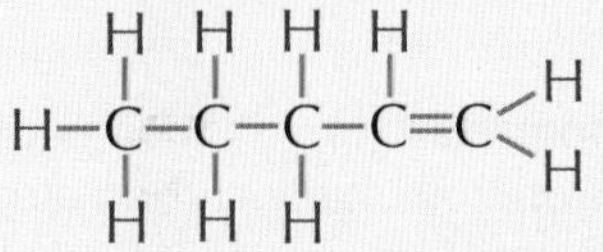

   a) Write down the molecular formula of pent-1-ene.

   b) Write down the structural formula of pent-1-ene.

   c) What is the empirical formula of pent-1-ene?

Q7 Draw skeletal formulas of the molecules below:

   a)

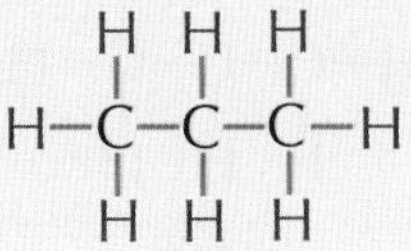

   b)

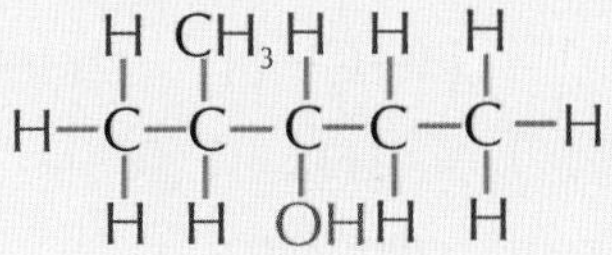

   c)

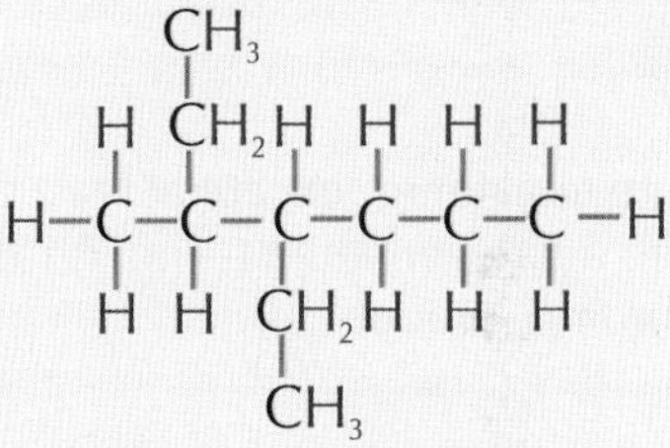

   d)

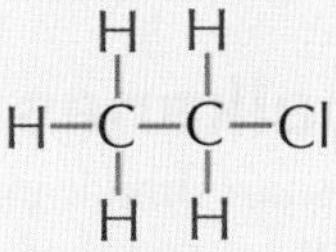

Q8 Give structural formulas for the molecules below:

   a)

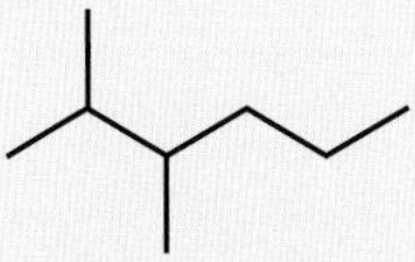

   b)

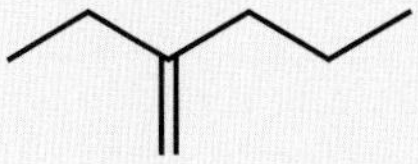

   c)

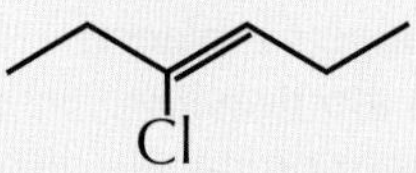

   d)

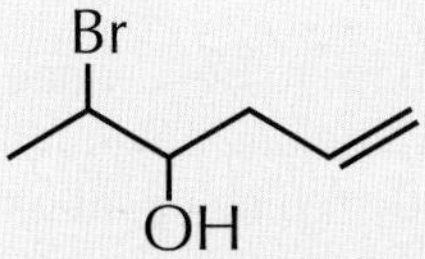

Exam Tip
It's really important to double-check your answers for questions like these. It's so easy to miscount — and you need to make sure you collect all the easy marks in the exam.

Tip: It doesn't matter whether you show atoms bonding above, below or to the side of a carbon atom — they all mean the same thing. It's which atoms they're bonding to that's the important thing.

Tip: When you're writing the molecular formulas of branched molecules, you put the branch in brackets. E.g. methylpropane...

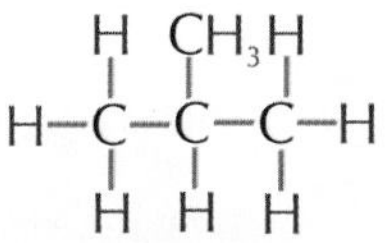

... has the structural formula:

$CH_3CH(CH_3)CH_3$

Practice Questions — Fact Recall

Q1 What is a molecular formula?

Q2 What does a displayed formula show?

Q3 How do you work out the empirical formula of a compound?

Q4 What is a homologous series?

2. Functional Groups

The functional groups are the parts of a molecule that define it. There are loads of different functional groups — all the ones you need to know about are described over the next few pages.

Homologous series

A homologous series is a series of molecules that all have the same functional group and the same general formula. If you know what homologous series a molecule is a part of, you can predict some of the ways that it will behave or react with other molecules. Below you're going to see a whole load of different homologous series, starting with the most basic of them — alkanes.

Alkanes

Alkanes have the general formula C_nH_{2n+2}. Their names all end in -ane, and the stem of the name depends on how many carbon atoms there are in the chain (see Figure 1). Naming alkanes is covered in more detail on pages 180-181). They've only got carbon and hydrogen atoms, so they're **hydrocarbons**. Every carbon atom in an alkane has four single bonds with other atoms. It's impossible for carbon to make more than four bonds, so alkanes are **saturated**.

No. of Carbon Atoms	Stem
1	meth-
2	eth-
3	prop-
4	but-
5	pent-
6	hex-

Figure 1: *Table showing the stems of organic compounds for up to six carbons.*

Examples

H—C—H (with H above and below)	H—C—C—H (with H's)	H—C—C—C—H (with H's)
methane	ethane	propane

Halogenoalkanes

Halogenoalkanes are similar in structure to alkanes, except at least one of the hydrogen atoms has been replaced with a halogen atom — i.e. F, Cl, Br or I. They have the prefix fluoro-, chloro-, bromo- or iodo-.

Examples

By replacing one hydrogen atom in methane with a chlorine atom, you get chloromethane.

Cl
|
H—C—H
|
H

chloromethane, CH_3Cl

It doesn't have to be just one hydrogen atom that gets replaced — you can replace any number of the hydrogen atoms with halogen. By replacing all of the hydrogen atoms in propane with fluorine atoms, you get octafluoropropane.

F   F   F
| | |
F—C—C—C—F
| | |
F   F   F

octafluoropropane, C_3F_8

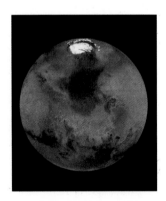

Figure 2: C_3F_8 *could potentially be used to create a habitable atmosphere on Mars.*

Tip: The 'octa-' tells you that there are eight fluorine atoms (see page 181 for more on this).

Cycloalkanes

Cycloalkanes have a ring of carbon atoms with two hydrogens attached to each carbon. Cycloalkanes have two fewer hydrogens than other alkanes (assuming they have only one ring), so cycloalkanes have a different general formula from that of normal alkanes (C_nH_{2n}), but they are still saturated. The molecules in this homologous series have the prefix cyclo- and the suffix -ane.

Examples

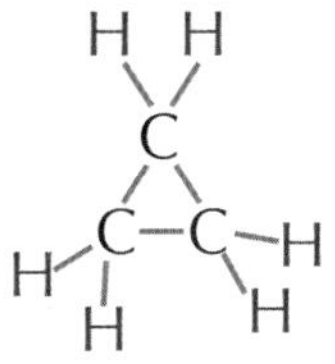

cyclopropane, C_3H_6

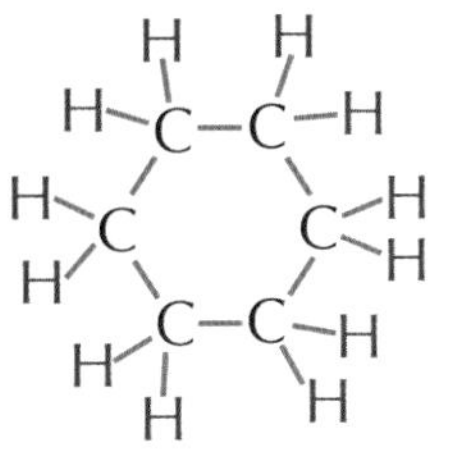

cyclohexane, C_6H_{12}

The smallest number of carbons you need to make a ring is three, so cyclopropane is the smallest cycloalkane.

Branched alkanes

A branched alkane is an alkane that doesn't have all the carbon atoms in one straight chain. They will have a main chain of carbons (whichever chain is the longest) and one or more carbons coming off this main chain. These branches are called alkyl groups. Branched alkanes have the same general formula as straight-chained alkanes.

Examples

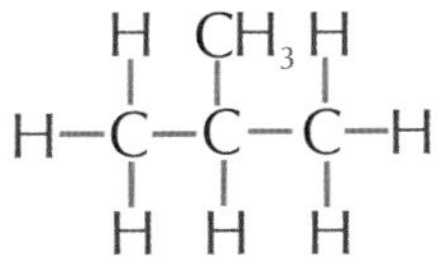

methylpropane, C_4H_{10}

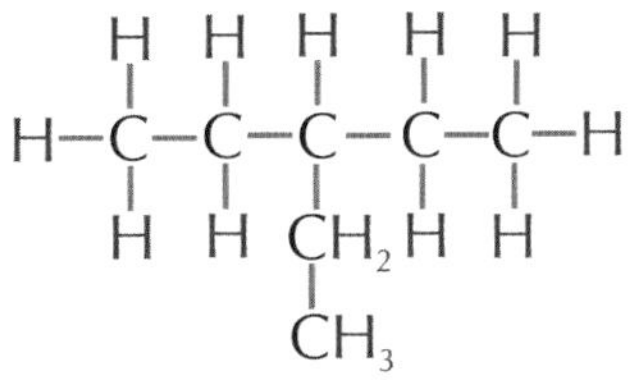

3-ethylpentane, C_7H_{16}

The alkyl group in the example on the left is just one carbon long, so it's called 'methyl-'. The alkyl group in the example on the right is two carbons long, so it's called 'ethyl-'.

Side Chain Length	Suffix
1	methyl-
2	ethyl-
3	propyl-
4	butyl-
5	pentyl-
6	hexyl-

Figure 3: *Table showing the suffixes for alkyl groups up to six carbons long.*

Tip: The '3' in 3-ethylpentane means that the branch is on the third carbon along the main chain (see page 180 for more details).

Alkenes

An alkene is a hydrocarbon with a carbon-carbon double bond. They have the general formula C_nH_{2n}. The carbons on either end of the double bond are only bonded to three atoms each, rather than the maximum of four. This means that they could form another bond, so they are unsaturated. This makes alkenes fairly reactive (see page 214 for more on this).

Examples

ethene

propene

Tip: The general formula C_nH_{2n} only applies to alkenes with exactly one C=C bond. The general formula's different for alkenes with two or more C=C bonds.

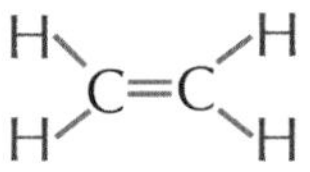

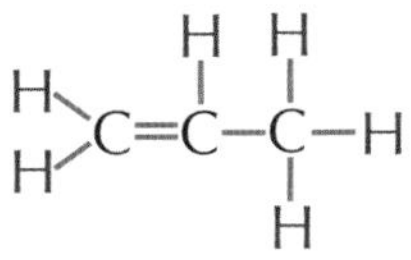

Alcohols

Alcohols are organic molecules that contain the –OH, or hydroxyl, functional group. They have the suffix -ol, and the general formula $C_nH_{2n+1}OH$. Alcohols can be reacted to give alkenes, and vice versa. These reactions are discussed in more detail on pages 227 and 230.

Figure 4: *Ethanol (C_2H_5OH) has been produced by humans for thousands of years.*

Examples

H–C–OH

methanol

H–C–C–C–C–H

butan-2-ol

Aldehydes

In aldehydes, one of the end carbons has a double bond to an oxygen atom and a single bond to a hydrogen atom, like this:

The suffix for aldehydes is -al. The general formula is written as R–CHO, where R is just an alkyl group or an H atom.

Tip: Anything with the functional group C=O is called a carbonyl. Aldehydes, ketones and carboxylic acids are all carbonyls.

Examples

The alkyl group can be a straight chain or a branched chain.

H–C–C–C–H

propanal

H–C–C–C–H

2-methylbutanal

Ketones

Tip: In the general formula for ketones, R or R' can't represent an H atom, otherwise it would be an aldehyde.

Like aldehydes, ketones also contain the C=O bond, except it isn't one of the end carbons. So the general structure of a ketone is this: Here, R and R' are alkyl groups, which may or may not be the same. The general formula is written R–CO–R'.

R–C–R'

Examples

In propanone, the alkyl groups R and R' are the same. In pentan-2-one, they're different.

H–C–C–C–H

propanone

H–C–C–C–C–C–H

pentan-2-one

Tip: Aldehydes, ketones and carboxylic acids can all be produced by oxidising alcohols — this is covered in detail on pages 234-237.

Carboxylic acids

Carboxylic acids all contain the carboxyl functional group:

Its suffix is -oic acid. The general formula is written R–COOH, where R is an alkyl group.

The alkyl group R can also represent a hydrogen atom, like in methanoic acid. This is the simplest carboxylic acid.

$$
\begin{array}{c}
O \\
\parallel \\
H-C-OH
\end{array}
$$

methanoic acid

$$
\begin{array}{c}
H \ \ H \ \ O \\
| \ \ \ | \ \ \parallel \\
H-C-C-C-OH \\
| \ \ \ | \\
H \ \ CH_3
\end{array}
$$

2-methylpropanoic acid

Figure 5: *Methanoic acid occurs naturally in the venom of some ants.*

Practice Questions — Fact Recall

Q1 Give the general formula for an alkane.

Q2 What is the stem for a carbon chain containing six carbon atoms?

Q3 Describe a cycloalkane.

Q4 What is the name for a carbon side chain containing two carbon atoms?

Q5 Which two homologous series have the general formula C_nH_{2n}?

Q6 What does the 'R' represent in the general formula R–CHO?

Q7 What is the difference between an aldehyde and a ketone?

Figure 1: *August Kekulé was one of the first scientists to recognise the need for a way to systematically name molecules.*

3. Nomenclature

Nomenclature is just a fancy word for naming organic compounds. You have to follow a strict set of rules for naming, but it's dead handy — this way anyone anywhere can know what compound you're talking about.

Naming alkanes

The IUPAC system for naming organic compounds is the agreed international language of chemistry. Years ago, organic compounds were given whatever names people fancied, such as acetic acid and ethylene. But these names caused confusion between different countries.

The IUPAC system means scientific ideas can be communicated across the globe more effectively. So it's easier for scientists to get on with testing each other's work, and either support or dispute new theories.

You need to be able to name straight-chain and branched alkanes using the IUPAC system for naming organic compounds.

Straight-chain alkanes

There are two parts to the name of a straight-chain alkane. The first part — the stem — states how many carbon atoms there are in the molecule (see Figure 1 on page 176). The second part is always "-ane". It's the "-ane" bit that lets people know it's an alkane.

┌─ **Example** ──────────────────────

$$H-\underset{\underset{H}{|}}{\overset{\overset{H}{|}}{C}}-\underset{\underset{H}{|}}{\overset{\overset{H}{|}}{C}}-\underset{\underset{H}{|}}{\overset{\overset{H}{|}}{C}}-\underset{\underset{H}{|}}{\overset{\overset{H}{|}}{C}}-\underset{\underset{H}{|}}{\overset{\overset{H}{|}}{C}}-H$$

pentane

There are 5 carbon atoms, so the stem is 'pent-' — the alkane is called pentane.

Branched alkanes

Branched alkanes have side chains. These are the carbon atoms that aren't part of the longest continuous chain. To name branched alkanes you first need to count how many carbon atoms are in the longest chain and work out the stem (just like you would for a straight-chain alkane). Once you've done that you can name the side chains.

The side chains are named according to how many carbon atoms they have (see Figure 3 on page 177) and which carbon atom they are attached to. If there's more than one side chain in a molecule, you place them in alphabetical order. So but- groups come before eth- groups, which come before meth- groups.

┌─ **Examples** ──────────────────────

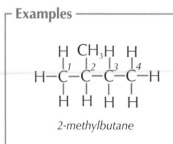

2-methylbutane

The longest continuous carbon chain is 4 carbon atoms, so the stem is butane.

There's one side chain, which has one carbon atom, so it's a methyl group.

It's joined to the main carbon chain at the 2nd carbon atom, so it's a 2-methyl group.

The alkane is called 2-methylbutane.

The longest continuous carbon chain is 5 carbon atoms, so the stem is pentane.

There are two side chains.

One side chain is a methyl group joined to the 2nd carbon atom: 2-methyl-.

The other is an ethyl group (2 carbons) joined to the 3rd carbon atom: 3-ethyl-.

Side chains go in alphabetical order, so the alkane is 3-ethyl-2-methylpentane.

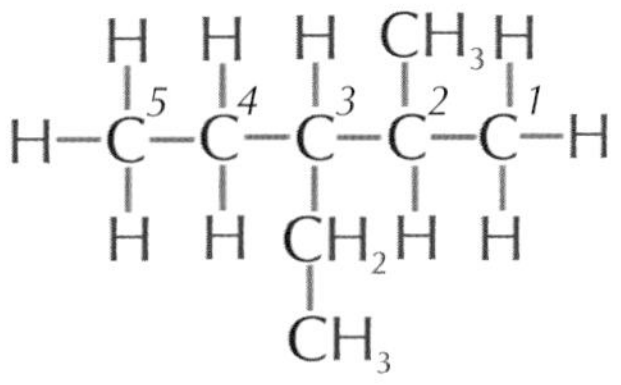

3-ethyl-2-methylpentane

Tip: Always number the longest continuous carbon chain so that the name contains the lowest numbers possible. For example, you could number this chain:

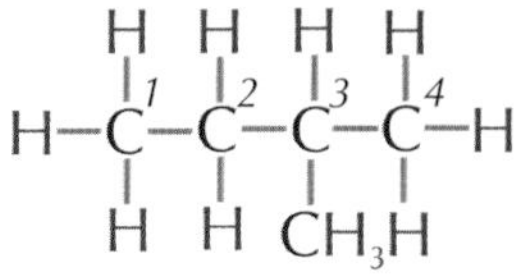

which would make it 3-methylbutane. But you should actually number it in the opposite direction to get 2-methylbutane.

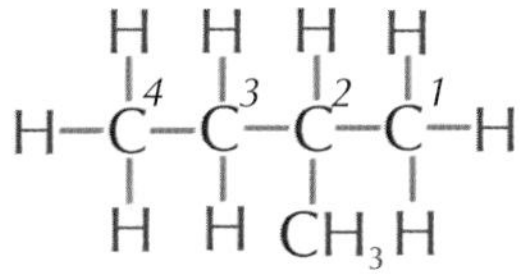

If there are two or more side chains of the same type then you add a prefix of di- for two, tri- for three, etc. (You should ignore these prefixes when you're putting the other prefixes in alphabetical order.)

Example

The longest carbon chain is 5 atoms long, so the stem is pentane.

There's an ethyl group on the 3rd carbon atom: 3-ethyl-.

There are methyl groups on the 2nd and the 4th carbon atoms: 2,4-dimethyl-.

The alkane is called 3-ethyl-2,4-dimethylpentane.

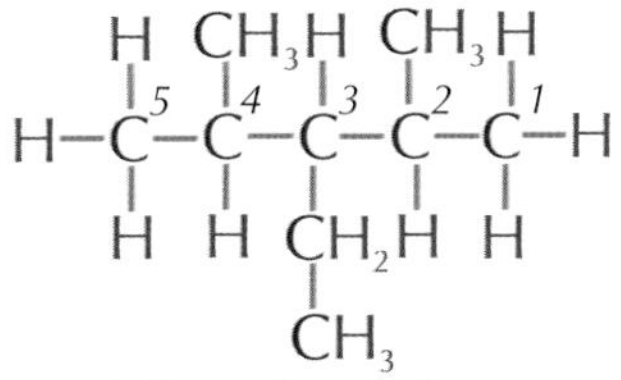

3-ethyl-2,4-dimethylpentane

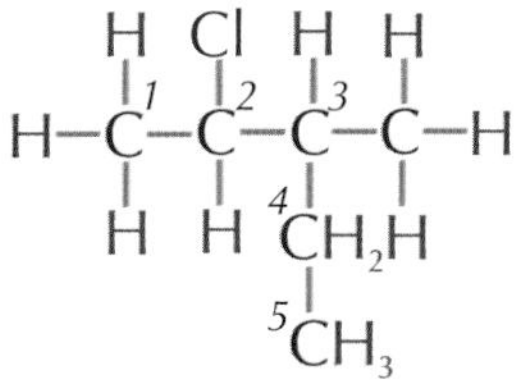

Cycloalkanes

Cycloalkanes have the same name as their straight-chain alkane equivalent, but with cyclo- attached to the front. If the cycloalkane has an alkyl group attached, then just add the alkyl prefix (you don't need a number). If there's more than one alkyl group, then make the numbers as low as possible, and the alkyl that's first alphabetically goes on the 1-carbon.

Tip: Be careful — the longest carbon chain may not be in a straight line:

Example

The carbon ring is 5 atoms long, so it's a cyclopentane.

There's a methyl group and an ethyl group. Ethyl comes first alphabetically: 1-ethyl.

Depending on which way round the ring you count, the methyl is on the 3rd or 4th carbon. Make the numbers as low as possible: 3-methyl.

So the molecule is 1-ethyl-3-methyl-cyclopentane.

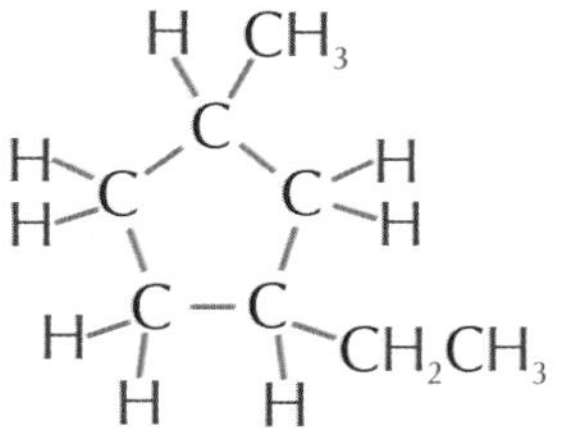

Tip: When you're naming molecules commas are put between numbers (for example 2,2) and dashes are put between numbers and letters (for example 2-methyl).

Naming other functional groups

Once you know how to name alkanes, the other functional groups follow nicely. The stem comes from the longest carbon chain that contains the functional group. Prefixes and suffixes come from the functional groups as well as any alkyl side chains. If you need to use a number to show the position of the functional group, give the carbon which the functional group is on the lowest number possible.

Examples

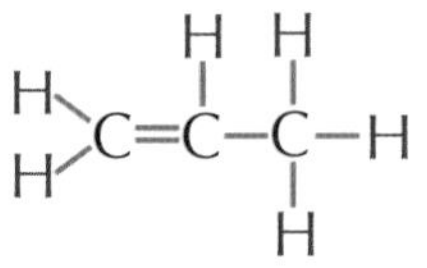

propene

There are three carbon atoms, so the stem is prop-. It's an alkene, so the suffix is -ene.

So this is propene. The double bond must always be on the first carbon in propene, so you don't need a number in the name.

This is an alkene with a straight chain of four carbon atoms — so it's butene.

The double bond is between the first and second carbon, so you say it's on the 1st carbon. So the name of the molecule is but-1-ene.

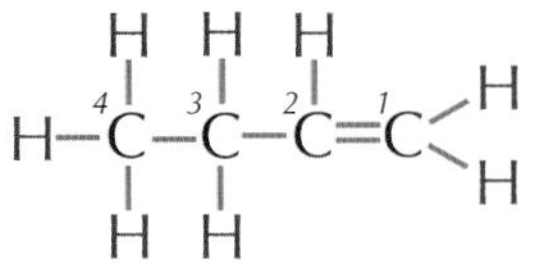

but-1-ene

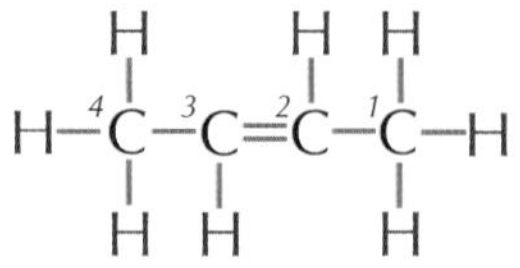

but-2-ene

This is also butene, but the double bond is between the second and third carbon atoms.

So the name of the molecule is but-2-ene.

If there's more than one functional group you have to work out which one has the highest priority (see Figure 2) — this is the main functional group. The stem of the name then comes from the longest carbon chain containing the main functional group, and you number the carbons so that the main functional group has the lowest number possible.

Tip: You might see molecules with several 'other functional groups', but you won't be asked to name them.

Halogens	Alkyl groups	Alkenes	Other functional groups
Lowest priority		→	*Highest priority*

Figure 2: *The order of priority of different functional groups.*

Examples

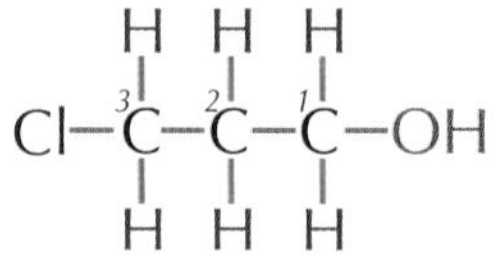

3-chloropropan-1-ol

This molecule has just one carbon chain, which is 3 atoms long, so the stem is prop-.

It's got two functional groups, Cl and OH, so it needs a chloro- prefix and an -ol suffix.

The alcohol group has a higher priority than the chlorine, so number the carbons to give the alcohol the lowest number possible. So this is 3-chloropropan-1-ol (not 1-chloropropan-3-ol).

Tip: If there are no double or triple carbon-carbon bonds in an aldehyde, you need to write '-an-' between the stem and the suffix. This is also true for alcohols, ketones and carboxylic acids.

The highest priority functional group on this molecule is the CHO group, so it's an aldehyde, and the suffix is -al. The longest carbon chain containing the CHO group is 4 atoms long, so the stem is but-.

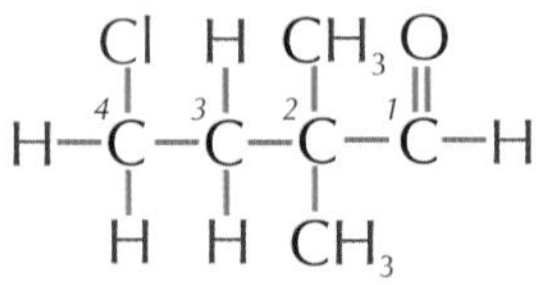

4-chloro-2,2-dimethylbutanal

Number the carbons in this chain starting from the carbonyl group, as it has the highest priority.

Both methyl groups are on the 2nd carbon: 2,2-dimethyl.

The chlorine atom is on the 4th carbon: 4-chloro.

Chloro- comes before methyl- alphabetically.

So the molecule is 4-chloro-2,2-dimethylbutanal.

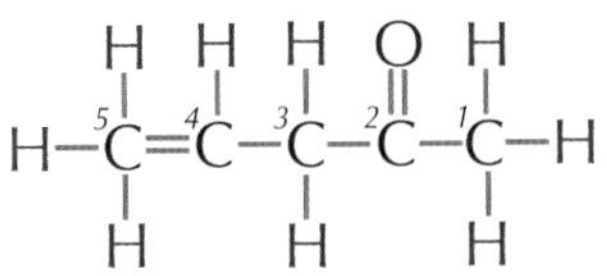

The molecule diagram (top left):

$$H-\underset{\underset{H}{|}}{\overset{\overset{H}{|}}{C}}=\underset{\underset{H}{|}}{\overset{\overset{H}{|}}{C}}-\underset{\underset{H}{|}}{\overset{\overset{H}{|}}{C}}-\underset{}{\overset{\overset{O}{\|}}{C}}-\underset{\underset{H}{|}}{\overset{\overset{H}{|}}{C}}-H$$

pent-4-en-2-one

The highest priority functional group here is the ketone. The longest carbon chain containing the ketone is 5 atoms long, so the stem is pent-.

It's a ketone, so the suffix is -one. It's also an alkene, so it ends '-enone' instead of '-anone'.

Number the carbons in the longest chain so that the carbonyl group has as low a number as possible (i.e. start on the right): -2-one.

The C=C bond is between the 4th and 5th carbons: -4-ene.

This molecule is called pent-4-en-2-one.

Figure 3: *Ketones can be used in tests for diabetes.*

Practice Questions — Application

Q1 Name the following branched alkanes:

a) 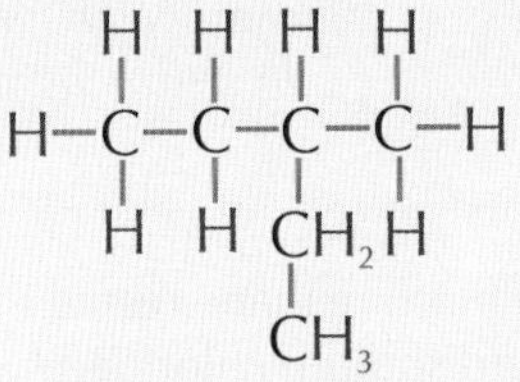
$$H-\overset{H}{\underset{H}{C}}-\overset{H}{\underset{H}{C}}-\overset{H}{\underset{CH_2H}{C}}-\overset{H}{\underset{CH_3}{C}}-H$$

b)
$$H-\overset{H}{\underset{H}{C}}-\overset{H}{\underset{H}{C}}-\overset{CH_2H}{\underset{CH_2H}{C}}-\overset{CH_3}{\underset{CH_3}{C}}-H$$

c)
$$H-\overset{H}{\underset{H}{C}}-\overset{H}{\underset{H}{C}}-\overset{CH_3}{\underset{CH_2H}{C}}-\overset{CH_2H}{C}-CH_3$$
$$H_3C-CH_2$$

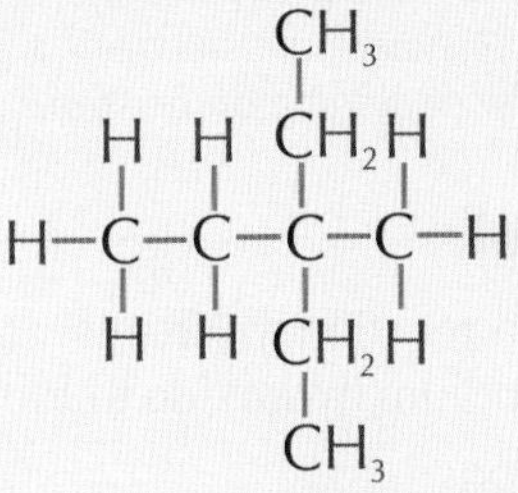

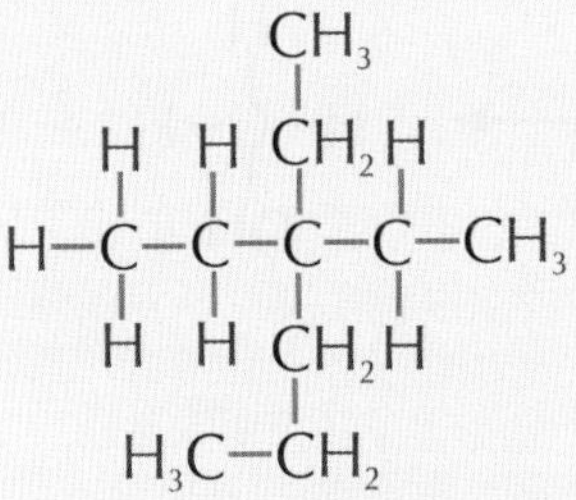

d) 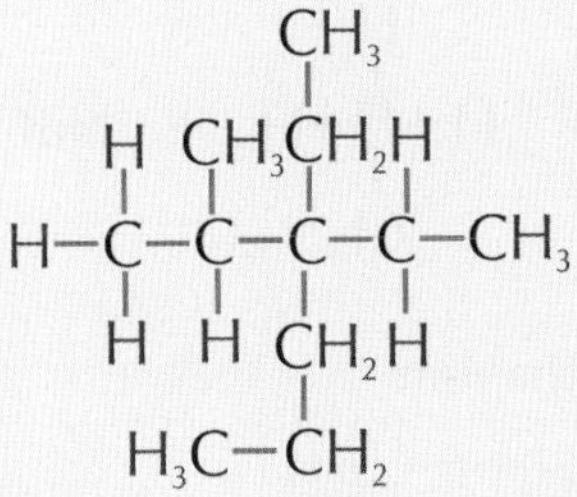
$$H-\overset{H}{\underset{H}{C}}-\overset{CH_3CH_2H}{\underset{H}{C}}-\overset{CH_3}{\underset{CH_2H}{C}}-C-CH_3$$
$$H_3C-CH_2$$

Q2 Name the following molecules:

a) 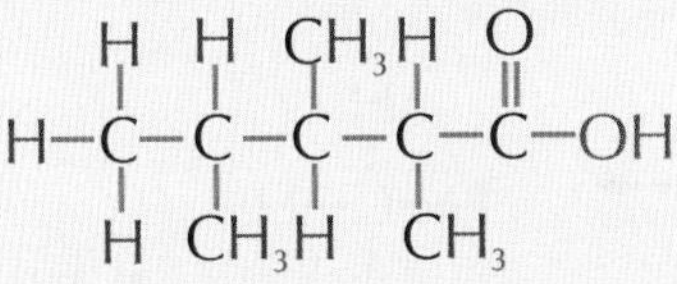
$$H-\overset{H}{\underset{H}{C}}-\overset{H}{\underset{CH_3H}{C}}-\overset{CH_3H}{\underset{CH_3}{C}}-\overset{O}{\underset{}{C}}-C-OH$$

b) 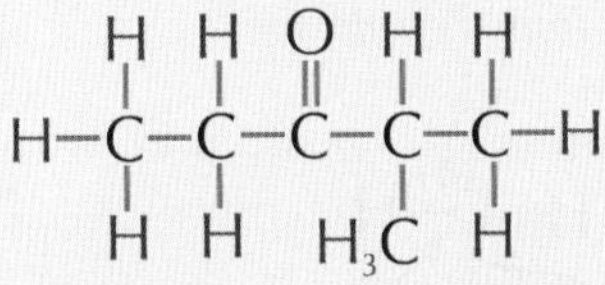
$$H-\overset{H}{\underset{H}{C}}-\overset{H}{\underset{H}{C}}-\overset{O}{\underset{H_3C}{C}}-\overset{H}{\underset{}{C}}-\overset{H}{\underset{H}{C}}-H$$

Q3 Draw the structure of each of the following molecules:

a) 2-methylhexane

b) 3-bromobutan-2-ol

c) 3-ethylpentan-2-one

d) 1,3-difluorobut-2-ene

Exam Tip
Make sure you know the order of priority of the functional groups.

Practice Questions — Fact Recall

Q1 If there are two methyl- side chains, what prefix should you add to methyl- when naming the molecule?

Q2 Put the following functional groups in order of priority, from highest to lowest: Alkene Alcohol Halogen Alkyl

Learning Objectives:

- Know that reactions of organic compounds can be explained using mechanisms.
- Know that the formation of a covalent bond is shown by a curly arrow that starts from a lone electron pair or from another covalent bond.
- Know that the breaking of a covalent bond is shown by a curly arrow starting from the bond.
- Be able to outline mechanisms by drawing the structures of the species involved and curly arrows to represent the movement of electron pairs.

Specification Reference 3.3.1.2

Tip: Free radical mechanisms, which are a different type of mechanism, are covered on pages 200-202.

Tip: There are lots of mechanisms coming up in the next two sections, so if it all seems a bit strange now, don't worry — before long you'll have seen loads of them.

4. Mechanisms

It's all very well knowing the outcome of a reaction, but it can also be useful to know how a reaction happens.

What are mechanisms?

Mechanisms break reactions down into a sequence of stages. Reaction mechanism diagrams show how molecules react together by using curly arrows to show which bonds are made or broken.

Curly arrows

In order to make or break a bond in a reaction, electrons have to move around. A curly arrow shows where a pair of electrons goes during a reaction. They look like this:

The arrow starts at the bond or lone pair where the electrons are at the beginning of the step.

The arrow points to where the new bond is formed at the end of the step.

Example

Draw a reaction mechanism to show how chloromethane reacts with sodium hydroxide to form methanol and sodium chloride.

Reaction:

$$H-\underset{\underset{Cl}{|}}{\overset{\overset{H}{|}}{C}}-H \ + \ NaOH \longrightarrow H-\underset{\underset{OH}{|}}{\overset{\overset{H}{|}}{C}}-H \ + \ NaCl$$

Mechanism:

1. The C–Cl bond is polar. The $C^{\delta+}$ attracts a lone pair of electrons from the OH⁻ ion.

3. A new bond forms between the C and the OH⁻ ion, making an alcohol...

2. The OH⁻ ion attacks the slightly positive carbon atom.

4. ... and the C–Cl bond breaks. Both the electrons from the bond are taken by the Cl.

NaOH and NaCl are both ionic compounds that are dissociated in a solution. This means that Na^+ doesn't get involved in the reaction — so you don't need to include it in the mechanism.

Practice Questions — Fact Recall

Q1 What does a curly arrow point from and to in a reaction mechanism diagram?

Q2 In a reaction between chloroethane and aqueous potassium hydroxide, why would potassium not feature in the mechanism?

5. Isomers

You can put the same atoms together in different ways to make completely different molecules. Two molecules that have the same molecular formula but are put together in a different way are isomers of each other.

Structural isomers

Structural isomers have the same molecular formula, but a different structural formula (i.e the atoms are connected in different ways). There are three types of structural isomers — chain isomers, position isomers and functional group isomers.

1. Chain isomers

Chain isomers have the same functional groups but different arrangements of the carbon skeleton. Some are straight chains and others are branched in different ways.

> **Examples**
>
> There are two chain isomers of C_4H_{10}. The diagrams below show the straight-chain isomer butane and the branched-chain isomer methylpropane.
>
> *Here the longest carbon chain is 3 carbon atoms.*
>
> *Here the longest carbon chain is 4 carbon atoms.*
>
> **butane**   **methylpropane**
>
> There are two chain isomers of C_3H_7COOH. The diagrams below show the straight-chain isomer butanoic acid and the branched-chain isomer methylpropanoic acid.
>
> *Here the longest carbon chain is 4 carbon atoms.*
>
> *Here the longest carbon chain is 3 carbon atoms.*
>
> **butanoic acid**   **methylpropanoic acid**

2. Position isomers

Position isomers have the same skeleton and the same atoms or groups of atoms attached. The difference is that the atoms or groups of atoms are attached to different carbon atoms.

> **Examples**
>
> There are two position isomers of C_4H_9Cl. The chlorine atom is attached to different carbon atoms in each isomer.
>
> *The Cl is attached to the first carbon atom.*
>
> **1-chlorobutane**

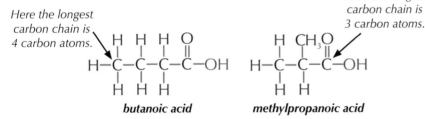

Learning Objectives:

- Know and understand the meaning of the term structural isomerism.
- Be able to draw the structures of chain, position and functional group isomers.

Specification Reference 3.3.1.3

Tip: When a functional group can only go in one place on a molecule (e.g. 2-methylpropane), you don't need to write the number (e.g. methylpropane).

Exam Tip
You don't always have to draw all of the bonds when you're drawing a molecule — writing CH_3 next to a bond is just as good as drawing out the carbon atom, three bonds and three hydrogen atoms. But if you're asked for a displayed formula you <u>must</u> draw out all of the bonds to get the marks.

Tip: When you're drawing isomers, always number the carbons. It makes it easier to see what the longest chain is and where side chains and atoms are attached:

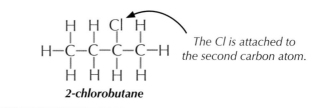

Tip: If the chlorine atom was attached to the second carbon atom from the left, it would still be the <u>same molecule</u> — just drawn the other way round. It would still be 2-chlorobutane.

The Cl is attached to the second carbon atom.

2-chlorobutane

3. Functional group isomers

Functional group isomers have the same atoms arranged into different functional groups.

Example

The formulas below show two functional group isomers of C_6H_{12}.

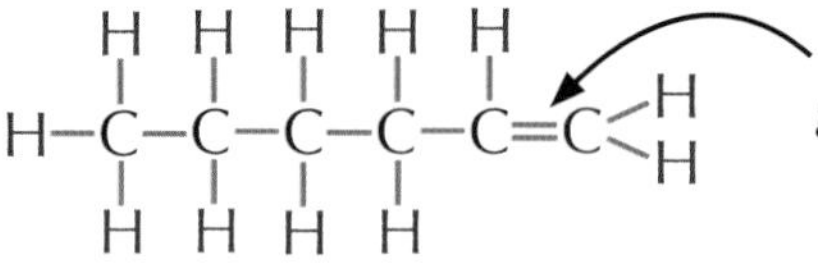

The functional group is the C=C — it's an alkene.

hex-1-ene

This molecule is an alkane.

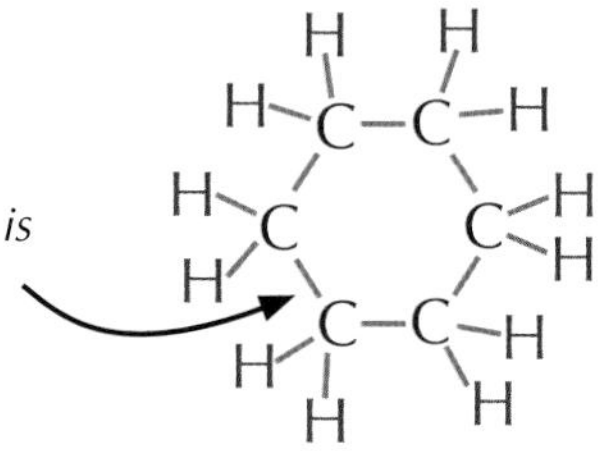

cyclohexane

Exam Tip
To avoid mistakes when you're identifying isomers in an exam, draw the molecule so the longest carbon chain goes left to right across the page. This will make it easier to see the isomers.

Identifying isomers

Atoms can rotate as much as they like around single C–C bonds. Remember this when you work out structural isomers — sometimes what looks like an isomer, isn't.

Examples

There are only two position isomers of C_3H_7Br — 1-bromopropane and 2-bromopropane.

1-bromopropane

The Br is always on the first carbon atom.

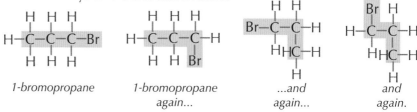

1-bromopropane

1-bromopropane again...

...and again...

and again.

All these molecules are the same — they're just drawn differently.

2-bromopropane

The Br is always on the second carbon atom.

2-bromopropane

2-bromopropane again

Tip: In propane, the Br can only really go on the first or second carbon atom. If it was on the "third" it would be the same as being on the first again because you start counting from whichever end the Br is on.

1-bromopropane

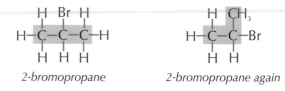

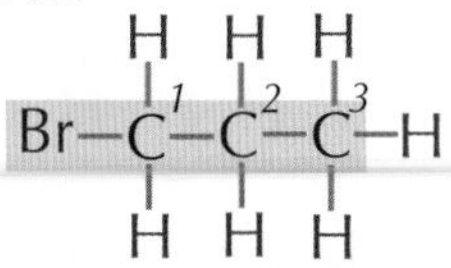

Q1 Here is an isomer of 2-chloro-2-methylpropane.

$$CH_3$$
$$H_3C-\underset{\underset{Cl}{|}}{\overset{\overset{CH_3}{|}}{C}}-CH_3$$

Draw the other position isomer of chloro-2-methylpropane.

Q2 Draw all the chain isomers of C_5H_{12}.

Q3 Here is the displayed formula of propanal.

$$H-\underset{\underset{H}{|}}{\overset{\overset{H}{|}}{C}}-\underset{\underset{H}{|}}{\overset{\overset{H}{|}}{C}}-\overset{\overset{O}{\|}}{C}-H$$

Propanal has the functional group $\overset{\overset{O}{\|}}{C}-H$.
Draw an isomer of propanal with a carbonyl group $\overset{\overset{O}{\|}}{C}$.

Q4 Here is the displayed formula of 1-chlorohexane.

$$H-\underset{\underset{H}{|}}{\overset{\overset{H}{|}}{C}}-\underset{\underset{H}{|}}{\overset{\overset{H}{|}}{C}}-\underset{\underset{H}{|}}{\overset{\overset{H}{|}}{C}}-\underset{\underset{H}{|}}{\overset{\overset{H}{|}}{C}}-\underset{\underset{H}{|}}{\overset{\overset{H}{|}}{C}}-\underset{\underset{H}{|}}{\overset{\overset{H}{|}}{C}}-Cl$$

a) For each of the molecules (i–iv), say whether they are isomers of 1-chlorohexane or not.

i)
$$H-\underset{\underset{H}{|}}{\overset{\overset{H}{|}}{C}}-\underset{\underset{H}{|}}{\overset{\overset{Cl}{|}}{C}}-\underset{\underset{CH_2H}{|}}{\overset{\overset{H}{|}}{C}}-\underset{\underset{H}{|}}{\overset{\overset{H}{|}}{C}}-H$$
$$CH_3$$

ii)
$$H-\underset{\underset{H}{|}}{\overset{\overset{H}{|}}{C}}-\underset{\underset{H}{|}}{\overset{\overset{Cl}{|}}{C}}-\underset{\underset{CH_3H}{|}}{\overset{\overset{CH_3}{|}}{C}}-\underset{\underset{H}{|}}{\overset{\overset{H}{|}}{C}}-H$$

iii)
$$H-\underset{\underset{H}{|}}{\overset{\overset{H}{|}}{C}}-\underset{\underset{H}{|}}{\overset{\overset{H}{|}}{C}}-\underset{\underset{CH_2H}{|}}{\overset{\overset{H}{|}}{C}}-\underset{\underset{H}{|}}{\overset{\overset{H}{|}}{C}}-H$$
$$CH_3$$

iv)
$$H-\underset{\underset{H}{|}}{\overset{\overset{H}{|}}{C}}-\underset{\underset{H}{|}}{\overset{\overset{H}{|}}{C}}-\underset{\underset{H}{|}}{\overset{\overset{Cl}{|}}{C}}-\underset{\underset{H}{|}}{\overset{\overset{H}{|}}{C}}-\underset{\underset{H}{|}}{\overset{\overset{H}{|}}{C}}-H$$

b) State the types of isomerism shown in part a).

Exam Tip
Remember, isomers have the same atoms arranged in a different way — you can do this type of question simply by counting the number of carbon, hydrogen and chlorine atoms.

Practice Questions — Fact Recall

Q1 What is a chain isomer?
Q2 What is a position isomer?
Q3 What is a functional group isomer?

6. *E/Z* Isomers

Learning Objectives:

- Know and understand the meaning of the term stereoisomerism.
- Understand that *E/Z*-isomerism is a form of stereoisomerism and that it occurs as a result of restricted rotation about the planar carbon-carbon double bond.
- Be able to draw the structural formulas of *E* and *Z* isomers.
- Know and be able to apply the Cahn-Ingold-Prelog priority rules to *E* and *Z* isomers.

Specification Reference 3.3.1.3

Structural isomers aren't the only isomers you need to know about. You also need to know about E/Z isomerism, which is a type of stereoisomerism.

Stereoisomers

Stereoisomers have the same structural formula, but their atoms are arranged differently in space. One type of stereoisomerism is *E/Z* isomerism, which you see in molecules with C=C double bonds. Before getting to that, you need to know a bit more about the structure of a C=C double bond. Read on...

Planar double bonds and restricted rotation

Carbon atoms in a C=C double bond and the atoms bonded to these carbons all lie in the same plane (they're planar). Because of the way they're arranged, they're said to be trigonal planar — the atoms attached to each double-bonded carbon form the corners of an imaginary equilateral triangle:

The bond angles in the planar unit are all 120°.

Ethene (C_2H_4) is totally planar. In larger alkenes only the C=C unit is planar.

─ **Example** ─────────────

This molecule is but-1-ene. The carbon-carbon double bond section of the molecule is planar. The section of the molecule that only contains single bonds is non-planar.

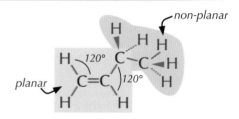

Another important thing about C=C double bonds is that atoms can't rotate around them like they can around single bonds. In fact, double bonds are fairly rigid — they don't bend much. Things can still rotate about any single bonds in the molecule though.

─ **Example** ─────────────

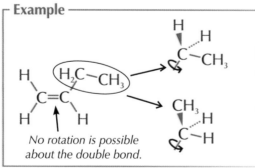

No rotation is possible about the double bond.

In this molecule of but-1-ene:

- The C=C double bond can't rotate.
- But the C–C single bonds can rotate.

Tip: Don't get confused by all those crazy green lines on the diagram. The dotted ones mean that the bond is pointing into the paper and the wedgy ones mean that the bond is pointing out of the paper. There's more on this on page 78.

E/Z isomerism in alkenes

The restricted rotation around the C=C double bond in alkenes causes a type of stereoisomerism called *E/Z* isomerism. If both double-bond carbons have two different atoms or groups attached to them, the arrangement of the groups around the double bond becomes important — you get two stereoisomers. One of these isomers is called the **'E-isomer'** and the other is the **'Z-isomer'**.

The simplest cases are when each carbon in the double bond has the same two 'different groups' attached. The *E*-isomer is the one that has the matching groups across the double bond from each other. The *Z*-isomer is the one with the matching groups both above or both below the double bond:

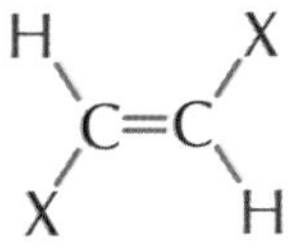

Tip: *E* stands for 'entgegen', a German word meaning 'opposite'. *Z* stands for 'zusammen', the German for 'together'.

E-isomer　　**Z-isomer**

In these diagrams X represents any group larger than a single H atom.

Example

The double-bonded carbon atoms in but-2-ene (C_4H_8) each have an H and a CH_3 group attached.

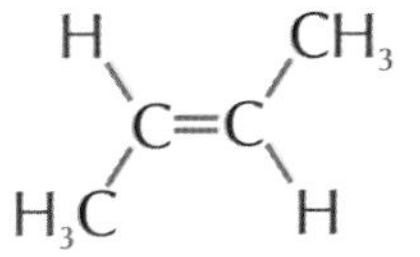

E-isomer

When the CH_3 groups are across the double bond then it's the *E*-isomer.
This molecule is *E*-but-2-ene.

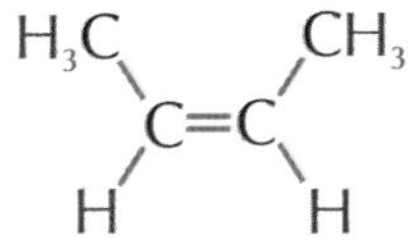

Z-isomer

When the CH_3 groups are both above or both below the double bond then it's the *Z*-isomer.
This molecule is *Z*-but-2-ene.

Tip: If all this isomer stuff is a bit confusing, try to get your hands on some molecular models and have a go making the isomers yourself — it should make everything a bit clearer.

In unbranched hydrocarbon chains, it is fairly straightforward to identify which isomer is which. The *E*-isomer is the one that has the carbon groups across the double bond from each other. The *Z*-isomer is the one which has the carbon groups both above or both below the double bond.

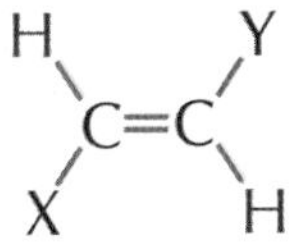

E-isomer 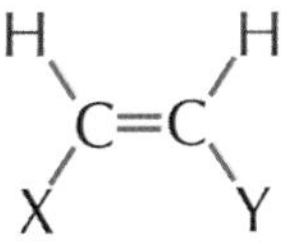　　**Z-isomer**

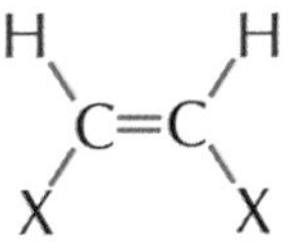

In these diagrams, X and Y are carbon chains.

Example

In pent-2-ene (C_5H_{10}) one of the double-bonded carbon atoms has an H and a CH_3 group attached to it. The other has an H and a CH_2CH_3 group attached.

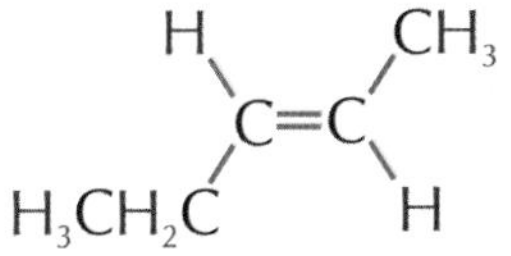

E-isomer

The high priority groups (CH_3 and CH_2CH_3) are across the double bond, so it's the *E*-isomer. This molecule is *E*-pent-2-ene.

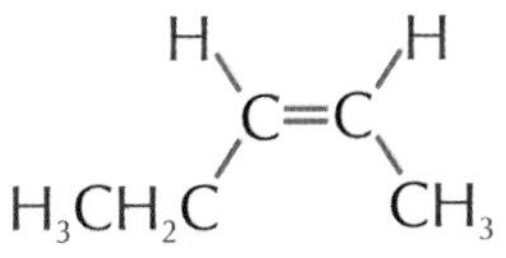

Z-isomer

The high priority groups are both below the double bond, so it's the *Z*-isomer.
This molecule is *Z*-pent-2-ene.

Cahn-Ingold-Prelog Priority Rules

A molecule that has a C=C bond surrounded by four different groups still has an E- and a Z-isomer — it's just harder to work out which is which. Fortunately, you can solve this problem using the Cahn-Ingold-Prelog (CIP) priority rules:

Figure 1: Sir Christopher Ingold contributed to the nomenclature of stereoisomers.

- Start by assigning a priority to the two atoms attached to each side of the double bond. To do this, you look at the atoms that are directly bonded to each of the C=C carbon atoms.

- The atom with the higher atomic number on each carbon is given the higher priority.

- If the atoms directly bonded to each carbon are the same, then you look at the next atom in the groups to work out which has the higher priority.

- To work out which isomer you have, just look at how the two highest priority groups are arranged. If they're positioned across the double bond from each other, you have the E-isomer. If they're both above or below the double bond, you have the Z-isomer.

Examples

A stereoisomer of 1-bromo-1-chloro-2-fluoro-ethene

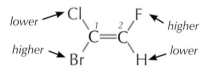

- The atoms directly attached to carbon-1 are bromine and chlorine. Bromine has an atomic number of 35 and chlorine has an atomic number of 17. So bromine is the higher priority group.

- The atoms directly attached to carbon-2 are fluorine and hydrogen. Fluorine has an atomic number of 9 and hydrogen has an atomic number of 1. So fluorine is the higher priority group.

- The two higher priority groups (Br and F) are positioned across the double bond from one another — so this is **E-1-bromo-1-chloro-2-fluoroethene**.

A stereoisomer of 1-bromo-1-chloro-2-methylbut-1-ene

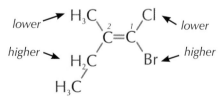

- The atoms attached to carbon-1 are bromine and chlorine. Bromine has the higher atomic number, so it is the higher priority group.

- The atoms attached to carbon-2 are both carbons, so you need to go further along the chain to work out the priority. The methyl carbon is attached to hydrogen (atomic number = 1), but the first ethyl carbon is attached to another carbon (atomic number = 6). So the ethyl group has higher priority.

- Both higher priority groups are below the double bond — so this molecule is **Z-1-bromo-1-chloro-2-methylbut-1-ene**.

Practice Questions — Application

Q1 State whether the following molecules are E-isomers or Z-isomers.

a)

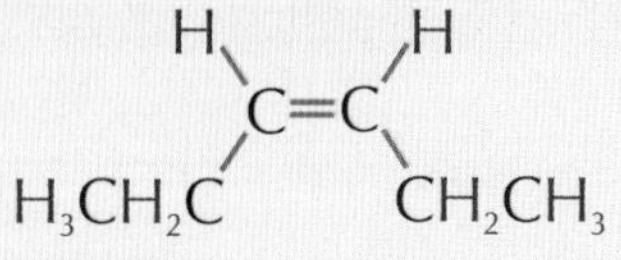

$$H_3CH_2C \underset{}{\overset{H}{\diagdown}} C = C \underset{CH_2CH_3}{\overset{H}{\diagup}}$$

b)

$$H_3CH_2C \underset{}{\overset{H}{\diagdown}} C = C \underset{CH_3}{\overset{CH_2CH_2CH_3}{\diagup}}$$

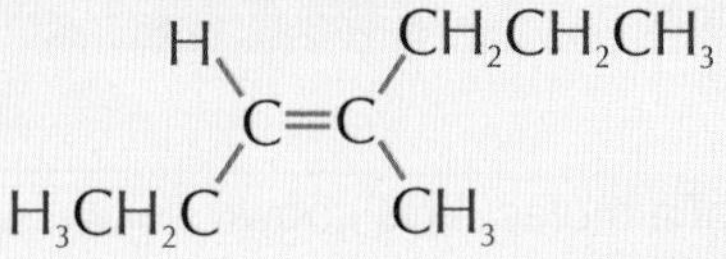

Q2 Draw the two stereoisomers of 3,4-dimethylhex-3-ene.
Label the E-isomer and the Z-isomer.
The structure of 3,4-dimethylhex-3-ene is shown below.

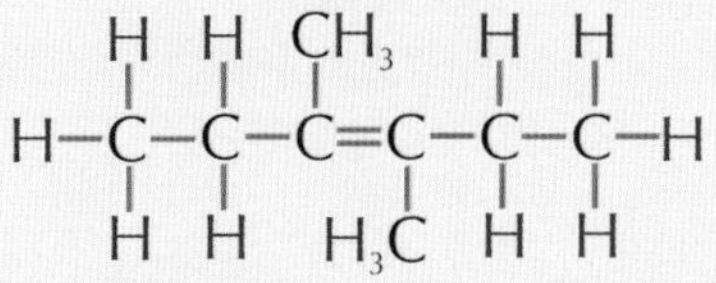

$$H-\overset{\overset{\displaystyle H}{|}}{\underset{\underset{\displaystyle H}{|}}{C}}-\overset{\overset{\displaystyle H}{|}}{\underset{\underset{\displaystyle H}{|}}{C}}-\overset{\overset{\displaystyle CH_3}{|}}{\underset{\underset{\displaystyle H_3C}{|}}{C}}=\overset{\overset{\displaystyle H}{|}}{\underset{\underset{\displaystyle H}{|}}{C}}-\overset{\overset{\displaystyle H}{|}}{\underset{\underset{\displaystyle H}{|}}{C}}-H$$

Practice Questions — Fact Recall

Q1 What is a stereoisomer?

Q2 a) What is a Z-isomer?

b) What is an E-isomer?

Q3 Each of the following pairs are joined to the same carbon in a carbon-carbon double bond. Use the CIP rules to decide which one has the higher priority:

a) CH_3 , H

b) CH_2CH_3 , Cl

c) $CH_2CH_2CH_3$, OH

d) $CH_2CH_2CH_2CH_2COOH$, $CH_2CH_2CH_2CH_2CH_2OH$

Tip: Remember — if the first atom in both chains is the same, you need to look at the next one (and so on...).

Section Summary

Make sure you know...

- What molecular formulas, structural formulas, displayed formulas, empirical formulas, general formulas, homologous series and skeletal formulas are. You also need to be able to use all of the different types of formulas.
- What alkanes are.
- How to name straight-chain and branched alkanes with up to 6 carbon atoms in the longest chain.
- How to draw reaction mechanisms using curly arrows.
- What structural isomerism is.
- How to draw the structures of chain, position and functional group isomers.
- What stereoisomerism is, and that it occurs as a result of carbon-carbon double bonds.
- That *E/Z*-isomerism is a form of stereoisomerism.
- How to identify *E*-isomers and *Z*-isomers.
- How to apply the Cahn-Ingold-Prelog priority rules to naming isomers.

Exam-style Questions

1   The skeletal formula of a molecule is shown below.

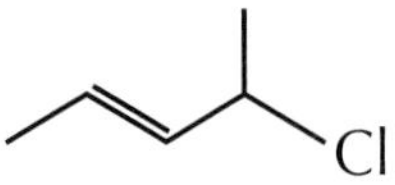

How many carbon atoms are in this molecule?

A   4

B   5

C   6

D   7

(1 mark)

2   Which of the options below represents a different molecule to the other three?

A

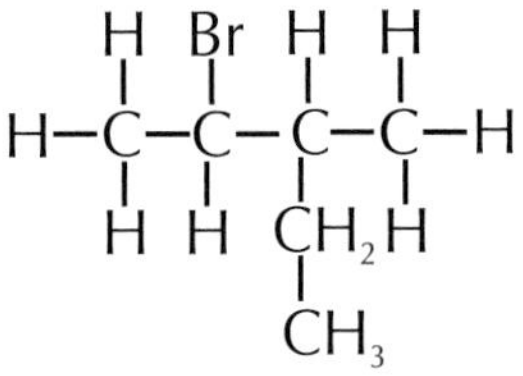

B $CH_3CHBrCH(CH_3)CH_2CH_3$

C   2-bromo-3-methylpentane

D $C_6H_{12}Br$

(1 mark)

3   Which of the skeletal formulas below represents a molecule that has E/Z-isomerism?

A

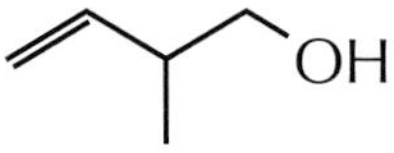

B

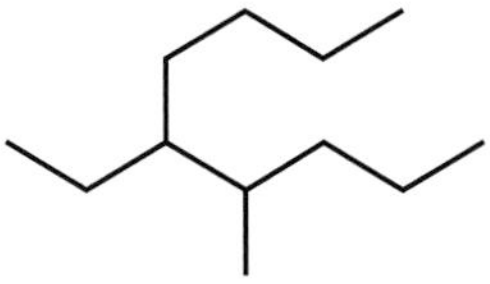

C

D

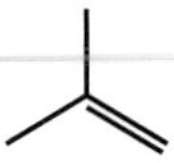

(1 mark)

4 The diagram below shows the displayed formula of molecule **A**.

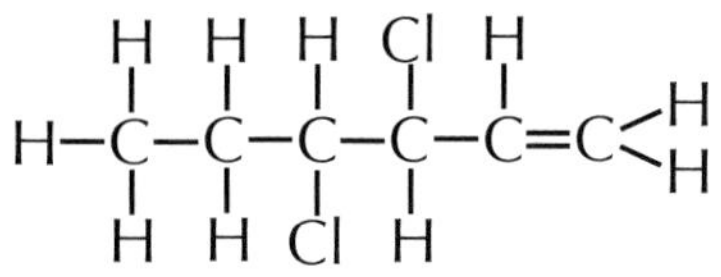

4.1 Name molecule **A**.

(1 mark)

4.2 Write down the molecular formula of molecule **A**.

(1 mark)

4.3 Give the empirical formula of molecule **A**.

(1 mark)

The diagram below shows a structural isomer of molecule **A** — molecule **B**.

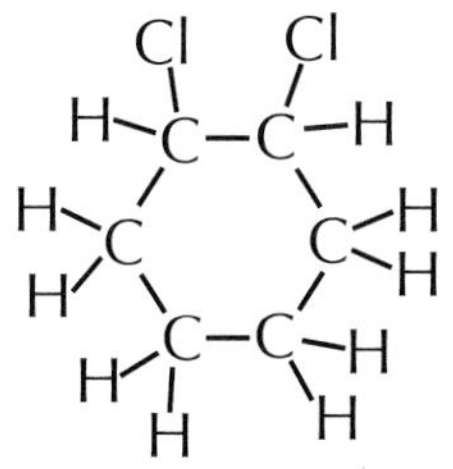

4.4 Identify what type of structural isomer molecule **B** is.

(1 mark)

4.5 Draw a position isomer of molecule **B**.

(1 mark)

The diagram below shows another isomer of molecule **A** — molecule **C**.

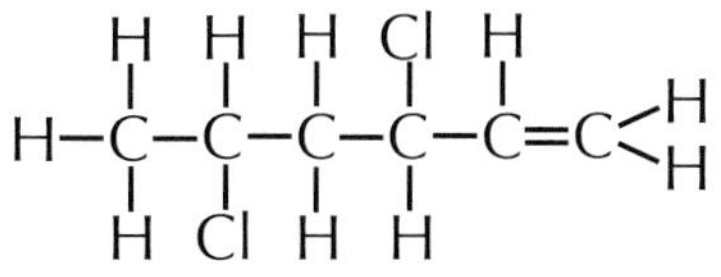

4.6 Identify what type of structural isomer of **A** molecule **C** is.

(1 mark)

4.7 Does molecule **C** show *E/Z*-isomerism? Explain your answer.

(2 marks)

5   Heptane is an alkane which is found in crude oil.

5.1   Give the general formula for an alkane.

(1 mark)

5.2   Below is the displayed formula for heptane.

$$H-\overset{\overset{\displaystyle H}{|}}{\underset{\underset{\displaystyle H}{|}}{C}}-\overset{\overset{\displaystyle H}{|}}{\underset{\underset{\displaystyle H}{|}}{C}}-\overset{\overset{\displaystyle H}{|}}{\underset{\underset{\displaystyle H}{|}}{C}}-\overset{\overset{\displaystyle H}{|}}{\underset{\underset{\displaystyle H}{|}}{C}}-\overset{\overset{\displaystyle H}{|}}{\underset{\underset{\displaystyle H}{|}}{C}}-\overset{\overset{\displaystyle H}{|}}{\underset{\underset{\displaystyle H}{|}}{C}}-\overset{\overset{\displaystyle H}{|}}{\underset{\underset{\displaystyle H}{|}}{C}}-H$$

Draw the displayed formula of a chain isomer of heptane.

(1 mark)

Lots of other alkanes can be found in crude oil.
Name the following alkanes.

5.3

$$H-\overset{\overset{\displaystyle H}{|}}{\underset{\underset{\displaystyle H}{|}}{C}}-\overset{\overset{\displaystyle H}{|}}{\underset{\underset{\displaystyle H}{|}}{C}}-\overset{\overset{\displaystyle H}{|}}{\underset{\underset{\displaystyle H}{|}}{C}}-\overset{\overset{\displaystyle H}{|}}{\underset{\underset{\displaystyle H}{|}}{C}}-\overset{\overset{\displaystyle H}{|}}{\underset{\underset{\displaystyle H}{|}}{C}}-H$$

(1 mark)

5.4

$$H-\overset{\overset{\displaystyle H}{|}}{\underset{\underset{\displaystyle H}{|}}{C}}-\overset{\overset{\displaystyle CH_3}{|}}{\underset{\underset{\displaystyle H}{|}}{C}}-\overset{\overset{\displaystyle H}{|}}{\underset{\underset{\displaystyle CH_3}{|}}{C}}-\overset{\overset{\displaystyle H}{|}}{\underset{\underset{\displaystyle H}{|}}{C}}-H$$

(1 mark)

6   A student has been given a sample of the alkene 3-methylpent-2-ene.
The structure of 3-methylpent-2-ene is shown below.

$$H-\overset{\overset{\displaystyle H}{|}}{\underset{\underset{\displaystyle H}{|}}{C}}-\overset{\overset{\displaystyle H}{|}}{\underset{\underset{\displaystyle H}{|}}{C}}-\overset{\overset{\displaystyle}{}}{\underset{\underset{\displaystyle CH_3}{|}}{C}}=\overset{\overset{\displaystyle H}{|}}{\underset{\underset{\displaystyle}{}}{C}}-\overset{\overset{\displaystyle H}{|}}{\underset{\underset{\displaystyle H}{|}}{C}}-H$$

3-methylpent-2-ene has a number of different stereoisomers.

6.1   Define the term stereoisomer.

(1 mark)

6.2   Draw two stereoisomers of 3-methylpent-2-ene.

(2 marks)

6.3   Name the two stereoisomers you have drawn in **6.2**.

(2 marks)

1. Alkanes and Petroleum

Petroleum is just a fancy word for crude oil — the sticky black stuff they get out of the ground with oil wells. It's a mixture that is mostly made up of alkanes. They range from small alkanes, like pentane, to massive alkanes with more than 50 carbons.

Alkanes

You've already met alkanes on page 176, but just to remind you — they're **saturated** hydrocarbons. This means they only contain carbon and hydrogen atoms, and each of their carbon atoms forms four single bonds (the most they can make).

Fractional distillation

Crude oil isn't very useful as it is, but you can separate it out into more useful bits (or fractions) by **fractional distillation**. Here's how fractional distillation works — don't try this at home.

- First, the crude oil is vaporised at about 350 °C.

- The vaporised crude oil goes into the bottom of the fractionating column and rises up through the trays.

- The largest hydrocarbons don't vaporise at all, because their boiling points are too high — they just run to the bottom and form a gooey residue.

- As the crude oil vapour goes up the fractionating column, it gets cooler, creating a temperature gradient.

- Because boiling points of alkanes increase as the molecules get bigger, each fraction condenses at a different temperature. The fractions are drawn off at different levels in the column.

- The hydrocarbons with the lowest boiling points don't condense. They're drawn off as gases at the top of the column.

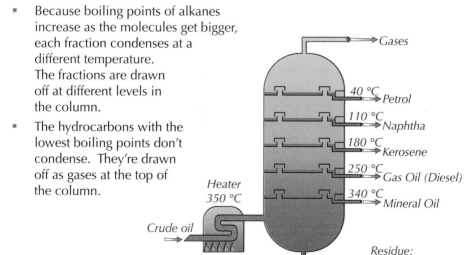

Figure 1: A fractionating column.

Learning Objectives:

- Know that alkanes are saturated hydrocarbons.

- Know that petroleum is a mixture consisting mainly of alkane hydrocarbons that can be separated by fractional distillation.

- Be able to explain the economic reasons for cracking alkanes.

- Know that cracking involves breaking C–C bonds in alkanes.

- Know that thermal cracking takes place at high pressure and high temperature and produces a high percentage of alkenes.

- Know that catalytic cracking takes place at a slight pressure, high temperature and in the presence of a zeolite catalyst and is used mainly to produce motor fuels and aromatic hydrocarbons.

Specification Reference 3.3.2.1, 3.3.2.2

Tip: You might do fractional distillation in the lab, but if you do you'll use a safer crude oil substitute instead. This could involve using high temperatures, so remember to carry out a risk assessment first.

Uses of crude oil fractions

Fraction	Carbon Chain	Uses
Gases	$C_1 - C_4$	Liquefied Petroleum Gas (LPG), camping gas
Petrol (gasoline)	$C_5 - C_{12}$	petrol
Naphtha	$C_7 - C_{14}$	processed to make petrochemicals
Kerosene (paraffin)	$C_{11} - C_{15}$	jet fuel, petrochemicals, central heating fuel
Gas oil (diesel)	$C_{15} - C_{19}$	diesel fuel, central heating fuel
Mineral Oil (lubricating)	$C_{20} - C_{30}$	lubricating oil
Fuel Oil	$C_{30} - C_{40}$	ships, power stations,
Wax, grease	$C_{40} - C_{50}$	candles, lubrication
Bitumen	C_{50+}	roofing, road surfacing

Figure 2: Fractions produced from fractional distillation of crude oil. The fractions are arranged in order of boiling point, with higher boiling points towards the left.

Figure 3: A table showing the products of fractional distillation of crude oil and their uses.

Cracking hydrocarbons

Most people want loads of light fractions, like petrol and naphtha. They don't want so much of the heavier stuff like bitumen though. Stuff that's in high demand is much more valuable than the stuff that isn't.

To meet this demand, the less popular heavier fractions are cracked. **Cracking** is breaking long-chain alkanes into smaller hydrocarbons (which can include alkenes). It involves breaking the C–C bonds.

Example

Decane could be cracked into smaller hydrocarbons like this:

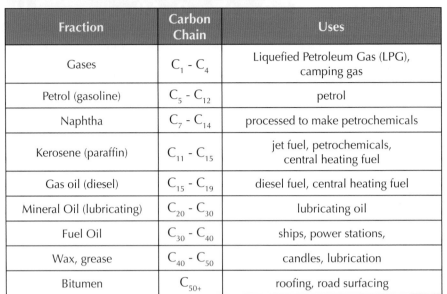

But, because the bond breaking in cracking is random, this isn't the only way that decane could be cracked — it could be cracked to produce different short chain hydrocarbons. For example...

Types of cracking

There are two types of cracking you need to know about — thermal cracking and catalytic cracking.

Thermal cracking

It takes place at high temperature (up to 1000 °C) and high pressure (up to 70 atm). It produces a lot of alkenes. These alkenes are used to make heaps of valuable products, like polymers. A good example is poly(ethene), which is made from ethene (have a look at pages 221-223 for more on polymers).

Catalytic cracking

Catalytic cracking uses something called a zeolite catalyst (hydrated aluminosilicate), at a slight pressure and high temperature (about 500 °C). This mostly produces aromatic hydrocarbons and the alkanes needed to produce motor fuels.

Using a catalyst cuts costs, because the reaction can be done at a low pressure and a lower temperature. The catalyst also speeds up the rate of reaction, saving time (and time is money).

Tip: Aromatic compounds contain substituted benzene rings. Benzene rings look like this:

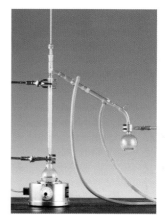

benzene

Practice Questions — Fact Recall

Q1 What is petroleum?

Q2 Why are alkanes described as saturated hydrocarbons?

Q3 Fractional distillation separates hydrocarbons.
What property are they separated by?

Q4 Explain why some fractions are drawn off higher up the fractional distillation column than others.

Q5 What is cracking?

Q6 Why do we crack heavier petroleum fractions?

Q7 Why does using a catalyst for catalytic cracking cut costs?

Figure 4: *Laboratory fractional distillation apparatus.*

- Know that alkanes are used as fuels.
- Know that the combustion of alkanes and other organic compounds can be complete or incomplete.
- Know that the internal combustion engine produces a number of pollutants including NO_x, CO, carbon and unburned hydrocarbons.
- Know that gaseous pollutants from internal combustion engines can be removed using catalytic converters.
- Know that the combustion of hydrocarbons containing sulfur leads to sulfur dioxide that causes air pollution.
- Be able to explain why sulfur dioxide can be removed from flue gases using calcium oxide or calcium carbonate.

Specification Reference 3.3.2.3

2. Alkanes as Fuels

Alkanes are found in fossil fuels. Alkanes make great fuels — burning just a small amount of methane releases a humongous amount of energy. They're burnt in power stations, central heating systems and, of course, to power car engines. Unfortunately, burning them can release pollutants.

Combustion

Complete combustion

If you burn (oxidise) alkanes (and other hydrocarbons) with plenty of oxygen, you get only carbon dioxide and water. This is **complete combustion**.

┌─ Example ──────────────────────────────

If you burn a molecule of propane in plenty of oxygen, you get three molecules of carbon dioxide and four water molecules. The equation for this is shown below.

$$C_3H_{8(g)} + 5O_{2(g)} \rightarrow 3CO_{2(g)} + 4H_2O_{(g)}$$

Incomplete combustion

If there's not enough oxygen around when you burn a hydrocarbon, you get **incomplete combustion** happening instead. This produces particulate carbon (soot) and carbon monoxide gas instead of, or as well as, carbon dioxide.

┌─ Example ──────────────────────────────

If you burn propane in a limited supply of oxygen you'll produce carbon monoxide and carbon as well as carbon dioxide and water.

$$C_3H_{8(g)} + 3\frac{1}{2}O_{2(g)} \rightarrow 3CO_{(g)} + 4H_2O_{(g)}$$

This is bad news because carbon monoxide gas is poisonous. Carbon monoxide molecules bind to the same sites on haemoglobin molecules in red blood cells as oxygen molecules. So oxygen can't be carried around the body. Luckily, carbon monoxide can be removed from exhaust gases by catalytic converters on cars.

Soot is also thought to cause breathing problems, and it can build up in engines, meaning they don't work properly.

Pollution from burning fuels

Unburnt hydrocarbons and oxides of nitrogen

Nitrogen oxides are a series of toxic and poisonous molecules which have the general formula NO_x. Nitrogen monoxide is produced when the high pressure and temperature in a car engine cause the nitrogen and oxygen atoms from the air to react together. Nitrogen monoxide can react further to produce nitrogen dioxide — the equations for these reactions are shown below.

$$N_{2(g)} + O_{2(g)} \rightarrow 2NO_{(g)}$$

$$2NO_{(g)} + O_{2(g)} \rightarrow 2NO_{2(g)}$$

Engines don't burn all the fuel molecules. Some of these come out as unburnt hydrocarbons. These hydrocarbons react with nitrogen oxides in the presence of sunlight to form ground-level ozone (O_3), which is a major component of smog. Ground-level ozone irritates people's eyes, aggravates respiratory problems and even causes lung damage (ozone isn't nice stuff, unless it is high up in the atmosphere as part of the ozone layer).

The three main pollutants from vehicle exhausts are nitrogen oxides, unburnt hydrocarbons and carbon monoxide. Catalytic converters on cars remove these pollutants from the exhaust by the following reactions:

$$C_3H_{8(g)} + 5O_{2(g)} \rightarrow 3CO_{2(g)} + 4H_2O_{(g)}$$

This equation is just an equation for the complete combustion of a hydrocarbon.

$$2NO_{(g)} \rightarrow N_{2(g)} + O_{2(g)}$$

$$2NO_{(g)} + 2CO_{(g)} \rightarrow N_{2(g)} + 2CO_{2(g)}$$

Tip: Catalytic converters are designed to have very large surface areas to make sure that the harmful pollutants have the best chance of being turned into less harmful chemicals.

Sulfur dioxide

Some fossil fuels contain sulfur. When they are burnt in, for example, car engines and power stations, the sulfur reacts to form sulfur dioxide gas (SO_2). If sulfur dioxide gets into the atmosphere, it dissolves in the moisture and is converted into sulfuric acid. This is what causes acid rain. The same process occurs when nitrogen dioxide escapes into the atmosphere — nitric acid is produced. Acid rain destroys trees and vegetation, as well as corroding buildings and statues and killing fish in lakes.

Fortunately, sulfur dioxide can be removed from power station flue gases before it gets into the atmosphere — you've already come across this process on page 156. Powdered calcium carbonate (limestone) or calcium oxide is mixed with water to make an alkaline slurry. When the flue gases mix with the alkaline slurry, the acidic sulfur dioxide gas reacts with the calcium compounds to form a harmless salt (calcium sulfate).

$$CaO_{(s)} + SO_{2(g)} \rightarrow CaSO_{3(s)}$$

Global warming

Burning fossil fuels produces carbon dioxide. Carbon dioxide is a greenhouse gas. Greenhouse gases in our atmosphere are very good at absorbing infrared energy (heat). They emit some of the energy they absorb back towards the Earth, keeping it warm. This is called the greenhouse effect. Most scientists agree that by increasing the amount of carbon dioxide in our atmosphere, we are making the Earth warmer. This process is known as global warming.

Figure 2: Trees killed by acid rain.

Tip: There's more about global warming and the greenhouse effect on page 250.

Practice Questions — Application

Q1 Write the equation for the complete combustion of pentane (C_5H_{12}).

Q2 Write the equation for the incomplete combustion of pentane (C_5H_{12}) to produce carbon monoxide and water only.

Practice Questions — Fact Recall

Q1 Give three pollutants produced by vehicle exhausts.

Q2 What can be used to remove pollutants from vehicle exhausts?

Q3 Explain how acid rain is caused by burning fossil fuels containing sulfur.

Q4 Describe one method for removing sulfur dioxide from flue gases.

Exam Tip
You could be asked to write equations for the complete or incomplete combustion of other alkanes. Make sure you get lots of practice writing out different equations.

3. Synthesis of Chloroalkanes

Learning Objectives:

- Know that the unpaired electron in a free radical is represented by a dot.

- Know the reaction of methane with chlorine and be able to explain this reaction as a free radical substitution mechanism involving initiation, propagation and termination steps.

- Be able to write balanced equations for the steps in a free radical mechanism.

- Know that ozone is beneficial because it absorbs UV radiation.

- Know that chlorine atoms are formed in the upper atmosphere when UV radiation causes CCl bonds in chlorofluorocarbons (CFCs) to break.

- Understand that chlorine atoms catalyse the decomposition of ozone and contribute to the hole in the ozone layer.

- Be able to use equations to explain how chlorine atoms catalyse decomposition of ozone.

- Appreciate that results of research by different groups in the scientific community provided evidence for legislation to ban the use of CFCs as solvents and refrigerants.

- Know that chemists have now developed chlorine-free alternatives to CFCs.

Specification Reference 3.3.1.2, 3.3.2.4, 3.3.3.3

Chloroalkanes are alkanes with one or more hydrogen atoms substituted by a chlorine atom. They are pretty important to chemists, so it's important to understand how they're made. That's where the synthesis part comes in — a synthesis is just a step-wise method detailing how to create a chemical.

Photochemical reactions

Halogens react with alkanes in photochemical reactions to form halogenoalkanes (see page 203 for more on halogenoalkanes).

Photochemical reactions are reactions started by ultraviolet (UV) light. A hydrogen atom is substituted (replaced) by chlorine or bromine. This is a **free radical** substitution reaction. A free radical is a particle with an unpaired electron. Free radicals form when a covalent bond splits equally, giving one electron to each species. The unpaired electron makes them very reactive. You can show something's a free radical in a mechanism by putting a dot next to it, like this: $Cl\bullet$ or $\bullet CH_3$. The dot represents the unpaired electron.

Synthesis of chloromethane

A mixture of methane and chlorine will not react on its own but when exposed to UV light it reacts with a bit of a bang to form chloromethane. The overall equation for this reaction is shown below.

$$CH_4 + Cl_2 \xrightarrow{UV} CH_3Cl + HCl$$

A reaction mechanism shows each step in the synthesis of a chemical. The reaction mechanism for the synthesis of chloromethane by a photochemical reaction has three stages — initiation, propagation and termination.

Initiation

In the initiation step, free radicals are produced. Sunlight provides enough energy to break some of the Cl–Cl bonds — this is photodissociation.

$$Cl_2 \xrightarrow{UV} 2Cl\bullet$$

The bond splits equally and each atom gets to keep one electron. The atom becomes a highly reactive free radical, $Cl\bullet$, because of its unpaired electron.

Propagation

During propagation, free radicals are used up and created in a chain reaction. First, $Cl\bullet$ attacks a methane molecule:

$$Cl\bullet + CH_4 \rightarrow \bullet CH_3 + HCl$$

The new methyl free radical, $CH_3\bullet$, can then attack another Cl_2 molecule:

$$\bullet CH_3 + Cl_2 \rightarrow CH_3Cl + Cl\bullet$$

The new $Cl\bullet$ can attack another CH_4 molecule, and so on, until all the Cl_2 or CH_4 molecules are used up.

Substitutions

If the chlorine's in excess, the hydrogen atoms on methane will eventually be replaced by chlorine atoms. This means you'll get dichloromethane CH_2Cl_2, trichloromethane $CHCl_3$, and tetrachloromethane CCl_4.

$$CH_4 + Cl_2 \rightarrow CH_3Cl + HCl$$

$$CH_3Cl + Cl_2 \rightarrow CH_2Cl_2 + HCl$$

$$CH_2Cl_2 + Cl_2 \rightarrow CHCl_3 + HCl$$

$$CHCl_3 + Cl_2 \rightarrow CCl_4 + HCl$$

But if the methane's in excess, then the chlorine will be used up quickly and the product will mostly be chloromethane.

$$CH_4 + Cl_2 \rightarrow CH_3Cl + HCl$$

Termination

In the termination step, free radicals are mopped up. If two free radicals join together, they make a stable molecule — the two unpaired electrons form a covalent bond. This terminates the chain reaction. Here are three possible termination reactions from the synthesis of chloromethane:

$$\bullet CH_3 + Cl\bullet \rightarrow CH_3Cl$$

$$\bullet CH_3 + CH_3\bullet \rightarrow C_2H_6$$

$$Cl\bullet + Cl\bullet \rightarrow Cl_2$$

Tip: Some of the products formed in the termination step will be trace impurities in the final sample.

Chlorofluorocarbons

Chlorofluorocarbons (CFCs) are halogenoalkane molecules where all of the hydrogen atoms have been replaced by chlorine and fluorine atoms.

Exam Tip
When you're writing radical equations you need to make sure that there's the same number of radicals on each side of the equation or that two radicals are combining to create a non-radical.

┌─ **Examples** ───────────────────────

trichlorofluoromethane   *chlorotrifluoromethane*

Tip: There's more on halogenoalkanes later on (see page 203).

Chlorofluorocarbons and the ozone layer

Ozone (O_3) in the upper atmosphere acts as a chemical sunscreen. It absorbs a lot of ultraviolet radiation from the Sun, stopping it from reaching us. Ultraviolet radiation can cause sunburn or even skin cancer. Ozone's formed naturally when an oxygen molecule is broken down into two free radicals by ultraviolet radiation:

$$O_2 + h\nu \rightarrow O\bullet + O\bullet$$

The free radicals attack other oxygen molecules forming ozone:

$$O_2 + O\bullet \rightarrow O_3$$

Tip: The $h\nu$ in the first equation is the notation for a quantum of UV radiation — a photon. It just means that the reaction needs to be initiated by electromagnetic radiation.

You've probably heard of how the ozone layer's being destroyed by CFCs, right. Well, here's what's happening. Chlorine free radicals, Cl•, are formed in the upper atmosphere when the C–Cl bonds in CFCs are broken down by ultraviolet radiation, like this:

$$CCl_3F_{(g)} \xrightarrow{UV} \bullet CCl_2F_{(g)} + Cl\bullet_{(g)}$$

These free radicals are **catalysts**. They react with ozone to form an **intermediate** (ClO•), and an oxygen molecule.

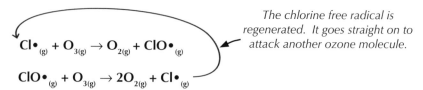

The chlorine free radical is regenerated. It goes straight on to attack another ozone molecule.

$$Cl\bullet_{(g)} + O_{3(g)} \rightarrow O_{2(g)} + ClO\bullet_{(g)}$$

$$ClO\bullet_{(g)} + O_{3(g)} \rightarrow 2O_{2(g)} + Cl\bullet_{(g)}$$

Because the Cl• free radical is regenerated, it only takes one little chlorine free radical to destroy loads of ozone molecules. So, the overall reaction is...

$$2O_{3(g)} \rightarrow 3O_{2(g)}$$

... and Cl• is the catalyst.

Environmental problems of CFCs

CFCs are pretty unreactive, non-flammable and non-toxic. They used to be used in fire extinguishers, as propellants in aerosols and as the coolant gas in fridges. They were also added to foam plastics to make insulation and packaging materials.

In the 1970s, research by several different scientific groups demonstrated that CFCs were causing damage to the ozone layer. The advantages of CFCs couldn't outweigh the environmental problems they were causing, so they were banned.

Chemists have developed safer alternatives to CFCs which contain no chlorine. HCFCs (hydrochlorofluorocarbons) and HFCs (hydrofluorocarbons) are less dangerous than CFCs, so they're being used as temporary alternatives until safer products are developed. Most aerosols now have been replaced by pump spray systems, or use nitrogen as the propellant. Many industrial fridges use ammonia or hydrocarbons as the coolant gas and carbon dioxide is used to make foamed polymers.

Practice Questions — Fact Recall

Q1 What is a photochemical reaction?

Q2 Write an equation for the initiation step of the synthesis of chloromethane by a photochemical reaction.

Q3 Describe what takes place in the termination step of a free radical substitution mechanism.

Q4 Why is ozone in the upper atmosphere beneficial?

Q5 Describe how chlorine free radicals are formed in the upper atmosphere.

Q6 Write two equations to show how chlorine atoms catalyse the decomposition of ozone.

Q7 Explain why CFCs were banned from use as solvents and refrigerants.

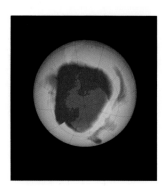

Figure 1: *Satellite image of the ozone layer over Antarctica in 2013. The 'hole' is shown by the blue area.*

4. Halogenoalkanes

Halogenoalkanes pop up a lot in chemistry so it's important that you know exactly what they are and how they react.

Learning Objective:

- Explain that halogenoalkanes contain polar bonds.

Specification Reference 3.3.3.1

What are halogenoalkanes?

A **halogenoalkane** is an alkane with at least one halogen atom in place of a hydrogen atom.

Examples

dichloromethane   *2-iodopropane*   *2-bromo-1,1-dichloroethane*

Tip: There's more about how to name halogenoalkanes on page 176.

Polarity of halogenoalkanes

Halogens are generally much more electronegative than carbon. So, most carbon-halogen bonds are **polar**.

Example

$$-\overset{|}{\underset{|}{C}}{}^{\delta+}\!-\!Br^{\delta-}$$

The bromine atom is more electronegative than the carbon atom and so withdraws electron density from the carbon atom. This leaves the carbon atom with a partial positive charge and the bromine atom with a partial negative charge.

Tip: Don't worry if you see halogenoalkanes called haloalkanes. It's a government conspiracy to confuse you.

The δ+ carbon doesn't have enough electrons. This means it can be attacked by a **nucleophile**. A nucleophile's an electron-pair donor. It donates an electron pair to somewhere without enough electrons.

Examples

Here are some examples of nucleophiles that will react with halogenoalkanes.

:C̄N   :NH$_3$:ŌH

cyanide ion   *ammonia*   *hydroxide ion*

The pairs of dots represent lone pairs of electrons.

Tip: Nucleophiles are often negative ions, and because they form by gaining electrons, they have extra electrons that they can donate. They don't <u>have</u> to be ions though. For example, NH$_3$ is a nucleophile — it's got a non-bonding pair of electrons that it can donate.

There are several examples of reactions where nucleophiles react with halogenoalkanes coming up on the next few pages.

Practice Questions — Fact Recall

Q1 What is a halogenoalkane?

Q2 Explain why halogen-carbon bonds are polar.

Q3 What is a nucleophile?

Q4 Give two examples of nucleophiles that will react with halogenoalkanes.

Q5 What does a pair of dots represent on a nucleophile?

Learning Objectives:

- Understand that halogenoalkanes undergo nucleophilic substitution reactions with the nucleophiles OH^-, CN^- and NH_3.
- Be able to outline the nucleophilic substitution mechanisms of the reactions of halogenalkanes with the nucleophiles OH^-, CN^- and NH_3.
- Be able to explain why the carbon–halogen bond enthalpy influences the rate of reaction.

Specification Reference 3.3.3.1

5. Nucleophilic Substitution

Nucleophilic substitution is a reaction where one functional group is substituted for another. You need to know about the nucleophilic substitution reactions of halogenoalkane molecules.

Nucleophilic substitution reactions

As you saw on page 184, **mechanisms** are diagrams that show how a reaction works. They show how the bonds in molecules are made and broken, how the electrons are transferred and how you get from the reactants to the products.

You need to know the mechanism for the **nucleophilic substitution** of halogenoalkanes. In a nucleophilic substitution reaction, a nucleophile attacks a polar molecule, kicks out a functional group and settles itself down in its place. The general equation for the nucleophilic substitution of a halogenoalkane is:

$$CH_3CH_2X + Nu^- \rightarrow CH_3CH_2Nu + X^-$$

And here's how it all works:

The X stands for one of the halogens (F, Cl, Br or I).

The carbon-halogen bond is polar, so there are δ+ and δ– signs drawn on the molecule to represent the charges.

The Nu⁻ stands for a nucleophile.

The lone pair of electrons on the nucleophile attacks the slightly positive charge on the carbon — this is shown by a black curly arrow. In mechanisms, curly arrows always show the movement of an electron pair. The lone pair of electrons creates a new bond between the nucleophile and the carbon.

The carbon can only be bonded to four other atoms so the addition of the nucleophile breaks the bond between the carbon and the halogen — this is shown by another curly arrow. The pair of electrons from the carbon-halogen bond are taken by the halogen and become a lone pair.

Reaction of halogenoalkanes with OH⁻

Halogenoalkanes will react with hydroxides to produce alcohols.

--- Example ---

Bromoethane can be changed to ethanol in a nucleophilic substitution reaction. You have to use warm aqueous sodium or potassium hydroxide or it won't work.

In the equation for the reaction, R represents an alkyl group. X stands for one of the halogens (F, Cl, Br or I). As it's a nucleophilic substitution reaction, the nucleophile ($^-$OH) kicks out the halogen (X) from the R–X molecule and takes its place. So the overall reaction can just be written as:

$$R–X + {}^-OH \rightarrow ROH + X^-$$

Here's how it happens:

1. The C–Br bond is polar. The $C^{\delta+}$ attracts a lone pair of electrons from the OH$^-$ ion.

3. A new bond forms between the C and the OH$^-$ ion, making an alcohol...

4. ... and the C–Br bond breaks. Both the electrons from the bond are taken by the Br.

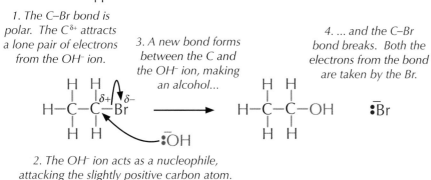

2. The OH$^-$ ion acts as a nucleophile, attacking the slightly positive carbon atom.

Tip: When you're drawing mechanisms make sure the charges balance. That way you'll know if you've managed to lose or gain electrons along the way. In this example, the left hand side of the equation has one negative charge on the hydroxide nucleophile and the right hand side has one negative charge from a bromide ion — so it's balanced.

Making nitriles from halogenoalkanes

Nitriles have CN groups. The carbon atom and nitrogen atom are held together with a triple bond.

┌─ Examples ─────────────

Nitriles are derived from hydrogen cyanide:

$$H–C\equiv N$$

hydrogen cyanide

Here is ethanenitrile:

$$H–\overset{\displaystyle H}{\underset{\displaystyle H}{C}}–C\equiv N$$

ethanenitrile

Tip: Hydrogen cyanide could also be called methanenitrile. Hydrogen cyanide is the molecule's old name and methane nitrile is its name assigned by the IUPAC naming conventions. Either name is correct.

If you warm a halogenoalkane with ethanolic potassium cyanide (that's just potassium cyanide dissolved in ethanol), you get a nitrile. It's yet another nucleophilic substitution reaction — the cyanide ion, CN$^-$, is the nucleophile.

┌─ Example ─────────────

Reacting bromoethane with potassium cyanide under reflux will produce propanenitrile and potassium bromide.

$$CH_3CH_2Br + KCN \rightarrow CH_3CH_2CN + KBr$$

The ethanolic potassium cyanide dissociates to form a K$^+$ ion and a CN$^-$ ion. It's the CN$^-$ ion that acts as the nucleophile in the reaction.

$$KCN \rightarrow K^+ + CN^-$$

The reaction mechanism follows the same pattern as above — the lone pair of electrons on the CN$^-$ ion attacks the $\delta+$ carbon, the C–Br bond breaks and the bromine leaves.

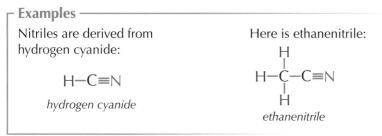

Tip: When you heat a liquid mixture, eventually it will start to boil and some of the mixture will be lost as vapour. When you heat under reflux, you use equipment that stops the vapour escaping from the reaction mixture. There's more about heating under reflux on page 236.

You have to use ethanol as a solvent here instead of water. If you used water, it could act as a competing nucleophile and you'd get some alcohol product.

Making amines from halogenoalkanes

An amine has the structure R_3N. The R groups can be hydrogens or another group. In amines, the nitrogen always has a lone pair (shown as a pair of dots next to the nitrogen atom).

Tip: Amines are derivatives of the ammonia molecule, shown below:

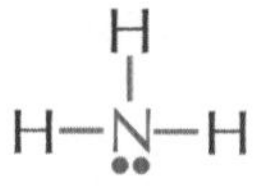

H
|
H–N–H
••

Examples

The molecules below are both amines.

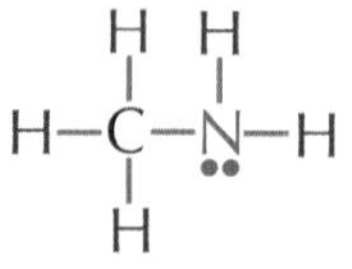

$$\begin{array}{c}
H \quad H \\
| \quad\quad | \\
H-C-N-H \\
| \quad\quad •• \\
H
\end{array}$$
methylamine

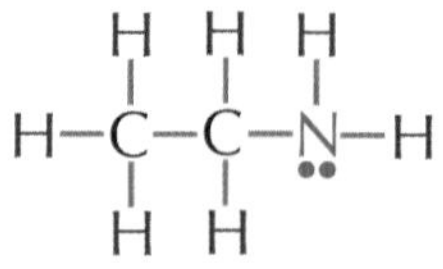

$$\begin{array}{c}
H \quad H \quad H \\
| \quad\; | \quad\; | \\
H-C-C-N-H \\
| \quad\; | \quad\; •• \\
H \quad H
\end{array}$$
ethylamine

If you warm a halogenoalkane with excess ethanolic ammonia (ammonia dissolved in ethanol) in a sealed tube, the ammonia swaps places with the halogen to form an amine — yes, it's another one of those nucleophilic substitution reactions.

Example

In this reaction bromoethane is reacting with ammonia to form ethylamine.

- The first step is the same as in the mechanism on the previous page, except this time the nucleophile is NH_3. The nitrogen atom donates its lone pair of electrons to the carbon atom to create a bond.
- The nitrogen atom was neutral to begin with, so this means the nitrogen is left with a positive charge.

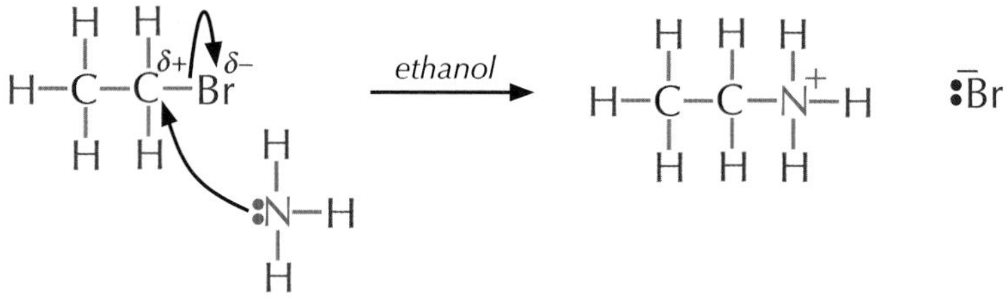

Exam Tip
When you're drawing amines in the exam, it's a good idea to draw the lone pair of electrons in so that you don't forget that they're there. And if the amine's part of a mechanism you'll <u>have</u> to draw them in to get all the marks.

- In the second step, a second ammonia molecule removes a hydrogen from the NH_3 group to form an ammonium ion (NH_4^+) and an amine.
- The ammonia molecule donates its lone pair of electrons to the hydrogen to form a bond, so the nitrogen atom in the ammonium ion now has a positive charge, and the amine has no charge.

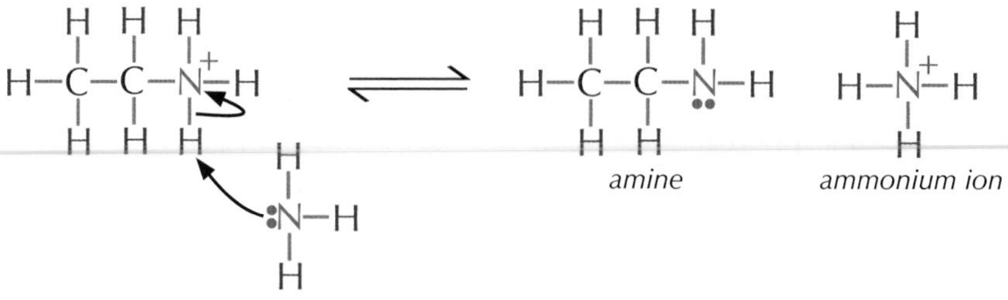

Exam Tip
This example shows ammonia reacting with bromoethane, but in the exam you could be given a question that involves a different halogenoalkane. Don't panic though — the mechanism is exactly the same.

amine   *ammonium ion*

The ammonium ion formed can react with the bromide ion to form ammonium bromide. Ammonium bromide is held together by an ionic bond (see page 69).

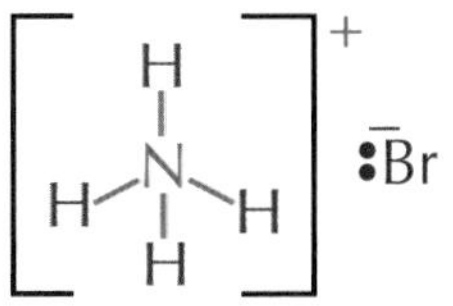

So the overall reaction is:

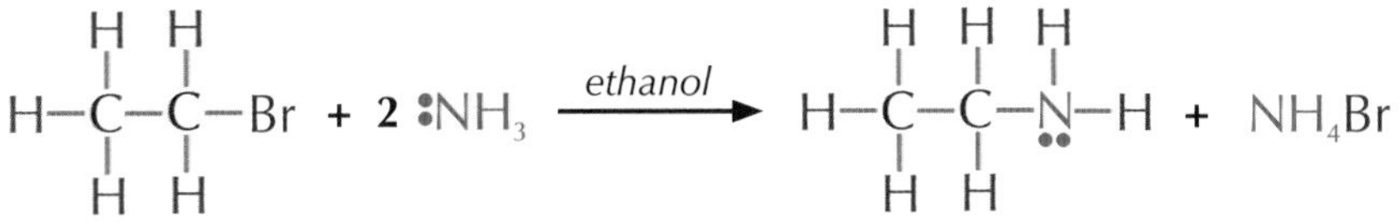

$$H-\overset{\overset{\displaystyle H}{|}}{\underset{\underset{\displaystyle H}{|}}{C}}-\overset{\overset{\displaystyle H}{|}}{\underset{\underset{\displaystyle H}{|}}{C}}-Br \ + \ 2\ \text{:}NH_3 \xrightarrow{\text{ethanol}} H-\overset{\overset{\displaystyle H}{|}}{\underset{\underset{\displaystyle H}{|}}{C}}-\overset{\overset{\displaystyle H}{|}}{\underset{\underset{\displaystyle H}{|}}{C}}-\overset{\overset{\displaystyle H}{|}}{\underset{\underset{\displaystyle \cdot\cdot}{}}{N}}-H \ + \ NH_4Br$$

The amine group in the product still has a lone pair of electrons. This means that it can also act as a nucleophile — so it may react with halogenoalkane molecules itself, giving a mixture of products.

Exam Tip
You could be asked for the mechanism for this reaction, or for the overall reaction equation, so make sure that you know them both.

Reactivity of halogenoalkanes

The carbon-halogen bond strength (or enthalpy) decides reactivity. For a reaction to occur the carbon-halogen bond needs to break. The C–F bond is the strongest — it has the highest bond enthalpy. So fluoroalkanes undergo nucleophilic substitution reactions more slowly than other halogenoalkanes. The C–I bond has the lowest bond enthalpy, so it's easier to break. This means that iodoalkanes are substituted more quickly.

bond	bond enthalpy kJ mol^{-1}
C–F	467
C–Cl	346
C–Br	290
C–I	228

Faster substitution as bond enthalpy decreases (the bonds are getting weaker).

Figure 1: Carbon-halogen bond enthalpies.

Tip: If you've got a molecule with more than one halogen in it, the halogen with the lowest bond enthalpy will get replaced first.

Summary of nucleophilic substitution

- Nucleophilic substitution reactions can occur between a halogenoalkane and a nucleophile.
- The nucleophile attacks the δ+ carbon atom, which breaks the carbon-halogen bond.
- One new bond is formed (between the nucleophile and the δ+ carbon atom) and one bond is broken (the carbon-halogen bond).
- When you're drawing mechanisms for nucleophilic substitution reactions, it's important to draw the curly arrows coming from the electrons and going to an atom. The electrons can come from either a bond or from a lone pair on an atom or ion.

Exam Tip
In the exam you could
be asked to draw
a mechanism for a
nucleophilic substitution
reaction you haven't
seen before. You
should practise drawing
mechanisms for lots of
different reactions before
the exam so that you get
into the swing of it.

- Make sure the charges are balanced at every stage of a mechanism
  — if you start with a negative charge you should end up with one too.
- And finally, it doesn't matter which nucleophile you use ($^-$CN, $^-$OH or
  NH_3), the mechanism for nucleophilic substitution of a halogenoalkane is
  always the same.

Practice Questions — Application

Q1 Draw the mechanism for the reaction of 1-chlorobutane with
warm ethanolic potassium cyanide. The molecule 1-chlorobutane
is shown below.

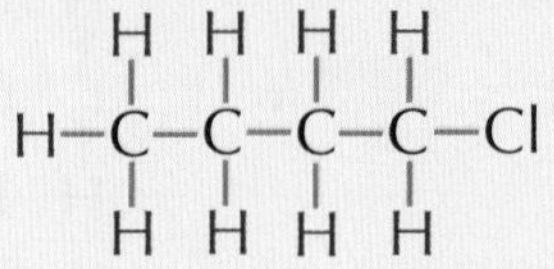

$$H-\overset{\overset{\displaystyle H}{|}}{\underset{\underset{\displaystyle H}{|}}{C}}-\overset{\overset{\displaystyle H}{|}}{\underset{\underset{\displaystyle H}{|}}{C}}-\overset{\overset{\displaystyle H}{|}}{\underset{\underset{\displaystyle H}{|}}{C}}-\overset{\overset{\displaystyle H}{|}}{\underset{\underset{\displaystyle H}{|}}{C}}-Cl$$

Q2 Which of the following reactions would be quickest?
Explain your answer.

A: $CH_3CH_2Cl + H_2O \rightarrow CH_3CH_2OH + HCl$

B: $CH_3CH_2Br + H_2O \rightarrow CH_3CH_2OH + HBr$

C: $CH_3CH_2I + H_2O \rightarrow CH_3CH_2OH + HI$

Q3 Draw the mechanism for the reaction of iodopropane with ammonia.
The reaction is done in a sealed tube in warm ethanol.
The reactants are shown below.

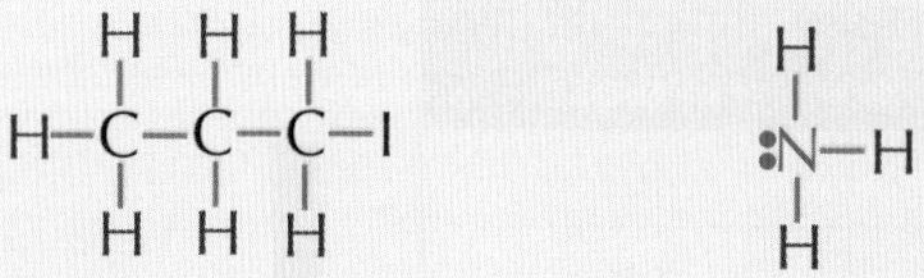

$$H-\overset{\overset{\displaystyle H}{|}}{\underset{\underset{\displaystyle H}{|}}{C}}-\overset{\overset{\displaystyle H}{|}}{\underset{\underset{\displaystyle H}{|}}{C}}-\overset{\overset{\displaystyle H}{|}}{\underset{\underset{\displaystyle H}{|}}{C}}-I \qquad \overset{\overset{\displaystyle H}{|}}{\underset{\underset{\displaystyle H}{|}}{:N}}-H$$

Q4 Draw the mechanism for the hydrolysis of chloroethane by warm
aqueous sodium hydroxide.

Practice Questions — Fact Recall

Q1 What happens in a nucleophilic substitution reaction?

Q2 What chemical would you react with bromoethane to get ethanol?

Q3 Name the nucleophile that is present when bromoethane reacts with
ethanolic potassium cyanide under reflux.

Q4 Under what reaction conditions do you react bromoethane with
ammonia to form ethylamine?

Q5 Explain why fluoroalkanes are substituted more slowly than other
halogenoalkanes.

6. Elimination Reactions

In an elimination reaction, a small group of atoms breaks away from a larger molecule. This small group is not replaced by anything else (whereas it would be in a substitution reaction).

Halogen elimination from a halogenoalkane

If you warm a halogenoalkane with hydroxide ions dissolved in ethanol instead of water, an elimination reaction happens and you end up with an alkene.

Example

Reacting 2-bromopropane with potassium hydroxide dissolved in warm ethanol under **reflux** produces an elimination reaction and forms propene, water and potassium bromide. Here's the equation for this reaction.

$$CH_3CHBrCH_3 + KOH \rightarrow CH_2CHCH_3 + H_2O + KBr$$

In the reaction, H and Br are eliminated from neighbouring carbon atoms in $CH_3CHBrCH_3$ to leave CH_2CHCH_3. Here's how the reaction works:

1. OH⁻ acts as a base and takes a proton, H⁺, from the carbon on the left (making water).

2. The left carbon now has a spare pair of electrons, so it forms a double bond with the middle carbon.

3. To form the double bond, the middle carbon has to let go of the Br, which drops off as a Br⁻ ion.

Nucleophilic substitution vs elimination

You can influence which type of reaction will happen most by changing the conditions. By reacting a halogenoalkane with water under reflux, the molecule will predominantly undergo nucleophilic substitution to form an alcohol. You'll still get a bit of elimination to form an alkene but not a lot.

Example

Reacting bromoethane with water under reflux will produce ethanol.

This is because under aqueous conditions, the OH⁻ acts as a nucleophile — it donates an electron pair to the δ+ carbon atom.

Here the OH⁻ nucleophile is attacking the δ+ carbon atom.

By reacting a halogenoalkane with ethanol under reflux, the molecule will predominantly undergo elimination to form an alkene.

Example

Reacting bromoethane with ethanol under reflux will produce ethene.

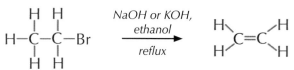

This is because the OH⁻ acts as a base — it removes a hydrogen atom from the halogenoalkane.

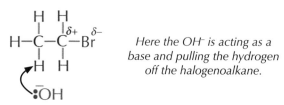

Here the OH⁻ is acting as a base and pulling the hydrogen off the halogenoalkane.

Figure 1: *Two students carrying out an organic reaction under reflux, to stop the vapour escaping from the reaction mixture.*

If you use a mixture of water and ethanol as the solvent, both reactions will happen and you'll get a mixture of the two products.

Practice Question — Application

Q1 Draw the mechanism for the main reaction of 1-bromopropane with ethanol under reflux. A molecule of 1-bromopropane is shown below.

$$\text{H}-\overset{\overset{\displaystyle H}{|}}{\underset{\underset{\displaystyle H}{|}}{C}}-\overset{\overset{\displaystyle H}{|}}{\underset{\underset{\displaystyle H}{|}}{C}}-\overset{\overset{\displaystyle H}{|}}{\underset{\underset{\displaystyle H}{|}}{C}}-\text{Br}$$

Practice Questions — Fact Recall

Q1 Briefly describe an elimination reaction.

Q2 a) Reacting bromoethane with water under reflux will produce mainly ethanol. What type of reagent does the ⁻OH act as in this reaction?

  b) Name the type of reaction that is occurring.

Q3 a) Reacting bromoethane with ethanol under reflux will produce mainly ethene. What type of reagent does the ⁻OH act as in this reaction?

  b) Name the type of reaction that is occurring.

Section Summary

Make sure you know...

- That alkanes are saturated hydrocarbons.
- That petroleum is a mixture, mostly consisting of alkanes.
- How petroleum can be separated by fractional distillation.
- That cracking breaks long-chain alkanes into smaller hydrocarbons.
- That cracking is a valuable process as smaller hydrocarbons are in much higher demand than long-chain hydrocarbons.
- The conditions needed for thermal cracking and catalytic cracking and what the products are.
- That alkanes are used as fuels.
- What complete combustion and incomplete combustion are.
- What pollutants are produced by internal combustion engines and how they are removed from exhaust gases.
- How air pollution is created.
- How sulfur dioxide can be removed from flue gases.
- That the unpaired electron in a free radical is represented by a dot.
- The reaction mechanism of methane with chlorine as a free radical substitution reaction involving initiation, propagation and termination steps.
- That ozone, which is formed naturally in the upper atmosphere, provides protection from the Sun's UV rays.
- That chlorine atoms are formed in the upper atmosphere when energy from ultraviolet radiation causes C–Cl bonds in chlorofluorocarbons (CFCs) to break.
- How chlorine atoms catalyse the decomposition of ozone and have helped form a hole in the ozone layer.
- That legislation to ban the use of CFCs was supported by chemists, and that alternative chlorine-free compounds have been developed to replace CFCs.
- That halogenoalkanes contain polar bonds and are susceptible to nucleophilic attack
- The mechanism of nucleophilic substitution in primary halogenoalkanes.
- That the carbon–halogen bond enthalpy influences the rate of reaction of reactions where carbon-halogen bonds break.
- That halogenoalkanes can undergo nucleophilic substitution and elimination reactions where the reagent can act as either a nucleophile or a base.
- The mechanisms of concurrent nucleophilic substitution and elimination reactions in halogenoalkanes.

Exam-style Questions

1   Bromoethane reacts with aqueous potassium hydroxide to form ethanol.
Which of the following statements about this reaction is **not** correct?

    A   The OH⁻ ions act as nucleophiles.

    B   Iodoethane will react more quickly than bromoethane in the same reaction.

    C   The reaction is an elimination reaction.

    D   The reaction needs to take place under reflux.

(1 mark)

2   Chloroethane reacts with ethanolic potassium cyanide under reflux.
The following steps describe the mechanism of the reaction.

    1)   A new bond forms between the C and the CN⁻ ion, making a nitrile.
    2)   The C–Cl bond breaks and both the electrons from the bond are taken by the Cl.
    3)   The $C^{\delta+}$ attracts a lone pair of electrons from the CN⁻ ion.
    4)   The CN⁻ ion acts as a nucleophile, attacking the slightly positive carbon atom.

    Which is the correct order of steps?

    A   1, 3, 2, 4

    B   3, 4, 1, 2

    C   3, 2, 4, 1

    D   4, 3, 2, 1

(1 mark)

3   Chlorine and methane react in ultraviolet light to form the halogenoalkane,
chloromethane. This reaction is initiated by the breaking of the Cl-Cl bond.

    3.1   Write two equations to show the propagation steps for this reaction.

(2 marks)

    3.2   Write an equation of a termination reaction showing the formation of chloromethane.

(1 mark)

    3.3   When chlorofluorocarbons enter the upper atmosphere, ultraviolet light breaks
the C-Cl bonds to form chlorine free radicals. Use equations to show how
this leads to the decomposition of ozone, and explain why this is a problem.

(4 marks)

4   Heptane is an alkane which is found in petroleum.

4.1   Fractional distillation can be used to separate out heptane.

Explain how fractional distillation allows the fractions in petroleum to be separated.

(3 marks)

4.2   Petroleum fractions can be burnt to generate energy.

Write an equation for the incomplete combustion of heptane.

(2 marks)

4.3   Explain why the incomplete combustion of heptane can be dangerous.

(3 marks)

4.4   Heptane can be cracked to form smaller chain hydrocarbons.

Explain why it is necessary to crack heptane into smaller chain hydrocarbons.

(1 mark)

4.5   Write an equation for the cracking of heptane into smaller chain hydrocarbons.

(1 mark)

4.6   In industry, a catalyst can be used to crack heptane.
Explain why a catalyst is used.

(2 marks)

5   Ethanol is a simple alcohol that can be used as a fuel, in alcoholic beverages,
as a solvent and also as a starting molecule for many organic synthesis reactions.
Its structure is shown below.

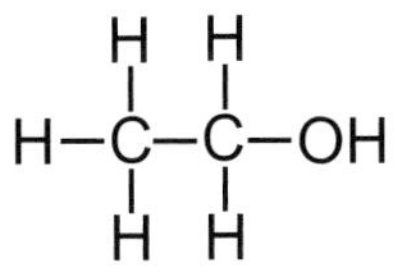

$$
\begin{array}{ccc}
 & H & H \\
 & | & | \\
H - & C - C & - OH \\
 & | & | \\
 & H & H
\end{array}
$$

5.1   Ethanol can be created by a nucleophilic substitution reaction
of bromoethane with aqueous sodium hydroxide.

Write the equation for this reaction and draw out the
mechanism by which it proceeds.

(2 marks)

5.2   Ethanol can also be produced by reaction of iodoethane
with aqueous sodium hydroxide.

Which of the reactions would proceed more quickly?
Explain your answer.

(3 marks)

5.3   Sodium hydroxide can be dissolved in warm ethanol, instead of water.

How will this affect the type of reaction that occurs with bromoethane?
Explain your answer.

(2 marks)

1. Alkenes

Alkenes might sound very similar to alkanes, but they're a whole different breed of organic compound...

What is an alkene?

Alkenes have the general formula C_nH_{2n}. They're just made of carbon and hydrogen atoms, so they're hydrocarbons. Alkene molecules all have at least one C=C double covalent bond. Molecules with C=C double bonds are **unsaturated** because they can make more bonds with extra atoms in **addition reactions**. Because there are two pairs of electrons in the C=C double bond, it has a really high electron density. This makes alkenes pretty reactive.

┌─ Examples ─────────────────────────────

Here are a few pretty diagrams of alkenes:

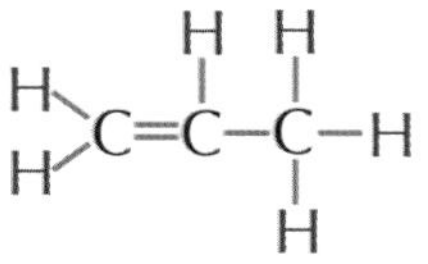

propene, CH_2CHCH_3

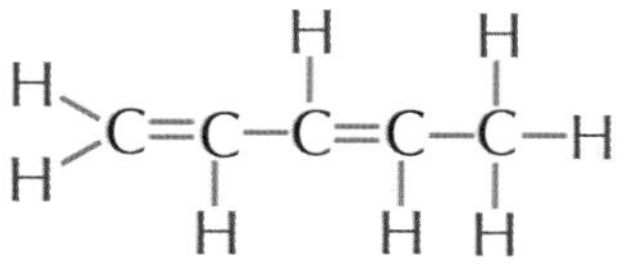

penta-1,3-diene, $CH_2CHCHCHCH_3$

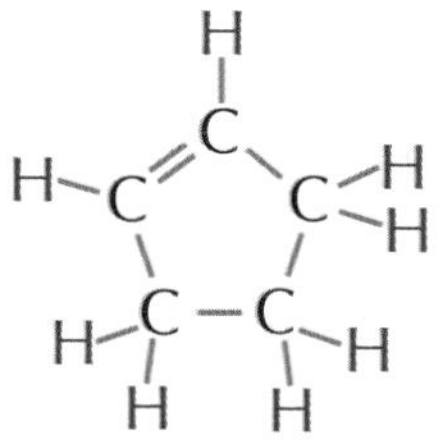

A cyclic alkene has two fewer hydrogen atoms than an open-chain alkene. Carbons can only have four bonds — a double bond means that the carbons can make one less bond with a hydrogen.

cyclopentene, C_5H_8

Tip: Alkenes with more than one double bond have fewer hydrogen atoms than the general formula suggests.

Tip: C=C double bonds are nucleophilic — they're attracted to places that don't have enough electrons.

Electrophilic addition reactions

Electrophilic addition reactions aren't too complicated. The double bond in an alkene opens up and atoms are added to the carbon atoms. Electrophilic addition reactions happen because the double bond has got plenty of electrons and is easily attacked by **electrophiles**. Electrophiles are electron-pair acceptors — they're usually a bit short of electrons, so they're attracted to areas where there's lots of electrons about.

Tip: Just as nucleophiles are often negatively charged ions (see page 203), electrophiles are often positively charged ions. Positive ions lose electrons as they form, so they're ready and waiting to accept any electrons that come their way.

┌─ Examples ─────────────────────────────

Here are a few examples of electrophiles.

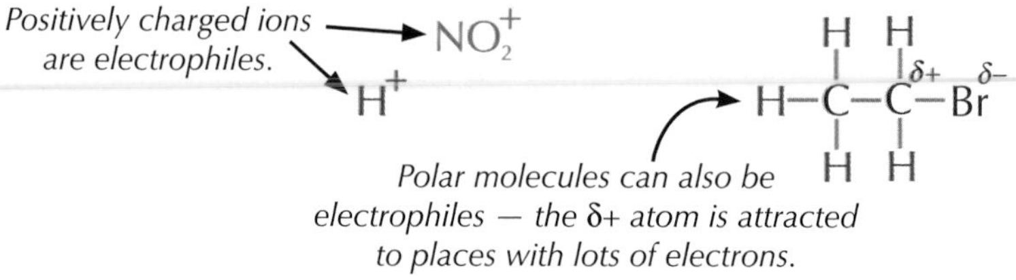

Positively charged ions are electrophiles.

NO_2^+

H^+

Polar molecules can also be electrophiles — the δ+ atom is attracted to places with lots of electrons.

Mechanism

You need to know how to draw mechanisms for electrophilic addition reactions with alkenes. Here's the general equation for this type of reaction, using ethene and an electrophile, X–Y.

$$CH_2CH_2 + X–Y \rightarrow CH_2XCH_2Y$$

And here's the mechanism for this reaction:

1. The C=C double bond repels the electrons in X–Y, which polarises the X–Y bond (or the bond could already be polar, as in HBr — see page 85).

2. Two electrons from the C=C double bond attack the δ+ X atom creating a new bond between carbon 1 and the X atom. The X–Y bond breaks and the electrons from the bond are taken by the Y atom to form a negative ion with a lone pair of electrons. Carbon 2 left with a positive charge (since when the double bond broke carbon 1 took the electrons to form a bond with the X atom) so you now have a **carbocation intermediate**.

3. The Y⁻ ion then acts as a nucleophile, attacking the positively charged carbocation, donating its lone pair of electrons and forming a new bond with carbon 2.

So overall, the X–Y molecule has been added to the alkene across the double bond to form a saturated compound.

Tip: Reactions of other alkenes look similar, but with longer carbon chains.

Tip: A carbocation is an organic ion containing a positively charged carbon atom.

Tip: An intermediate is a short-lived, reactive species that forms in the middle of a reaction mechanism — you can't easily isolate them from the reaction mixture.

Tip: If you're drawing this mechanism for a reaction involving an unsymmetrical alkene, they'll be two different carbocations that could form during step 2. The more stable carbocation will be more likely to form, so you need to make sure you draw the right one. Don't panic though — there's lots about the stability of carbocations coming up on page 219.

Example

Heating ethene with water in the presence of concentrated sulfuric acid produces ethanol. The overall equation for this reaction is shown below.

$$CH_2=CH_2 + H_2O \xrightarrow{H_2SO_4} C_2H_5OH$$

You have to do the reaction in two steps. First, concentrated sulfuric acid reacts with ethene in an electrophilic addition reaction. This forms ethyl hydrogen sulfate.

$$CH_2=CH_2 + H_2SO_4 \rightarrow CH_3CH_2OSO_2OH$$

If you then add cold water and warm the product, it's hydrolysed to form ethanol.

$$CH_3CH_2OSO_2OH + H_2O \rightarrow CH_3CH_2OH + H_2SO_4$$

The sulfuric acid isn't used up — it acts as a catalyst.

Mechanism

In the first step of this reaction, the carbon-carbon double bond attacks a $\delta+$ hydrogen atom on the sulfuric acid molecule. A new bond is formed between one of the carbons and the hydrogen, and the electrons from the O–H bond are taken by the oxygen atom to form a lone pair. The second carbon is left with a positive charge because it has lost the electron from the double bond.

Exam Tip
You could be asked about this reaction in your exams, but you should only be asked to draw the mechanism for the first part (i.e. the reaction of an alkene with H_2SO_4 — the bit before the reaction with water). Read the question carefully, so you're sure you know what it's asking for.

The negative ion created in the first step then acts as a nucleophile and attacks the carbocation creating a new intermediate.

Once this stage of the reaction is over, water can be added to produce sulfuric acid and ethanol.

Figure 1: Bromine water test. The test tube on the right contains hex-1-ene, a compound with a C=C that has reacted with the bromine water. The one on the left contains hexane, a saturated substance that doesn't react with bromine water.

Tip: Because they turn it from orange to colourless, alkenes are sometimes described as 'decolourising' the bromine water.

Testing for unsaturation

When you shake an alkene with orange bromine water, the solution quickly turns from orange to colourless (see Figure 1 and 2). Bromine is added across the double bond to form a colourless dibromoalkane — this happens by electrophilic addition.

Figure 2: Adding bromine water to a solution containing a carbon-carbon double bond turns the bromine water colourless.

Example

When you shake ethene orange bromine water, the solution turns from orange to colourless. Here's the equation for this reaction:

$$H_2C=CH_2 + Br_2 \rightarrow CH_2BrCH_2Br$$

Here's the mechanism...

The double bond repels the electrons in Br_2, polarising Br–Br. This is called an induced dipole.

A pair of electrons in the double bond attracts the $Br^{\delta+}$ and forms a bond with it. This repels electrons in the Br–Br bond further, until it breaks.

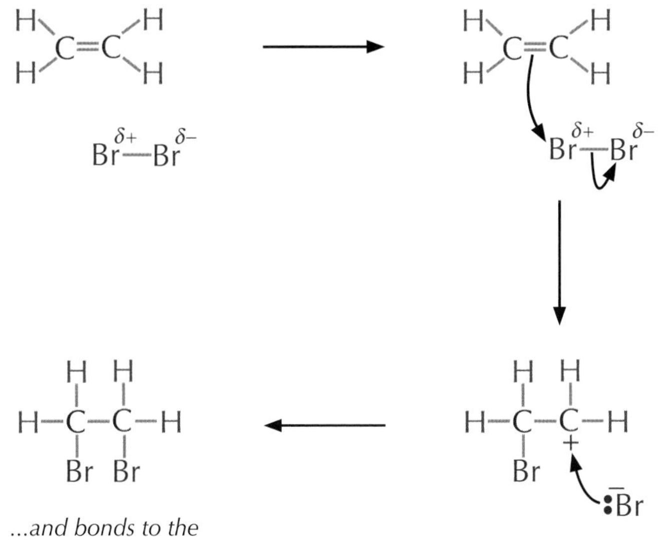

Exam Tip
Make sure the first curly arrow comes from the carbon-carbon double bond.

...and bonds to the other C atom, forming 1,2-dibromoethane.

You get a positively charged carbocation intermediate. The Br^- now zooms over...

Practice Question — Application

Q1 Draw the mechanism for the reaction of but-2-ene with bromine. The structures of the reactants are shown below.

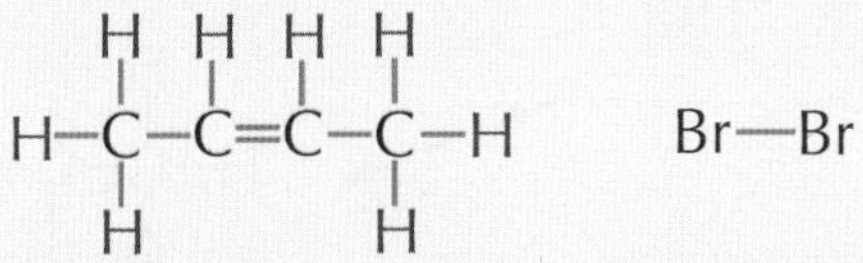

Tip: Remember to be careful where your curly arrows start and finish — they should come from bonds or lone pairs, and go to atoms.

Practice Questions — Fact Recall

Q1 Give the general formula for an alkene.

Q2 Explain why alkenes are unsaturated.

Q3 Explain why alkenes can undergo electrophilic addition reactions.

Q4 What is an electrophile?

Q5 Give two examples of electrophiles.

Q6 What can you use bromine water to test for?

- Understand and be able to outline the mechanism of electrophilic addition reactions of alkenes with HBr.

- Explain the formation of major and minor products in addition reactions of unsymmetrical alkenes by reference to the relative stabilities of primary, secondary and tertiary carbocation intermediates.

Specification Reference 3.3.4.2

2. Reactions of Alkenes

Sometimes a chemical reaction has more than one product — you've got to be able to decide which product is more likely to form. Don't panic, it's not just a wild stab in the dark — there are some handy rules to help you out.

Reactions with hydrogen halides

Alkenes undergo electrophilic addition reactions with hydrogen halides to form halogenoalkanes.

┌ Example

This is the reaction between ethene and hydrogen bromide, to form bromoethane.

$$C_2H_4 + HBr \rightarrow C_2H_5Br$$

It's an electrophilic addition reaction so the mechanism follows the pattern that you saw on page 215.

Addition of hydrogen halides to unsymmetrical alkenes

If the hydrogen halide adds to an unsymmetrical alkene, there are two possible products.

┌ Example

If you add hydrogen bromide to propene, the bromine atom could add to either the first carbon or the second carbon. This means you could produce 1-bromopropane or 2-bromopropane.

propene

1-bromopropane

2-bromopropane

Exam Tip
Other alkenes react in a similar way with HBr. Don't be put off if they give you a different alkene in the exam — the mechanism works in exactly the same way.

Tip: "Primary carbocation" can also be written as 1° carbocation — the 1° stands for primary. Secondary carbocation can be written as 2° carbocation, and tertiary as 3° carbocation.

The amount of each product formed depends on how stable the carbocation formed in the middle of the reaction is. This is known as the carbocation intermediate. The three possible carbocations are:

primary carbocation   *secondary carbocation*   *tertiary carbocation*

R is an alkyl group — an alkane with a hydrogen removed, e.g. –CH$_3$.

Carbocations with more alkyl groups are more stable because the alkyl groups feed electrons towards the positive charge.

You can show that an alkyl group is donating electrons by drawing an arrow on the bond that points to where the electrons are donated.

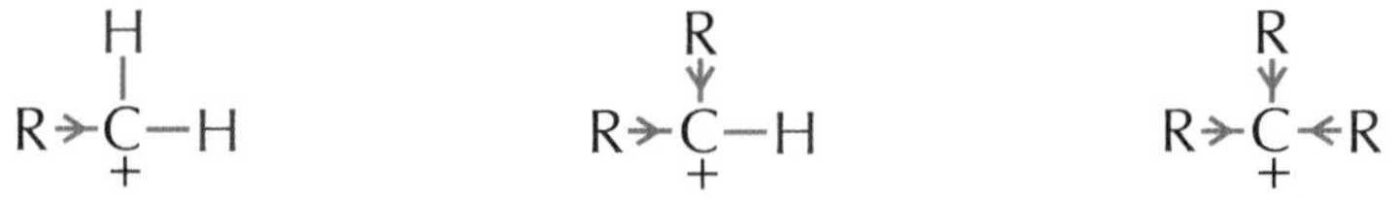

primary carbocation   secondary carbocation   tertiary carbocation

Least stable ⟶ **Most stable**

Tip: The alkyl groups don't give up their electrons to the carbon atom — they just move some of their negatively charged electrons nearer to it, which helps to stabilise the positive charge.

More stable carbocations are much more likely to form than less stable ones. This means that there will be more of the product formed via the more stable carbocation than there is via the less stable carbocation.

Tip: The product that there's most of is called the <u>major</u> product, or the <u>Markovnikov</u> product — after the Russian scientist, Vladimir Markovnikov, who came up with the theory that the product formed most often is formed via a more stable carbocation.

┌─ **Examples** ─────────────────────

Here's how hydrogen bromide reacts with propene:

$H_2C=CHCH_3 + HBr \rightarrow CH_3CHBrCH_3$
2-bromopropane
major product

$H_2C=CHCH_3 + HBr \rightarrow CH_2BrCH_2CH_3$
1-bromopropane
minor product

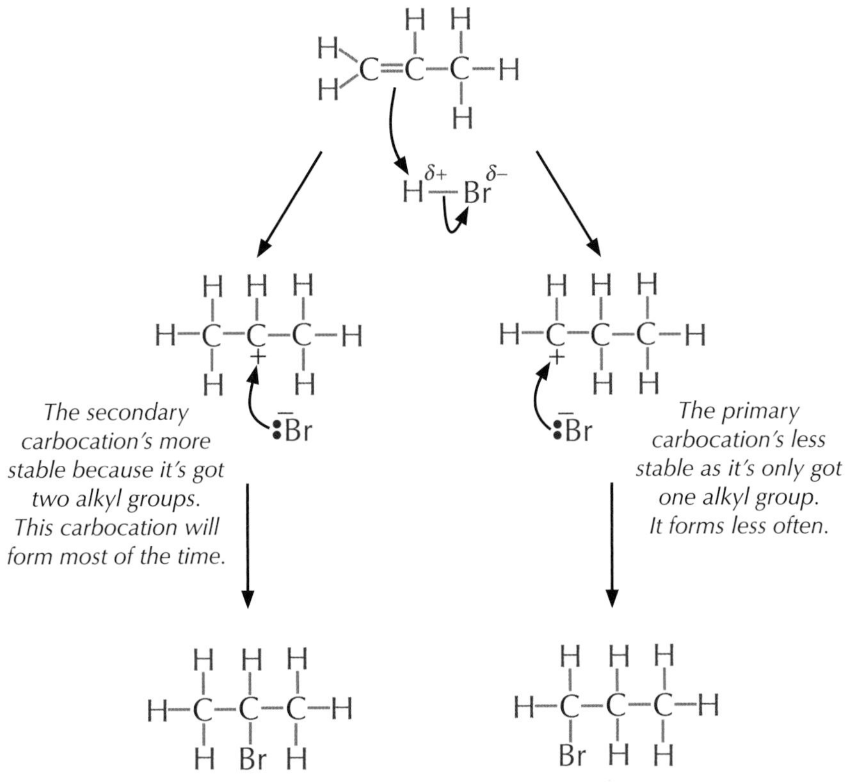

The secondary carbocation's more stable because it's got two alkyl groups. This carbocation will form most of the time.

The primary carbocation's less stable as it's only got one alkyl group. It forms less often.

2-bromopropane
major product

1-bromopropane
minor product

Tip: If you were adding Br_2 to propene instead, they'd only be one possible product (1,2-dibromopropane) — but the reaction would still be more likely to go by the route with a secondary carbocation intermediate.

Exam Tip
It makes it easier to see what the main product is if you draw out all the possible carbocations each time — then there's less chance of making a mistake.

Here's how hydrogen bromide reacts with 2-methylbut-2-ene:

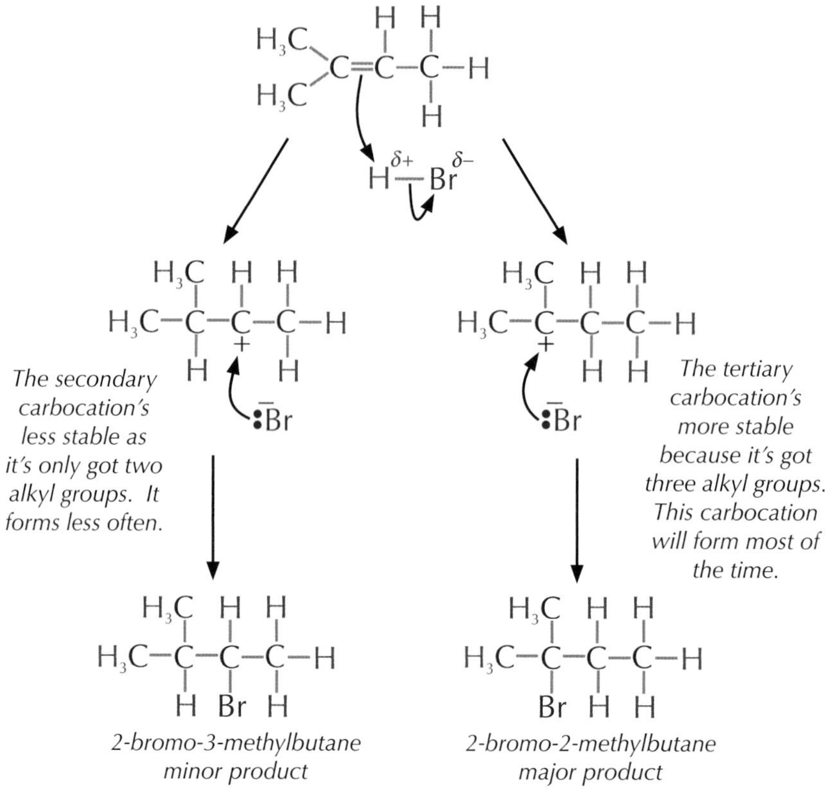

The secondary carbocation's less stable as it's only got two alkyl groups. It forms less often.

The tertiary carbocation's more stable because it's got three alkyl groups. This carbocation will form most of the time.

Tip: The bigger the difference in stability of the carbocations, the more of the major product you'll get at the end.

2-bromo-3-methylbutane
minor product

2-bromo-2-methylbutane
major product

Practice Questions — Application

Q1 a) Draw the mechanism for the reaction between but-2-ene and hydrogen bromide. The reactants for this reaction are shown below.

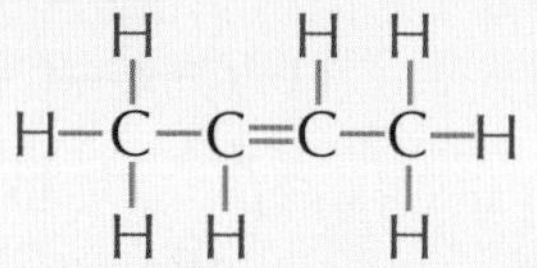

HBr

b) Write the overall equation for this reaction.

Q2 Hydrogen bromide reacts with but-1-ene to form either 1-bromobutane or 2-bromobutane. Explain why 2-bromobutane is the major product of the reaction. The structures of 1-bromobutane and 2-bromobutane are shown below.

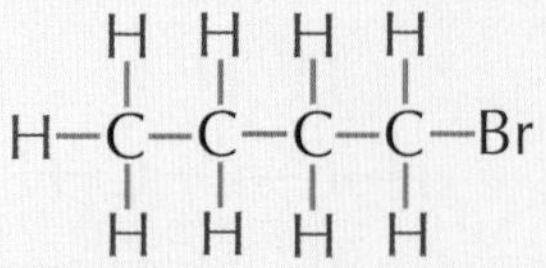

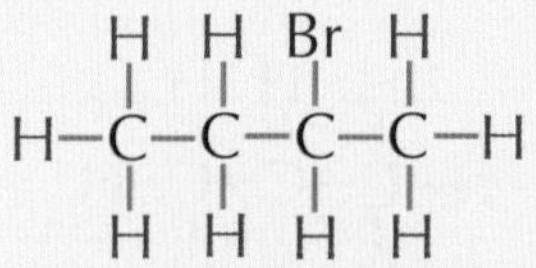

Practice Questions — Fact Recall

Q1 What could you react with ethene in order to produce bromoethane?

Q2 Place the following carbocations in order of stability from most to least stable: secondary, primary and tertiary.

3. Addition Polymers

There is a way of joining up lots of alkene molecules to make all sorts of different materials — these are called polymers.

Polymers

Polymers are long chain molecules formed when lots of small molecules, called **monomers**, join together.

Polymers can be natural, e.g. DNA, or synthetic (man-made), e.g. polythene. We use them for all sorts of things in everyday life, including in plastic bags, rain coats, non-stick pans and car tyres. People have used natural polymers to make things like fabrics and jewellery for many years.

During the 19th century, researchers managed to synthesise artificial polymers, such as artificial silk and hard rubber. Further developments in polymers came during the 20th century, when materials such as nylon and Kevlar® were developed. Polymers are still being developed today — scientists are still looking to develop materials that are cheaper to produce or that perform their functions better than current materials.

Addition polymers

The double bonds in alkenes can open up and join together to make long chains called polymers. It's kind of like they're holding hands in a big line. The individual, small alkenes are called monomers. This is called **addition polymerisation**.

┌─ **Example** ──────────────────────────────

Poly(ethene) is made by the addition polymerisation of ethene.

ethene monomers   *poly(ethene)*

└──────────────────────────────

Addition polymerisation reactions can be written like this...

monomer   *polymer*

...where the n stands for the number of repeating units in the polymer.

You can also use **substituted alkenes** as monomers in addition polymerisation. A substituted alkene is just an alkene where one of the hydrogen atoms has been swapped for another atom or group. For example, if you swap one of the hydrogen atoms in ethene for a chlorine atom, you get chloroethene. Polymerising chloroethene makes poly(chloroethene) — see page 223.

see page 223

Learning Objectives:

- Appreciate that knowledge and understanding of the production and properties of polymers has developed over time.
- Know that addition polymers are formed from alkenes and substituted alkenes.
- Be able to draw the repeating unit from a monomer structure, and the repeating unit or monomer from a section of the polymer chain.
- Know IUPAC rules for naming addition polymers.
- Be able to explain why addition polymers are unreactive.
- Be able to explain the nature of intermolecular forces between molecules of polyalkenes.
- Know typical uses of poly(chloroethene) and how its properties can be modified using a plasticiser.

Specification Reference 3.3.4.3

Exam Tip
If you're asked for the <u>formula</u> of a polymer, you need to include the brackets and the n. If you're asked for the <u>repeating unit</u>, you should just draw the bit inside the brackets.

Tip: Remember to show the 'trailing bonds' at the ends of the molecule. This shows that the polymer continues.

To find the monomer used to form an addition polymer, take the repeating unit, remove unnecessary side bonds and add a double bond.

Example

To find the monomer used to make the polymer below you first need to look for the repeating unit.

$$\begin{array}{c} \text{H} \quad \text{CH}_3\ \text{H} \quad \text{CH}_3\ \text{H} \quad \text{CH}_3 \\ | \quad | \quad | \quad | \quad | \quad | \\ -\text{C}-\text{C}-\text{C}-\text{C}-\text{C}-\text{C}- \\ | \quad | \quad | \quad | \quad | \quad | \\ \text{H} \quad \text{H} \quad \text{H} \quad \text{H} \quad \text{H} \quad \text{H} \end{array} \longrightarrow \begin{array}{c} \text{H} \quad \text{CH}_3 \\ | \quad | \\ -\text{C}-\text{C}- \\ | \quad | \\ \text{H} \quad \text{H} \end{array}$$

polymer　　　　　　　　　　*repeating unit*

Then replace the horizontal carbon-carbon bond with a double bond and remove the unnecessary side bonds to find the monomer.

$$\begin{array}{c} \text{H} \quad \text{CH}_3 \\ | \quad | \\ -\text{C}-\text{C}- \\ | \quad | \\ \text{H} \quad \text{H} \end{array} \longrightarrow \begin{array}{c} \text{H} \diagdown \quad \diagup \text{CH}_3 \\ \text{C}=\text{C} \\ \text{H} \diagup \quad \diagdown \text{H} \end{array}$$

repeating unit　　　　　　　　*monomer — propene*

IUPAC nomenclature

Naming addition polymers is fairly straightforward once you've found the monomer used to form the addition polymer — they have the form **poly(X)**, where X is the name of the monomer. For example, if the monomer is but-2-ene, the polymer it forms will be called poly(but-2-ene).

If the name of the monomer doesn't have a number in it, then you can write it without the brackets. So in the example above, the addition polymer is called poly(propene), or just polypropene.

Properties of polymers

Alkene monomers are unsaturated (they contain one or more double covalent bonds), but once they form polymers they become saturated (there are only single bonds in the carbon chain). The main carbon chain of polyalkenes is also usually non-polar. These factors result in addition polymers being very unreactive — polyalkenes are chemically inert.

The monomers within a polymer chain have strong covalent bonds. However, the intermolecular forces between polymer chains are much weaker, which affects the properties of the polymer. Longer chains with fewer branches have stronger intermolecular forces, making these polymer materials stronger and more rigid.

Tip: The carbon chain of a polyalkene can be polar in cases where the monomer contains electronegative atoms — the main example of this is poly(chloroethene) (see next page), which contains chlorine atoms.

Tip: Look back at page 86 for more information on van der Waals forces.

Examples

Polyethene

A polymer with few or no branches, such as polyethene, can pack closely together (see Figure 1). The polymer chains are attracted to each other by van der Waals forces. This makes a strong, rigid material.

Figure 1: Skeletal diagram of packed polyethene chains.

Polystyrene

Poly(phenylethene), more commonly known as polystyrene, is formed from phenylethene.

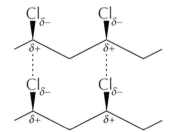

The benzene ring coming off the main carbon chain of poly(phenylethene) is a large branch. This makes it difficult for the chains to pack closely together, so they only form weak van der Waals forces. This makes poly(phenylethene) a more flexible material than polyethene.

Poly(chloroethene)

Poly(chloroethene), also known as polyvinyl chloride, or **PVC**, is an addition polymer formed from chloroethene monomers.

chloroethene monomer   *poly(chloroethene) polymer*

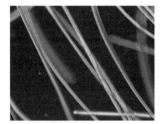

Figure 2: *Polyvinyl chloride (PVC) fibres. PVC is an addition polymer.*

The covalent bonds between the chlorine and the carbon atoms are polar, with chlorine being more electronegative. The $\delta-$ charges on the chlorine atoms and the $\delta+$ charges on the carbon atoms mean that there are permanent dipole-dipole forces between the polymer chains (see Figure 3). This makes PVC a hard but brittle material. It is used to make drain pipes and window frames.

Figure 3: *Skeletal formula showing the permanent dipole-dipole forces in PVC.*

Plasticisers

You can add chemicals, such as **plasticisers**, to polymers to modify their properties. Adding a plasticiser makes a polymer bendier. The plasticiser molecules get between the polymer chains and push them apart. This reduces the strength of the intermolecular forces between the chains — so the chains can slide around more, making them more flexible.

Plasticised PVC is much more flexible than rigid PVC. It's used to make electrical cable insulation, flooring tiles and clothing.

Exam Tip
Make sure you know how to convert between the monomer structure, the repeating unit and the polymer structure.

Practice Questions — Application

Q1 a) Write a reaction for the addition polymerisation of the monomer fluoroethene. The structure of fluoroethene is shown below.

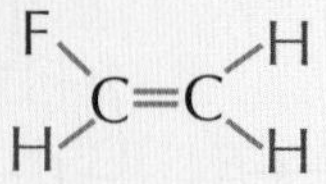

b) Name the polymer that is formed in the reaction.

Q2 Draw the structure of the monomer used to form the polymer shown below.

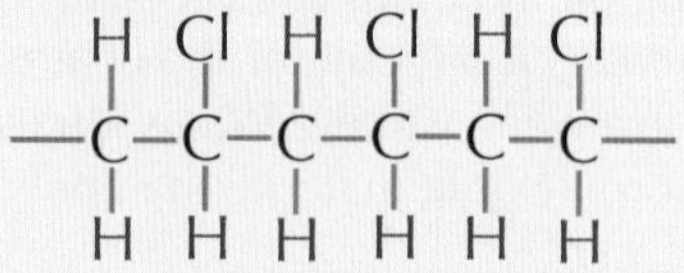

Q3 Draw the repeating unit of the polymer shown below.

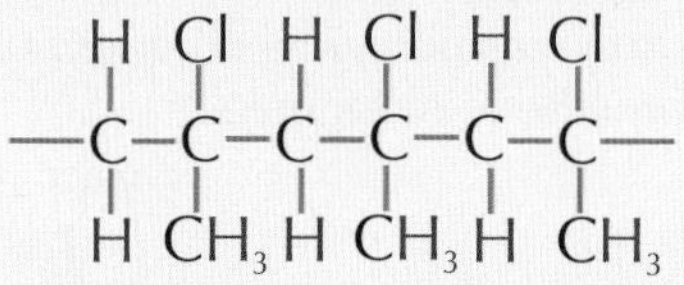

Tip: Plasticisers are just chemicals that make a polymer more flexible.

Practice Questions — Fact Recall

Q1 Briefly describe addition polymerisation.

Q2 Why are poly(alkenes) unreactive?

Q3 a) Describe and explain the intermolecular forces that exist between the polymer chains in unplasticised poly(chloroethene).

b) Give two uses of rigid poly(chloroethene).

Q4 a) Briefly describe how plasticisers work.

b) Give two uses of flexible poly(chloroethene).

4. Alcohols

These pages on alcohols are pretty important — this topic is packed full of real life applications of chemistry. But before we get onto all that fun stuff here's a bit more nomenclature for you to learn.

Nomenclature of alcohols

The alcohol homologous series has the general formula $C_nH_{2n+1}OH$. Alcohols are named using the same IUPAC naming rules found on pages 180-183, but the suffix -ol is added in place of the -e on the end of the name. You also need to indicate which carbon atom the alcohol functional group is attached to — the carbon number(s) comes before the -ol suffix. If there are two –OH groups the molecule is a -diol and if there are three it's a -triol.

Examples

The longest continuous carbon chain is 2 carbon atoms, so the stem is ethane.

There's one –OH attached to the carbon chain so the suffix is -ol.

There are two carbon atoms it could be attached to, but they are equivalent (they'd both be labelled carbon atom 1) so there's no need to put a number.

So, the alcohol is called ethanol.

ethanol

The longest continuous carbon chain is 3 carbon atoms, so the stem is propane.

There's one –OH attached to the carbon chain so the suffix is -ol.

It's attached to the second carbon so there's a 2 before the -ol.

There's also a methyl group attached to the second carbon so there's also a 2-methyl- prefix.

The alcohol is called 2-methylpropan-2-ol.

2-methylpropan-2-ol

The longest continuous carbon chain is 2 carbon atoms, so the stem is ethane.

There are two –OH groups attached to the carbon chain so the suffix is -diol.

There's one –OH attached to each carbon atom so there's a 1,2- before the -diol.

So, the alcohol is called ethane-1,2-diol.

ethane-1,2-diol

Tip: When you're naming alcohols with only one -OH group, you lose the 'e' at the end of the alkane stem, as usual — but when you're naming diols and triols, you keep the 'e' For example:

• butanol (not butaneol),
• hexane-2,4-diol (not hexan-2,4-diol).

Primary, secondary and tertiary alcohols

An alcohol is primary, secondary or tertiary, depending on which carbon atom the hydroxyl group –OH is bonded to. **Primary alcohols** are given the notation 1° and the –OH group is attached to a carbon with one alkyl group attached (see Figure 1). **Secondary alcohols** are given the notation 2° and the –OH group is attached to a carbon with two alkyl groups attached. **Tertiary alcohols** are given the notation 3° (you can see where I'm going with this) and the –OH group is attached to a carbon with three alkyl groups attached.

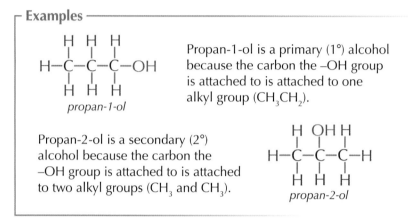

primary alcohol   *secondary alcohol*   *tertiary alcohol*

Figure 1: Diagrams of 1°, 2° and 3° alcohols. R = alkyl group.

Examples

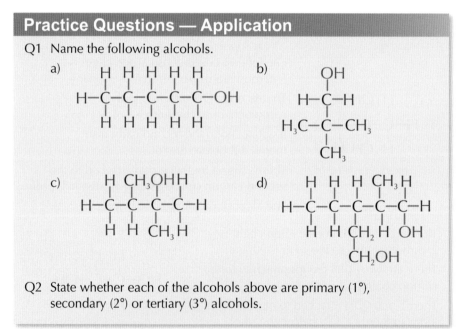

propan-1-ol

Propan-1-ol is a primary (1°) alcohol because the carbon the –OH group is attached to is attached to one alkyl group (CH_3CH_2).

Propan-2-ol is a secondary (2°) alcohol because the carbon the –OH group is attached to is attached to two alkyl groups (CH_3 and CH_3).

propan-2-ol

Practice Questions — Application

Q1 Name the following alcohols.

a)

b)

c)

d)

Q2 State whether each of the alcohols above are primary (1°), secondary (2°) or tertiary (3°) alcohols.

Practice Questions — Fact Recall

Q1 Give the general formula for the alcohol homologous series.

Q2 What is a secondary alcohol?

5. Dehydrating Alcohols

Making ethene from ethanol means kicking out a molecule of water, so it's called 'dehydration'. The opposite reaction is in the next topic (on page 230).

How to dehydrate an alcohol

You can make alkenes by eliminating water from alcohols in a dehydration reaction (i.e. elimination of water).

$$C_nH_{2n+1}OH \rightarrow C_nH_{2n} + H_2O$$

This reaction allows you to produce alkenes from renewable resources — you can produce ethanol by fermentation of glucose, which you can get from plants. This is important, because it means that you can produce polymers (poly(ethene), for example) without needing oil.

One of the main industrial uses for alkenes is as the starting material for polymers. Here's how you can make ethene from ethanol:

┌─ Example ─────────────────────────────

Water can be eliminated from ethanol in a dehydration reaction. Ethanol is heated with a concentrated sulfuric acid catalyst.

$$C_2H_5OH \xrightarrow{H_2SO_4} CH_2=CH_2 + H_2O$$

The product is usually in a mixture with water, acid and reactant in it, so the alkene has to be separated out. Here is the mechanism:

1. A lone pair of electrons from the oxygen bonds to an H⁺ from the acid. The alcohol is protonated, giving the oxygen a positive charge.

2. The positively charged oxygen pulls electrons away from the carbon. An H_2O molecule leaves, creating an unstable carbocation intermediate.

4. ...and the alkene is formed.

3. The carbocation loses an H⁺...

Dehydration of longer, unsymmetrical alcohols results in more than one product, because the double bond can go on either side of the carbon that had the OH group on it.

┌─ Example ─────────────────────────────

Butan-2-ol   But-2-ene   But-1-ene

Learning Objectives:

- Know that alkenes can be formed from alcohols by acid-catalysed elimination reactions.

- Know that alkenes produced by this method can be used to produce addition polymers without using monomers derived from crude oil.

- Be able to outline the mechanism for the elimination of water from alcohols.

- Know how to distil a product from a reaction (Required Practical 5).

Specification Reference 3.3.5.3

Tip: In an elimination reaction, a small group of atoms breaks away from a larger molecule. It's not replaced by anything else.

Tip: Phosphoric acid can also be used as a catalyst in this reaction.

Tip: The acid catalysed elimination of water from ethanol is the reverse of the acid catalysed hydration of ethene — see page 230.

Tip: Butan-2-ol actually forms three products, because but-2-ene exists in two isomer forms — see pages 185-189 for more on isomerism.

Purifying the product of a reaction

The products of organic reactions are often impure — so you definitely need to know how to get rid of any unwanted by-products or leftover reactants from the reaction mixture.

In the dehydration reaction of alcohols to form alkenes, the mixture at the end contains the product, the reactant, acid, water and other impurities. To get a pure alkene, you need a way to separate it from the other substances.

Distillation is a technique which uses the fact that different chemicals have different boiling points, to separate them. You need to know how to distil a product from a reaction — there's a description of how to do this in the example below.

Sometimes you'll need to perform a series of steps to collect and purify the product of a reaction. A good example of this is preparing an alkene from an alcohol.

Tip: Remember to consider any safety precautions that you might need to take before you start doing an experiment like this.

┌ Example

Here's how to produce cyclohexene from cyclohexanol and separate and purify the product.

Stage 1 — reaction and first distillation

1) Add concentrated H_2SO_4 and H_3PO_4 to a round-bottom flask containing cyclohexanol. Mix the solution by swirling the flask and add 2-3 carborundum boiling chips (these make the mixture boil more calmly).

2) Connect the flask to the rest of the distillation apparatus, including a thermometer, condenser and a cooled collection flask. Figure 1, below, shows how the distillation apparatus should be set up.

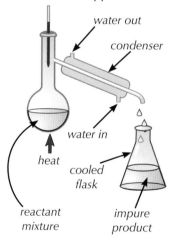

water out
condenser
water in
heat
cooled flask
reactant mixture
impure product

Figure 1: *Set-up of distillation apparatus.*

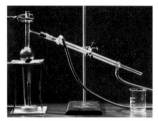

Figure 2: *Photograph of distillation apparatus.*

Tip: You should use a heating method without a flame here because the reactants and the products are flammable.

3) Gently heat the mixture in the flask to around 83 °C (the boiling point of cyclohexene) using a water bath or electric heater.

4) Chemicals with boiling points up to 83 °C will evaporate. The warm gas will rise out of the flask and into the condenser

5) The condenser has cold water running through the outside. The cooler temperatures turn the gas back into a liquid.

6) The liquid product can then be collected in a cooled flask.

Stage 2 — separation

1) The product collected after the first distillation will still contain some impurities which need to be removed.

2) Transfer the product mixture to a separating funnel (see Figure 3, below) and add water to dissolve water soluble impurities and create an aqueous solution.

3) Allow the mixture to settle into layers. Drain off the aqueous layer at the bottom, leaving behind the impure cyclohexene.

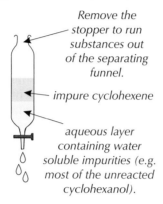

Remove the stopper to run substances out of the separating funnel.

impure cyclohexene

aqueous layer containing water soluble impurities (e.g. most of the unreacted cyclohexanol).

Figure 3: Set-up of separation apparatus.

Tip: The water in the aqueous layer is polar and the cyclohexene is non-polar, so the two liquids won't mix — like oil and water. This come's in really handy when you're trying to separate them...

Stage 3 — purification

1) Drain off the impure cyclohexene into a round-bottomed flask.

2) Add anhydrous $CaCl_2$ (a drying agent — it removes any remaining traces of water) and stopper the flask. Let the mixture dry for at least 20 minutes with occasional swirling.

3) The cyclohexene may still have small amounts of impurities so distil the mixture one last time. This time, only collect the product that is released when the mixture is at around 83 °C — this will be the pure cyclohexene.

Tip: The cyclohexene will be fairly pure by the end of the second purification step, so you may not be asked to do the second distillation.

Practice Question — Application

Q1 a) Write an equation for the dehydration of propan-1-ol to form propene.

    b) Draw out a the mechanism for this reaction.

Practice Questions — Fact Recall

Q1 Write out the general equation for the dehydration of an alcohol to form an alkene.

Q2 Draw and label a diagram to show how you would set up distillation apparatus.

Q3 Imagine you are making cyclohexene from cyclohexanol. You heat the alcohol with acid in distillation apparatus, collect the resulting product and separate it using a separating funnel. You are left with impure cyclohexene. Describe how you would purify it.

6. Ethanol Production

- Know that alcohols are produced industrially by hydration of alkenes in the presence of an acid catalyst.

- Be able to outline the mechanism for the formation of an alcohol by the reaction of an alkene with steam in the presence of an acid catalyst.

- Be able to describe how ethanol is produced industrially by fermentation of glucose.

- Be able to justify the conditions used in the production of ethanol by fermentation of glucose.

- Know that ethanol produced industrially by fermentation is separated by fractional distillation and can then be used as a biofuel.

- Be able to explain the meaning of the term biofuel.

- Be able to write equations to support the statement that ethanol produced by fermentation is a carbon neutral fuel, and give reasons why this statement is not valid.

- Be able to discuss the environmental (including ethical) issues linked to decision making about biofuel use.

Specification Reference 3.3.5.1

There are two main methods that are used to produce ethanol and other alcohols industrially — hydrating alkenes and fermenting sugars. You need to know the details of both methods, so here they come...

Hydrating alkenes

The standard industrial method for producing alcohols is to hydrate an alkene using steam in the presence of an acid catalyst. Here's the general equation for this type of reaction:

$$C_nH_{2n} + H_2O \overset{H^+}{\rightleftharpoons} C_nH_{2n+1}OH$$

Steam hydration of ethene is used industrially to produce ethanol. Ethene can be hydrated by steam at 300 °C and a pressure of 60 atm. It needs a solid phosphoric(V) acid catalyst. Here's the equation for the industrial hydration of ethene:

$$CH_2{=}CH_{2(g)} + H_2O_{(g)} \overset{H_3PO_4}{\underset{\substack{300\,°C \\ 60\,atm}}{\rightleftharpoons}} CH_3CH_2OH_{(g)}$$

The reaction's reversible and the reaction yield is low — only about 5%. (This sounds rubbish, but you can recycle the unreacted ethene gas, making the overall yield a much more profitable 95%.)

Mechanism

Here's the mechanism for the reaction of ethene with steam (it's the reverse of the dehydration mechanism from page 227):

1. *A pair of electrons from the double bond bonds to an H+ from the acid.*

2. *A lone pair of electrons from a water molecule bonds to the carbocation.*

4. *...and the alcohol is formed.*

3. *The water loses an H+...*

Make sure you're familiar with how this mechanism works — you could be asked to draw the mechanism for the reaction of steam with other alcohols too.

(This reaction is similar to the reaction of ethene with sulfuric acid (see pages 215-216), but because the reaction conditions are different the mechanism's slightly different too.)

Fermentation of glucose

At the moment most industrial ethanol is produced by steam hydration of ethene with a phosphoric acid catalyst (see page 230). The ethene comes from cracking heavy fractions of crude oil. But in the future, when crude oil supplies start running out, petrochemicals like ethene will be expensive — so producing ethanol by fermentation will become much more important...

Industrial production of ethanol by fermentation

Fermentation is an exothermic process, carried out by yeast in anaerobic conditions (without oxygen). Here's the equation for the reaction.

$$C_6H_{12}O_{6(aq)} \xrightarrow[\text{yeast}]{30\text{-}40°C} 2C_2H_5OH_{(aq)} + 2CO_{2(g)}$$

Yeast produces enzymes which convert glucose ($C_6H_{12}O_6$) into ethanol and carbon dioxide. The enzyme works at an optimum (ideal) temperature of 30-40 °C. If it's too cold, the reaction is slow — if it's too hot, the enzyme is denatured (damaged). Figure 2 shows how the rate of reaction of fermentation is affected by temperature.

Exam Tip
When you're writing out this equation make sure you always include the conditions above and below the arrow.

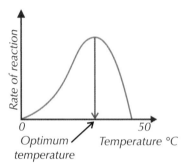

Figure 2: Graph to show the effect of temperature on fermentation.

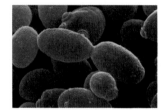

Figure 1: A scanning electron micrograph (SEM) of yeast cells.

When the solution reaches about 15% ethanol, the yeast dies. Fractional distillation is used to increase the concentration of the ethanol. Fermentation is low-tech — it uses cheap equipment and renewable resources. But the fractional distillation step that is needed to purify the ethanol produced using this method takes extra time and money.

Comparison of ethanol production methods

Figure 4 shows a quick summary of the advantages and disadvantages of the two main industrial methods of making ethanol.

	Hydration of Ethene	Fermentation
Rate of Reaction	Very fast	Very slow
Quality of Product	Pure	Very impure — needs further processing.
Raw Material	Ethene from oil — a finite resource.	Sugars — a renewable resource.
Process/Costs	Continuous process, so expensive equipment needed, but low labour costs.	Batch process, so cheap equipment needed, but high labour costs.

Figure 4: Table comparing methods of ethanol production.

Figure 3: Vat for the fermentation of yeast.

Issues with biofuels

A **biofuel** is a fuel that's made from biological material that's recently died. For example, sugars from sugar cane can be fermented to produce ethanol, which can be added to petrol. Ethanol produced in this way is a biofuel (sometimes called bioethanol)

You need to know about both the advantages and the disadvantages of using biofuels.

Figure 5: A maize field that grows crops for the production of biofuel.

Advantages of biofuel use

One of the big advantages of using biofuels instead of fuels that come from crude oil is that biofuels are renewable energy sources. Unlike fossil fuels, biofuels won't run out. This makes them more sustainable.

Like conventional fuels, biofuels do produce carbon dioxide when they're burnt. But burning a biofuel only releases the same amount of carbon dioxide that the crop plant took in as it was growing. So most biofuels are considered to be **carbon neutral** (although this is not quite true — see below).

Disadvantages of biofuel use

The main ethical problem with biofuel production is known as the "food vs. fuel" debate. When you use land used to grow crops for fuel, that land can't be used to grow food. If countries start using land to grow biofuel crops instead of food, they may be unable to feed everyone in the country.

There are also environmental problems with the production of biofuels. In some places, trees may be cut down in order to create more land to grow crops for biofuels. Deforestation destroys habitats and removes trees, which are very efficient at taking carbon dioxide out of the air themselves. The trees that are cut down are often burnt, releasing more carbon dioxide.

Fertilisers are often added to soils in order to increase biofuel crop production. Fertilisers can pollute waterways, and some fertilisers also release nitrous oxide, which is a greenhouse gas (see page 199).

There are also some practical problems with switching from fossil fuels to biofuels. For example, most current car engines would be unable to run on fuels with high ethanol concentrations without being modified.

Tip: Carbon dioxide is a greenhouse gas — See page 199 for more details.

Is ethanol a carbon neutral biofuel?

Just like burning the hydrocarbons from fossil fuels, burning ethanol produces carbon dioxide (CO_2). But the plants that are grown to produce bioethanol take in carbon dioxide from the atmosphere as they grow. When you burn the fuel produced from the plants, you only release the same amount of carbon dioxide that the plant took in in the first place — this is described as being carbon neutral. So bioethanol is sometimes thought of as a carbon neutral fuel. Here are the chemical equations to support that argument:

1. During photosynthesis, plants use carbon dioxide from the atmosphere to produce glucose.

$$6CO_2 + 6H_2O \longrightarrow C_6H_{12}O_6 + 6O_2$$

6 moles of carbon dioxide are taken from the atmosphere to produce 1 mole of glucose.

2.   In the fermentation process, glucose is converted into ethanol.

$$C_6H_{12}O_6 \longrightarrow 2C_2H_5OH + 2CO_2$$

2 moles of carbon dioxide are released into the atmosphere when 1 mole of glucose is converted to 2 moles of ethanol.

3.   When ethanol is burned, carbon dioxide and water are produced.

$$2C_2H_5OH + 6O_2 \longrightarrow 4CO_2 + 6H_2O$$

4 moles of carbon dioxide are released into the atmosphere when 2 moles of ethanol are burned completely.

If you combine these three equations, you'll see that exactly 6 moles of CO_2 are taken in and exactly 6 moles of CO_2 are given out.

However, fossil fuels will need to be burned to power the machinery used to make fertilisers for the crops and the machinery used to harvest the crops. Refining and transporting the bioethanol also uses energy. It's usually fossil fuels that are being burnt in order to produce the energy needed to carry out these processes, and burning that fuel will produce carbon dioxide. So bioethanol isn't a completely carbon neutral fuel.

Tip: If these equations are combined, all of the species on the left and right sides completely cancel each other out. Overall, CO_2 isn't taken from or put into the atmosphere.

Practice Question — Application

Q1   Ethene reacts with steam in the presence of an acid catalyst.
Draw the mechanism for this reaction.

Practice Questions — Fact Recall

Q1   Write down the equation for the production of ethanol by fermentation.

Q2   Why is it necessary for the reaction to take place between 30 °C and 40 °C?

Q3   What is a biofuel?

Q4   a)   Write down three equations which support the statement "bioethanol is a carbon neutral fuel".

   b)   Explain why bioethanol is not a carbon neutral fuel.

Q5   a)   Give one advantage of using biofuels rather than fossil fuels.

   b)   Give three disadvantages of using biofuels.

7. Oxidising Alcohols

Oxidising an alcohol creates a carbon-oxygen double bond. Substances that contain these carbon-oxygen double bonds are known as carbonyl compounds — they're great fun. Honest.

Learning Objectives:

- Be able to apply IUPAC rules for nomenclature to naming aldehydes, ketones and carboxylic acids limited to chains with up to 6 carbon atoms.

- Know that primary alcohols can be oxidised to aldehydes, which can be further oxidised to carboxylic acids.

- Know that secondary alcohols can be oxidised to ketones.

- Know that tertiary alcohols are not easily oxidised.

- Know that acidified potassium dichromate(VI) is a suitable oxidising agent.

- Be able to write equations for these oxidation reactions, showing the oxidant as [O].

- Be able to explain how the method used to oxidise a primary alcohol determines whether an aldehyde or carboxylic acid is obtained.

- Be able to use chemical tests to distinguish between aldehydes and ketones including Fehling's solution and Tollens' reagent.

Specification Reference 3.3.1.1, 3.3.5.2

The basics

The simple way to oxidise alcohols is to burn them. But you don't get the most exciting products by doing this. If you want to end up with something more interesting, you need a more sophisticated way of oxidising. You can use the oxidising agent acidified potassium dichromate(VI), $K_2Cr_2O_7$, to mildly oxidise 1° and 2° alcohols. In the reaction the orange dichromate(VI) ion, $Cr_2O_7^{2-}$, is reduced to the green chromium(III) ion, Cr^{3+}. Primary alcohols are oxidised to aldehydes and then to carboxylic acids. Secondary alcohols are oxidised to ketones only. Tertiary alcohols aren't oxidised.

Aldehydes, ketones and carboxylic acids

Aldehydes

Aldehydes and ketones are carbonyl compounds — they have the functional group C=O. Their general formula is $C_nH_{2n}O$. Aldehydes have a hydrogen and one alkyl group attached to the **carbonyl** carbon atom...

This is the aldehyde functional group.

Aldehydes have the suffix -al. You don't have to say which carbon the functional group is on — it's always on carbon-1. Naming aldehydes follows very similar rules to the naming of alcohols (see page 225).

┌─ **Examples** ─────────────────

propanal

The longest continuous carbon chain is 3 carbon atoms, so the stem is propane. So, the aldehyde is called propanal.

The longest continuous carbon chain is 4 carbon atoms, so the stem is butane.

There's a methyl group attached to the second carbon atom so there's a 2-methyl- prefix.

So, the aldehyde is called 2-methylbutanal.

2-methylbutanal

Ketones

Ketones have two alkyl groups attached to the carbonyl carbon atom.

This is the ketone functional group.

Tip: A molecule has to contain at least 3 carbon atoms for it to be a ketone.

The suffix for ketones is -one. For ketones with five or more carbons, you need to say which carbon the functional group is on.

Tip: Remember that a suffix comes at the end of a name and a prefix comes at the beginning.

Examples

propanone

The longest continuous carbon chain is 3 carbon atoms, so the stem is propane.

So, the ketone is called propanone.

The longest continuous carbon chain is 5 carbon atoms, so the stem is pentane. The carbonyl is found on the second carbon atom.

So, the ketone is called pentan-2-one.

pentan-2-one

Figure 1: The ketone propanone (also known as acetone) is commonly used as a nail varnish remover.

Carboxylic acids

Carboxylic acids have a COOH group at the end of their carbon chain. Their general formula is $C_nH_{2n+1}COOH$.

This is the carboxylic acid functional group.

Tip: The carboxylic acid functional group is usually written COOH and not CO_2H to show that the two oxygens are different — one is part of a carbonyl group (CO) and the other is part of an OH group.

The suffix for carboxylic acids is -oic. You also add the word 'acid' to the end of the name.

Examples

propanoic acid

The longest continuous carbon chain is 3 carbon atoms, so the stem is propane.

So, the carboxylic acid is called propanoic acid.

The longest continuous carbon chain is 3 carbon atoms, so the stem is propane.

There's a COOH group at each end of the carbon chain so it has a -dioic acid suffix.

So, the carboxylic acid is called propanedioic acid.

propanedioic acid

Exam Tip
Don't get all these functional groups mixed up in the exam — you could lose easy marks. The only way to learn them is practice, practice and more practice.

Oxidation of primary alcohols

A primary alcohol is first oxidised to an aldehyde. This aldehyde can then be oxidised to a carboxylic acid. You can use the notation [O] to represent an oxidising agent. This means you can write equations like this:

$$R-CH_2-OH + [O] \longrightarrow R-\overset{O}{\overset{\|}{C}}-H + H_2O$$

primary alcohol   aldehyde

$$R-\overset{O}{\overset{\|}{C}}-H + [O] \xrightarrow{reflux} R-\overset{O}{\overset{\|}{C}}-OH$$

aldehyde   carboxylic acid

Figure 2: Alcohol oxidation. The acidified potassium dichromate(VI) ion turns from orange to green when it oxidises an alcohol.

You can control how far the alcohol is oxidised by controlling the reaction conditions.

Oxidising primary alcohols to aldehydes

Gently heating ethanol with potassium dichromate(VI) solution and sulfuric acid in a test tube should produce "apple" smelling ethanal (an aldehyde).

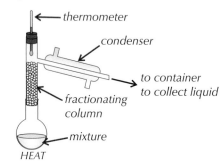

However, it's really tricky to control the amount of heat and the aldehyde is usually oxidised to form "vinegar" smelling ethanoic acid.

To get just the aldehyde, you need to get it out of the oxidising solution as soon as it forms.

You can do this by gently heating excess alcohol with a controlled amount of oxidising agent in distillation apparatus (see Figure 3). The aldehyde (which boils at a lower temperature than the alcohol) is distilled off immediately.

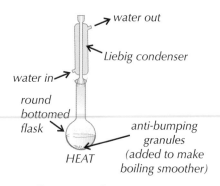

Figure 3: Distillation apparatus.

Oxidising primary alcohols to carboxylic acids

To produce the carboxylic acid, the alcohol has to be vigorously oxidised.

The alcohol is mixed with excess oxidising agent and heated under reflux (see Figures 4 and 5). Heating under reflux means you can increase the temperature of an organic reaction to boiling without losing volatile solvents, reactants or products. Any vapourised compounds are cooled, condense and drip back into the reaction mixture. So the aldehyde stays in the reaction mixture and is oxidised to carboxylic acid.

Figure 4: Refluxing apparatus.

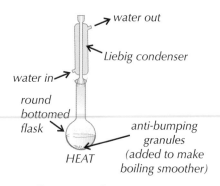

Figure 5: Refluxing apparatus.

Oxidation of secondary alcohols

Refluxing a secondary alcohol with acidified dichromate(VI) will produce a ketone.

$$R_1-\overset{\overset{\displaystyle R_2}{|}}{\underset{\underset{\displaystyle H}{|}}{C}}-OH \ + \ [O] \ \xrightarrow[\substack{\text{acidic}\\\text{conditions}}]{\text{reflux}} \ R_1-\overset{\overset{\displaystyle O}{\|}}{C}-R_2 \ + \ H_2O$$

secondary alcohol   *ketone*

Example

$$H-\overset{\overset{\displaystyle H}{|}}{\underset{\underset{\displaystyle H}{|}}{C}}-\overset{\overset{\displaystyle OH}{|}}{\underset{\underset{\displaystyle H}{|}}{C}}-\overset{\overset{\displaystyle H}{|}}{\underset{\underset{\displaystyle H}{|}}{C}}-H \ + \ [O] \ \xrightarrow[\substack{\text{acidic}\\\text{conditions}}]{\text{reflux}} \ H-\overset{\overset{\displaystyle H}{|}}{\underset{\underset{\displaystyle H}{|}}{C}}-\overset{\overset{\displaystyle O}{\|}}{C}-\overset{\overset{\displaystyle H}{|}}{\underset{\underset{\displaystyle H}{|}}{C}}-H \ + \ H_2O$$

propan-2-ol   *propanone*

Ketones can't be oxidised easily, so even prolonged refluxing won't produce anything more.

Oxidation of tertiary alcohols

Tertiary alcohols don't react with acidified potassium dichromate(VI) at all — the solution stays orange. The only way to oxidise tertiary alcohols is by burning them.

Testing for aldehydes and ketones

Aldehydes and ketones can be distinguished using oxidising agents — aldehydes are easily oxidised but ketones aren't. Fehling's solution and Benedict's solution are both deep blue Cu^{2+} complexes (alkaline solutions of copper(II) sulfate), which reduce to a brick-red Cu_2O precipitate when warmed with an aldehyde, but stay blue with a ketone (see Figure 6). Tollens' reagent is a colourless $[Ag(NH_3)_2]^+$ complex — it's reduced to silver when warmed with an aldehyde, but not with a ketone. The silver will coat the inside of the apparatus to form a silver mirror (see Figure 7).

Figure 6: *Fehling's solution. The test-tube on the left shows the unreacted Fehling's solution. The test-tube on the right shows the result of the reaction of Fehling's solution with an aldehyde.*

Figure 7: *The test-tube on the left shows the result of warming Tollens' reagent with an aldehyde. The test-tube on the right shows the result of warming Tollens' reagent with an ketone.*

Practice Question — Application

Q1 Draw the structures of the organic products of the following reactions.

    a) A reaction between butan-2-ol and acidified potassium dichromate(VI) under reflux.

    b) A reaction between butan-1-ol and acidified potassium dichromate(VI) using distillation apparatus.

    c) A reaction between butan-1-ol and acidified potassium dichromate(VI) under reflux.

Practice Questions — Fact Recall

Q1 What are the functional groups of aldehydes, ketones and carboxylic acids?

Q2 Write a general equation for the reaction of a primary alcohol with an oxidising agent under reflux.

Q3 Name two reagents you could use to distinguish between an aldehyde and a ketone.

Section Summary

Make sure you know...

- That alkenes are unsaturated hydrocarbons which contain a double covalent bond.
- That the double bond in an alkene is a centre of high electron density.
- The mechanism of electrophilic addition reactions of alkenes with HBr, H_2SO_4 and Br_2.
- That bromine water can be used to test for unsaturation.
- How to predict the products of addition to unsymmetrical alkenes.
- How addition polymers are formed from alkenes.
- How to recognise and draw the repeating unit in a polyalkene.
- How to draw the structure of a monomer when given a section of the polymer.
- How to name addition polymers.
- That addition polymers are unreactive.
- The nature of intermolecular forces between molecules of polyalkenes.
- Some typical uses of poly(chloroethene) and how its properties can be modified using a plasticiser.
- How to name alcohols.
- That alcohols can be primary, secondary or tertiary.
- That alkenes can be formed from alcohols by acid catalysed elimination reactions and that this method provides a possible route to polymers without using monomers derived from oil.
- The mechanism for the elimination of water from alcohols.
- That alcohols are produced industrially by hydration of alkenes in the presence of an acid catalyst.
- The typical conditions for the industrial production of ethanol from ethene.
- The mechanism for the formation of an alcohol by the reaction of an alkene with steam i n the presence of an acid catalyst.
- How ethanol is produced industrially by fermentation, including the conditions for the reaction.
- What a biofuel is and what carbon neutral means.
- Equations to show that ethanol, produced by fermentation, can be thought of as a carbon-neutral biofuel, but that this statement is invalid.
- The environmental and ethical issues linked to decision-making about biofuel use.
- How to name aldehydes, ketones and carboxylic acids.
- That primary and secondary alcohols can be oxidised to aldehydes, carboxylic acids and ketones by using an oxidising agent such as acidified potassium dichromate(VI).
- How to use Fehling's and Benedict's solution or Tollens' reagent to distinguish between aldehydes and ketones.

Exam-style Questions

1   Which substance is not involved in the reaction during the
    dehydration of propanol using a phosphoric acid catalyst?

    A   propene

    B   propane

    C   phosphoric acid

    D   water

    (1 mark)

2   What type of reaction produces bromoethane from ethene and hydrogen bromide?

    A   nucleophilic addition

    B   electrophilic substitution

    C   electrophilic addition

    D   nucleophilic substitution

    (1 mark)

3   Ethanol is a simple alcohol that can be used as a fuel, in alcoholic beverages,
    as a solvent and also as a starting molecule for many organic synthesis reactions.
    Its structure is shown below.

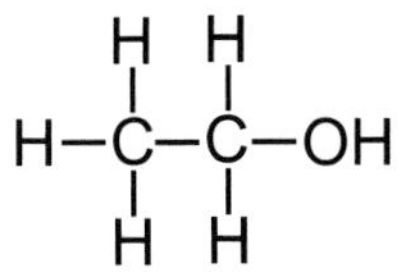

$$H-\underset{\underset{H}{|}}{\overset{\overset{H}{|}}{C}}-\underset{\underset{H}{|}}{\overset{\overset{H}{|}}{C}}-OH$$

    A fermentation reaction can be used to produce ethanol.

3.1 Write down the equation for this reaction and state the conditions needed for the
    reaction to occur.

    (2 marks)

3.2 Explain why production of ethanol by fermentation may be important in the future.

    (1 mark)

3.3 Industrially, ethanol is also produced by steam hydration.
    Describe the conditions required for this reaction.

    (2 marks)

3.4 Draw the mechanism for the production of ethanol by steam hydration.

    (4 marks)

Ethanol can be used as a carbon neutral biofuel.

3.5 Define the term biofuel.

(1 mark)

3.6 By using equations, show that ethanol made by fermentation is a carbon neutral fuel.

(4 marks)

3.7 Explain why your answer to **3.6** is not a valid conclusion.

(2 marks)

3.8 Outline two environmental issues associated with biofuels.

(2 marks)

3.9 Outline one ethical issue associated with biofuels.

(1 mark)

4 A student has been given a sample of the alkene 3-methylpent-2-ene. The structure of 3-methylpent-2-ene is shown below.

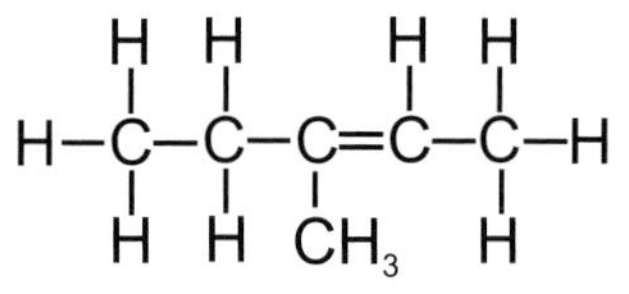

$$H-\overset{\overset{\displaystyle H}{|}}{\underset{\underset{\displaystyle H}{|}}{C}}-\overset{\overset{\displaystyle H}{|}}{\underset{\underset{\displaystyle H}{|}}{C}}-\overset{}{\underset{\underset{\displaystyle CH_3}{|}}{C}}=\overset{\overset{\displaystyle H}{|}}{\underset{\underset{\displaystyle H}{|}}{C}}-\overset{\overset{\displaystyle H}{|}}{\underset{\underset{\displaystyle H}{|}}{C}}-H$$

4.1 Describe how the student could prove that the sample is unsaturated.

(2 marks)

The student reacts 3-methylpent-2-ene with hydrogen bromide (HBr).

4.2 Write the equation for the reaction.

(1 mark)

4.3 Draw the structure of the major product of the reaction.

(1 mark)

4.4 Use your knowledge of carbocation stability to explain why the structure given in **4.3** is the major product of this reaction.

(3 marks)

4.5 3-methylpent-2-ene can be polymerised using an addition polymerisation reaction. Draw the repeating unit of the polymer formed in this reaction.

(1 mark)

5 Poly(tetrafluoroethene) is a polymer, more commonly known as Teflon®.
Teflon® is formed by addition polymerisation from its monomer.

5.1 What is a monomer?

(1 mark)

5.2 Give the IUPAC name of the monomer of Teflon®.

(1 mark)

5.3 Explain why poly(tetrafluoroethene) is unreactive.

(2 marks)

5.4 A plasticiser is sometimes added to a polymer.
How does a plasticiser affect the properties of a polymer?

(1 mark)

6 The structure of an isomer of butanol is shown below.

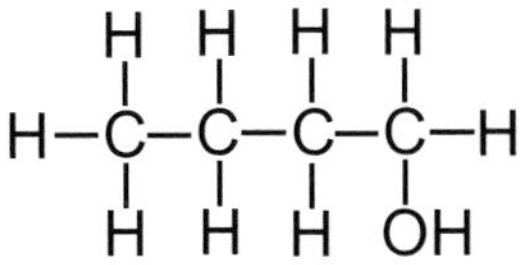

6.1 Give the IUPAC name of this isomer.

(1 mark)

The isomer is oxidised to produce butanal.

6.2 Name a suitable oxidising agent for this reaction.

(1 mark)

6.3 Describe the method used to carry out the oxidation.

(3 marks)

6.4 Give the equation for the reaction.
You may use [O] to represent the oxidising agent.

(1 mark)

6.5 A student is given the oxidised product, but she is not told whether
it is an aldehyde or a ketone. She must carry out a test to determine
what the oxidised product is. Describe two tests that she could carry out,
and the expected outcome of each.

(4 marks)

6.6 Draw the structure of an isomer of butanol that will not oxidise.

(1 mark)

Learning Objectives:

- Be able to identify functional groups using reactions in the specification.
- Know the tests for alcohols, aldehydes, alkenes and carboxylic acids (Required Practical 6).

Specification Reference 3.3.6.1

Tip: Primary alcohols would be oxidised to carboxylic acids if the aldehyde product was not distilled off when it formed.

Tip: Look back at pages 235-237 for more on these reactions.

Figure 1: *With a primary or secondary alcohol, the colour changes from orange to green as Cr(VI) changes to Cr(III). With a tertiary alcohol there is no reaction, so it stays orange.*

Tip: If you're doing any of the tests shown on pages 242-244 in the lab, make sure you're aware of any hazards or safety issues involved.

1. Tests for Functional Groups

REQUIRED PRACTICAL **6**

Organic compounds can be a bit tricky to identify. But handily there are a few simple tests that you can do that will help you tell them apart.

Testing for primary, secondary and tertiary alcohols

Potassium dichromate(VI) is an oxidising agent. It can oxidise primary and secondary alcohols to form aldehydes and ketones respectively (tertiary alcohols can't be oxidised). You can use the notation [O] to represent an oxidising agent when you write out a reaction .

$$R{-}CH_2{-}OH \ + \ [O] \ \xrightarrow{\text{distil}} \ R{-}\overset{\displaystyle O}{\underset{}{C}}{-}H \ + \ H_2O$$
primary alcohol   *aldehyde*

$$R_1{-}\overset{\displaystyle R_2}{\underset{\displaystyle H}{C}}{-}OH \ + \ [O] \ \xrightarrow[\text{acidic conditions}]{\text{reflux}} \ R_1{-}\overset{\displaystyle O}{\underset{}{C}}{-}R_2 \ + \ H_2O$$
secondary alcohol   *ketone*

$$R_1{-}\overset{\displaystyle R_2}{\underset{\displaystyle R_3}{C}}{-}OH \ + \ [O] \ \longrightarrow \ \text{no reaction}$$
tertiary alcohol

As primary and secondary alcohols are oxidised, as in the reactions above, potassium dichromate(VI) is reduced. This is accompanied by a colour change (see Figure 1):

$$Cr_2O_7{}^{2-} \ + \ 6e^- \ + \ 14H^+ \ \rightarrow \ 2Cr^{3+} \ + \ 7H_2O$$

orange dichromate(VI) ions are reduced   *green chromium(III) ions are formed*

You can use this colour change to test for the presence of primary, secondary or tertiary alcohols. Here's the test you you'll need to carry out:

1. Add 10 drops of the alcohol to 2 cm³ of acidified potassium dichromate solution in a test tube.

2. Warm the mixture gently in a hot water bath.

3. Watch for a colour change — with primary and secondary alcohols, the orange solution slowly turns green as an aldehyde or ketone forms. No colour change is seen with tertiary alcohols.

This test is useful, but there is a problem. This test doesn't help to work out whether an alcohol is a primary or a secondary alcohol — it gives the same result for both. There are a few more tests you can carry out, however, to tell whether an unknown alcohol is primary or secondary, using the oxidised versions of the primary or secondary alcohol:

- If you oxidise an alcohol under reflux and it tests positive for being a carboxylic acid, then it's a primary alcohol.

- If you oxidise an alcohol under distillation conditions and it tests positive for being an aldehyde, then it's a primary alcohol.

- If you oxidise an alcohol under reflux (or distillation) and it tests positive for being a ketone, then it's a secondary alcohol.

The tests for aldehydes, ketones and carboxylic acids are covered on the next two pages.

Testing for aldehydes and ketones

As you saw on pages 235-237, aldehydes are easily oxidised to carboxylic acids, whereas it's not easy to oxidise ketones further. You can use this property to tell the difference between them.

Fehling's and Benedict's solution

Fehling's solution is a blue solution of complexed copper(II) ions dissolved in sodium hydroxide. **Benedict's solution** is effectively the same as Fehling's solution except the copper(II) ions are dissolved in sodium carbonate instead of sodium hydroxide. To test an aldehyde or ketone with Benedict's or Fehling's solution, follow this method:

1. Add 2 cm³ of Fehling's or Benedict's solution to a test tube. (Whichever one you use, it should be a clear blue solution.)

2. Add 5 drops of the aldehyde or ketone to the test tube.

3. Put the test tube in a hot water bath to warm it for a few minutes.

Benedict's and Fehling's solutions will both reduce to a brick red Cu_2O precipitate when warmed with an aldehyde. No reaction happens with ketones, so the solution will stay blue (see Figure 2).

Copper(II) ions in Fehling's/ Benedict's solution are reduced. *Blue* *Brick-red* $2Cu^{2+}_{(aq)} + 2OH^-_{(aq)} + 2e^- \rightarrow Cu_2O_{(s)} + H_2O_{(l)}$ *The copper(I) ions produced form a brick red precipitate of copper(I) oxide.*

Electrons come from the oxidation of the aldehyde.

Tollens' reagent

Tollens' reagent contains a $[Ag(NH_3)_2]^+$ complex. It can be made using the following method.

1. Put 2 cm³ of 0.10 mol dm⁻³ silver nitrate solution in a test tube.

2. Add a few drops of dilute sodium hydroxide solution. A light brown precipitate should form.

3. Add drops of dilute ammonia solution until the brown precipitate dissolves completely — this solution is Tollens' reagent.

Tip: You can also test for alcohols using sodium metal. If you add a small piece of sodium to a pure alcohol, it will fizz as it gives off H_2 gas. There are lots of other chemicals which react with sodium like this though, so it may not be conclusive. Also, sodium reacts violently with acids, so you have to be very sure that the solution you're testing isn't acidic first.

Figure 2: *From left to right, these test tubes show: Fehling's solution, the brick-red precipitate made by reacting Fehling's solution with an aldehyde, and the result of reacting Fehling's solution with an ketone (i.e. no change).*

Tip: Don't panic — you don't need to know this equation for what happens to the ions in the oxidising agent for your exams.

Tip: You don't need to learn this equation for what happens to the silver ions here.

The silver ions in Tollens' reagent are reduced to silver metal when warmed with an aldehyde, but not with a ketone. The silver will coat the inside of the apparatus to form a silver mirror (see Figure 3).

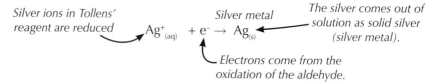

Silver ions in Tollens' reagent are reduced

Silver metal

The silver comes out of solution as solid silver (silver metal).

$$Ag^+_{(aq)} + e^- \rightarrow Ag_{(s)}$$

Electrons come from the oxidation of the aldehyde.

This doesn't always produce a lovely even, shiny silver coating, so don't worry if you end up with a silvery-grey precipitate — that's a positive result too.

 Aldehydes and ketones are flammable so you have to take great care when heating them (such as in these tests). Aldehydes and ketones should always be warmed using a water bath, rather than using a Bunsen burner, to prevent them from catching alight.

Figure 3: The test-tube on the left contains unreacted Tollens' reagent. The one on the right shows the result of its reaction with an aldehyde.

Testing for carboxylic acids

Carboxylic acids are formed by oxidising aldehydes or primary alcohols — there's more about how this happens on page 236.

 If you've got a sample of a substance that you think might be a carboxylic acid, you can test it using the following method:

1. Add 2 cm³ of the solution that you want to test to a test tube.
2. Add 1 small spatula of solid sodium carbonate (or 2 cm³ of sodium carbonate solution).
3. If the solution begins to fizz, bubble the gas that it produces through some limewater in a second test tube.

If the solution tested contains a carboxylic acid, carbon dioxide gas will be produced. When carbon dioxide is bubbled through limewater, the limewater turns cloudy.

 Be careful though — this test will give a positive result with any acid, so you can only use it to distinguish between organic compounds when you already know that one of them is a carboxylic acid.

Figure 4: Limewater turns from clear to cloudy when carbon dioxide is bubbled through it.

Tip: When carbon dioxide is bubbled through limewater, a calcium carbonate precipitate is formed. It's this that makes the limewater turn cloudy.

Testing for alkenes

Testing for alkenes involves testing for the presence of unsaturation. In the case of alkenes, this is testing for double bonds.

1. Add 2 cm³ of the solution that you want to test to a test tube.
2. Add 2 cm³ of bromine water to the test tube.
3. Shake the test tube.

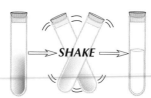

➤ **SHAKE** ➤

Figure 6: Shaking alkenes with bromine water causes orange bromine water to turn colourless.

Figure 5: Bromine water turns colourless when shaken with alkenes.

If an alkene is present, the bromine water will turn from orange to colourless.

Q1 A student has an unknown organic compound. It contains only carbon, oxygen and hydrogen atoms. He adds it to a test tube containing a solution of Tollens' reagent. He warms the test tube for a while, and silver metal starts to coat the inside of the test tube. What homologous series does his compound belong to?

Q2 A student has two compounds, A and B. She knows one is a ketone. She adds the two compounds, A and B, to separate test tubes containing Benedict's solution. A red precipitate forms in the test tube containing compound A, but nothing happens with compound B. Which compound, A or B, is the ketone?

Q3 A student is investigating the behaviour of primary alcohols.

a) She firstly adds a primary alcohol to a solution containing potassium dichromate(VI) ions and refluxes the mixture. What colour change would you expect her to see?

b) She then adds a spatula of calcium carbonate to the resulting solution. The solution starts to fizz. The student bubbles the resulting gas through a test tube containing limewater. What would you expect the student to observe?

Q4 A student has three test tubes. Each test tube contains one of three carbonyl compounds: propanal, propanoic acid or propanone. Outline a series of tests the student could carry out to identify which test tube contains which compound. You should include details of any reagents, conditions and expected observations.

Q5 a) State why warming samples of a substance with acidified potassium dichromate(VI) solution is not enough on its own to distinguish whether it is a primary alcohol or a secondary alcohol.

b) Describe an experiment that you could perform to distinguish between samples of a primary alcohol and a secondary alcohol.

Tip: This topic will be so much easier if you know the chemistry of alcohols and carbonyl compounds inside out. Have a look back at pages 225-237 for all this chemistry.

Q1 What colour precipitate forms when Fehling's solution is mixed with an aldehyde?

Q2 Describe the procedure for making Tollens' reagent.

Q3 What observation would you make when an alkene was shaken with bromine water?

- Know that mass spectrometry can be used to determine the molecular formula of a compound.
- Be able to use precise atomic masses and the precise molecular mass to determine the molecular formula of a compound.

Specification Reference 3.3.6.2

2. Mass Spectrometry

An analytical technique is a method of analysing a substance to learn more about it. This topic deals with one specific analytic technique — mass spectrometry. Mass spectrometry uses the mass of a compound to identify it.

Finding relative molecular masses

You saw on pages 19-24 how mass spectrometry can be used to find relative isotopic masses, the abundance of different isotopes of an element, and the relative molecular mass, M_r, of a compound. Remember — the M_r of a compound is given by the molecular ion peak on the spectrum. The mass/charge (m/z) value of the molecular ion peak is equal to the M_r of the molecule.

─ Example ────────────────

The mass spectrum of a straight chain alkane contains a molecular ion peak with $m/z = 72$. Identify the compound.

1. The m/z value of the molecular ion peak is 72, so the M_r of the compound must be 72.
2. If you calculate the molecular masses of the first few straight-chain alkanes, you'll find that the one with a molecular mass of 72 is pentane (C_5H_{12}): M_r of pentane $= (5 \times 12.0) + (12 \times 1.0) = 72.0$
3. So the compound must be pentane.

***Figure 1:** Mass spectrometer.*

High resolution mass spectrometry

High resolution mass spectrometers can measure atomic and molecular masses extremely accurately (to several decimal places). This can be useful for identifying compounds that appear to have the same M_r when they're rounded to the nearest whole number.

For example, propane (C_3H_8) and ethanal (CH_3CHO) both have an M_r of 44 to the nearest whole number. But on a high resolution mass spectrum, propane has a molecular ion peak with $m/z = 44.0624$ and ethanal has a molecular ion peak with $m/z = 44.0302$.

Tip: On a normal (low resolution) mass spectrum, all of these molecules would show up as having an m/z of 98.

─ Example ────────────────

On a high resolution mass spectrum, a compound has a molecular ion peak with $m/z = 98.0336$. What is its molecular formula?

A $C_5H_{10}N_2$	B $C_6H_{10}O$	C C_7H_{14}	D $C_5H_6O_2$

Use these precise atomic masses to work out your answer:

$^1H — 1.0078$ $^{12}C — 12.0000$ $^{14}N — 14.0031$ $^{16}O — 15.9949$

Work out the precise molecular mass of each compound:

$C_5H_{10}N_2$: $M_r = (5 \times 12.0000) + (10 \times 1.0078) + (2 \times 14.0031) = 98.0842$

$C_6H_{10}O$: $M_r = (6 \times 12.0000) + (10 \times 1.0078) + 15.9949$ $\qquad = 98.0729$

C_7H_{14} : $M_r = (7 \times 12.0000) + (14 \times 1.0078)$ $\qquad\qquad = 98.1092$

$C_5H_6O_2$: $M_r = (5 \times 12.0000) + (6 \times 1.0078) + (2 \times 15.9949)$ $= 98.0336$

So the answer is **D**, $C_5H_6O_2$.

Q1 A student runs low resolution mass spectrometry on a sample of a compound, which he knows is either C_3H_6O, C_3H_8N or C_4H_{10}.

a) Why might low resolution mass spectrometry not be able to distinguish between these molecules?

b) The sample is injected into a high resolution mass spectrometer. A molecular ion peak is seen at $m/z = 58.0655$.
What is the molecular formula of the compound?
Use these precise atomic masses to work out your answer:

^{1}H: 1.0078 ^{12}C: 12.0000
^{14}N: 14.0031 ^{16}O: 15.9949

Q2 A mixture of two compounds was analysed in a high resolution time of flight mass spectrometer. The sample produced the two molecular ion peaks shown on the spectrum below.

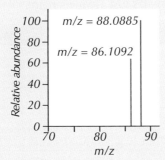

The mixture consists of two of the compounds listed below. Using the precise atomic masses given in Q1, work out which two of the compounds make up the mixture.

Molecule	Formula
butanoic acid	$CH_3CH_2CH_2COOH$
pentan-1-ol	$CH_3CH_2CH_2CH_2CH_2OH$
pentan-3-one	$CH_3CH_2COCH_2CH_3$
hexane	$CH_3CH_2CH_2CH_2CH_2CH_3$

Learning Objectives:

- Know that bonds in a molecule absorb infrared radiation at characteristic wavenumbers.

- Know that 'fingerprinting' allows identification of a particular molecule by comparison of spectra.

- Be able to use infrared spectra and the Chemistry Data Sheet or Booklet to identify particular bonds, and therefore functional groups, and also to identify impurities.

- Understand the link between absorption of infrared radiation by bonds in CO_2, methane, water vapour and global warming.

Specification Reference 3.3.6.3

3. Infrared Spectroscopy

Infrared spectroscopy is another analytical technique. It uses the fact that bonds in different functional groups absorb different frequencies of infrared light. We can use an infrared spectrum of a molecule to identify its functional groups.

The basics

In **infrared (IR) spectroscopy**, a beam of IR radiation is passed through a sample of a chemical. The IR radiation is absorbed by the covalent bonds in the molecules, increasing their vibrational energy. Bonds between different atoms absorb different frequencies of IR radiation. Bonds in different places in a molecule absorb different frequencies too — so the O–H bond in an alcohol and the O–H bond in a carboxylic acid absorb different frequencies. Figure 1 shows what frequencies different bonds absorb — you don't need to learn this data, but you do need to understand how to use it. Wavenumber is the measure used for the frequency (it's just 1/wavelength).

Bond	Where it's found	Wavenumber (cm⁻¹)
N–H (amines)	amines (e.g. CH_3NH_2)	3300 - 3500
O–H (alcohols)	alcohols	3230 - 3550
C–H	most organic molecules	2850 - 3300
O–H (acids)	carboxylic acids	2500 - 3000
C≡N	nitriles (e.g. CH_3CN)	2220 - 2260
C=O	aldehydes, ketones, carboxylic acids, esters	1680 - 1750
C=C	alkenes	1620 - 1680
C–O	alcohols, carboxylic acids	1000 - 1300
C–C	most organic molecules	750 - 1100

Figure 1: Table showing the absorption of different bonds.

An infrared spectrometer produces a graph that shows you what frequencies of radiation the bond in the molecules are absorbing. So you can use it to identify the functional groups in a molecule. The peaks show you where radiation is being absorbed — the 'peaks' on IR spectra are upside-down.

Exam Tip
You'll get a table like the one in Figure 1 on the Data Sheet in your exam. So there's no need to memorise all those numbers — yay.

Tip: Most organic molecules will have loads of C–H bonds in them so the region at ~3000 cm⁻¹ on an IR spectrum isn't always very useful.

┌ **Examples** ─ **Maths Skills** ─────────────

The structure of ethanal is shown on the right:
This is the infrared spectrum of ethanal:

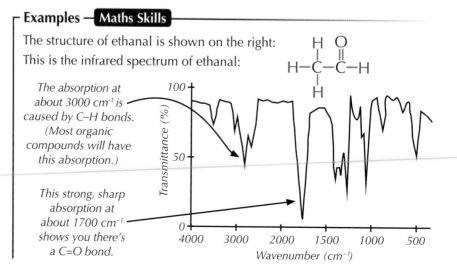

The absorption at about 3000 cm⁻¹ is caused by C–H bonds. (Most organic compounds will have this absorption.)

This strong, sharp absorption at about 1700 cm⁻¹ shows you there's a C=O bond.

Here is the structure and infrared spectrum of ethylamine.

ethylamine

Infrared spectrum of ethylamine

This strong, sharp absorption at about 2900 cm⁻¹ shows you there are C–H bonds in the molecule.

This strong absorption at about 3350 cm⁻¹ shows you there are N–H bonds.

Transmittance (%)

Wavenumber (cm⁻¹)

Tip: When you're reading an infrared spectrum, always double check the scale. The wavenumbers increase from right to left — don't get caught out.

The fingerprint region

The region between 1000 cm⁻¹ and 1550 cm⁻¹ on the spectrum is called the **fingerprint region**. It's unique to a particular compound. You can check this region of an unknown compound's IR spectrum against those of known compounds. If it matches one of them, you know what the molecule is.

Tip: There are computer databases that store the infrared spectra of thousands of pure organic compounds. So you can do this checking and comparing relatively quickly using a computer.

─ **Example** ── **Maths Skills**

Here is the structure and the infrared spectrum of ethanoic acid.

ethanoic acid

This medium, broad absorption at about 3000 cm⁻¹ shows you there's an O–H bond in a carboxylic acid.

Infrared spectrum of ethanoic acid

Transmittance (%)

This strong, sharp absorption at about 1720 cm⁻¹ shows you there's a C=O bond.

Wavenumber (cm⁻¹)

This is the fingerprint region. If you see an infrared spectrum of an unknown molecule that has the same pattern in this area, you can be sure that it's ethanoic acid.

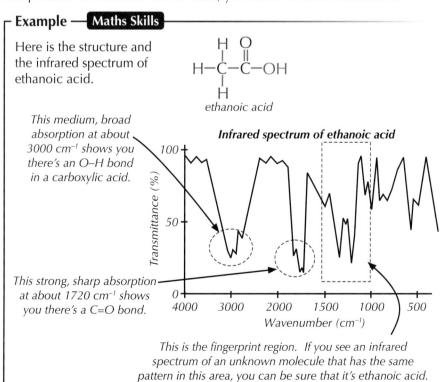

Infrared spectroscopy can also be used to assess how pure a compound is and identify impurities — impurities produce extra peaks in the fingerprint region.

Infrared absorption and global warming

The Sun emits mainly UV/visible radiation which is absorbed by the Earth's surface and re-emitted as IR radiation. Molecules of greenhouse gases, like carbon dioxide, methane and water vapour, have bonds that are really good at absorbing infrared energy — so if the amounts of these gases in the atmosphere increase, more IR radiation is absorbed which leads to global warming. The more IR radiation a molecule absorbs, the more effective they are as greenhouse gases.

Figure 2: *The greenhouse effect.*

Tip: You can use the table on page 248 to help you out with these questions.

Practice Questions — Application

Q1 The spectrum below is the infrared spectrum of a carboxylic acid with $M_r = 74$.

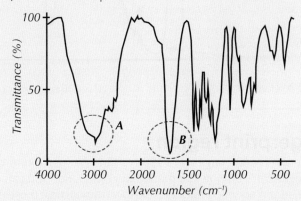

a) Identify the bonds that create the peaks marked **A** and **B** in the diagram.

b) Draw the displayed formula of the molecule.

Q2 The spectrum below shows the infrared spectrum for an unknown molecule. Use the spectrum to identify one important bond that can be found in the molecule.

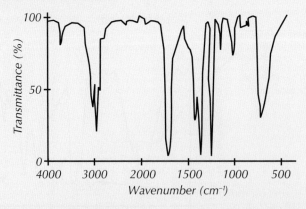

Practice Questions — Fact Recall

Q1 Give a brief explanation of how an infrared spectrum is created.

Q2 Over what frequency range is the fingerprint region of an IR spectrum found?

Section Summary

Make sure you know...

- How to use potassium dichromate(VI) to distinguish between primary and secondary and tertiary alcohols.
- How to use Fehling's (or Benedict's) solution to distinguish between aldehydes and ketones.
- How to make Tollens' reagent and use it to distinguish between aldehydes and ketones.
- How to use calcium carbonate as a test for carboxylic acids.
- How to use bromine water to test for alkenes.
- How to use mass spectrometry to identify the molecular mass of a compound.
- How to use mass spectrometry to determine the molecular formula of a compound.
- That high resolution mass spectrometry can be used to identify compounds with similar M_r values.
- How to use precise atomic masses and precise molecular masses to determine the molecular formula of a compound.
- That certain functional groups absorb infrared radiation at characteristic frequencies.
- That the 'fingerprint region' of an infrared spectrum allows identification of a molecule by comparison of spectra.
- How to use infrared spectra to identify particular functional groups and to identify impurities.
- That greenhouse gases, such as CO_2, water and methane, absorb infrared radiation and so increasing the amounts of them in the atmosphere can cause global warming.

Exam-style Questions

1   A scientist has synthesised two molecules — molecule **A** and molecule **B**.
Both of the molecules were synthesised by reacting 1-bromopropane
with OH⁻ ions. The structure of 1-bromopropane is shown below.

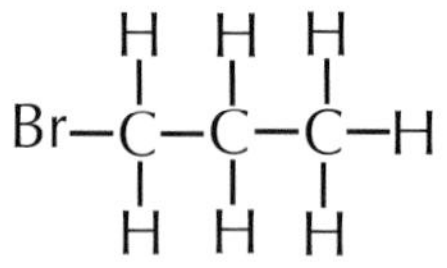

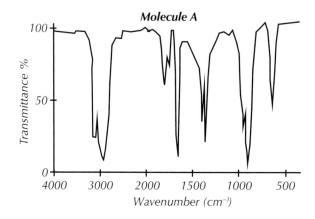

The infrared spectra of the molecules are shown below.

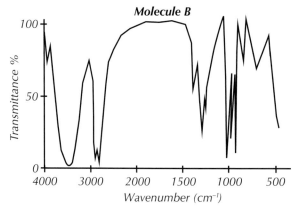

1.1   Neither molecule **A** nor molecule **B** contains halogen atoms.
Use the table on page 248 to help you predict the structures
of molecule **A** and molecule **B**. Explain your reasoning.

(4 marks)

1.2   Name molecule **A** and molecule **B**.

(2 marks)

1.3   Give the reagents and conditions that are needed
to produce each molecule from 1-bromopropane.

(2 marks)

2   A student is investigating the nature of various greenhouse gases using infrared spectroscopy. The graphs below show the spectra of water vapour, carbon dioxide and methane.

Spectrum of water vapour

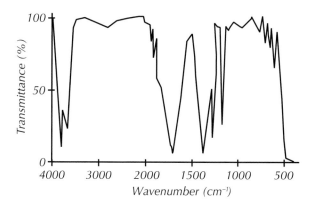

Spectrum of carbon dioxide

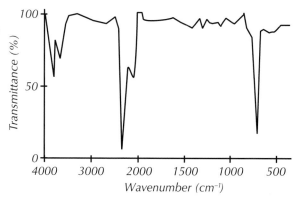

Spectrum of methane

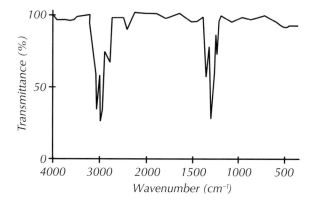

Predict, with reasoning, whether water vapour, carbon dioxide or methane is the most effective greenhouse gas.

(2 marks)

3   A student has three organic compounds — butanal, propanoic acid and ethanol. The substances are each in a separate test tube, labelled **A**, **B** and **C**.

The student carries out a series of tests to work out which compound is contained in each test tube.

Her results are summarised in the table below.

	Test		
	Addition to potassium dichromate(VI) solution and warmed	Addition of a spatula of calcium carbonate	Addition to Tollens' reagent and warmed
Compound A	Solution turns from orange to green	No reaction	No reaction
Compound B	Solution turns from orange to green	No reaction	Silver mirror coats the inside of the test tube
Compound C	No reaction	Fizzing — gas produced turns limewater turns cloudy	No reaction

With reasoning, correctly assign the identity of compounds **A**, **B** and **C**.

(3 marks)

4   A student has two molecules — molecule **X** and molecule **Y**.

She knows each molecule is either propanal or propanone.

4.1   Draw out the displayed formulae of propanal.

(1 mark)

4.2   Draw out the displayed formula of propanone.

(1 mark)

4.3   Explain why the infrared spectroscopy would not be a suitable technique to use to distinguish between molecule **X** and molecule **Y**.

(1 mark)

4.4   Explain why high resolution mass spectrometry would not be a suitable technique to use to distinguish between molecule **X** and molecule **Y**.

(1 mark)

4.5   Outline a simple test that the student could use to identify molecule **X** and molecule **Y**.

You should include the names of any reagents used, any specific safety precautions that should be taken and how the test results would show the identity of each molecule.

(3 marks)

5   Three organic compounds, **A**, **B** and **C** were analysed using high resolution mass spectrometry and infrared spectroscopy. None of the compounds contain any atoms other than hydrogen, carbon and oxygen.

The tables below show the m/z value of the molecular ion peak in the mass spectrum of each compound and the precise atomic masses of hydrogen, carbon and oxygen.

Compound	m/z
A	72.0573
B	72.0936
C	70.0780

Atom	Atomic mass
^{1}H	1.0078
^{12}C	12.0000
^{16}O	15.9949

Each of the infrared spectra below matches one of compounds **A**, **B** and **C**.

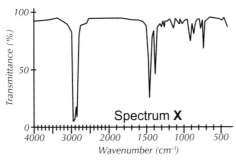

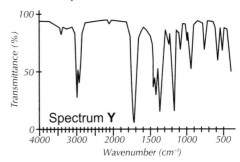

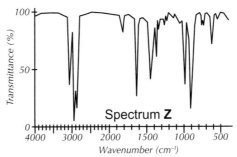

5.1   Using your knowledge of organic chemistry and analytical techniques, along with data given above and in the table on page 248, find the molecular formula of each of compounds **A**, **B** and **C**, and to match each of the infrared spectra above to one of the three compounds. Explain your reasoning.

(8 marks)

5.2   Given that none of compounds **A**, **B** and **C** contain branched carbon chains, suggest one possible identity for each of the three compounds. (There may be more than one possible answer for each.)

(3 marks)

5.3   What feature of infrared spectra would allow you to check whether your suggestions in **5.2** were correct?

(1 mark)

Maths crops up a lot in AS and A level Chemistry so there are lots of maths skills you need to master for your exams. These skills are covered throughout the book but here's an extra little section, just on maths, to help you out.

1. Calculations and Diagrams

There's no getting away from those pesky calculations and diagrams...

Calculations

The most important thing to remember in calculations is to show your working. You've probably heard it a million times before but it makes sense. It only takes a few seconds to write down what's in your head and it'll stop you from making silly errors and losing out on marks. You won't get a mark for a wrong answer but you could get marks for the method you used to work out the answer.

Units

Make sure you always give the correct units for your answer.

┌─ **Example** ── `Maths Skills` ──────────────

Here's an example of a question where you need to change the units so they match the answer the examiner wants.

1   In an experiment, 1 g of a liquid fuel was completely burned in oxygen. The heat formed during this reaction raised the temperature of 50 g of water by 40 K.

1.1   Calculate the heat energy given out by this reaction in kJ.

When you use $q = mc\Delta T$ to calculate the heat given out, you get an answer in joules. You'll need to convert the units to kilojoules by dividing by 1000.

Standard form

You might be asked to give your answer in standard form. Standard form is used for writing very big or very small numbers in a more convenient way. Standard form must always look like this:

This number must always be between 1 and 10. ⟶ $A \times 10^n$ ⟵ *This number is the number of places the decimal point moves.*

┌─ **Examples** ── `Maths Skills` ──────────────

Here's how to write 3 500 000 in standard form.

- First write the non-zero digits with a decimal point after the first digit and a '× 10' after the last digit: 3.5×10

- Then count how many places the decimal point has moved to the left. (This is the same as n — the number that sits to the top right of the 10.)

$$3\,500\,000 = 3.5 \times 10^6$$

- Et voilà... that's 3 500 000 written in standard form.

Here are some more examples.

- You can write 450 000 as 4.5×10^5.

- The number 0.000056 is 5.6×10^{-5} in standard form — the number to the top right of the 10 is negative because the decimal point has moved to the right instead of the left.

- You can write 0.003456 as 3.456×10^{-3}.

Exam Tip
If you're asked specifically to give a number in ordinary or standard form, make sure you follow the instruction.

You need to be able to convert numbers written in standard form into ordinary form too.

Examples — Maths Skills

Here's how to write 7.2×10^3 in ordinary form.

- Take the number in standard form and move the decimal point n places to the right (remember, n is the number to the top right of the 10) — so in this case, three places to the right. Fill in any gaps with zeros.

$$7.2\overset{1}{0}\overset{2}{0}\overset{3}{0} = 7200$$

- There you go... that's 7.2×10^3 written in standard form.

Here are some more examples.

- You can write 9.1×10^5 as 910 000.

- The number 3.3×10^{-4} is 0.00033 in ordinary form — the n is negative so the decimal point has moved to the left instead of the right.

- You can write 1.765×10^{-3} as 0.001765.

Exam Tip
Make sure you know how to type numbers in standard form into your own calculator — it'll make calculations involving standard form easier.

Significant figures

Use the number of significant figures given in the data as a guide for how many you need to give in your answer. Whether you're doing calculations with the results of an experiment or in an exam, the rule is the same — round your answer to the lowest number of significant figures in the data you're using.

You should always write down the number of significant figures you've rounded to after your answer, so that other people can see what rounding you've done.

Tip: The first significant figure of a number is the first digit that isn't a zero. The second, third and fourth significant figures follow on immediately after the first (even if they're zeros).

Example — Maths Skills

In this question the data given to you is a good indication of how many significant figures you should give your answer to.

1.2 Calculate how many moles of sodium oxide are present in a pure 12.5 g sample of the compound. (Mr Na_2O = 62.0)

As all of the data in the question is given to 3 s.f., you should give your final answer to 3 s.f. too. So if your calculator gave you the answer 0.20161290 g, you should write down your final answer as 0.202 g (3 s.f.).

Tip: Careful though — don't round the answers to any intermediate steps in your calculation. Rounding too early will make your final answer less accurate.

┌─ **Example** — **Maths Skills** ─────────────

3.2 13.5 cm³ of a 0.51 mol dm⁻³ solution of sodium hydroxide reacts with 1.5 mol dm⁻³ hydrochloric acid. Calculate the volume of hydrochloric acid required to neutralise the sodium hydroxide.

There are two types of data in this question, volume data and concentration data. The volume data is given to 3 s.f. and the concentration data is given to 2 s.f.. You should always give your answer to the lowest number of significant figures given — in this case that's to 2 s.f. The answer in full is 4.59 cm³ so the answer rounded correctly would be 4.6 cm³ (2 s.f.).

When you're converting between ordinary and standard form, you need to make sure the number you've converted to has the same number of significant figures as the number you've converted from.

┌─ **Example** — **Maths Skills** ─────────────

Convert 130.50 kJ from ordinary form to standard form.

The number 130.50 kJ has 5 significant figures. When you convert it from ordinary to standard form, the number still needs to have 5 significant figures. So the correct answer is:

$$1.3050 \times 10^2 \text{ kJ}$$

Diagrams of molecules

When you're asked to draw a diagram of a molecule in an exam it's important that you draw everything correctly. There's more about how to draw the displayed and skeletal formulas of molecules on pages 172 and 174, but you're also going to have to tackle how to represent the 3D shapes of molecules on the page. Here's a reminder of the main things to remember.

┌─ **Examples** — **Maths Skills** ─────────────

Here's how to draw a 2D representation of the 3D shape of an ammonia molecule (NH_3):

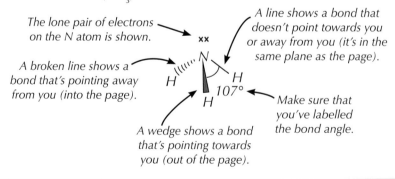

The lone pair of electrons on the N atom is shown.

A line shows a bond that doesn't point towards you or away from you (it's in the same plane as the page).

A broken line shows a bond that's pointing away from you (into the page).

A wedge shows a bond that's pointing towards you (out of the page).

Make sure that you've labelled the bond angle.

Figure 1: *An ammonia molecule. This is the 3D shape you are trying to represent in your drawing.*

When you're drawing any diagram make sure it's really clear what you're drawing. Draw diagrams nice and big, so you can see all of the details clearly. But do stay within the answer space — you won't get marks for anything that's drawn in the margin.

2. Formulas and Symbols

There's quite a lot of mathsy type stuff in the exams that involves using formulas — here are the ones you need to learn to get it all right.

Formulas

First up is perhaps the most useful formula of all:

$$\text{Number of moles} = \frac{\text{Mass of substance}}{M_r} \quad \text{also written as...} \quad n = \frac{m}{M_r}$$

Then there's the one that uses Avogadro's constant (6.02×10^{23}):

$$\text{Number of particles} = \text{Number of moles} \times \text{Avogadro's constant}$$

You'll need these ones when you're dealing with solutions:

$$\text{Number of moles} = \frac{\text{Concentration (mol dm}^{-3}) \times \text{Volume (cm}^3)}{1000}$$

$$\text{Number of moles} = \text{Concentration (mol dm}^{-3}) \times \text{Volume (in dm}^3)$$

Here's the ideal gas equation:

$$\underset{\text{(Pa)}}{\overset{\text{(m}^3)}{pV}} = nRT \quad \begin{array}{l}\text{(8.31 J K}^{-1}\text{mol}^{-1})\\ \text{(K)}\\ \text{(moles)}\end{array}$$

And the ones to do with atom economy and percentage yield:

$$\%\text{ atom economy} = \frac{\text{molecular mass of desired product}}{\text{sum of molecular masses of all reactants}} \times 100$$

$$\%\text{ yield} = \frac{\text{Actual yield}}{\text{Theoretical yield}} \times 100$$

Here's the formula for finding the enthalpy change of a reaction:

$$\underset{\text{(J)}}{q} = mc\Delta T \quad \begin{array}{l}\text{(g)}\\ \text{(K)}\\ \text{(J g}^{-1}\text{K}^{-1})\end{array}$$

The official unit for ΔT is K, but actually you can use °C here — it's the change in temperature, and that will be the same if you use K or °C.

Here's the general formula for finding the rate of a reaction:

$$\text{rate of reaction} = \frac{\text{amount of reactant used or product formed}}{\text{time}}$$

And finally, here's the formula for the equilibrium constant:

For the general reaction $aA + bB \rightleftharpoons dD + eE$:
$$K_c = \frac{[D]^d[E]^e}{[A]^a[B]^b}$$

Tip: You'll find all of these formulas dotted throughout Unit 1 of the book — all of them come from Physical chemistry.

Tip: M_r is relative molecular mass (or relative formula mass). You work it out by adding up all the A_rs (atomic masses) of all the atoms in the molecule (or compound).

Exam Tip
All these formulas are really important — you have to learn them because they won't be given to you in the exam (except for the values of the gas constant, R, and specific heat capacity, c). Make sure you can rearrange them (see next page) and give the units that go with each formula too.

Tip: In the equilibrium constant formula, the lower-case letters a, b, d and e are the number of moles of each substance in the equation. The square brackets, [ ], mean concentration in mol dm^{-3}.

Rearranging formulas

Being able to rearrange formulas is a must in chemistry, since you'll often need to make a different quantity the subject of a formula. Just remember the golden rule — whatever you do to one side of the formula, you must do to the other side of the formula.

Exam Tip
Once you've rearranged your formula, all you need to do is to pop the values from the question into the right places — making sure that they're in the right units first, of course.

┌─ **Example** ─ **Maths Skills** ─────────────

The ideal gas equation is $pV = nRT$.
Rearrange the equation to make T the subject.

$pV = nRT$

$T = \dfrac{pV}{nR}$ ⟩ Divide both sides by nR

Formula triangles

Formula triangles are useful tools for changing the subject of a formula.

If three things are related by a formula like this: $a = b \times c$ or like this: $b = \dfrac{a}{c}$

then you can put them into a formula triangle:

┌─ **Example** ─ **Maths Skills** ─────────────

If you have this formula:

number of moles (n) = mass (m) ÷ M_r

then you can turn it into a formula triangle like this:

- As m is divided by M_r, m goes on top, leaving $n \times M_r$ on the bottom:

- If you wanted to find the number of moles (n) you would just cover up n, which leaves $m \div M_r$.
- So, number of moles = mass ÷ M_r.

Tip: You don't have to use formula triangles to rearrange formulas. If you're happy rearranging formulas without them, that's fine.

Symbols

You'll need to know these symbols which might be used in equations in the exam. You'll have seen many of them before but here's a quick refresher:

Symbol	Meaning
=	equal to
<	less than
<<	much less than
>	greater than
>>	much greater than
∝	proportional to
~	approximately
⇌	reversible

3. Units

Units can trip you up if you're not sure which ones to use or how to convert between them. Here are some handy hints for using units.

Exam Tip
You really need to know these conversions — it'll save you time if you're confident changing between units.

Working with units

Here's the key thing to remember with regard to units when you do any calculation: whatever you do to the numbers, do the same thing to the units.

Example — **Maths Skills**

If you're dividing a number of moles by a volume, you need to make sure that you've divided 'moles' by the volume units too. For example:

2 moles $\div$ 4 dm^3 = 2 mol/dm^3 = 2 mol dm^{-3}

Common unit conversions

Volume units

Volume can be measured in m^3, dm^3 and cm^3.

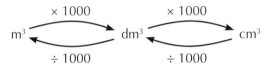

$$m^3 \underset{\div\ 1000}{\overset{\times\ 1000}{\rightleftarrows}} dm^3 \underset{\div\ 1000}{\overset{\times\ 1000}{\rightleftarrows}} cm^3$$

Tip: These two units are the same because multiplying something by x^{-3} is the same as dividing it by x^3.

Examples — **Maths Skills**

Write 6 dm^3 in m^3 and cm^3.

First, to convert 6 dm^3 into m^3 you need to divide by 1000.

6 dm^3 $\div$ 1000 = 0.006 m^3 = 6 $\times$ 10^{-3} m^3

Then, to convert 6 dm^3 into cm^3 you need to multiply by 1000.

6 dm^3 $\times$ 1000 = 6000 cm^3 = 6 $\times$ 10^3 cm^3

Write 0.4 cm^3 in dm^3 and m^3.

First, to convert 0.4 cm^3 into dm^3 you need to divide by 1000.

0.4 cm^3 $\div$ 1000 = 0.0004 dm^3 = 4 $\times$ 10^{-4} dm^3

Then, to convert 0.0004 dm^3 into m^3 you need to divide by 1000.

0.0004 dm^3 $\div$ 1000 = 0.0000004 m^3 = 4 $\times$ 10^{-7} m^3

Tip: The answers that look like this:
$\quad$ 6 $\times$ 10^{-3} cm^3
are shown in standard form. There's more about standard form on pages 256-257.

Temperature units

Temperature can be measured in K and °C.

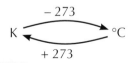

$$K \underset{+\ 273}{\overset{-\ 273}{\rightleftarrows}} °C$$

Examples — **Maths Skills**

Write 21 °C in Kelvin.

To convert 21 °C into K you need to add 273: $\quad$ 21 °C + 273 = 294 K

Write 298 K in °C.

To convert 298 K into °C you need to subtract 273: $\quad$ 298 K – 273 = 25 °C

Figure 1: *A calculator. In an exam, don't be afraid to put even simple calculations into the calculator even if it's just to check your working— if it stops you making a mistake then it's worth it.*

Pressure units

Pressure can be measured in Pa and kPa.

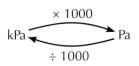

Example ── Maths Skills

Write 2100 Pa in kPa.

To convert 2100 Pa into kPa you need to divide by 1000.

$$2100 \text{ Pa} \div 1000 = 2.1 \text{ kPa}$$

Mass units

Mass can be measured in kg and g.

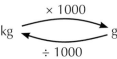

Tip: If you're unsure about converting between units like these just think about a conversion you know and use that to help you. For example, if you know that 1 kg is 1000 g you know that to get from kg to g you must have to multiply by 1000 — simple.

Examples ── Maths Skills

Write 4.6 kg in g.

To convert 4.6 kg into g you need to multiply by 1000.

$$4.6 \text{ kg} \times 1000 = 4600 \text{ g (or } 4.6 \times 10^3 \text{ g)}$$

Write 320 g in kg.

To convert 320 g into kg you need to divide by 1000.

$$320 \text{ g} \div 1000 = 0.32 \text{ kg}$$

Energy units

Energy can be measured in kJ and J.

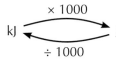

Tip: A kJ is bigger than a J, so you'd expect the number to get smaller when you convert from J to kJ — each unit is worth more so you'll have fewer of them.

Examples ── Maths Skills

Write 56 kJ in J.

To convert 56 kJ into J you need to multiply by 1000.

$$56 \text{ kJ} \times 1000 = 56\,000 \text{ J} = 5.6 \times 10^4 \text{ J}$$

Write 48 000 J in kJ.

To convert 48 000 J into kJ you need to divide by 1000.

$$48\,000 \text{ J} \div 1000 = 48 \text{ kJ}$$

Exam Tip
Always, always, always give units with your answer. It's really important that the examiner knows what units you're working in — 10 g is very different from 10 kg.

Life can get a bit confusing if you have to do lots of calculations, one after the other — sometimes it can be difficult to keep track of your units. To avoid this, always write down the units that you're using with each line of the calculation. Then, when you get to the end, you'll know what units to give with your answer.

1. Exam Structure and Technique

Exam Tip
If you're taking A-level Chemistry, you'll sit a different set of exams to the ones described here.

Passing exams isn't all about revision — it really helps if you know how the exam is structured and have got your exam technique nailed so that you pick up every mark you can. These pages are about the AS Level exams.

Course structure

AQA AS level Chemistry is split into three units:

Unit 1 — Physical chemistry

Unit 2 — Inorganic chemistry

Unit 3 — Organic chemistry

Figure 1: *Chemistry lesson — witness the joy.*

Exam structure

For AQA AS Level Chemistry you're going to have to sit two exams — Paper 1 and Paper 2:

Paper	Content Assessed	*Where this content is covered in this book:*
1	▪ Unit 1: Physical chemistry Specification references 3.1.1.1 to 3.1.4.4, and 3.1.6.1 to 3.1.7. ◀ ▪ Unit 2: Inorganic chemistry Specification references 3.2.1.1 to 3.2.3.2. ◀ ▪ Relevant practical skills (see below)	*Unit 1 Sections 1 to 4 and 6* *Unit 2 Sections 1 and 2*
2	▪ Unit 1: Physical chemistry Specification references 3.1.2.1 to 3.1.6.2. ◀ ▪ Unit 3: Organic chemistry Specification references 3.3.1.1 to 3.3.6.3. ◀ ▪ Relevant practical skills (see below)	*Unit 1 Sections 2 to 6* *Unit 3 Sections 1 to 4*

Exam Tip
Make sure you have a good read through of this exam structure. It might not seem important now but you don't want to get any nasty surprises just before an exam.

Both exams are 1 hour and 30 minutes long. Both papers are worth 80 marks, and they're each worth 50% of your total mark.

Each paper is split into two sections. Section A has 65 marks' worth of short and long answer questions. Section B has 15 marks' worth of multiple choice questions.

Make sure you know which units and sections will be assessed in each exam. That way, you can make sure that you're properly prepared when you actually come to sit the papers.

Exam Tip
Short answer questions are broken down into parts, but they can still be worth lots of marks overall.

Relevant practical skills

At least 15% of the marks on your AS Level Chemistry exams will focus on practical skills. This means you'll be given questions where you're asked to do things like comment on the design of experiments, make predictions, draw graphs, calculate means and percentage uncertainties — basically, anything to do with planning experiments or analysing results. Handily, the Practical Skills section of this book covers these skills, so make sure you've read through it.

Exam Tip
You could also be asked questions about the Required Practicals for your course in the exam — so make sure you've revised those too.

Quality of written communication

Your AS Level Chemistry exam papers will have some extended response questions — in these questions you'll be tested on your ability to write clearly as well as on your chemistry knowledge. So for extended response questions, you need to make doubly sure that:

- your writing is legible.
- your spelling, punctuation and grammar are accurate.
- you organise your answer clearly and coherently — make sure everything is in a logical order and it's clear how your points are linked.
- you use specialist scientific vocabulary where it's appropriate.

Don't worry too much about extended response questions — they sound a bit scary, but as long as you write full and coherent answers whenever you tackle a long answer question, you'll be fine.

Time management

This is one of the most important exam skills to have. How long you spend on each question is really important in an exam — it could make all the difference to your grade. Some questions will require lots of work for only a few marks but other questions will be much quicker. Don't spend ages struggling with questions that are only worth a couple of marks — move on. You can come back to them later when you've bagged loads of other marks elsewhere.

┌─ Example ────────────────────────────────

The questions below are both worth the same number of marks but require different amounts of work.

1.1 Define the term 'standard enthalpy change of combustion'.

(2 marks)

2.2 Draw a structural isomer of molecule **B** and state the type of structural isomerism it shows.

(2 marks)

Question 1.1 only requires you to write down a definition — if you can remember it this shouldn't take you too long.

Question 2.2 requires you to draw an isomer and then work out what type of isomer it is — this may take a lot longer than writing down a definition, especially if you have to draw out a few structures before getting it right.

So, if you're running out of time it makes sense to do questions like 1.1 first and come back to 2.2 if you've got time at the end.

└──

It's worth keeping in mind that the multiple choice questions are only worth 1 mark each and some of them can be quite time-consuming to answer. If you're pressed for time, it's usually a good idea to focus on the written answer questions first, where there are more marks available, and then go back to the harder multiple choice questions later.

Don't leave any questions blank if you can avoid it though. For example, to answer a multiple choice question, all you have to do is colour in a circle — even if you're getting short on time towards the end of the exam it will only take a moment to fill in an answer (and even if you're not absolutely sure what the answer is, you can still make an educated guess).

Exam Tip
'Extended response' sounds a bit technical, but all it really means is a particularly big long answer question — they're usually worth about 6 marks and have loads of space for you to write your answer.

Exam Tip
Don't forget to go back and do any questions that you left the first time round — you don't want to miss out on marks because you forgot to do the question.

Exam Tip
It's a really good idea to do as many practice papers as you can before you actually sit the exams — that way you'll get a good feel for how to divide up your time. You could ask your teacher if they have any practice papers you can do, or look on the AQA website to see if there are any specimen papers or past papers for you to download.

Command words

Command words are just the bit of the question that tell you what to do. You'll find answering exam questions much easier if you understand exactly what they mean, so here's a summary of the most common command words.

Command word	What to do
Give / State	Write a concise answer, from fact recall or from information that you've been given in the question.
Name	Give the correct technical term for a chemical or a process.
Identify	Say what something is.
Describe	Write about what something is like or how it happens.
Explain	Give reasons for.
Suggest / Predict	Use your scientific knowledge to work out what the answer might be.
Outline	Give a brief description of the main characteristics of a process or an issue.
Calculate	Work out the solution to a mathematical problem.
Estimate	Give an approximate answer.
Determine	Use the information given in the question to work something out.
Compare	Give the similarities and differences between two things.
Draw	Produce a diagram or graph.
Sketch	Draw something approximately — for example, draw a rough line graph to show the main trend of some data.
Justify	Give the case for or against, supported by evidence.

Not all of the questions will have a command word like this — instead they may just ask a which / what / how type of question.

Some questions will also ask you to answer 'using the information (or data) provided' (e.g. a graph, table, equation, etc.). If so, make sure that you do use it in your answer, or you may not get all the marks.

Exam data booklet

When you sit your exams, you'll be given a data booklet with the exam paper. In it you'll find some useful information to help you, including...

- the characteristic infrared absorptions of some bonds in organic molecules.
- a copy of the periodic table.

You might have seen a few slightly different versions of the periodic table — in the exams you should use the information from the one in the data booklet, even if it's slightly different to something you've seen elsewhere. The information in the data booklet will be what the examiners use to mark the exam papers.

Exam Tip
Some questions might contain more than one command word. For example, a question could start 'state and explain'. In this case, you should treat the question a little bit like two questions rolled into one — start by stating what the questions asks for and then explain it.

Exam Tip
The same data booklet is usually used for both AS and A-level exams. If you're sitting AS, there'll be some information on the data sheet that you may not be familiar with. Don't be put off by it — it's there for people doing A-level exams and you won't need to use it. Phew!

Exam Tip
It's a good idea to have a look at the data booklet before the exams — you should be able to find it on the AQA website.

2. Diagrams

When you're asked to draw diagrams or mechanisms in an exam it's important that you draw everything correctly and include all the details that are needed.

Organic reaction mechanisms

Organic reaction mechanisms are used to show what happens during a chemical reaction. One of the most common mistakes people make when drawing these is to get the curly arrows wrong.

Tip: It's important that the curly arrows come from a lone pair or a bond because curly arrows show the movement of electrons and that's where the electrons are found.

Exam Tip
Make sure you draw full charges (+ and –) or dipoles (partial charges shown using $\delta+$ and $\delta-$) clearly — you could lose marks if it's not clear which type of charge you mean.

Example

When you're drawing organic reaction mechanisms the curly arrows must come from either a lone pair of electrons or from a bond, like this:

The examples below are incorrect — you wouldn't get marks for them:

You won't get marks if the curly arrows come from atoms, like this...

...or if they come from a charge or from thin air like these.

Displayed and skeletal formulas

Displayed formulas show how all the atoms are connected in a molecule.

Examples

If a question asks you for a displayed formula you have to show all of the bonds and all of the atoms in the molecule. That means you have to draw displayed formulas like this:

And not like this:

Some of the bonds between the carbon atoms and the hydrogen atoms haven't been shown, so it's not a displayed formula and you wouldn't get the marks.

If you're not asked specifically for a displayed formula then either of the diagrams above will do. Just make sure that the bonds are always drawn between the right atoms. For example, ethanol should be drawn like this:

And not like this:

It's the oxygen that's bonded to the carbon, not the hydrogen, so drawing it like this is wrong.

Skeletal formulas are handy when you're drawing large organic molecules. You might have to either draw or interpret skeletal formulas in your exam, so make sure that you're happy drawing and using them. Remember — bonds between carbon atoms are shown by a line and carbon atoms are found at each end. Atoms that aren't carbon or hydrogen have to be drawn on:

Tip: If you're not totally comfortable drawing skeletal formulas, it might help to draw the displayed formula first. That will help you to see what atoms need to be drawn in the skeletal formula.

┌─ **Example** ─────────────────────────────

1,5-difluoropentane ($FCH_2CH_2CH_2CH_2CH_2F$)

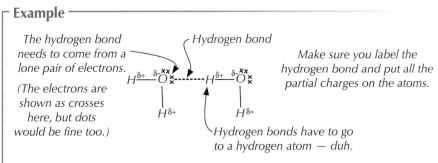

The carbon-carbon bonds are shown by lines.

Each junction represents one carbon atom.

You still have to show the atoms that aren't carbon or hydrogen.

You don't draw any carbon or hydrogen atoms from the main carbon chain when you're drawing a skeletal formula, so both of the diagrams below are wrong.

You don't show the carbon atoms or the hydrogen atoms.

Hydrogen bonds

Drawing a diagram showing hydrogen bonding (see pages 88-89) is a fairly common exam question. You need to know how to draw hydrogen bonds properly to pick up all the marks you can.

┌─ **Example** ─────────────────────────────

The hydrogen bond needs to come from a lone pair of electrons.

(The electrons are shown as crosses here, but dots would be fine too.)

Hydrogen bond

Make sure you label the hydrogen bond and put all the partial charges on the atoms.

Hydrogen bonds have to go to a hydrogen atom — duh.

Exam Tip
Make sure you include everything the question asks for in your answer. For example, if the question asks you to show lone pairs and dipoles in a diagram, don't forget to add them.

General advice on diagrams

These pages cover some of the types of diagram that are likely to come up in your exams. But you could be asked to draw other diagrams. Whatever diagram you're drawing, make sure it's really clear. A small scribble in the bottom corner of a page isn't going to show enough detail to get you the marks. Draw the diagrams nice and big, but make sure that you stay within the space given for that answer.

If you've drawn a diagram incorrectly don't scribble part of it out and try to fix it — it'll look messy and be hard for the examiner to figure out what you're trying to show. Cross the whole thing out and start again. And always double check that you've included all the things that you should have done.

3. The Periodic Table — Facts and Trends

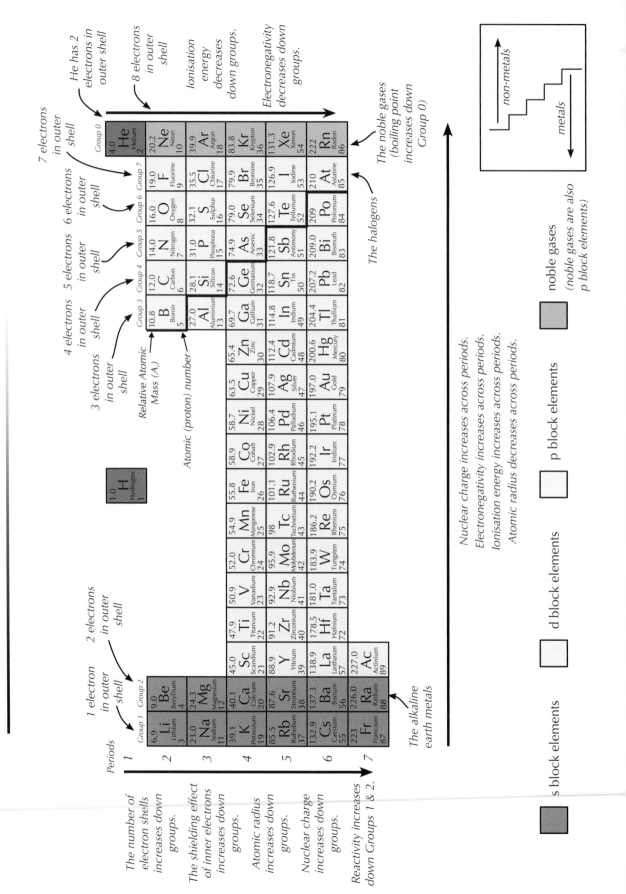

He has 2 electrons in outer shell

8 electrons in outer shell

Ionisation energy decreases down groups.

Electronegativity decreases down groups.

7 electrons in outer shell

6 electrons in outer shell

5 electrons in outer shell

4 electrons in outer shell

3 electrons in outer shell

Relative Atomic Mass (A_r)

Atomic (proton) number

The noble gases (boiling point increases down Group 0)

The halogens

1 electron in outer shell

2 electrons in outer shell

Periods

The alkaline earth metals

The number of electron shells increases down groups.

The shielding effect of inner electrons increases down groups.

Atomic radius increases down groups.

Nuclear charge increases down groups.

Reactivity increases down Groups 1 & 2.

Nuclear charge increases across periods.
Electronegativity increases across periods.
Ionisation energy increases across periods.
Atomic radius decreases across periods.

non-metals

metals

s block elements

d block elements

p block elements

noble gases (noble gases are also p block elements)

Answers

Unit 1

Section 1: Atomic Structure

1. The Atom
Page 14 — Application Questions
Q1 a) 13
    b) 13
    c) 27 – 13 = **14**
Q2 a) 19
    b) 19 + 20 = **39**
    c) $^{39}_{19}\text{K}$
    d) 19 – 1 = **18**
Q3 a) 20 – 2 = **18**
    b) 40 – 20 = **20**
Q4 Isotope X is an isotope of niobium. Its nuclear symbol is:

$^{93}_{41}\text{Nb}$

Looking at the periodic table, niobium's atomic number is 41. Isotope X has 41 protons, so it must be an isotope of niobium. Then, mass number = protons + neutrons = 41 + 52 = 93.
Q5 a) A and C both have 10 electrons.
    b) A and D both have 8 protons.
    c) B and C both have 10 neutrons.
       (17 – 7 = 10 and 20 – 10 = 10)
    d) B and D both have 10 neutrons.
       (17 – 7 = 10 and 18 – 8 = 10)
    e) A and D are isotopes of each other because they have the same number of protons (8) but different numbers of neutrons.
       (A has 16 – 8 = 8 neutrons and D has 18 – 8 = 10 neutrons.)

Page 14 — Fact Recall Questions
Q1 proton, neutron, electron
Q2 Protons and neutrons are found in the nucleus. Electrons are found in orbitals around the nucleus.
Q3 proton: 1, neutron: 1, electron: 1/2000
Q4 The total number of protons and neutrons in the nucleus of an atom.
Q5 The number of protons in the nucleus of an atom.
Q6 By subtracting the atomic number from the mass number.
Q7 Atoms with the same number of protons but different numbers of neutrons.
Q8 The chemical properties of an element are decided by its electron configuration. Isotopes have the same configuration of electrons, so have the same chemical properties.
Q9 Physical properties depend on the mass of an atom. Isotopes have different masses, so can have different physical properties.

2. Atomic Models
Page 16 — Fact Recall Questions
Q1 Dalton described atoms as solid spheres. J. J. Thomson suggested that atoms were not solid spheres — he thought they contained small negatively charged particles (electrons) in a positively charged "pudding".

Q2 If Thomson's model was correct the alpha particles fired at the sheet of gold should have been deflected very slightly by the positive "pudding" that made up most of the atom. Instead, most of the alpha particles passed straight through the gold atoms, and a very small number were deflected backwards. So the plum pudding model couldn't be right.
Q3 Rutherford's model has a tiny positively charged nucleus at the centre surrounded by a "cloud" of negative electrons. Most of the atom is empty space.
Q4 In Bohr's model the electrons only exist in fixed shells and not anywhere in between. Each shell has a fixed energy. When an electron moves between shells electromagnetic radiation is emitted or absorbed. Because the energy of the shells is fixed, the radiation will have a fixed frequency.

3. Relative Mass
Page 18 — Application Questions
Q1 a) 85.5
    b) 200.6
    c) 65.4
Q2 a) 14.0 + (3 × 1.0) = **17.0**
    b) 12.0 + (16.0 × 2) = **44.0**
    c) (12.0 × 2) + (1.0 × 4) + (16.0 × 6) + (14.0 × 2) = **152.0**
Q3 a) 40.1 + (35.5 × 2) = **111.1**
    b) 24.3 + 32.1 + (16.0 × 4) = **120.4**
    c) 23.0 + 16.0 + 1.0 = **40.0**
Q4 A_r = ((0.1 × 180) + (26.5 × 182) + (14.3 × 183) + (30.7 × 184) + (28.4 × 186)) ÷ 100 = **183.9 (to 1 d.p.)**
Q5 A_r = ((51.5 × 90) + (11.2 × 91) + (17.1 × 92) + (17.4 × 94) + (2.8 × 96)) ÷ 100 = **91.3 (to 1 d.p.)**

Page 18 — Fact Recall Questions
Q1 The average mass of an atom of an element on a scale where an atom of carbon-12 is exactly 12.
Q2 The average mass of a molecule on a scale where an atom of carbon-12 is exactly 12.
Q3 The average mass of a formula unit on a scale where an atom of carbon-12 is exactly 12.

4. The Mass Spectrometer
Page 20 — Application Question
Q1 a) 2
    b) 63, 65
    c) ^{63}Cu = 69.1%, ^{65}Cu = 30.9%

Page 21 — Application Question
Q1 E.g. It's unlikely to be magnesium, as the abundance of the particle with the smallest mass/charge is about 90%, which is too high for magnesium. It's unlikely to be silicon, as you'd expect the second peak to be higher than the third peak in the mass spectrum for silicon. It can't be indium, as the mass spectrum for indium would only have two peaks.

Page 21 — Fact Recall Questions
Q1 ionisation, acceleration, ion drift, detection

Q2 The ions are accelerated in an electric field to give them constant kinetic energy. Ions with different masses are accelerated by different amounts, so they take a different length of time to travel through the ion drift region of the mass spectrometer and arrive at the detector.

Q3 mass/charge

Q4 The number of isotopes in the sample is equal to the number of peaks on the mass spectrum.

5. Using Mass Spectra

Page 23 — Application Questions

Q1 $50.5 \times 79 = 3989.5$ $49.5 \times 81 = 4009.5$
$3989.5 + 4009.5 = 7999$
$7999 \div 100 = \mathbf{80.0\ (to\ 3\ s.f.)}$

Q2 $20 \times 10 = 200$ $80 \times 11 = 880$
$200 + 880 = 1080$
$1080 \div 100 = \mathbf{10.8}$

Q3 $8.0 \times 6 = 48$ $100 \times 7 = 700$
$700 + 48 = 748$
$748 \div (100 + 8) = \mathbf{6.9\ (to\ 2\ s.f.)}$

Q4 $100 \times 69 = 6900$ $65.5 \times 71 = 4650.5$
$6900 + 4650.5 = 11550.5$
$11550.5 \div (100 + 65.5) = \mathbf{69.8\ (to\ 3\ s.f.)}$

Page 24 — Application Questions

Q1 a) $(3 \times 12.0) + (6 \times 1.0) + 16.0 = \mathbf{58.0}$
b) $(4 \times 12.0) + (8 \times 1.0) = \mathbf{56.0}$
c) $(3 \times 12.0) + (6 \times 1.0) + (2 \times 16.0) = \mathbf{74.0}$
The mass/charge value is equal to the M_r of the compound.

Q2 C
M_r of $N_2 = 28.0$, M_r of $CH_2CH_2 = 28.0$, M_r of $CH_3NH_2 = 31.0$, and M_r of $CO = 28.0$. So the gas could be N_2, CH_2CH_2 or CO, but not CH_3NH_2.

Q3 B
M_r of $CH_3CH_3 = 30.0$, M_r of $CH_3F = 34.0$, M_r of $CO_2 = 44.0$, and M_r of $HCN = 27.0$. The only one of these with a molecular ion of $m/z = 34$ is CH_3F.

Q4 The spectrum has two peaks, one at $m/z = 18$ and one at $m/z = 46$.
M_r of $NH_3 = 14.0 + (3 \times 1.0) = 17.0$
M_r of $H_2O = (2 \times 1.0) + 16.0 = 18.0$
M_r of $CH_4 = 12.0 + (4 \times 1.0) = 16.0$
M_r of $CH_3CH_2OH = (2 \times 12.0) + (6 \times 1.0) + 16.0 = 46.0$
M_r of $CH_3CH_2CH_3 = (3 \times 12.0) + (8 \times 1.0) = 44.0$
The compounds in the mixture must be **water and ethanol**.

6. Electronic Structure

Page 27 — Application Questions

Q1 a) $1s^2\ 2s^1$
b) $1s^2\ 2s^2\ 2p^6\ 3s^2\ 3p^6\ 3d^2\ 4s^2$
(or $1s^2\ 2s^2\ 2p^6\ 3s^2\ 3p^6\ 4s^2\ 3d^2$)
c) $1s^2\ 2s^2\ 2p^6\ 3s^2\ 3p^6\ 3d^{10}\ 4s^2\ 4p^1$
d) $1s^2\ 2s^2\ 2p^3$

Q2 a)
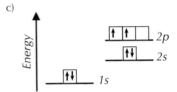
b)

Remember that for each sub-shell you add, you should fill up each orbital singly before they start to share.

Q2 (continued)
c)
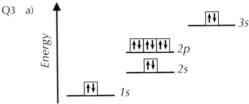
d)

Q3 a)
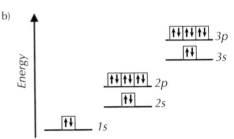

b)

c)
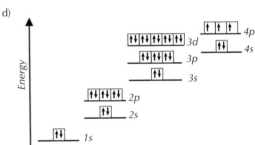

d)

Q4 a) $1s^2\ 2s^2\ 2p^6$
b) $1s^2\ 2s^2\ 2p^6$
c) $1s^2\ 2s^2\ 2p^6$
d) $1s^2\ 2s^2\ 2p^6\ 3s^2\ 3p^6$

Q5 a) bromine
b) phosphorus
c) vanadium

Page 28 — Application Questions

Q1 $1s^2\ 2s^2\ 2p^6\ 3s^2\ 3p^6\ 3d^4$
Q2 $1s^2\ 2s^2\ 2p^6\ 3s^2\ 3p^6\ 3d^8$
Q3 $1s^2\ 2s^2\ 2p^6\ 3s^2\ 3p^6\ 3d^2$

Page 28 — Fact Recall Questions

Q1 3
Q2 6 (it can hold two electrons in each orbital)
Q3 18
Q4 The number of electrons that an atom or ion has and how they are arranged.
Q5 Electrons fill orbitals singly before they start sharing, so the electrons in the 2p sub-shell should be in separate orbitals.

Q6 $1s^2 2s^2 2p^6 3s^2 3p^6 3d^5 4s^1$

Q7 Copper donates one of its 4s electrons to the 3d sub-shell so that the 3d sub-shell is full, making it more stable.

Q8 They form negative ions with an inert gas electron configuration.

7. Ionisation Energies

Pages 32-33 — Application Questions

Q1 a) $Cl_{(g)} \rightarrow Cl^+_{(g)} + e^-$

b) $Cl^+_{(g)} \rightarrow Cl^{2+}_{(g)} + e^-$

Q2

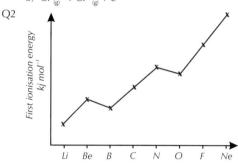

Q3 In both nitrogen and oxygen, the first electron to be removed is in the same sub-shell and the shielding is identical in the two atoms. However, the electron being removed from oxygen is in an orbital where there are two electrons. The repulsion between these two electrons means that it's easier to remove the electron than it would be if it was unpaired (like in nitrogen), so the first ionisation energy of oxygen is lower than that of nitrogen.

Q4 Boron's outer electron is in a 2p orbital rather than a 2s (like beryllium's), which means it has a higher energy and is located further from the nucleus. The 2p orbital also has additional shielding provided by the 2s electrons. These two factors override the effect of the increased nuclear charge of the boron atom, and result in the first ionisation energy of beryllium being higher than the first ionisation energy of boron.

Q5 The first electron in lithium is removed from the 2s orbital, whereas the second and third electrons are removed from the 1s orbital. The 2s orbital is further from the nucleus and is shielded by the inner electrons, so it takes much less energy to remove the first electron than the second. The second and third electrons have no shielding and are the same distance from the nucleus, so there's less difference between their ionisation energies.

Q6 a) Group 6

b) 2 electrons in the first shell and 6 electrons in the second shell.

c) Oxygen

Q7 a)

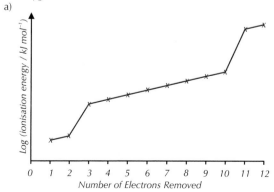

b) Within each shell, successive ionisation energies increase. This is because electrons are being removed from an increasingly positive ion. There's less repulsion amongst the remaining electrons, so they're held more strongly by the nucleus. The big jumps in ionisation energy happen when a new shell that's closer to the nucleus is broken into — the first shell that electrons are removed from has 2 electrons in it, the second shell has 8 electrons and the third shell has 2 electrons.

Page 33 — Fact Recall Questions

Q1 The first ionisation energy is the energy needed to remove 1 electron from each atom in 1 mole of gaseous atoms to form one mole of gaseous 1+ ions.

Q2 The more protons there are, the more positively charged the nucleus is, the stronger the attraction for the electrons and the higher the first ionisation energy.

Q3 The distance between the outer electron and the nucleus, and the shielding effect of inner electrons.

Q4 The second ionisation energy is the energy needed to remove 1 electron from each ion in 1 mole of gaseous 1+ ions to form one mole of gaseous 2+ ions.

Q5 Within each shell, successive ionisation energies increase because electrons are being removed from an increasingly positive ion — there's less repulsion amongst the remaining electrons, so they're held more strongly by the nucleus.

Q6 It decreases.

Q7 The first ionisation energy increases.

Exam-style Questions — pages 35-37

1.1 silicon *(1 mark)*

1.2 The p block *(1 mark)*

1.3 $1s^2 2s^2 2p^6 3s^2 3p^1$ *(1 mark)*

1.4 three *(1 mark)*

1.5 $^{28}_{14}\text{Si}$

(2 marks for correct nuclear symbol, otherwise 1 mark for a correct mass number of 28.)

1.6 The isotopes would have the same chemical properties, as they have the same electron arrangement and it's this that determines the chemical properties of an element *(1 mark)*.

2.1 electrospray ionisation *(1 mark)*

2.2 The ions are accelerated to constant kinetic energy *(1 mark)* by an electric field *(1 mark)*. Lighter ions are accelerated more than heavier ions *(1 mark)*, so ions with different masses take different amounts of time to travel through the mass spectrometer and reach the detector *(1 mark)*.

3.1 The first ionisation energy increases across Period 3 *(1 mark)*.

3.2 $Na_{(g)} \rightarrow Na^+_{(g)} + e^-$ *(1 mark)*

3.3 Magnesium's outer electron is in a 3s orbital and aluminium's outer electron is in a 3p orbital *(1 mark)*. The 3p orbital has a higher energy than the 3s orbital, so the electron is further from the nucleus *(1 mark)*. The 3p orbital also has additional shielding provided by the 3s electrons *(1 mark)*.

3.4 B *(1 mark)*

3.5 Aluminium, silicon and phosphorus all have their outer electron in the same/3p sub-shell *(1 mark)*. So the shielding effect and the distance between the nucleus and the outer electron is very similar for all three elements *(1 mark)*. But the nuclear charge of silicon is higher than aluminium and lower than phosphorus *(1 mark)*. So the energy needed to remove the outer electron/first ionisation energy of silicon should be greater than aluminium, but lower than phosphorus *(1 mark)*.

3.6 In phosphorus, the electron is being removed from a singly-occupied orbital, but in sulfur the electron is being removed from an orbital containing two electrons *(1 mark)*. The repulsion between the two electrons means that electrons are easier to remove from shared orbitals and so the first ionisation energy of sulfur is lower than that of phosphorus *(1 mark)*.

4.1 $1s^2 2s^2 2p^6 3s^2 3p^6 3d^3 4s^2$ *(1 mark)*

4.2 V^{2+}: $1s^2 2s^2 2p^6 3s^2 3p^6 3d^3$ *(1 mark)*
V^{3+}: $1s^2 2s^2 2p^6 3s^2 3p^6 3d^2$ *(1 mark)*

4.3 $1s^2 2s^2 2p^6 3s^2 3p^6 3d^{10} 4s^1$ *(1 mark)*
Copper donates one of its 4s electrons to the 3d sub-shell to make a more stable full 3d sub-shell *(1 mark)*.

4.4 iron *(1 mark)*

4.5 manganese *(1 mark)*

5.1 $\dfrac{(20 \times 90.48) + (21 \times 0.27) + (22 \times 9.25)}{90.48 + 0.27 + 9.25} = \mathbf{20.2}$
(1 mark for correct calculation, 1 mark for correct answer.)
Element X is neon *(1 mark)*.

5.2 ^{20}X has 10 protons, 10 electrons and 20 – 10 = **10** neutrons *(1 mark)*.
^{21}X has 10 protons, 10 electrons and 21 – 10 = **11** neutrons *(1 mark)*.
^{22}X has 10 protons, 10 electrons and 22 – 10 = **12** neutrons *(1 mark)*.

5.3 The mass number of an atom is the total number of protons and neutrons in the nucleus of the atom *(1 mark)*.

5.4 The proton number of an atom is the number of protons in the nucleus of the atom *(1 mark)*.

5.5 The first ionisation energy is the energy needed to remove 1 electron from each atom in 1 mole of gaseous atoms *(1 mark)* to form 1 mole of gaseous 1+ ions *(1 mark)*.

5.6 The first ionisation energy of element A would be lower than the first ionisation energy of element X. Element A has more electrons than element X, so the distance between the outer electrons and the nucleus is greater *(1 mark)*. The shielding effect of the inner electrons is greater in element A than in element X *(1 mark)*.

5.7 The eighth electron is being removed from the second electron shell, but the ninth electron is being removed from the first electron shell *(1 mark)*. The ninth electron is much closer to the nucleus than the eighth and experiences less shielding *(1 mark)*, so it takes much more energy to remove it *(1 mark)*.

Section 2: Amount of Substance

1. The Mole

Page 39 — Application Questions
Q1 Number of molecules = $0.360 \times (6.02 \times 10^{23})$ = **2.17 × 10²³**
Q2 Number of ions = $0.0550 \times (6.02 \times 10^{23})$ = **3.31 × 10²²**
Q3 $M_r = 66 \div 1.5 = \mathbf{44}$
Q4 $M_r = 23.0 + 14.0 + (16.0 \times 3) = 85.0$
number of moles = $212.5 \div 85.0$ = **2.50 moles**
Q5 $M_r = 65.4 + (35.5 \times 2) = 136.4$
number of moles = $15.5 \div 136.4$ = **0.114 moles**
Q6 $M_r = 23.0 + 35.5 = 58.5$
Mass = 58.5×2 = **117 g**

Page 41 — Application Questions
Q1 Number of moles = $(2 \times 50) \div 1000$ = **0.1 moles**
Q2 Number of moles = 0.08×0.5 = **0.04 moles**
Q3 Number of moles = $(0.70 \times 30) \div 1000$ = **0.021 moles**
Q4 Concentration = $0.25 \div 0.50$ = **0.50 mol dm⁻³**
Q5 Concentration = $0.080 \div 0.75$ = **0.11 mol dm⁻³**
Q6 Concentration = $0.10 \div (36 \div 1000)$ = **2.8 mol dm⁻³**

Q7 Volume = $0.46 \div 1.8$ = **0.26 dm³**
Q8 Volume = $0.010 \div 0.55$ = **0.018 dm³**
Q9 Number of moles = concentration × volume (dm³)
= $0.80 \times (75 \div 1000)$ = 0.060
M_r of Na_2O = $(23.0 \times 2) + 16.0 = 62.0$
Mass = moles × molar mass = 0.060×62.0 = **3.7 g**
Q10 Number of moles = concentration × volume (dm³)
= $0.50 \times (30 \div 1000)$ = 0.015
M_r of $CoBr_2$ = $58.9 + (79.9 \times 2) = 218.7$
Mass = number of moles × molar mass
= 0.015×218.7 = **3.3 g**
Q11 Number of moles = concentration × volume (dm³)
= $1.20 \times (100 \div 1000)$ = 0.120
M_r = mass ÷ number of moles
= $4.08 \div 0.120$ = **34.0**

Page 41 — Fact Recall Questions
Q1 a) 6.02×10^{23}
b) The Avogadro constant
Q2 number of particles = number of moles × Avogadro constant
Q3 Number of moles = mass of substance ÷ M_r
Q4 1000
Q5 E.g mol dm⁻³
Q6 Number of moles = $\dfrac{\text{concentration} \times \text{volume (in cm}^3)}{1000}$
Number of moles = concentration × volume (dm³)

2. Gases and the Mole

Page 43 — Application Questions
Q1 n = $pV \div RT$
= $(70\,000 \times 0.040) \div (8.31 \times 350)$ = **0.96 moles**
Q2 V = $nRT \div p$
= $(0.65 \times 8.31 \times 280) \div 100\,000$ = **0.015 m³**
Q3 0.55 dm³ = 5.5×10^{-4} m³   35 °C = 308 K
n = $pV \div RT$
= $(90\,000 \times (5.5 \times 10^{-4})) \div (8.31 \times 308)$
= **0.019 moles**
Q4 1200 cm³ = 1.2×10^{-3} m³
T = $pV \div nR$
= $(110\,000 \times (1.2 \times 10^{-3})) \div (0.0500 \times 8.31)$ = 318 K
318 K = $(318 - 273)$ °C = **45 °C**
Q5 75 kPa = 75 000 Pa   22 °C = 295 K
V = $nRT \div p$
= $(0.75 \times 8.31 \times 295) \div 75\,000$ = **0.025 m³**
Q6 80 kPa = 80 000 Pa   1.5 dm³ = 1.5×10^{-3} m³
n = $pV \div RT$
= $(80\,000 \times (1.5 \times 10^{-3})) \div (8.31 \times 300)$
= 0.048... moles
M_r = mass ÷ moles = $2.6 \div 0.048...$ = 54
So the relative molecular mass is **54**.
Q7 44 °C = 317 K   100 kPa = 100 000 Pa
n = $pV \div RT$
= $(100\,000 \times 0.00300) \div (8.31 \times 317)$
= 0.113... moles
M_r of neon = 20.2
mass = number of moles × M_r
= $0.113... \times 20.2$ = **2.30 g**

Page 43 — Fact Recall Question
Q1 $pV = nRT$
p = pressure measured in pascals (Pa)
V = volume measured in m³
n = number of moles
R = 8.31 J K⁻¹ mol⁻¹. R is the gas constant.
T = temperature measured in kelvin (K)

3. Chemical Equations

Page 45 — Application Questions

Q1 a) $Mg + 2HCl \rightarrow MgCl_2 + H_2$

b) $S_8 + 24F_2 \rightarrow 8SF_6$

c) $Ca(OH)_2 + H_2SO_4 \rightarrow CaSO_4 + 2H_2O$

d) $Na_2CO_3 + 2HCl \rightarrow 2NaCl + CO_2 + H_2O$

e) $C_4H_{10} + 6\frac{1}{2}O_2 \rightarrow 4CO_2 + 5H_2O$

Q2 a) $Fe + Cu^{2+} \rightarrow Fe^{2+} + Cu$

b) $Ba^{2+} + SO_4^{2-} \rightarrow BaSO_4$

This reaction looks like it has the same ions on each side of the equation, so wouldn't have an ionic equation. But the state symbols show you that $BaSO_4$ is a solid, so you shouldn't split it up into ions when writing your ionic equation.

c) $CO_3^{2-} + 2H^+ \rightarrow H_2O + CO_2$

4. Equations and Calculations

Page 47 — Application Questions

Q1 a) $Zn + 2HCl \rightarrow ZnCl_2 + H_2$

b) A_r of $Zn = 65.4$
number of moles = mass $\div A_r$
$= 3.4 \div 65.4 = \textbf{0.052 moles}$

c) The molar ratio of $Zn : ZnCl_2$ is 1 : 1. So 0.052 moles of Zn will give **0.052 moles** of $ZnCl_2$.

d) M_r of $ZnCl_2 = 65.4 + (2 \times 35.5) = 136.4$
mass = number of moles $\times M_r = 0.052 \times 136.4 = \textbf{7.1 g}$

Q2 a) $C_2H_4 + 3O_2 \rightarrow 2CO_2 + 2H_2O$

b) M_r of $H_2O = (2 \times 1.0) + 16.0 = 18.0$
number of moles = mass $\div M_r = 15 \div 18.0 = \textbf{0.83 moles}$

c) The molar ratio of $H_2O : C_2H_4$ is 2 : 1.
So 0.83 moles of H_2O must be made from
$(0.83 \div 2) = \textbf{0.42 moles}$ of C_2H_4.

d) M_r of $C_2H_4 = (2 \times 12.0) + (4 \times 1.0) = 28.0$
mass = number of moles $\times M_r = 0.42 \times 28.0 = \textbf{12 g}$

Q3 $Na_2CO_3 + BaCl_2 \rightarrow 2NaCl + BaCO_3$
M_r of $BaCl_2 = 137.3 + (2 \times 35.5) = 208.3$
number of moles = mass $\div M_r$
$= 4.58 \div 208.3 = 0.0219...$ moles
The molar ratio of $BaCl_2 : BaCO_3$ is 1 : 1.
So 0.0219... moles of $BaCO_3$ must be made from 0.0219... moles of $BaCl_2$.
M_r of $BaCO_3 = 137.3 + 12.0 + (16.0 \times 3) = 197.3$
mass = number of moles $\times M_r = 0.0219... \times 197.3 = \textbf{4.34 g}$

Page 48 — Application Questions

Q1 a) aq
b) s
c) l
d) aq
e) g
f) s

Q2 a) $2H_2O_{(l)} \rightarrow 2H_{2(g)} + O_{2(g)}$

b) M_r of $H_2O = (2 \times 1.0) + 16.0 = 18.0$
number of moles = mass $\div M_r = 9.00 \div 18.0 = \textbf{0.500}$

c) The molar ratio of H_2O to O_2 is 2 : 1.
So 0.500 moles of H_2O will produce
$(0.500 \div 2) = \textbf{0.250 moles}$ of O_2.

d) Using the ideal gas equation:
$V = nRT \div p$
$= (0.0250 \times 8.31 \times 298) \div 100\ 000$
$= \textbf{0.00619 m}^3$

Q3 a) $ZnS_{(s)} + 1\frac{1}{2}O_{2(g)} \rightarrow ZnO_{(s)} + SO_{2(g)}$

b) M_r of $ZnS = 65.4 + 32.1 = 97.5$
number of moles = mass $\div M_r$
$= 7.0 \div 97.5 = \textbf{0.072 moles}$

c) The molar ratio of ZnS to SO_2 is 1 : 1.
So 0.072 moles of ZnS will give **0.072 moles** of SO_2.

d) Using the ideal gas equation:
$V = nRT \div p$
$= (0.072 \times 8.31 \times 298) \div 100\ 000$
$= \textbf{0.0018 m}^3$

Q4 a) $C_6H_{14\ (g)} \rightarrow C_4H_{10\ (g)} + C_2H_{4\ (g)}$

b) M_r of $C_4H_{10} = (4 \times 12.0) + (10 \times 1.0) = 58.0$
number of moles = mass $\div M_r$
$= 3.0 \div 58.0 = \textbf{0.052 moles}$

c) The molar ratio of C_4H_{10} to C_6H_{14} is 1 : 1.
So 0.052 moles of C_4H_{10} must be made from
0.052 moles of C_6H_{14}.

d) Using the ideal gas equation:
$V = nRT \div p$
$= (0.052 \times 8.31 \times 308) \div 100\ 000$
$= \textbf{0.0013 m}^3$

Q5 $Mg_{(s)} + H_2O_{(g)} \rightarrow MgO_{(s)} + H_{2\ (g)}$
M_r of $MgO = 24.3 + 16.0 = 40.3$
number of moles = mass $\div M_r = 10 \div 40.3 = 0.248...$ moles
The molar ratio of $MgO : H_2O$ is 1 : 1. So 0.248... moles of MgO is made from 0.248... moles of H_2O.
Using the ideal gas equation:
$V = nRT \div p$
$= (0.248... \times 8.31 \times (100 + 273)) \div 101\ 325$
$= \textbf{0.0076 m}^3$

5. Titrations

Page 52 — Application Questions

Q1 a) $HCl_{(aq)} + KOH_{(aq)} \rightarrow KCl_{(aq)} + H_2O_{(l)}$

b) moles HCl = (conc. $\times$ volume $(cm^3)) \div 1000$
$= (0.75 \times 28) \div 1000 = \textbf{0.021 moles}$

c) 1 mole of HCl reacts with 1 mole of KOH.
So 0.021 moles of HCl must react with
0.021 moles of KOH.

d) concentration = (moles KOH $\times$ 1000) $\div$ vol. (cm^3)
$= (0.021 \times 1000) \div 40 = \textbf{0.53 mol dm}^{-3}$

Q2 a) $NaOH_{(aq)} + HNO_{3\ (aq)} \rightarrow NaNO_{3\ (aq)} + H_2O_{(l)}$

b) moles NaOH = (conc. $\times$ volume $(cm^3)) \div 1000$
$= (1.5 \times 15.3) \div 1000 = \textbf{0.023 moles}$

c) 1 mole of NaOH reacts with 1 mole of HNO_3.
So 0.023 moles of NaOH must react with
0.023 moles of HNO_3.

d) concentration = (moles HNO_3 $\times$ 1000) $\div$ vol. (cm^3)
$= (0.023 \times 1000) \div 35 = \textbf{0.66 mol dm}^{-3}$

Q3 $KOH_{(aq)} + HCl_{(aq)} \rightarrow KCl_{(aq)} + H_2O_{(l)}$
moles HCl = (conc. $\times$ volume $(cm^3)) \div 1000$
$= (0.50 \times 12) \div 1000 = 0.0060$ moles
1 mole of HCl reacts with 1 mole of KOH, so 0.0060 moles of HCl must react with 0.0060 moles of KOH.
concentration = (moles KOH $\times$ 1000) $\div$ vol. (cm^3)
$= (0.0060 \times 1000) \div 24 = \textbf{0.25 mol dm}^{-3}$

Page 53 — Application Questions

Q1 a) $HNO_{3\ (aq)} + KOH_{(aq)} \rightarrow KNO_{3\ (aq)} + H_2O_{(l)}$

b) moles HNO_3 = (conc. $\times$ volume $(cm^3)) \div 1000$
$= (0.20 \times 18.8) \div 1000 = \textbf{0.0038 moles}$

c) 1 mole of HNO_3 reacts with 1 mole of KOH.
So 0.0038 moles of HNO_3 must react with
0.0038 moles of KOH.

d) volume = (moles KOH $\times$ 1000) $\div$ concentration
$= (0.0038 \times 1000) \div 0.45 = \textbf{8.4 cm}^3$

Q2 a) $KOH_{(aq)} + CH_3COOH_{(aq)} \rightarrow CH_3COOK_{(aq)} + H_2O_{(l)}$

b) moles KOH = (conc. × volume (cm³)) ÷ 1000
   = (0.420 × 37.3) ÷ 1000 = **0.0157 moles**
c) 1 mole of KOH reacts with 1 mole of CH_3COOH.
   So 0.0157 moles of KOH must react with
   0.0157 moles of CH_3COOH.
d) volume = (moles CH_3COOH × 1000) ÷ conc.
   = (0.0157 × 1000) ÷ 1.10 = **14.3 cm³ (3 s.f.)**

Q3 $2NaOH_{(aq)} + H_2SO_{4\ (aq)} \rightarrow Na_2SO_{4\ (aq)} + 2H_2O_{(l)}$
    2 moles of NaOH = (conc. × volume (cm³)) ÷ 1000
    = (14 × 1.5) ÷ 1000 = 0.021 moles
    2 moles of NaOH react with 1 mole of H_2SO_4.
    So, 0.021 moles of NaOH must react with 0.0105 moles
    of H_2SO_4.
    volume = (moles H_2SO_4 × 1000) ÷ conc.
    = (0.0105 × 1000) ÷ 0.60 = **18 cm³**

Page 53 — Fact Recall Questions
Q1 Any solution that you know the exact concentration of.
Q2 pipette
Q3 burette
Q4 The exact point at which the indicator changes colour
    (at this point the amount of acid added is just enough to
    neutralise the alkali).

6. Formulas
Page 55 — Application Questions
Q1 empirical mass = (4 × 12.0) + (9 × 1.0) = 57.0
    M_r = 171, so there are (171 ÷ 57.0) = 3 empirical units in
    the molecule.
    molecular formula = $C_{12}H_{27}$
Q2 empirical mass = (3 × 12.0) + (5 × 1.0) + (2 × 16.0) = 73.0
    M_r = 146, so there are (146 ÷ 73.0) = 2 empirical units in
    the molecule.
    molecular formula = $C_6H_{10}O_4$
Q3 empirical mass = (2 × 12.0) + (6 × 1.0) + (1 × 16.0) = 46.0
    M_r = 46, so there is (46 ÷ 46.0) = 1 empirical unit in the
    molecule.
    molecular formula = C_2H_6O
Q4 empirical mass = (4 × 12.0) + (6 × 1.0) + (2 × 35.5)
                    + (1 × 16.0) = 141.0
    M_r = 423, so there are (423 ÷ 141.0) = 3 empirical units
    in the molecule.
    molecular formula = $C_{12}H_{18}Cl_6O_3$

Page 57 — Application Questions
Q1 Mass of each element:
    H = 5.9 g   O = 94.1 g
    Moles of each element:
    H = (5.9 ÷ 1.0) = 5.9 moles
    O = (94.1 ÷ 16.0) = 5.9 moles
    Divide each by 5.9:
    H = (5.9 ÷ 5.9) = 1   O = (5.9 ÷ 5.9) = 1
    The ratio of H : O is 1 : 1.
    So the empirical formula is **HO**.
Q2 Mass of each element:
    Al = 20.2 g   Cl = 79.8 g
    Moles of each element:
    Al = (20.2 ÷ 27.0) = 0.748 moles
    Cl = (79.8 ÷ 35.5) = 2.25 moles
    Divide each by 0.748:
    Al = (0.748 ÷ 0.748) = 1   Cl = (2.25 ÷ 0.748) = 3
    The ratio of Al : Cl is 1 : 3.
    So the empirical formula is **$AlCl_3$**.

Q3 Mass of each element:
    C = 8.5 g   H = 1.4 g   I = 90.1 g
    Moles of each element:
    C = (8.5 ÷ 12.0) = 0.71 moles
    H = (1.4 ÷ 1.0) = 1.4 moles
    I = (90.1 ÷ 126.9) = 0.71 moles
    Divide each by 0.71:
    C = (0.71 ÷ 0.71) = 1
    H = (1.4 ÷ 0.71) = 2
    I = (0.71 ÷ 0.71) = 1
    The ratio of C : H : I is 1 : 2 : 1.
    So the empirical formula is **CH_2I**.
Q4 Mass of each element:
    Cu = 50.1 g   P = 16.3 g   O = 33.6 g
    Moles of each element:
    Cu = (50.1 ÷ 63.5) = 0.789 moles
    P = (16.3 ÷ 31.0) = 0.526 moles
    O = (33.6 ÷ 16.0) = 2.10 moles
    Divide each by 0.526:
    Cu = (0.789 ÷ 0.526) = 1.5
    P = (0.526 ÷ 0.526) = 1.0
    O = (2.10 ÷ 0.526) = 4.0
    The ratio of Cu : P : O is 1.5 : 1.0 : 4.0.
    Multiply by 2 — 2 × (1.5 : 1.0 : 4.0) = 3 : 2 : 8.
    So the empirical formula is **$Cu_3P_2O_8$**.
Q5 % V = 32.3   % Cl = 100 − 32.3 = 67.7
    Mass of each element:
    V = 32.3 g   Cl = 67.7 g
    Moles of each element:
    V = (32.3 ÷ 50.9) = 0.635 moles
    Cl = (67.7 ÷ 35.5) = 1.91 moles
    Divide each by 0.635:
    V = (0.635 ÷ 0.635) = 1   Cl = (1.91 ÷ 0.635) = 3
    The ratio of V : Cl is 1 : 3.
    So the empirical formula is **VCl_3**.
Q6 % O = 31.58   % Cr = 100 − 31.58 = 68.42
    Mass of each element:
    O = 31.58 g   Cr = 68.42 g
    Moles of each element:
    O = (31.58 ÷ 16.0) = 1.97 moles
    Cr = (68.42 ÷ 52.0) = 1.32 moles
    Divide each by 1.32:
    O = (1.97 ÷ 1.32) = 1.5   Cr = (1.32 ÷ 1.32) = 1.0
    The ratio of Cr : O is 1.0 : 1.5.
    Multiply by 2 — 2 × (1.0 : 1.5) = 2 : 3.
    So the empirical formula is **Cr_2O_3**.
Q7 Mass of each reactant:
    P = 2.00 g   O = 4.58 − 2.00 = 2.58 g
    Moles of each reactant:
    P = (2.00 ÷ 31.0) = 0.0645 moles
    O = (2.58 ÷ 16.0) = 0.161 moles
    Divide each by 0.0645:
    P = (0.0645 ÷ 0.0645) = 1.0
    O = (0.161 ÷ 0.0645) = 2.5
    The ratio of P : O is 1.0 : 2.5.
    Multiply by 2 — 2 × (1.0 : 2.5) = 2 : 5.
    So the empirical formula is **P_2O_5**.
Q8 Mass of each reactant:
    Ag = 0.503 g   Cl = 0.669 − 0.503 = 0.166 g
    Moles of each reactant:
    Ag = (0.503 ÷ 107.9) = 0.00466 moles
    Cl = (0.166 ÷ 35.5) = 0.00468 moles
    Divide each by 0.00466:
    Ag = (0.00466 ÷ 0.00466) = 1
    Cl = (0.00468 ÷ 0.00466) = 1
    The ratio of Ag : Cl is 1 : 1.
    So the empirical formula is **AgCl**.

Q9 M_r of $CO_2 = (12.0 + (2 \times 16.0)) = 44.0$
M_r of $H_2O = (16.0 + (2 \times 1.0)) = 18.0$
moles of $CO_2 = (9.70 \div 44.0) = 0.220$ moles
moles of $H_2O = (7.92 \div 18.0) = 0.440$ moles
So the hydrocarbon must contain 0.220 moles of carbon
and $2 \times 0.440 = 0.880$ moles of hydrogen.
Divide each by 0.220:
$C = (0.220 \div 0.220) = 1$
$H = (0.880 \div 0.220) = 4$
The ratio of C : H is 1 : 4.
So the empirical formula is **CH_4**.

Page 57 — Fact Recall Questions
Q1 The empirical formula gives the smallest whole number
ratio of atoms present in a compound.
Q2 The molecular formula gives the actual numbers
of atoms in a molecule.

7. Chemical Yield
Page 60 — Application Questions
Q1 % yield $= (1.76 \div 3.24) \times 100 = $ **54.3%**
Q2 % yield $= (3.7 \div 6.1) \times 100 = $ **61%**
Q3 % yield $= (138 \div 143) \times 100 = $ **96.5%**
Q4 a) M_r of Fe $= 55.8$
moles of Fe $=$ mass $\div M_r$
$= 3.0 \div 55.8 = $ **0.054 moles**
b) From the equation: 4 moles of Fe produces 2 moles of
Fe_2O_3, so 0.054 moles of Fe will produce
$(0.054 \div 2) = 0.027$ moles of Fe_2O_3.
M_r of $Fe_2O_3 = (2 \times 55.8) + (3 \times 16.0) = 159.6$
theoretical yield $=$ moles $Fe_2O_3 \times M_r$
$= 0.027 \times 159.6 = $ **4.3 g**
c) % yield $=$ (actual yield $\div$ theoretical yield) $\times 100$
$= (3.6 \div 4.3) \times 100 = $ **84%**
Q5 M_r of $Al_2O_3 = (2 \times 27.0) + (3 \times 16.0) = 102.0$
Number of moles $Al_2O_3 =$ mass $\div M_r$
$= 1000 \div 102.0 = 9.80$ moles
From the equation: 2 moles of Al_2O_3 produce
4 moles of Al, so 9.80 moles of Al_2O_3 will produce
$(9.80 \times 2) = 19.6$ moles of Al.
M_r of Al $= 27.0$
theoretical yield $=$ moles Al $\times M_r$
$= 19.6 \times 27.0 = $ **529 g**
Q6 M_r of NaOH $= 23.0 + 16.0 + 1.0 = 40.0$
Number of moles NaOH $=$ mass $\div M_r$
$= 4.70 \div 40.0 = 0.118$ moles
From the equation: 2 moles of NaOH produce
1 mole of Na_2SO_4, so 0.118 moles of NaOH will produce
$(0.118 \div 2) = 0.0590$ moles of Na_2SO_4.
M_r of $Na_2SO_4 = (2 \times 23.0) + 32.1 + (4 \times 16.0) = 142.1$
theoretical yield $=$ moles $Na_2SO_4 \times M_r$
$= 0.0590 \times 142.1 = 8.38...$ g
% yield $=$ (actual yield $\div$ theoretical yield) $\times 100$
$= (6.04 \div 8.38...) \times 100 = $ **72.0%**
Q7 M_r of Mg $= 24.3$
Number of moles Mg $=$ mass $\div M_r$
$= 40.0 \div 24.3 = 1.64...$ moles
From the equation: 1 mole of Mg produces
1 mole of H_2, so 1.64... moles of Mg will produce
1.64... moles of H_2.
M_r of $H_2 = 2 \times 1.0 = 2.0$
theoretical yield $=$ moles $H_2 \times M_r$
$= 1.64... \times 2.0 = 3.29...$ g
% yield $=$ (actual yield $\div$ theoretical yield) $\times 100$
$= (1.70 \div 3.29...) \times 100 = $ **51.6%**

Page 60 — Fact Recall Questions
Q1 The theoretical yield is the mass of product that should be
formed in a chemical reaction.

Q2 percentage yield $= \dfrac{\text{actual yield}}{\text{theoretical yield}} \times 100$

8. Atom Economy
Page 63 — Application Questions
Q1 a) mass of reactants $= (12.0 + (4 \times 1.0)) + (2 \times 35.5) = $ **87.0**
b) mass of $CH_3Cl = 12.0 + (3 \times 1.0) + 35.5 = $ **50.5**

c) % atom economy $=$
$\dfrac{\text{molecular mass of desired product}}{\text{sum of molecular masses of all reactants}} \times 100$
$= (50.5 \div 87.0) \times 100 = $ **58.0%**
d) E.g. sell the HCl so it can be used in other chemical
reactions / use the HCl as a reactant in another reaction.
Q2 % atom economy $= $ **100%**
Any reaction where there's only one product will have 100%
atom economy. If you don't notice this, you can just do the
calculations as usual:
mass of reactants $= (2 \times 27.0) + (3 \times (2 \times 35.5)) = 267$
mass of $2AlCl_3 = 2 \times (27.0 + (3 \times 35.5)) = 267$
% atom economy $= (267 \div 267) \times 100 = 100\%$
Q3 mass of reactants $=$
$[2 \times ((2 \times 55.8) + (3 \times 16.0))] + [3 \times 12.0] = 355.2$
mass of 4Fe $= 4 \times 55.8 = 223.2$

% atom economy $=$
$\dfrac{\text{molecular mass of desired product}}{\text{sum of molecular masses of all reactants}} \times 100$
$= (223.2 \div 355.2) \times 100 = $ **62.8%**
Q4 a) Reaction 1:
% atom economy $= $ **100%**
There's only one product so the atom economy has to
be 100%. If you didn't spot this, the calculations would
have been:
mass of reactants $= (2 \times 14.0) + (3 \times (2 \times 1.0)) = 34.0$
mass of $2NH_3 = 2 \times (14.0 + (3 \times 1.0)) = 34.0$
% atom economy $= (34.0 \div 34.0) \times 100 = 100\%$
Reaction 2:
mass of reactants $= (2 \times (14.0 + (4 \times 1.0) + 35.5)) +$
$(40.1 + ((16.0 + 1.0) \times 2)) = 107 + 74.1 = 181.1$
mass of $2NH_3 = 2 \times (14.0 + (3 \times 1.0)) = 34.0$

% atom economy $=$
$\dfrac{\text{molecular mass of desired product}}{\text{sum of molecular masses of all reactants}} \times 100$
$= (34.0 \div 181.1) \times 100 = $ **18.8%**
b) E.g. reaction 1 has a much higher atom economy /
produces no waste.

Page 63 — Fact Recall Questions
Q1 Atom economy is a measure of the proportion of reactant
atoms that become part of the desired product (rather than
by-products) in the balanced chemical equation.
Q2 E.g. Processes with high atom economies are better for the
environment because they use fewer raw materials and
produce less waste. They're also less expensive. A company
using a process with a high atom economy will spend less
on raw materials, and also less on treating waste.
Q3 % atom economy $=$
$\dfrac{\text{molecular mass of desired product}}{\text{sum of molecular masses of all reactants}} \times 100$

Exam-style Questions — pages 65-67

1 B *(1 mark)*
   One mole of any substance contains 6.02×10^{23} particles, so the substance with the largest number of particles will be the one with the most number of moles.

2 C *(1 mark)*
   M_r of CO = 12.0 + 16.0 = 28.0
   Moles of CO = 5.00 ÷ 28.0 = 0.178... moles
   From the equation, 0.178... moles of CO will produce 0.178... moles of CO_2.
   Theoretical yield = moles × M_r = 0.178... × 44.0 = 7.85... g
   Percentage yield = 6.40 ÷ 7.85... = 81.5%

3.1 M_r = 23.0 + 35.5 = 58.5 *(1 mark)*
     Number of moles = 20.0 ÷ 58.5 = **0.342 moles** *(1 mark)*

3.2 2 moles of NaCl react to form 1 mole of Cl_2, so the number of moles of Cl_2 produced from 0.342 moles NaCl is:
     0.342 ÷ 2 = **0.171 moles**
     (1 mark)
     Even if you got the first part wrong you can still get the marks for the second part as long as you've used the correct method. This will happen for all of the calculation questions.

3.3 98 kPa = 98 000 Pa
     $pV = nRT$
     $V = nRT \div p$
     = (0.65 × 8.31 × 330) ÷ 98 000 = **0.018 m³**
     (3 marks for correct answer, otherwise 1 mark for converting 98 kPa into Pa and 1 mark for correctly rearranging the equation to find V.)

3.4 mass of reactants = (2 × (23.0 + 35.5)) +
     (2 × ((2 × 1.0) + 16.0)) = 153
     mass of Cl_2 = 2 × 35.5 = 71.0
     % atom economy = (71.0 ÷ 153) × 100 = **46.4%**
     (2 marks for correct answer, otherwise 1 mark for correct masses.)

3.5 E.g. the other products (H_2 and NaOH) are useful starting chemicals for other reactions/can be sold to make money *(1 mark)*.

4.1 O = 43.6   P = 100 − 43.6 = 56.4 *(1 mark)*
     Moles of each element:
     P = (56.4 ÷ 31.0) = 1.82 moles
     O = (43.6 ÷ 16.0) = 2.73 moles
     Divide each by 1.82:
     P = (1.82 ÷ 1.82) = 1.0   O = (2.73 ÷ 1.82) = 1.5
     The ratio of P : O is 1.0 : 1.5 *(1 mark)*.
     Multiply by 2: 2 × (1.0 : 1.5) = 2 : 3.
     So the empirical formula is P_2O_3 *(1 mark)*.
     All the numbers in an empirical formula must be whole numbers — that's why you need to multiply the ratio by two here.

4.2 empirical mass = (2 × 31.0) + (3 × 16.0) = 110 g
     molecular mass = 220 g
     (220 ÷ 110) = 2 empirical units in the molecular formula *(1 mark)*
     Molecular formula = P_4O_6 *(1 mark)*

4.3 M_r of NH_3 = 14.0 + (3 × 1.0) = 17.0 *(1 mark)*
     number of moles = mass ÷ M_r
     = 2.50 ÷ 17 = **0.147** *(1 mark)*

4.4 Number of moles = 0.147 ÷ 2 = **0.0735** *(1 mark)*
     The equation tells you that the molar ratio of NH_3 : $(NH_4)_2HPO_4$ is 2 : 1. So to find the number of moles of $(NH_4)_2HPO_4$ you divide the number of moles of NH_3 by 2.

4.5 M_r of $(NH_4)_2HPO_4$ = (2 × (14.0 + (4 × 1.0))) + 1.0
     + 31.0 + (4 × 16.0)
     = 132 *(1 mark)*
     mass = number of moles × M_r
     = 0.0735 × 132 = **9.70 g** *(1 mark)*

5.1 The atom economy is 100% *(1 mark)* because the reaction only has one product *(1 mark)*.
     If the reaction only has one product, all of the reactants end up in the desired product.

5.2 M_r of Ca = 40.1 *(1 mark)*
     number of moles = mass ÷ M_r
     = 3.40 ÷ 40.1 = **0.0848** *(1 mark)*

5.3 Number of moles = **0.0848** *(1 mark)*
     You can see from the equation that the molar ratio of Ca : CaO is 2 : 2. So the number of moles of CaO must be the same as the number of moles of Ca.

5.4 M_r of CaO = 40.1 + 16.0 = 56.1 *(1 mark)*
     mass = number of moles × M_r
     = 0.0848 × 56.1 = **4.76 g** *(1 mark)*

5.5 % yield = (actual yield ÷ theoretical yield) × 100
     = (3.70 ÷ 4.76) × 100 = **77.7%** *(1 mark)*

6.1 $C_8H_{18\,(l)} + 12\frac{1}{2}O_{2\,(g)} \rightarrow 8CO_{2\,(g)} + 9H_2O_{(l)}$
     (1 mark for balanced equation, 1 mark for state symbols. Allow any correct multiple of the balanced equation. Allow (g) as the state symbol for water.)

6.2 $pV = nRT$
     $n = pV \div RT$ *(1 mark)*
     = (101 000 × 0.020) ÷ (8.31 × 308) = **0.79 moles** *(1 mark)*

6.3 Number of moles = 0.79 ÷ 8 = 0.099 *(1 mark)*
     From the balanced equation you wrote in part 6.1, you know that the molar ratio of CO_2 : C_8H_{18} is 8 : 1. So, to find how many moles of octane were burnt, you can divide the number of moles of CO_2 by 8.

6.4 C = 85.7   H = 100 − 85.7 = 14.3 *(1 mark)*
     Moles of each element:
     C = (85.7 ÷ 12) = 7.14 moles
     H = (14.3 ÷ 1) = 14.3 moles
     Divide each by 7.14:
     C = (7.14 ÷ 7.14) = 1   H = (14.3 ÷ 7.14) = 2
     The ratio of C : H is 1 : 2 *(1 mark)*.
     So the empirical formula is CH_2 *(1 mark)*.

7.1 moles KOH = concentration × volume (dm³)
     = 0.5 × (150 ÷ 1000) = 0.075 *(1 mark)*
     M_r of KOH = 39.1 + 16.0 + 1.0 = 56.1 *(1 mark)*
     Mass = number of moles × M_r
     = 0.075 × 56.1 = **4.2 g** *(1 mark)*

7.2 Average titre = (26.00 + 26.05 + 26.00) ÷ 3
     = 26.02 cm³ *(1 mark)*
     Titration 3 is an anomalous result so you should ignore it when calculating the average titre.
     moles KOH = concentration × volume (dm³)
     = 0.5 × (26.02 ÷ 1000) = 0.013 *(1 mark)*
     moles HCl = 0.013 *(1 mark)*
     concentration of HCl = moles ÷ volume (dm³)
     = 0.013 ÷ (20 ÷ 1000)
     = **0.65 mol dm⁻³** *(1 mark)*

7.3 moles HX = concentration × volume (dm³)
     = 0.12 × 0.20 *(1 mark)*
     = 0.024 *(1 mark)*
     M_r of HX = mass ÷ number of moles
     = 3.07 ÷ 0.024 *(1 mark)*
     = 127.9 *(1 mark)*
     A_r of X = M_r of HX − A_r of H
     = 127.9 − 1.0 = 126.9 *(1 mark)*
     So the halogen, X, is iodine (I) *(1 mark)*.

Section 3: Bonding

1. Ionic Bonding
Page 72 — Application Questions
Q1 a) –1
    b) +1
    c) +2
Q2 a) +2
    b) –1
    c) CaI_2
Q3 a) LiF
    b) A lithium atom (Li) loses 1 electron to form a lithium ion (Li^+). The fluorine atom (F) gains 1 electron to form a fluoride ion (F^-). Electrostatic attraction holds the positive and negative ions together — this is an ionic bond.
Q4 Magnesium sulfate is an ionic compound, so will have a giant ionic lattice structure where the ions are held together by very strong electrostatic forces. These bonds require a lot of energy to break, so magnesium sulfate will have a very high melting point.

Page 72 — Fact Recall Questions
Q1 a) SO_4^{2-}
    b) NH_4^+
Q2 It holds positive and negative ions together.
Q3 A regular structure made up of ions.
Q4 E.g

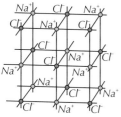

Q5 The ions in a liquid are free to move and carry a charge.
Q6 It will have a high melting point. It will dissolve in water.

2. Covalent Bonding
Page 76 — Application Questions
Q1 a) 5
    b) 8
    c) phosphorus
    d)

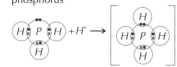

You could also draw PH_4^+ like this:

Q2 SiO_2 is a giant covalent compound so the bonds between the atoms are very strong covalent bonds which require a lot of energy to break, so it will have a very high melting point. All the outer electrons in SiO_2 are held in localised bonds, so it won't conduct electricity. As the covalent bonds are very difficult to break, SiO_2 will be insoluble.

Page 76 — Fact Recall Questions
Q1 It forms when two atoms share electrons so that they've both got full outer shells of electrons.

Q2 (diagram)

Q3 It is a covalent bond formed when two atoms share three pairs of electrons.
Q4 The weak bonds between layers are easily broken, so the sheets can slide over each other.
Q5 Diamond is a giant covalent structure made up of carbon atoms. Each carbon atom is covalently bonded to four other carbon atoms and the atoms arrange themselves in a tetrahedral shape.
Q6 A bond formed between two atoms where one of the atoms provides both of the shared electrons.
Q7 The arrow shows a pair of electrons from one atom shared between 2 atoms in a co-ordinate bond. The direction of the arrow shows which atom is the donor atom.

3. Charge Clouds
Page 77 — Fact Recall Questions
Q1 Electrons in an atom that are unshared.
Q2 A charge cloud is an area where you have a really big chance of finding an electron pair.
Q3 Lone-pair charge clouds repel more than bonding-pair charge clouds. So, the greatest angles are between lone pairs of electrons, and bond angles between bonding pairs are often reduced because they are pushed together by lone-pair repulsion.

4. Shapes of Molecules
Page 83 — Application Questions
Q1 a) Sulfur has 6 outer electrons and 2 hydrogen atoms donate one electron each. So there are 8 electrons on the S atom, which is **4 electron pairs**.
    b) 2 electron pairs are involved in bonding, so there are **2 lone pairs**.
    c)

    d) non-linear/bent
    e) 104.5°
Q2 a) Oxygen has 6 outer electrons and 3 hydrogen atoms donate one electron each. It's a positive ion so one electron has been removed. So there are 8 electrons on the O atom, which is **4 electron pairs**.
    b) 3 electron pairs are involved in bonding, so there is **1 lone pair**.
    c)

    The shape is trigonal pyramidal.
    d) 107°
Q3 a)

(diagram)

    The shape is trigonal pyramidal.
    Arsenic has 5 outer electrons and 3 hydrogen atoms donate one electron each. So there are 8 electrons on the As atom, which is 4 electron pairs. 3 electron pairs are involved in bonding, so there is 1 lone pair.

b) 107°

Q4

The shape is tetrahedral.
Carbon has 4 outer electrons and 2 chlorine and 2 fluorine atoms donate one electron each. So there are 8 electrons on the C atom, which is 4 electron pairs. All the electron pairs are involved in bonding.

Page 83 — Fact Recall Questions
Q1 120°
Q2 4
Q3 seesaw

5. Polarisation
Page 85 — Application Questions
Q1 a)

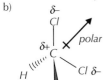

The polar B–Cl bonds cancel each other out, so the molecule has no permanent dipole (it's non-polar).

b)

The two C–Cl bonds point in roughly the same direction, so the molecule has a permanent dipole (it's polar).

c)

The P–F bonds all point in roughly the same direction, so the molecule has a permanent dipole (it's polar).

Q2 Chlorine has a much higher electronegativity than silicon, so $SiCl_4$ will have polar bonds — the Si–Cl bonds will be polarised towards chlorine. The shape of the molecule is tetrahedral, so the four polar Si–Cl will balance each other out, and the molecule won't have a permanent dipole.

Page 85 — Fact Recall Questions
Q1 Electronegativity is the ability to attract the bonding electrons in a covalent bond. So a chlorine atom is better able to attract the bonding electrons than a hydrogen atom.
Q2 Fluorine is more electronegative than hydrogen so attracts the electrons in the H—F covalent bond more than hydrogen. The bonding electrons are pulled towards the fluorine atom. This makes the bond polar.
Q3 A dipole is a difference in charge between two atoms caused by a shift in the electron density in the bond between them.

6. Intermolecular Forces
Page 91 — Applications Questions
Q1 van der Waals forces / induced dipole-dipole forces
Q2 a) The weak van der Waals forces between the chlorine molecules are easily broken.
   b) No — chlorine wouldn't conduct electricity because there are no free ions to carry the charge.
Q3 Decane is a larger molecule/contains more atoms than methane, therefore it has a larger electron cloud and stronger van der Waals forces between the molecules. This means more energy is needed to break the forces between the molecules.
Q4 a) Oxygen is more electronegative than chlorine so it has a greater ability to pull the bonding electrons away from hydrogen atoms. So the bonds are more polarised in H_2O than in HCl, which means that hydrogen bonds form in H_2O but not in HCl.
   b) fluorine/F
   c) carbon/C
Q5 a) NH_3 has hydrogen bonds between molecules whereas PH_3 only has van der Waals forces, as the electronegativity values of P and H are very similar. It takes less energy to break van der Waals forces than hydrogen bonds so the boiling point of PH_3 is lower.
   b) lower

Page 91 — Fact Recall Questions
Q1 There are covalent bonds within iodine molecules and van der Waals forces between iodine molecules.
Q2 Permanent dipole-dipole forces are weak electrostatic forces of attraction between polar molecules.
Q3 hydrogen bonding
Q4 a) hydrogen bonding
   b) E.g.

Make sure you draw the hydrogen bonds coming from the lone pair of electrons on the nitrogen atoms.
Q5 Ice has more hydrogen bonds than liquid water, and hydrogen bonds are relatively long. So the H_2O molecules in ice are further apart on average than in liquid water, making ice less dense than liquid water.

7. Metallic Bonding
Page 92 — Fact Recall Questions
Q1 Magnesium exists as a giant metallic lattice structure. The outermost shell of electrons of a magnesium atom is delocalised — the electrons are free to move about the metal. This leaves positive metal ions, Mg^{2+}, which are attracted to the delocalised negative electrons. They form a lattice of closely packed positive ions in a sea of delocalised electrons.
Q2 metallic bonding
Q3 a) As there are no bonds holding specific ions together, the copper ions can slide over each other when the structure is pulled, so it can be drawn into a wire.
   b) Copper has delocalised electrons which can pass kinetic energy to each other, making copper a good thermal conductor.

8. Properties of Materials

Page 95 — Application Questions

Q1 a) Giant covalent/macromolecular.
   b) Silicon dioxide has a high melting point because the strong covalent forces between all the atoms have to be broken to turn silicon dioxide from a solid to a liquid. This takes a lot of energy.

Q2 Simple covalent/molecular
   The sample won't conduct electricity when solid, so it isn't metallic. It won't dissolve in water, so it isn't ionic. It has a low melting point, so it isn't giant covalent. That just leaves simple covalent (molecular), which fits all three properties.

Page 95 — Fact Recall Questions

Q1 The particles go from vibrating about a fixed point and being unable to move about freely, to being able to move about freely and randomly.

Q2 To melt a simple covalent substance you only have to overcome the intermolecular forces that hold the molecules together. To melt a giant covalent substance you need to break the much stronger covalent bonds that hold the structure together. This takes a lot more energy, so the melting points of giant covalent substances are higher.

Q3 Three from: e.g. high melting and boiling points / typically solid at room temperature / conducts electricity as a solid and a liquid / insoluble in water / malleable.

Exam-style Questions — pages 97-99

1 C *(1 mark)*

2 B *(1 mark)*

3.1 Covalent bonding *(1 mark)*. A germanium atom and a hydrogen atom share a pair of electrons, with each atom donating one electron *(1 mark)*.

3.2

(2 marks — 1 mark for correct shape, 1 mark for correct bond angle)
The shape is tetrahedral *(1 mark)*.
Ge has 4 outer electrons and each H atom donates 1 electron, so there are 8 electrons on the Ge atom, which is 4 electron pairs. There are 4 bonding pairs, so there are no lone pairs.

3.3 It will not conduct electricity *(1 mark)* as there are no free ions or electrons to carry the charge *(1 mark)*.

3.4
$$\overset{\times\times}{Ge}$$
Cl   Cl *(1 mark)*
The shape is non-linear/bent *(1 mark)*
Ge has 4 outer electrons and each Cl atom donates 1 electron, so there are 6 outer electrons on the Ge atom, which is 3 electron pairs. There are 2 bonding pairs, so there is 1 lone pair.

3.5 Accept 112°-119° *(1 mark)* There are 3 pairs of electrons on the central atom, but lone pair/bonding pair repulsion is greater than bonding pair/bonding pair repulsion, so the bond angle will be less than 120° *(1 mark)*.

4.1 As you go down Group 5 the atoms have more electrons, so the van der Waals forces between molecules increase *(1 mark)*. It takes more energy to break the stronger van der Waals forces so the boiling points increase from PH_3 to SbH_3 *(1 mark)*.

4.2 hydrogen bonding *(1 mark)*

4.3 It is a dative/co-ordinate bond *(1 mark)*. The ammonia molecule has a lone pair of electrons *(1 mark)* which it donates to the hydrogen ion to form a co-ordinate bond *(1 mark)*.

4.4 NH_3 has one lone pair of electrons and three bonding pairs whereas NH_4^+ has four bonding pairs *(1 mark)*. As lone-pair/bonding pair repulsion is greater than bonding-pair/bonding-pair repulsion *(1 mark)*, the bond angle is pushed smaller in the NH_3 molecule than in NH_4^+ *(1 mark)*.

5.1 Sodium metal has a giant metallic lattice structure *(1 mark)* made up of Na^+ ions surrounded by delocalised electrons *(1 mark)*. The atoms in sodium are held together by metallic bonds formed due to the electrostatic attraction between the positively charged metal ions and the delocalised sea of electrons *(1 mark)*.

5.2 As there are no bonds holding specific ions together, the sodium ions can slide over each other when the structure is pulled *(1 mark)*.

5.3 Oppositely charged ions held together by electrostatic attraction *(1 mark)*.

5.4 Sodium chloride is a giant ionic lattice *(1 mark)* with a cube shape made up of alternating sodium and chloride ions *(1 mark)*.

6.1 Electronegativity is the ability to attract the bonding electrons in a covalent bond *(1 mark)*.
   If there's a difference in the electronegativities of two covalently bonded atoms, there's a shift in the electron density towards the more electronegative atom, giving the bond a dipole and causing it to be polar *(1 mark)*. If the shape of the molecule means the dipoles aren't cancelled out then the molecule will have a permanent dipole *(1 mark)* and there will be weak electrostatic forces of attraction, known as permanent dipole-dipole interactions, between molecules *(1 mark)*.

6.2 HCl: van der Waals forces / induced dipole-dipole forces and permanent dipole-dipole forces *(1 mark)*
   CH_4: van der Waals forces / induced dipole-dipole forces *(1 mark)*
   H_2O: van der Waals forces / induced dipole-dipole forces, permanent dipole-dipole forces and hydrogen bonds *(1 mark)*

6.3
$$\overset{\delta+}{H}\!\!-\!\!\overset{\delta-}{\underset{\times\times}{\overset{\times\times}{F}}}\text{----}\overset{\delta+}{H}\!\!-\!\!\overset{\delta-}{\underset{\times\times}{\overset{\times\times}{F}}}$$
(3 marks — 1 mark for showing all lone pairs, 1 mark for showing the partial charges and 1 mark for showing the hydrogen bond going from a lone pair on an F atom to an H atom.)

6.4 The Cl atoms in Cl_2 have equal electronegativities so the covalent bond is non-polar so only van der Waals forces will form between the molecules (permanent dipole-dipole forces and hydrogen bonds can't form) *(1 mark)*.

7.1 Giant covalent/macromolecular *(1 mark)*

7.2 Graphite consists of flat sheets of carbon atoms covalently bonded to three other carbon atoms and arranged in hexagons *(1 mark)*. The sheets of hexagons are bonded together by weak van der Waals forces *(1 mark)*. Each carbon atom in diamond is covalently bonded to four other carbon atoms *(1 mark)*. The atoms arrange themselves in a tetrahedral shape *(1 mark)*.

7.3 The delocalised electrons in graphite are free to move along the sheets, so an electric current can flow, unlike in diamond where there are no free electrons *(1 mark)*.

7.4 Van der Waals forces / induced dipole-dipole forces *(1 mark)* The forces between the C_3H_8 molecules would be stronger because each molecule contains more atoms so has larger electron clouds *(1 mark)*.

7.5 For diamond to boil the covalent bonds between carbon atoms have to be broken *(1 mark)*. This would need a lot more energy than breaking the van der Waals forces between methane molecules *(1 mark)*.

Section 4: Energetics

1. Enthalpy
Page 100 — Fact Recall Questions
Q1 ΔH_{298}°

Q2 Exothermic reactions give out energy, and endothermic reactions absorb energy. For exothermic reactions, the enthalpy change (ΔH) is negative. For endothermic reactions it is positive.

2. Bond Enthalpies
Page 103 — Application Questions
Q1 a) Bonds broken = $(1 \times C=C) + (1 \times H–H)$
So total energy absorbed = $612 + 436$
= 1048 kJ mol^{-1}.
Bonds formed = $(2 \times C–H) + (1 \times C–C)$
So total energy released = $(2 \times 413) + 347$
= 1173 kJ mol^{-1}.
Enthalpy change of reaction
= total energy absorbed – total energy released
= $1048 – 1173$ = **–125 kJ mol^{-1}**.

b) Bonds broken = $(1 \times C–O) + (1 \times H–Cl)$
So total energy absorbed = $358 + 432$
= 790 kJ mol^{-1}.
Bonds formed = $(1 \times C–Cl) + (1 \times O–H)$
So total energy released = $346 + 464$
= 810 kJ mol^{-1}.
Enthalpy change of reaction
= total energy absorbed – total energy released
= $790 – 810$ = **–20 kJ mol^{-1}**.

c) Bonds broken =
$(2 \times C–C) + (8 \times C–H) + (5 \times O=O)$
So total energy absorbed =
$(2 \times 347) + (8 \times 413) + (5 \times 498)$ = 6488 kJ mol^{-1}.
Bonds formed = $(6 \times C=O) + (8 \times O–H)$
So total energy released = $(6 \times 805) + (8 \times 464)$
= 8542 kJ mol^{-1}.
Enthalpy change of reaction/combustion
= total energy absorbed – total energy released
= $6488 – 8542$ = **–2054 kJ mol^{-1}**.

It really helps if you've drawn a sketch for this question.

d) Bonds broken = $(1 \times C–Cl) + (1 \times N–H)$
So total energy absorbed = $346 + 391$
= 737 kJ mol^{-1}.
Bonds formed = $(1 \times C–N) + (1 \times H–Cl)$
So total energy released = $286 + 432$
= 718 kJ mol^{-1}.
Enthalpy change of reaction
= total energy absorbed – total energy released
= $737 – 718$ = **+19 kJ mol^{-1}**.

Q2 The balanced equation for the combustion of ethene is:
$C_2H_4 + 3O_2 \rightarrow 2CO_2 + 2H_2O$.
Bonds broken =
$(1 \times C=C) + (4 \times C–H) + (3 \times O=O)$
So total energy absorbed =
$(1 \times 612) + (4 \times 413) + (3 \times 498)$ = 3758 kJ mol^{-1}.

Bonds formed = $(4 \times C=O) + (4 \times O–H)$
So total energy released = $(4 \times 805) + (4 \times 464)$
= 5076 kJ mol^{-1}.
Enthalpy change of combustion
= total energy absorbed – total energy released
= $3758 – 5076$ = **–1318 kJ mol^{-1}**.

Q3 The balanced equation for the formation of 1 mole of HCl is: $\frac{1}{2}H_2 + \frac{1}{2}Cl_2 \rightarrow HCl$.
The enthalpy change of formation is the enthalpy change when 1 mole of a compound is formed, so your equation needs to have 1 mole of HCl on the RHS, which means you need half a mole of H_2 and half a mole of Cl_2 on the LHS of the equation.
Bonds broken = $\frac{1}{2}(1 \times H–H) + \frac{1}{2}(1 \times Cl–Cl)$
So total energy absorbed = $(\frac{1}{2} \times 436) + (\frac{1}{2} \times 243)$
= 339.5 kJ mol^{-1}.
Bonds formed = $1 \times H–Cl$
So total energy released = 432 kJ mol^{-1}.
Enthalpy change of formation
= total energy absorbed – total energy released
= $339.7 – 432$ = **–92.5 kJ mol^{-1}**.

Q4 Call the unknown bond enthalpy between N and O 'X'.
Bonds broken = $2 \times X$
So total energy absorbed = $2X$ kJ mol^{-1}.
Bonds formed = $(1 \times N≡N) + (1 \times O=O)$
So total energy released = $945 + 498$
= 1443 kJ mol^{-1}.
Enthalpy change of reaction = –181 kJ mol^{-1}
= total energy absorbed – total energy released.
So: $–181 = 2X – 1443$
$2X = –181 + 1443 = 1262$
$X = 1262 \div 2$ = **+631 kJ mol^{-1}**.

Page 103 — Fact Recall Questions
Q1 a) $\Delta_f H^{\circ}$
b) $\Delta_c H^{\circ}$

Q2 Standard enthalpy change of formation, $\Delta_f H^{\circ}$, is the enthalpy change when 1 mole of a compound is formed from its elements in their standard states under standard conditions.

3. Measuring Enthalpy Changes
Page 107 — Application Questions
Q1 $q = mc\Delta T = 220 \times 4.18 \times (301 – 298) = 2758.8$ J
= 2.7588 kJ
$\Delta H = \frac{q}{n} = -\frac{2.7588 \text{ kJ}}{0.0500 \text{ mol}}$ = **–55.2 kJ mol^{-1}** (to 3 s.f.).

Don't forget — the enthalpy change must be negative because it's an exothermic reaction (you can tell because the temperature increased).

Q2 a) $q = mc\Delta T = 200 \times 4.18 \times 29.0 = 24244$ J
= 24.244 kJ
$n = \frac{\text{mass}}{M} = \frac{0.500 \text{ g}}{72 \text{ g mol}^{-1}} = 0.00694$ moles of fuel
$\Delta H = \frac{q}{n} = -\frac{24.244 \text{ kJ}}{0.00694 \text{ mol}}$
= **–3490 kJ mol^{-1}** (to 3 s.f.).

b) E.g. some heat from the combustion will have been lost to the surroundings (rather than being transferred to the water). / Some of the combustion may have been incomplete combustion. / If the fuel was volatile, some of it may have been lost to evaporation. / The experiment may not have taken place under standard conditions.

Q3 $q = mc\Delta T = 300 \times 4.18 \times 55 = 68\,970$ J
$\quad = 68.97$ kJ
$\Delta_c H^\circ$ octane $= -5470$ kJ mol$^{-1} = \dfrac{q}{n}$
$n = \dfrac{q}{\Delta H} = \dfrac{68.97\,\text{kJ}}{5470\,\text{kJ mol}^{-1}} = 0.0126...$ mol.
$n = \dfrac{\text{mass}}{M}$, so mass $= n \times M = 0.0125... \times 114$
$\quad = \textbf{1.44 g}$ of octane (to 3 s.f.).

Page 107 — Fact Recall Questions
Q1 The temperature change due to the reaction, the mass of the reactant (which is used to calculate the number of moles that has reacted), and the mass of the stuff that's being heated.

Q2 E.g.

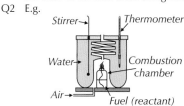

Q3 a) q is the heat lost or gained during a reaction.
　　b) joules (J)

Q4 Find the number of moles of that reactant that react in the balanced chemical equation, then calculate $\Delta_c H^\circ$ using:
$\Delta_c H^\circ = \dfrac{q}{n} \times$ number of moles reacting in balanced chemical equation

4. Hess's Law
Page 111 — Application Questions
Q1 a) First draw out a reaction scheme with an alternative reaction route that includes balanced equations for the formation of each compound:

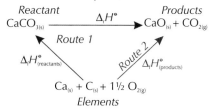

$\Delta_f H^\circ_{\text{(reactants)}} = \Delta_f H^\circ_{[\text{CaCO}_3]} = -1207$ kJ mol^{-1}.
$\Delta_f H^\circ_{\text{(products)}} = \Delta_f H^\circ_{[\text{CaO}]} + \Delta_f H^\circ_{[\text{CO}_2]}$
$\Delta_f H^\circ_{\text{(products)}} = -635 + -394 = -1029$ kJ mol^{-1}.

Using Hess's Law: Route 1 = Route 2, so:
$\Delta_f H^\circ_{\text{(reactants)}} + \Delta_r H^\circ = \Delta_f H^\circ_{\text{(products)}}$
$-1207 + \Delta_r H^\circ = -1029$
$\Delta_r H^\circ = -1029 + 1207 = \textbf{+178 kJ mol}^{-1}$.

b)

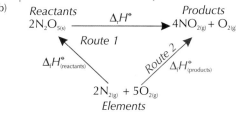

$\Delta_f H^\circ_{\text{(reactants)}} = 2 \times \Delta_f H^\circ_{[\text{N}_2\text{O}_5]}$
$\Delta_f H^\circ_{\text{(reactants)}} = 2 \times -41 = -82$ kJ mol^{-1}.
$\Delta_f H^\circ_{\text{(products)}} = (4 \times \Delta_f H^\circ_{[\text{NO}_2]}) + \Delta_f H^\circ_{[\text{O}_2]}$

$\Delta_f H^\circ_{\text{(products)}} = (4 \times 33) + 0 = 132$ kJ mol^{-1}.
Remember that the enthalpy change of formation of O_2 is zero because it's an element.

Using Hess's Law: Route 1 = Route 2, so:
$\Delta_f H^\circ_{\text{(reactants)}} + \Delta_r H^\circ = \Delta_f H^\circ_{\text{(products)}}$
$-82 + \Delta_r H^\circ = 132$
$\Delta_r H^\circ = 132 + 82 = \textbf{+214 kJ mol}^{-1}$.

Q2 a) First draw out balanced reactions for the formation of the compound, and the combustion of the reactants and product:

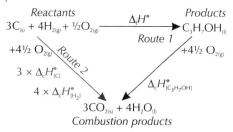

Using Hess's Law: Route 1 = Route 2, so:
$\Delta_f H^\circ + \Delta_c H^\circ_{[\text{C}_3\text{H}_7\text{OH}]} = (3 \times \Delta_c H^\circ_{[\text{C}]}) + (4 \times \Delta_c H^\circ_{[\text{H}_2]})$
$\Delta_f H^\circ + (-2021) = (3 \times -394) + (4 \times -286)$
$\Delta_f H^\circ = -1182 - 1144 + 2021 = \textbf{-305 kJ mol}^{-1}$.

b)

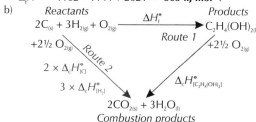

Using Hess's Law: Route 1 = Route 2, so:
$\Delta_f H^\circ + \Delta_c H^\circ_{[\text{C}_2\text{H}_4(\text{OH})_2]} = (2 \times \Delta_c H^\circ_{[\text{C}]}) + (3 \times \Delta_c H^\circ_{[\text{H}_2]})$
$\Delta_f H^\circ + (-1180) = (2 \times -394) + (3 \times -286)$
$\Delta_f H^\circ = -788 - 858 + 1180 = \textbf{-466 kJ mol}^{-1}$.

c)

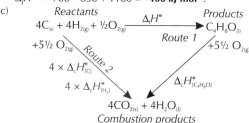

Using Hess's Law: Route 1 = Route 2, so:
$\Delta_f H^\circ + \Delta_c H^\circ_{[\text{C}_4\text{H}_8\text{O}]} = (4 \times \Delta_c H^\circ_{[\text{C}]}) + (4 \times \Delta_c H^\circ_{[\text{H}_2]})$
$\Delta_f H^\circ + (-2442) = (4 \times -394) + (4 \times -286)$
$\Delta_f H^\circ = -1576 - 1144 + 2442 = \textbf{-278 kJ mol}^{-1}$.

Exam-style Questions — pages 112-113
1.1 $q = mc\Delta T = 50.0 \times 2.46 \times 1.00 = 123$ J $= 0.123$ kJ
$\Delta H = \dfrac{q}{n} = -\dfrac{0.123\,\text{kJ}}{0.0500\,\text{mol}} = \textbf{-2.46 kJ mol}^{-1}$.

(3 marks for correct answer, otherwise 1 mark for $q = mc\Delta T$, 1 mark for 235 J or 0.235 kJ)
You've got to remember the negative sign on your answer — the temperature rises so it's an exothermic reaction.

1.2 The reaction must be carried out at a pressure of 100 kPa *(1 mark)* with all reactants and products in their standard states at that pressure *(1 mark)*.

2.1 Hess's Law says that the total enthalpy change for a reaction is independent of the route taken *(1 mark)*.

2.2 $C_8H_{18(l)} + 12\frac{1}{2}O_{2(g)} \rightarrow 8CO_{2(g)} + 9H_2O_{(l)}$ *(1 mark)*

2.3

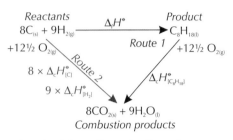

Using Hess's Law: Route 1 = Route 2, so:
$\Delta_f H° + \Delta_c H°_{[C_8H_{18}]} = (8 \times \Delta_c H°_{[C]}) + (9 \times \Delta_c H°_{[H_2]})$
$\Delta_f H° + (-5470) = (8 \times -394) + (9 \times -286)$
$\Delta_f H° = -3152 - 2574 + 5470 = \textbf{-256 kJ mol}^{-1}$.
(3 marks for correct answer, otherwise 1 mark for correct equation using Hess's Law and 1 mark for correct molar quantities.)

2.4 Exothermic *(1 mark)*. The enthalpy change for the formation of octane is negative *(1 mark)*.

3.1 Standard enthalpy of combustion, $\Delta_c H°$, is the enthalpy change when 1 mole of a substance *(1 mark)* is completely burned in oxygen *(1 mark)* under standard conditions with all reactants and products in their standard states *(1 mark)*.

3.2 The balanced equation for the combustion of but-1-ene is: $C_4H_8 + 6O_2 \rightarrow 4CO_2 + 4H_2O$.
Bonds broken =
$(1 \times C=C) + (2 \times C–C) + (8 \times C–H) + (6 \times O=O)$
So total energy absorbed =
$(1 \times 612) + (2 \times 347) + (8 \times 413) + (6 \times 498)$
$= 7598$ kJ mol^{-1}.
Bonds formed = $(8 \times C=O) + (8 \times O–H)$
So total energy released = $(8 \times 805) + (8 \times 464)$
$= 10\,152$ kJ mol^{-1}.
Enthalpy change of combustion
= total energy absorbed – total energy released
$= 7598 - 10\,152 = \textbf{-2554 kJ mol}^{-1}$.
(3 marks for correct answer, otherwise 1 mark for 'total energy absorbed – total energy released', and 1 mark for correct value for either energy released or energy absorbed.)

3.3 Some of the mean bond enthalpies are average values for the bonds in many different compounds, so they are not accurate for the specific molecules involved in this combustion *(1 mark)*.

4.1 Standard enthalpy change of formation, $\Delta_f H°$, is the enthalpy change when 1 mole *(1 mark)* of a compound is formed from its elements *(1 mark)* in their standard states under standard conditions *(1 mark)*.

4.2

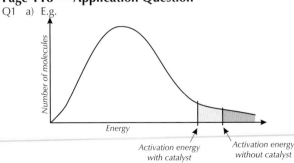

$\Delta_f H°_{(reactants)} = (2 \times \Delta_f H°_{[KOH]}) + \Delta_f H°_{[H_2SO_4]}$
$\Delta_f H°_{(reactants)} = (2 \times -425) + -814 = -1664$ kJ mol^{-1}.
$\Delta_f H°_{(products)} = \Delta_f H°_{[K_2SO_4]} + (2 \times \Delta_f H°_{[H_2O]})$
$\Delta_f H°_{(products)} = -1438 + (2 \times -286) = -2010$ kJ mol^{-1}.
Using Hess's Law: Route 1 = Route 2, so:
$\Delta_f H°_{(reactants)} + \Delta_r H° = \Delta_f H°_{(products)}$
$-1664 + \Delta_r H° = -2010$
$\Delta_r H° = -2010 + 1664 = \textbf{-346 kJ mol}^{-1}$.
(3 marks for correct answer, otherwise 1 mark for correct equation using Hess's Law and 1 mark for correct molar quantities.)

Section 5: Kinetics

1. Reaction Rates

Page 116 — Application Question
Q1 B is the curve for the gas at a higher temperature because it is shifted over to the right showing that more molecules have more energy.

Page 116 — Fact Recall Questions
Q1 The particles must collide in the right direction (facing each other the right way) and with at least a certain minimum amount of kinetic energy.
Q2 The minimum amount of kinetic energy that particles need to have in order to react when they collide.
Q3 A small increase in temperature gives all molecules more energy, so a greater number of them have at least the activation energy to react when they collide. They will also collide more frequently because they will be moving about faster.
Q4 If you increase the concentration of reactants in a solution, the particles will be closer together in a given volume and so collide more frequently, increasing the reaction rate.

2. Catalysts

Page 118 — Application Question
Q1 a) E.g.

Number of molecules

Energy

Activation energy with catalyst

Activation energy without catalyst

You can draw the activation energy line anywhere as long as it is lower than the activation energy for the uncatalysed reaction. The shape of the graph should stay the same.

b) Adding a catalyst would lower the activation energy for the reaction so that it would not need such a high temperature in order to take place. Being able to carry out the reaction at a lower temperature would save energy and money.

Page 118 — Fact Recall Questions
Q1 A substance that increases the rate of a reaction by providing an alternative reaction pathway with a lower activation energy. The catalyst is chemically unchanged at the end of the reaction.
Q2 A catalyst increases the rate of a reaction by providing an alternative reaction pathway with a lower activation energy. This means that more of the molecules collide with energies above the activation energy, and so can react.

3. Measuring Reaction Rates
Page 121 — Application Question
Q1 a) One of the products is a gas so the student could measure the change in mass of the open reaction vessel over time / use a gas syringe to measure the volume of gas produced by the reaction mixture over time.
    b) If the student is measuring the change in mass, then the reaction is finished when the mass of the reaction vessel stops decreasing. If the student is measuring the change in gas volume, then the reaction is finished when the volume stops increasing.
    c) 188-196 s.

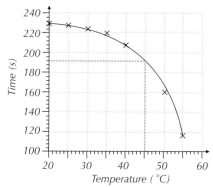

The best way to get an estimate is to draw a graph and plot the data points from the table. You can then draw a curve and read off the value on the time axis (y-axis in the example above) at 45 °C. For the curve drawn above, the estimate of time taken is 192 s. Everyone will draw a slightly different curve though so any answer from 188 s to 196 s is fine.

Page 121 — Fact Recall Questions
Q1 The rate of reaction is the change in the amount of a reactant or product over time.
Q2 Mix the reactants in a conical flask placed on a black cross. Using a stop clock, measure the time taken for enough precipitate to form so that the cross is no longer visible through the reaction mixture.

Exam-style Questions — pages 123-124
1   B *(1 mark)*
2   C *(1 mark)*
3   A *(1 mark)*
4   D *(1 mark)*
5.1 The minimum amount of kinetic energy that particles need to have in order to react when they collide *(1 mark)*.

5.2 E.g.

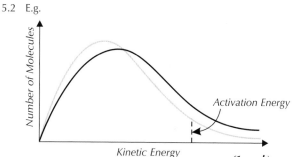

(1 mark)

There isn't just one right answer here. Your curve just needs to be pushed over to the right, with a greater number of molecules having at least the activation energy.

5.3 A catalyst is a substance that increases the rate of a reaction by providing an alternative reaction pathway with a lower activation energy. The catalyst is chemically unchanged at the end of the reaction *(1 mark)*.
5.4 The shape doesn't change *(1 mark)* because the molecules still have the same amount of energy *(1 mark)*.
5.5 The rate of reaction will increase *(1 mark)*. Heating the reactants gives the molecules on average more kinetic energy and they will move faster *(1 mark)*. A greater proportion of molecules will have at least the activation energy, and because the molecules are moving about faster, the frequency of collisions increases *(1 mark)*.
5.6 Lowering the pressure will reduce the rate of reaction *(1 mark)*. This is because there will be fewer gas molecules in a given volume/the concentration will be reduced/the molecules will be further apart *(1 mark)*, so the frequency of collisions between molecules that result in a reaction decreases *(1 mark)*.

Section 6: Equilibria and Redox Reactions

1. Reversible Reactions
Page 128 — Application Questions
Q1 a) Increasing the concentration of A will shift the equilibrium to the right (favouring the forwards reaction) in order to get rid of the excess A.
    b) There are 3 moles on the left and only 2 on the right. Increasing the pressure will shift the equilibrium to the right (favouring the forwards reaction) in order to reduce the number of moles to reduce the pressure again.
    c) The forwards reaction is exothermic, so the backwards reaction must be endothermic. Increasing the temperature will shift the equilibrium to the left (favouring the endothermic backwards reaction) in order to remove the extra heat.
    d) The reaction should ideally be performed with a high concentration of A and B, at a high pressure and low temperature.
Q2 There are the same number of moles on either side of the reaction. Increasing the pressure favours the reaction producing the fewest moles, but since both reactions are equal in this respect, increasing the pressure will not shift the position of equilibrium.

Page 128 — Fact Recall Questions
Q1 At dynamic equilibrium, the concentrations of reactants and products are constant, and the forwards reaction and the backwards reaction are going at the same rate.

Q2 For a dynamic equilibrium to be established it must be a closed system and the temperature must be constant.

Q3 Le Chatelier's principle states that if there's a change in concentration, pressure or temperature, the equilibrium will move to help counteract the change.

Q4 The addition of a catalyst has no effect on the position of equilibrium in a reversible reaction.

2. Industrial Processes

Page 129 — Fact Recall Question

Q1 The temperature and pressure used in the industrial production of ethanol are a compromise. Using a low temperature increases the yield of the reaction, but at low temperatures the reaction rate becomes much slower. So a moderate temperature is used as a compromise between a good yield and a fast reaction. Using a high pressure also increases the yield of the reaction, but high pressures are expensive to produce. You need stronger pipes and containers to withstand high pressure. So a moderate pressure is used as a compromise between maximum yield and minimum expense.

3. The Equilibrium Constant

Page 132 — Application Questions

Q1 a) $K_c = \dfrac{[C_2H_5OH]}{[C_2H_4][H_2O]}$

b) The equation tells you that if 1 mole of C_2H_5OH decomposes, 1 mole of C_2H_4 and 1 mole of H_2O are formed. So if 1.85 moles of C_2H_4 are produced at equilibrium, there will also be **1.85** moles of H_2O. 1.85 moles of C_2H_5OH has decomposed so there must be 5.00 – 1.85 = **3.15** moles of C_2H_5OH remaining.

c) The volume of the reaction is 15.0 dm³. So the molar concentrations are:
For H_2O and C_2H_4: 1.85 ÷ 15.0 = **0.123 mol dm⁻³**.
For C_2H_5OH: 3.15 ÷ 15.0 = **0.210 mol dm⁻³**.

d) $K_c = \dfrac{[C_2H_5OH]}{[C_2H_4][H_2O]} = \dfrac{0.210}{(0.123)(0.123)} = 13.9$

Units of $K_c = \dfrac{\text{mol dm}^{-3}}{(\text{mol dm}^{-3})(\text{mol dm}^{-3})} = \dfrac{1}{(\text{mol dm}^{-3})}$

$K_c = $ **13.9 mol⁻¹ dm³**

For the units here, you've ended up with mol dm⁻³ on its own on the bottom of the fraction. So you simplify it by swapping the signs of the powers — it becomes mol⁻¹ dm³.

e) $K_c = \dfrac{[C_2H_5OH]}{[C_2H_4][H_2O]}$ so $3.8 = \dfrac{0.80}{[C_2H_4][H_2O]}$

$[C_2H_4][H_2O] = 0.8 \div 3.8 = 0.21$
$[C_2H_4]$ and $[H_2O] = \sqrt{0.21} = $ **0.46 mol dm⁻³**

Q2 a) $K_c = \dfrac{[SO_3]^2}{[SO_2]^2[O_2]}$

b) $K_c = \dfrac{[SO_3]^2}{[SO_2]^2[O_2]} = \dfrac{0.36^2}{(0.25)^2(0.18)} = 11.5$

Units of $K_c = \dfrac{(\text{mol dm}^{-3})^2}{(\text{mol dm}^{-3})^2(\text{mol dm}^{-3})^2} = \dfrac{1}{\text{mol dm}^{-3}}$

$K_c = $ **11.5 mol⁻¹ dm³**

c) $[SO_2]^2 = \dfrac{[SO_3]^2}{K_c \times [O_2]} = \dfrac{0.360^2}{15.0 \times 0.180} = 0.0480$

$[SO_2] = \sqrt{0.0480} = $ **0.219 mol dm⁻³**

4. Factors Affecting the Equilibrium Constant

Page 134 — Application Questions

Q1 a) No effect — if the concentration of C_2F_4 increases the equilibrium will shift to counteract the change and K_c will stay the same.

b) The reaction is endothermic in the forward direction so increasing the temperature will shift the equilibrium to the right. As a result more product will be produced, so K_c will increase.

c) No effect — catalysts only affect the time taken to reach equilibrium and not the position of the equilibrium itself.

Remember, it's only temperature that affects the value of K_c.

Q2 Exothermic. If decreasing the temperature increases K_c then it must increase the amount of product formed. The equilibrium must have shifted to the right, so the forward reaction must be exothermic.

Page 134 — Fact Recall Questions

Q1 a) It will increase K_c.
b) It will decrease K_c.

Q2 If the concentration of a reagent is changed the equilibrium will shift and the concentrations of other reagents will also change. So K_c will stay the same.

Q3 Adding a catalyst doesn't change K_c, but it decreases the time taken to reach equilibrium.

5. Redox Reactions

Pages 137-138 — Application Questions

Q1 a) +1
b) −1
c) +2

Q2 a) −1
b) −2
c) −1

Q3 a) H: +1, Cl: −1
b) S: +4, O: −2
c) C: +4, O: −2

Oxygen has an oxidation state of -2. There are 3 oxygen atoms here so the total is −6. The overall oxidation state of the ion is −2. So, carbon must have an oxidation state of +4 (as −6 + 4 = −2).

d) Cl: +7, O: −2
e) Cu: +1, O: −2
f) H: +1, S: +6, O: −2

Oxygen has an oxidation state of −2. There are 4 oxygen atoms here so the total is −8. The overall oxidation state of the ion is −1. Hydrogen has an oxidation state of +1, so sulfur must have an oxidation state of +6 (as −8 + 1 + 6 = −1).

Q4 a) +2
b) +4
c) +4
d) 0
e) +4

Hydrogen has an oxidation state of +1, so in C_3H_6 carbon must have an oxidation state of −2 (as $(6 \times +1) + (3 \times -2) = 0$).

Q5 a) 0
b) −3
c) +5
d) +2

Fluorine is the most electronegative element so its oxidation state is equal to its ionic charge, −1. There are 4 fluorine atoms here so the total is −4. So, phosphorus must have an oxidation state of +2 (as $(4 \times -1) + (2 \times +2) = 0$).

e) +5
f) −2

Q6 a) beginning: 0, end: +2
b) beginning: +6, end: +6
c) beginning: +1, end: 0
d) beginning: −2, end: −2

Page 138 — Fact Recall Questions

Q1 Oxidation is a loss of electrons.

Q2 Reduction is a gain of electrons.

Q3 An oxidising agent accepts electrons from another reactant and is reduced.

Q4 A reducing agent donates electrons to another reactant and is oxidised.

Q5 0

Q6 0

Q7 −1

Q8 −1

6. Redox Equations

Page 140 — Application Questions

Q1 $Zn + 2Ag^+ \rightarrow Zn^{2+} + 2Ag$

You need to multiply everything in the silver half-equation by 2 so that the e^- will cancel when you combine the two half-equations.

Q2 Oxidation equation: $Ca \rightarrow Ca^{2+} + 2e^-$
Reduction equation: $Cl_2 + 2e^- \rightarrow 2Cl^-$

Q3 $2NO_3^- + 12H^+ + 10e^- \rightarrow N_2 + 6H_2O$

Q4 $Cr_2O_7^{2-} + 14H^+ + 6e^- \rightarrow 2Cr^{3+} + 7H_2O$

Q5 $H_2SO_4 + 8H^+ + 8e^- \rightarrow H_2S + 4H_2O$

Page 141 — Fact Recall Questions

Q1 An ionic half-equation shows oxidation or reduction.

Q2 **B**

Exam-style Questions — pages 142-144

1 C *(1 mark)*

2 D *(1 mark)*

3 A *(1 mark)*

4 B *(1 mark)*

5.1 In a reversible reaction, dynamic equilibrium is reached when the concentrations of reactants and products are constant *(1 mark)*, and the forwards reaction and the backwards reaction are going at the same rate *(1 mark)*.

5.2 If there's a change in concentration, pressure or temperature, the equilibrium will move to help counteract the change *(1 mark)*.

5.3 The higher the pressure, the faster the reaction rate *(1 mark)*. A high pressure also favours the forwards reaction (which produces fewer moles) so the higher the pressure, the greater the yield of ethanol *(1 mark)*. However, high pressures are very expensive/produce side reactions/require strong and expensive equipment, so the pressure used is limited by these factors *(1 mark)*.

5.4 Reducing the amount of H_2O will shift the position of equilibrium to the left *(1 mark)* in order to increase the amount of H_2O present *(1 mark)*. This shift will reduce the maximum yield of ethanol from the forwards reaction *(1 mark)*.

6.1 It has no effect on the position of equilibrium *(1 mark)*.
Catalysts increase the rate at which equilibrium is reached but don't affect the position of equilibrium.

6.2 exothermic

6.3 The forwards reaction is exothermic, so the backwards reaction is endothermic. Increasing the temperature will shift the position of equilibrium to the left *(1 mark)*, favouring the endothermic backwards reaction *(1 mark)* in order to remove the excess heat *(1 mark)*.

6.4 Any two from: e.g. increasing the pressure/increasing the concentration of N_2 and H_2/reducing the concentration of NH_3 (e.g. by removing it) *(1 mark for each — maximum of 2 marks overall)*.

7.1 $K_c = \dfrac{[CO_2][H_2]^4}{[CH_4][H_2O]^2}$ *(1 mark)*.

7.2 $K_c = (0.200 \times (0.280)^4) \div (0.0800 \times (0.320)^2) = 0.150$
$K_c = (mol\ dm^{-3} \times (mol\ dm^{-3})^4) \div (mol\ dm^{-3} \times (mol\ dm^{-3})^2) = mol^2\ dm^{-6}$ so $K_c = $ **0.150 mol² dm⁻⁶**
(3 marks for correct answer, otherwise 1 mark for correct method and 1 mark for correct units.)

7.3 $[CH_4] = \dfrac{[CO_2][H_2]^4}{K_c \times [H_2O]^2}$
$= (0.420 \times 0.480^4) \div (0.0800 \times 0.560^2)$
$= $ **0.889 mol dm⁻³** *(2 marks for correct answer, otherwise 1 mark for correct equation.)*

7.4 Lower *(1 mark)*. K_c is lower at temperature Z than at Y. This means at Z the equilibrium is being shifted to the left *(1 mark)*. As the reaction is endothermic in the forward direction, the temperature must be lower to make it shift in the exothermic direction *(1 mark)*.

7.5 The value of K_c would not change *(1 mark)*. Catalysts do not affect the position of the equilibrium, only the time taken to reach equilibrium *(1 mark)*.

8.1 $3Cl_2 + 6e^- \rightarrow 6Cl^-$ *(1 mark)*
$2Al \rightarrow 2Al^{3+} + 6e^-$ *(1 mark)*

8.2 Chlorine is the oxidising agent *(1 mark)*.

8.3 +6 *(1 mark)*

Unit 2

Section 1: Periodicity

1. The Periodic Table

Page 147 — Application Questions

Q1 a) 3
b) 2
c) 4
d) 2
e) 5

Q2 a) 6
b) 1
c) 7
d) 3
e) 2

Q3 a) $1s^2\ 2s^2\ 2p^6\ 3s^1$
b) $1s^2\ 2s^2\ 2p^6\ 3s^2\ 3p^6\ 4s^2$
c) $1s^2\ 2s^2\ 2p^6\ 3s^2\ 3p^5$
d) $1s^2\ 2s^2\ 2p^6\ 3s^2\ 3p^6\ 3d^{10}\ 4s^2\ 4p^3$
e) $1s^2\ 2s^2\ 2p^6\ 3s^2\ 3p^6\ 3d^3\ 4s^2$
f) $1s^2\ 2s^2\ 2p^6\ 3s^2\ 3p^6\ 3d^1\ 4s^2$

Page 147 — Fact Recall Questions

Q1 The periodic table is arranged into periods (rows) and groups (columns) by atomic (proton) number.

Q2 a) Z
b) Y
c) X

2. Periodicity

Page 150 — Application Questions
Q1 a) Aluminium has 13 protons and sulfur has 16 protons. So the positive charge of the nucleus of sulfur is greater. This means electrons are pulled closer to the nucleus, making the atomic radius of sulfur smaller than the atomic radius of aluminium.

b) sodium/magnesium

Q2 Sulfur has more protons than aluminium, so its electrons are attracted more strongly towards the nucleus. This means it takes more energy to remove an electron from each atom, so it has a higher first ionisation energy.

Q3 a) Silicon is macromolecular so has strong covalent bonds linking all its atoms together. Phosphorus is a molecular substance with van der Waals forces between its molecules. It takes much less energy to break van der Waals forces than covalent bonds so the melting point of phosphorus is much lower than the melting point of silicon.

b) chlorine / argon

Page 150 — Fact Recall Questions
Q1 The atomic radius decreases across Period 3.
Q2 The melting points increase from sodium to silicon, but then generally decrease from silicon to argon.
Q3 There's a general increase in the first ionisation energy as you go across Period 3.

Exam-style Questions — page 151
1 B *(1 mark)*
2 C *(1 mark)*
   Sulfur is in the p block of the periodic table.
3 B *(1 mark)*
   First ionisation energy generally increases across Period 3.
4.1 The atomic radius of aluminium is smaller than that of sodium because an aluminium atom contains more protons, which increases the positive charge of the nucleus *(1 mark)*. This means the electrons are pulled closer to the nucleus, making the atomic radius smaller *(1 mark)*.
4.2 Magnesium ions have a 2+ charge, whereas sodium ions only have a 1+ charge *(1 mark)*. Magnesium ions also have more delocalised electrons and a smaller radius than sodium ions *(1 mark)*. So the metal-metal bonds are stronger in magnesium than in sodium *(1 mark)*.
4.3 Sodium, magnesium and aluminium are all metals with strong metallic bonds holding the atoms together, so they have quite high melting points *(1 mark)*. However, argon exists as individual atoms with only weak van der Waals forces between the atoms, so it has a very low melting point *(1 mark)*.

Section 2: Group 2 and Group 7 Elements

1. Group 2 — The Alkaline Earth Metals
Page 154 — Application Questions
Q1 Strontium with dilute hydrochloric acid.
Q2 a) Element X
    b) Element Y

Page 154 — Fact Recall Questions
Q1 Atomic radius increases down the group.

Q2 First ionisation energy decreases down the group. This is because each element down Group 2 has an extra electron shell compared to the one above. The extra inner shells shield the outer electrons from the attraction of the nucleus. Also, the extra shell means that the outer electrons are further away from the nucleus, which greatly reduces the nucleus's attraction. Both of these factors make it easier to remove outer electrons, resulting in a lower first ionisation energy.

Q3 a) Barium has a smaller atomic radius than radium, so its two delocalised electrons will be closer to the positive ion/nucleus. This means they will be more strongly attracted to the positive ion/nucleus than the delocalised electrons in radium. So it will take more energy to break the bonds in barium, which means it has a higher melting point.

b) Magnesium — the crystal structure changes.

2. Group 2 Compounds
Page 157 — Application Questions
Q1 The element with the lower ionisation energy will react more readily because it will be oxidised more easily.
Q2 There are no sulfate ions in the solution.
   If there were sulfate ions in the sample, a white precipitate of barium sulfate would form.

Page 157 — Fact Recall Questions
Q1 The elements react more readily down the group.
Q2 They become more soluble down the group.
Q3 They become less soluble down the group.
Q4 To get rid of any sulfites or carbonates that might affect the result of the test.
Q5 It is a suspension of barium sulfate that a patient swallows before an X-ray. It is opaque to X-rays so will show up the structure of the oesophagus, stomach or intestines.
Q6 Titanium(IV) oxide is first converted to titanium(IV) chloride by heating it with carbon in a stream of chlorine gas. The titanium chloride is then purified by fractional distillation, before being reduced by magnesium in a furnace at almost 1000 °C.
Q7 Calcium oxide and calcium carbonate.
Q8 Calcium hydroxide is used in agriculture to neutralise acidic soils.

3. Group 7 — The Halogens
Page 161 — Application Questions
Q1 a) A — bromide, B — chloride/fluoride, C — iodide
    b) There would be no change in the colours of the halide solutions. Iodine is below bromine and chlorine in Group 7 so it is less oxidising than them and cannot displace them from a halide solution.
Q2 When chlorine reacts with sodium hydroxide solution it produces sodium chlorate solution. This is bleach, so it will turn the litmus paper white by bleaching it.

Page 161 — Fact Recall Questions
Q1 The boiling points increase down the group.
Q2 fluorine
Q3 bromide and iodide
Q4 a) The solution turns from colourless to brown.
    b) $Br_{2(aq)} + 2KI_{(aq)} \rightarrow 2KBr_{(aq)} + I_{2(aq)}$
    c) $Br_{2(aq)} + 2I^-_{(aq)} \rightarrow 2Br^-_{(aq)} + I_{2(aq)}$

Q5 a) sodium chlorate(I) solution, sodium chloride, water

b) $2NaOH_{(aq)} + Cl_{2(g)} \rightarrow NaClO_{(aq)} + NaCl_{(aq)} + H_2O_{(l)}$

Q6 When you mix chlorine with water, it undergoes disproportionation. You end up with a mixture of chloride ions and chlorate(I) ions. In sunlight, chlorine can also decompose water to form chloride ions and oxygen.

Q7 a) Chlorine kills disease-causing microorganisms. It also prevents the growth of algae, eliminating bad tastes and smells, and removes discolouration caused by organic compounds.

b) Chlorine gas is very harmful if it's breathed in — it irritates the respiratory system. Liquid chlorine on the skin or eyes causes severe chemical burns. Accidents involving chlorine could be really serious, even fatal. Water contains a variety of organic compounds, e.g. from the decomposition of plants. Chlorine reacts with these compounds to form chlorinated hydrocarbons, e.g. chloromethane (CH_3Cl) — and many of these chlorinated hydrocarbons are carcinogenic (cancer-causing).

4. Halide Ions
Page 164 — Application Questions

Q1 He is correct for sodium chloride — it will only produce hydrogen chloride. However, the hydrogen bromide produced in the sodium bromide reaction is a strong reducing agent, so it will reduce the sulfuric acid further to sodium dioxide gas and bromine gas.

Q2 A — iodide
B — fluoride
C — bromide

Page 164 — Fact Recall Questions

Q1 How easy it is for a halide ion to lose an electron depends on the attraction between the nucleus and the outer electrons. As you go down the group, the attraction gets weaker because the ions get bigger, so the electrons are further away from the positive nucleus. There are extra inner electron shells, so there's a greater shielding effect too. Therefore, the reducing power of the halides increases down the group.

Q2 a) $NaF_{(s)} + H_2SO_{4(l)} \rightarrow NaHSO_{4(s)} + HF_{(g)}$

b) $NaI_{(s)} + H_2SO_{4(l)} \rightarrow NaHSO_{4(s)} + HI_{(g)}$
$2HI_{(g)} + H_2SO_{4(l)} \rightarrow I_{2(s)} + SO_{2(g)} + 2H_2O_{(l)}$
$6HI_{(g)} + SO_{2(g)} \rightarrow H_2S_{(g)} + 3I_{2(s)} + 2H_2O_{(l)}$

Q3 a) You can use the silver nitrate test. First add dilute nitric acid (to remove ions which might interfere with the test). Then add silver nitrate solution ($AgNO_{3\,(aq)}$). Chloride ions give a white precipitate, whereas fluoride ions give no precipitate.

b) A precipitate of silver chloride will dissolve in dilute ammonia solution.

5. Tests for Ions
Page 167 — Fact Recall Questions

Q1 a) pale green
b) brick red
c) red

Q2 sodium hydroxide

Q3 Add a little dilute hydrochloric acid, followed by barium chloride solution. If a white precipitate of barium sulfate forms, it means the original compound contained a sulfate.

Q4 Dip a piece of red litmus paper into the solution and if hydroxide ions are present, the paper will turn blue.

Q5 Dilute nitric acid and silver nitrate solution.

Q6 If you add dilute hydrochloric acid to a solution containing carbonate ions, carbon dioxide will be given off. Carbon dioxide turns limewater cloudy so if you bubble the gas through a test tube of limewater and it goes cloudy, your solution contains carbonate ions.

Exam-style Questions — pages 168-170

1 D *(1 mark)*
When you add hydrochloric acid and barium chloride to a solution, a white precipitate means that sulfate ions are present. In a flame test, a brick red flame means that calcium ions are present. So the substance must be calcium sulfate.

2 B *(1 mark)*
Hydroxide ions react with ammonium ions to release ammonia gas, which turns damp red litmus paper blue.

3.1 $Cl_{2(g)} + H_2O_{(l)} \rightleftharpoons 2H^+_{(aq)} + Cl^-_{(aq)} + ClO^-_{(aq)}$ *(1 mark)*

3.2 It kills disease-causing microorganisms *(1 mark)*. It persists in the water and prevents reinfection further down the supply *(1 mark)*.

3.3 E.g. chlorine reacts with organic compounds in the water to form chlorinated hydrocarbons, e.g. chloromethane, many of which are carcinogenic *(1 mark)*.

3.4 E.g. the increased risk of cancer is small compared to the risk of thousands of people dying from untreated water *(1 mark)*.

4.1 Chlorine has a lower boiling point than bromine *(1 mark)*. This is because chlorine molecules are smaller than bromine molecules *(1 mark)*. So chlorine molecules have weaker van der Waals forces holding them together *(1 mark)*.

4.2 Potassium bromide *(1 mark)*. Chlorine displaces the halide ions, so the halogen must be below it in Group 7 *(1 mark)*. However, there's no reaction with bromine water so the halide ion can't be less reactive than bromine *(1 mark)*.

4.3 Potassium iodide *(1 mark)*.
$Cl_2 + 2I^- \rightarrow 2Cl^- + I_2$ *(1 mark)*
You must make sure you balance ionic equations or you won't get the marks in the exam.

4.4 NaClO is used as bleach *(1 mark)*.

4.5 Dilute nitric acid is added to the solution to remove ions which might interfere with the test *(1 mark)*.

4.6 A cream precipitate would form *(1 mark)*.

4.7 The precipitate of silver bromide would dissolve in concentrated (but not dilute) ammonia solution *(1 mark)*.

5.1 D *(1 mark)*
Of the three elements listed, magnesium is the first in Period 2, so it will have the smallest atomic radius, the highest 1st ionisation energy and the lowest melting point.

5.2 Metal E has an extra electron shell compared to metal D. The extra inner shells shield the outer electrons from the attraction of the nucleus *(1 mark)*. The outer electrons in E are further away from the nucleus, which greatly reduces the nucleus's attraction *(1 mark)*. This makes it easier to remove outer electrons, resulting in a lower ionisation energy in metal E *(1 mark)*.

5.3 Metal F will react more quickly with water *(1 mark)* because it has a lower first ionisation energy *(1 mark)*.

5.4 Barium has a larger atomic radius than metal F *(1 mark)*. So its delocalised electrons will be further away from the positive ion/nucleus than those in metal F *(1 mark)*. This means they will be less strongly attracted to the positive ion/nucleus than in metal F so the metallic bonding is weaker *(1 mark)*.

5.5 It is sparingly soluble / has very low solubility *(1 mark)*.

5.6 It is used in indigestion tablets *(1 mark)* to neutralise acid in the stomach *(1 mark)*.

5.7 $TiCl_{4(g)} + 2Mg_{(l)} \rightarrow Ti_{(s)} + 2MgCl_{2(l)}$ *(1 mark)*

Unit 3

Section 1: Introduction to Organic Chemistry

1. Formulas

Pages 174-175 — Application Questions

Q1

It doesn't matter if you draw the bromine atom above or below the carbon atom — it means the same thing.

Q2 C_8H_{18}

Q3 a) CH_2
    b) C_4H_7Br
    c) $C_9H_{17}Cl_3$

Q4 a) C_4H_8
    b) Heptene contains 14 H atoms.

Q5 a) $C_3H_6Br_2$
    b)

    c) $C_3H_6Br_2$
For this molecule the empirical formula is the same as the molecular formula because you can't cancel the numbers of atoms down and still have whole numbers.

Q6 a) C_5H_{10}
    b) $CH_3CH_2CH_2CHCH_2$
    c) CH_2

Q7 a)

Skeletal formulas have a carbon atom at each end and at each junction.

    b)

    c) e.g.

    d)

Q8 a) $CH_3CH(CH_3)CH(CH_3)CH_2CH_2CH_3$
    b) $CH_3CH_2C(CH_2)CH_2CH_2CH_3$
    c) $CH_3CH_2CClCHCH_2CH_3$
    d) $CH_3CHBrCH(OH)CH_2CHCH_2$

Page 175 — Fact Recall Questions

Q1 A molecular formula is a formula which gives the actual number of atoms of each element in a molecule.

Q2 A displayed formula shows how all the atoms are arranged, and all the bonds between them.

Q3 To find the empirical formula you have to divide the molecular formula by the highest number that goes into each number given in the molecular formula.

Q4 A homologous series is a family of organic compounds which have the same general formula and similar chemical properties.

2. Functional Groups

Page 179 — Fact Recall Questions

Q1 C_nH_{2n+2}

Q2 hex-

Q3 A cycloalkane is a ring of carbon atoms with two hydrogens attached to each carbon (assuming there's only one ring).

Q4 ethyl group

Q5 cycloalkanes and alkenes

Q6 An alkyl group or a hydrogen atom.

Q7 An aldehyde has a C=O at the end of a carbon chain, while a ketone has a C=O between two alkyl groups.

3. Nomenclature

Page 183 — Application Questions

Q1 a) 3-methylpentane
    b) 3-ethyl-3-methylpentane
    c) 3,3-diethylhexane
    d) 3,3-diethyl-2-methylhexane

Q2 a) 2,3,4-trimethylpentanoic acid
    b) 2-methlypentan-3-one

Q3 a)

    b)

    c)

    d)

These could all be drawn the other way round (i.e. with the 1-carbon on the other side).

Page 183 — Fact Recall Questions

Q1 di-

Q2 Alcohol, Alkene, Alkyl, Halogen

4. Mechanisms

Page 184 — Fact Recall Questions

Q1 The arrow points from where the electrons are moving from, and points to where they move to.

Q2 Potassium hydroxide dissociates in aqueous solution, giving K^+ and OH^- ions. It is the OH^- ion that interacts with the chloroethane. In the reaction, ethanol and potassium chloride, KCl, are formed. So K^+ ions are unchanged in the reaction, so they play no part in the mechanism.

5. Isomers
Page 187 — Application Questions

Q1

$$Cl-\underset{\underset{H}{|}}{\overset{\overset{H}{|}}{C}}-\underset{\underset{H}{|}}{\overset{\overset{CH_3}{|}}{C}}-CH_3$$

You could draw the chlorine atom attached to any other carbon atom apart from the one it was on originally.

Q2 There are three chain isomers of C_5H_{12}.

$$H-\underset{\underset{H}{|}}{\overset{\overset{H}{|}}{C}}-\underset{\underset{H}{|}}{\overset{\overset{H}{|}}{C}}-\underset{\underset{H}{|}}{\overset{\overset{H}{|}}{C}}-\underset{\underset{H}{|}}{\overset{\overset{H}{|}}{C}}-\underset{\underset{H}{|}}{\overset{\overset{H}{|}}{C}}-H$$

$$H-\underset{\underset{H}{|}}{\overset{\overset{H}{|}}{C}}-\underset{\underset{H}{|}}{\overset{\overset{CH_3}{|}}{C}}-\underset{\underset{H}{|}}{\overset{\overset{H}{|}}{C}}-\underset{\underset{H}{|}}{\overset{\overset{H}{|}}{C}}-H$$

$$H_3C-\underset{\underset{CH_3}{|}}{\overset{\overset{CH_3}{|}}{C}}-CH_3$$

Q3

$$H-\underset{\underset{H}{|}}{\overset{\overset{H}{|}}{C}}-\overset{\overset{O}{\|}}{C}-\underset{\underset{H}{|}}{\overset{\overset{H}{|}}{C}}-H$$

Q4 a) i) Yes
　　 ii) Yes
　　 iii) No
　　 iv) No
　 b) chain isomerism and positional isomerism

Page 187 — Fact Recall Questions

Q1 A chain isomer is a molecule that has the same molecular formula but a different arrangement of the carbon skeleton to another molecule. Some are straight chains and others branched in different ways.

Q2 A position isomer has the same skeleton and the same atoms or groups of atoms attached as another molecule. The difference is that the atoms or groups of atoms are attached to different carbon atoms.

Q3 A functional group isomer has the same atoms as another molecule but the atoms are arranged into different functional groups.

6. *E/Z* Isomers
Page 191 — Application Questions

Q1 a) *Z*-isomer
　 b) *E*-isomer

Q2

$$\underset{H_3CH_2C}{\overset{H_3C}{\diagdown}}C=C\underset{\diagup CH_3}{\overset{CH_2CH_3}{\diagup}} \quad \textit{E}\text{-isomer}$$

$$\underset{H_3CH_2C}{\overset{H_3C}{\diagdown}}C=C\underset{\diagup CH_2CH_3}{\overset{CH_3}{\diagup}} \quad \textit{Z}\text{-isomer}$$

Page 191 — Fact Recall Questions

Q1 A stereoisomer is one of two or more forms of a molecule having the same structural formula but a different arrangement in space.

Q2 a) A *Z*-isomer is an isomer which has the higher priority groups both above or both below the double bond.
　 b) An *E*-isomer is an isomer that has the higher priority groups across the double bond from each other.

Q3 a) CH_3
　 b) Cl
　 c) OH
　 d) $CH_2CH_2CH_2CH_2COOH$

Exam-style Questions — pages 192-194

1　B *(1 mark)*
2　D *(1 mark)*
3　C *(1 mark)*
4.1　3,4-dichlorohex-1-ene *(1 mark)*
4.2　$C_6H_{10}Cl_2$ *(1 mark)*
4.3　C_3H_5Cl *(1 mark)*
4.4　functional group isomer *(1 mark)*
4.5　E.g.

$$\begin{array}{c}
H\quad Cl \\
H-C-C-H \\
Cl-C\quad\quad C-H \\
H\quad\quad H \\
H-C-C-H \\
H\quad\quad H
\end{array}$$

(1 mark)

Any position isomer where the two chlorine atoms aren't on adjacent carbons and the carbon skeleton is the same as the other isomer will get the marks.

4.6　position isomer *(1 mark)*
4.7　It does not show *E/Z*-isomerism *(1 mark)*. This is because one of the carbons in the C=C double bond has two identical groups (the carbon on the right of the diagram has two Hs) *(1 mark)*.
5.1　C_nH_{2n+2} *(1 mark)*
5.2　E.g.

$$H-\underset{\underset{H}{|}}{\overset{\overset{H}{|}}{C}}-\underset{\underset{H}{|}}{\overset{\overset{H}{|}}{C}}-\underset{\underset{\underset{\underset{\underset{H}{|}}{H-C-H}}{|}}{\overset{\overset{H}{|}}{H-C-H}}}{\overset{\overset{H}{|}}{C}}-\underset{\underset{H}{|}}{\overset{\overset{H}{|}}{C}}-\underset{\underset{H}{|}}{\overset{\overset{H}{|}}{C}}-H$$

(1 mark)

There are loads of possible answers for this question. As long as you've drawn a molecule with seven carbon atoms, sixteen hydrogen atoms and have arranged the carbon skeleton so there is at least one branch from the main carbon chain you'll pick up the mark.

5.3　pentane *(1 mark)*
5.4　2,3-dimethylbutane *(1 mark)*
6.1　A stereoisomer is a molecule that has the same structural formula as another molecule but its atoms are arranged differently in space *(1 mark)*.
6.2　E.g.

$$\underset{H_3CH_2C}{\overset{CH_3}{\diagdown}}C=C\underset{\diagup H}{\overset{CH_3}{\diagup}}$$

(1 mark)

$$CH_3 \quad H$$
$$C=C$$
$$H_3CH_2C \quad CH_3$$
(1 mark)

The two isomers shown above would still be correct if they were rotated and reflected in any direction.

6.3 The top isomer is *E*-3-methylpent-2-ene *(1 mark)*.
The bottom isomer is *Z*-3-methylpent-2-ene *(1 mark)*.

Section 2: Alkanes and Halogenoalkanes

1. Alkanes and Petroleum

Page 197 — Fact Recall Questions

Q1 A mixture that consists mainly of alkane hydrocarbons.
Q2 They only contain carbon and hydrogen atoms, and each of their carbon atoms forms four single bonds — there are no C=C double bonds present.
Q3 They are separated by boiling point.
Q4 Some fractions have lower boiling points than others. This means they condense further up the column, so are drawn off higher up.
Q5 Cracking is breaking long-chain alkanes into smaller hydrocarbons.
Q6 There is more demand for lighter petroleum fractions so, to meet the demand, the heavier fractions are cracked into lighter fractions.
Q7 Using a catalyst cuts costs, because the reaction can be done at a lower temperature and pressure, and at an increased speed.

2. Alkanes as Fuels

Page 199 — Application Questions

Q1 $C_5H_{12} + 8O_2 \rightarrow 5CO_2 + 6H_2O$
Q2 $C_5H_{12} + 5\frac{1}{2}O_2 \rightarrow 5CO + 6H_2O$

Page 199 — Fact Recall Questions

Q1 Any three from: e.g. nitrogen oxides / carbon monoxide / carbon (soot) / unburned hydrocarbons / carbon dioxide.
Q2 A catalytic converter.
Q3 The sulfur burns to produce sulfur dioxide gas. If sulfur dioxide enters the atmosphere, it can dissolve in the moisture, and form sulfuric acid.
Q4 Powdered calcium carbonate or calcium oxide can be mixed with water to make an alkaline slurry. When the flue gases mix with the alkaline slurry, the acidic sulfur dioxide gas reacts with the calcium compounds to form a harmless salt (calcium sulfate).

3. Synthesis of Chloroalkanes

Page 202 — Fact Recall Questions

Q1 Reactions that are started by light.
Q2 $Cl_2 \xrightarrow{UV} 2Cl\bullet$
Q3 Two free radicals join together to make a stable molecule. This terminates the chain reaction.
Q4 It acts as a chemical sunscreen by absorbing a lot of ultraviolet radiation from the Sun, and stopping it from reaching us. This helps to prevent sunburn and even skin cancer.
Q5 Chlorine free radicals, $Cl\bullet$, are formed in the upper atmosphere when the C–Cl bonds in CFCs are broken down by ultraviolet radiation.

Q6 $Cl\bullet_{(g)} + O_{3(g)} \rightarrow O_{2(g)} + ClO\bullet_{(g)}$
$ClO\bullet_{(g)} + O_{3(g)} \rightarrow 2O_{2(g)} + Cl\bullet_{(g)}$

Q7 Research by several different scientific groups demonstrated that CFCs were causing damage to the ozone layer. The advantages of CFCs couldn't outweigh the environmental problems they were causing, so they were banned.

4. Halogenoalkanes

Page 203 — Fact Recall Questions

Q1 An alkane with at least one halogen atom in place of a hydrogen atom.
Q2 Halogen atoms are generally more electronegative than carbon atoms, and so they withdraw electron density from carbon atoms. This leaves the carbon atoms with a partial positive charge and the halogen atoms with a partial negative charge — resulting in a polar bond.
Q3 An electron-pair donor.
Q4 Any two from: e.g. CN^- / NH_3 / OH^-.
Q5 A pair of dots represents a lone pair of electrons.

5. Nucleophilic Substitution

Page 208 — Application Questions

Q1

Q2 Reaction C would happen the quickest because the C–I bond has the lowest bond enthalpy of all the carbon-halogen bonds. This means that the C–I bond is the easiest to break, and therefore this reaction will happen the quickest.

Q3

Q4

Page 208 — Fact Recall Questions

Q1 In nucleophilic substitution, one functional group is substituted for another.
Q2 Aqueous sodium hydroxide or potassium hydroxide.
Q3 e.g. $^-$CN / cyanide ion
Q4 Warm in ethanol in a sealed tube.
Q5 The C–F bond is the strongest — it has the highest bond enthalpy. So fluoroalkanes are substituted more slowly than other halogenoalkanes.

6. Elimination Reactions

Page 210 — Application Question

Q1 [reaction scheme: but-2-yl bromide with OH⁻ under reflux in ethanol → alkene + H₂O + :Br⁻]

$$H_2O \quad :Br^-$$

Page 210 — Fact Recall Questions

Q1 An elimination reaction happens when a molecule loses atoms or groups of atoms from two neighbouring carbon atoms and forms a carbon-carbon double bond.

Q2 a) The ⁻OH acts as a nucleophile.
   b) This is a nucleophilic substitution reaction.

Q3 a) The ⁻OH acts as a base.
   b) This is an elimination reaction.

Exam-style Questions — pages 212-213

1 C *(1 mark)*
   In aqueous conditions, the OH⁻ acts as a nucleophile, so a nucleophilic substitution reaction will dominate.

2 B *(1 mark)*

3.1 $Cl\bullet + CH_4 \rightarrow \bullet CH_3 + HCl$ *(1 mark)*
    $\bullet CH_3 + Cl_2 \rightarrow CH_3Cl + Cl\bullet$ *(1 mark)*

3.2 $\bullet CH_3 + Cl\bullet \rightarrow CH_3Cl$ *(1 mark)*

3.3 The chlorine free radicals act as catalysts. They react with ozone to form an intermediate (ClO·), and an oxygen molecule in the following reaction:
    $Cl\bullet_{(g)} + O_{3(g)} \rightarrow O_{2(g)} + ClO\bullet_{(g)}$ *(1 mark)*
    The ClO• then reacts with more ozone to regenerate the chlorine free radical in this reaction:
    $ClO\bullet_{(g)} + O_{3(g)} \rightarrow 2O_{2(g)} + Cl\bullet_{(g)}$ *(1 mark)*
    Because the chlorine free radical is regenerated, just one chlorine free radical can destroy lots of ozone molecules *(1 mark)*. This is a problem as ozone absorbs ultraviolet radiation, and acts as a chemical sunscreen. When ozone is destroyed, it will increase people's risk of getting sunburn and skin cancer *(1 mark)*.

4.1 Because the boiling points of alkanes increase as the molecules get bigger, each fraction condenses at a different temperature *(1 mark)*. As the crude oil vapour goes up the fractionating column, it gets cooler *(1 mark)*. So the fractions are drawn off at different levels in the column depending on where they condense *(1 mark)*.

4.2 E.g. $C_7H_{16(g)} + 7\frac{1}{2}O_{2(g)} \rightarrow 7CO_{(g)} + 8H_2O_{(g)}$
    (1 mark for the correct products and 1 mark for a correctly balanced equation)
    There's more than one correct answer here. You get both marks if you've shown carbon monoxide as one of the products (as well as water) and your equation is balanced. The other possible products are carbon and carbon dioxide.

4.3 It can be dangerous because carbon monoxide gas is poisonous *(1 mark)*. Carbon monoxide molecules bind to the same sites on haemoglobin molecules in red blood cells as oxygen molecules *(1 mark)*. So oxygen can't be carried around the body *(1 mark)*.

4.4 There is more demand for light fractions. / Light fractions are more useful *(1 mark)*.

4.5 E.g. $C_7H_{16} \rightarrow C_4H_8 + C_3H_8$ *(1 mark)*
    Any balanced equation including an alkane and alkene gets a mark here.

4.6 Using a catalyst cuts costs, because the reaction can be done at a lower temperature and pressure *(1 mark)*. The catalyst also speeds up the rate of reaction *(1 mark)*.

5.1 $CH_3CH_2Br + OH^- \rightarrow CH_3CH_2OH + Br^-$ *(1 mark)*

[reaction mechanism diagram: bromoethane + OH⁻ → ethanol + :Br⁻]

(1 mark for each curly arrow, up to a maximum of 2 marks)

5.2 The reaction of water with iodoethane would be quicker than the reaction of bromoethane with water *(1 mark)*. This is because the reaction involves the breaking of a carbon-halogen bond and the C–I bond has a lower bond enthalpy than the C–Br bond *(1 mark)*, which means it is more easily broken *(1 mark)*.

5.3 It will predominantly undergo an elimination reaction, instead of a nucleophilic reaction *(1 mark)*. This is because the OH– acts as a base and removes a hydrogen atom from bromoethane *(1 mark)*.

Section 3: Alkenes and Alcohols

1. Alkenes

Page 217 — Application Question

Q1 [reaction scheme: but-2-ene + Br₂ → intermediate carbocation + :Br⁻ → 2,3-dibromobutane]

Page 217 — Fact Recall Questions

Q1 C_nH_{2n}

Q2 Alkenes are unsaturated because they can make more bonds with extra atoms in addition reactions across the carbon-carbon double bond.

Q3 Alkenes can undergo electrophilic addition reactions because they have a double bond which has a high electron density and is easily attacked by electrophiles.

Q4 Electrophiles are electron-pair acceptors.

Q5 Any two from: e.g. NO_2^+ / H^+ / CH_3CH_2Br.

Q6 Carbon-carbon double bonds/unsaturation/alkenes.

2. Reactions of Alkenes

Page 220 — Application Questions

Q1 a) [reaction scheme: but-2-ene + HBr → carbocation intermediate + :Br⁻ → 2-bromobutane]

It doesn't matter which carbon you add the bromine to as you'll always end up with the same product (2-bromobutane).

b) $C_4H_8 + HBr \rightarrow C_4H_9Br$

Q2 The reaction mechanism for the production of 2-bromobutane contains a secondary carbocation, which is more stable than the primary carbocation formed in the reaction mechanism for 1-bromobutane. More stable carbocations are more likely to form, so 2-bromobutane is the major product of this reaction.

Page 220 — Fact Recall Questions
Q1 hydrogen bromide
Q2 Tertiary carbocations are more stable than secondary carbocations, which are more stable than primary carbocations.

3. Addition Polymers
Page 224 — Application Questions
Q1 a)
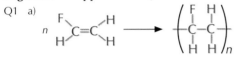

b) poly(fluoroethene) / polyfluoroethene
Q2

Q3

H Cl
| |
—C—C—
| |
H CH$_3$

Page 224 — Fact Recall Questions
Q1 The double bonds in alkenes (monomers) open up and join together to make long chains called polymers.
Q2 Poly(alkenes) are unreactive because they have lost their carbon-carbon double bonds/they are saturated. Also, the carbon chain is non-polar.
Q3 a) The chlorine-carbon bonds are polar, with the chlorine atoms being $\delta-$. The chlorine and carbon atoms of different polymer chains have permanent dipole-dipole forces bonding them.
b) E.g. window frames, drain pipes.
Q4 a) Plasticisers are molecules that get between polymer chains. This pushes them apart, which reduces the strength of the intermolecular forces between the chains, which makes the polymer more flexible.
b) E.g. electric cable insulation, clothing.

4. Alcohols
Page 226 — Application Questions
Q1 a) pentan-1-ol
b) 2,2-dimethylpropan-1-ol
c) 2,3-dimethylbutan-2-ol
d) 3-ethyl-2-methylpentane-1,5-diol
That last one is a tricky one... Make sure you have the side chains in alphabetical order and the name has the lowest possible numbers in it.
Q2 a) primary
b) primary
c) tertiary
d) primary

Page 226 — Fact Recall Questions
Q1 $C_nH_{2n+1}OH$
Q2 A secondary alcohol is an alcohol with the –OH group attached to a carbon with two alkyl groups attached.

5. Dehydrating Alcohols
Page 229 — Application Question
Q1 a) $C_3H_7OH \rightarrow C_3H_6 + H_2O$
b)
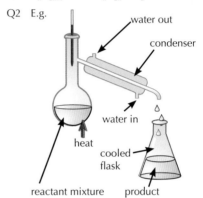

Page 229 — Fact Recall Questions
Q1 $C_nH_{2n+1}OH \rightarrow C_nH_{2n} + H_2O$

Q2 E.g.

water out
condenser
water in
heat
cooled flask
reactant mixture   product

Q3 Put impure cyclohexene in a round-bottomed flask. Add anhydrous $CaCl_2$ and stopper the flask. Let the mixture dry for at least 20 minutes with occasional swirling. Distil the resulting mixture. Collect the product that is released when the mixture is at around 83 °C — this will be the pure cyclohexene.

6. Ethanol Production
Page 233 — Application Question
Q1

Page 233 — Fact Recall Questions
Q1 $C_6H_{12}O_{6(aq)} \xrightarrow[\text{yeast}]{30\text{-}40°C} 2C_2H_5OH_{(aq)} + 2CO_{2(g)}$
Q2 If it's too cold, the reaction is slow — if it's too hot, the enzyme is denatured (damaged).
Q3 A biofuel is a fuel that's made from biological material that's recently died.

Q4 a) $6CO_2 + 6H_2O \rightarrow C_6H_{12}O_6 + 6O_2$

$C_6H_{12}O_6 \rightarrow 2C_2H_5OH + 2CO_2$

$2C_2H_5OH + 6O_2 \rightarrow 4CO_2 + 6H_2O$

b) These equations don't take into account the carbon dioxide produced by other stages in the process, e.g. making fertilisers, powering agricultural machinery, and transporting the fuel.

Q5 a) E.g. unlike fossil fuels, biofuels are sustainable/ renewable. / Burning a biofuel releases the same amount of carbon dioxide that the plant took in as it grew, so biofuels are nearly carbon neutral/don't contribute to global warming as much as fossil fuels.

b) Any three from: e.g. land which is being used to grow crops for fuel, can't be used to grow food. / Trees may be cut down to create more land to grow crops for biofuels, which destroys habitats/removes trees/releases carbon dioxide if they are burnt. / Fertilisers, which are added to soils to increase crop production, can pollute waterways/release nitrous oxide. / Most current car engines couldn't run on biofuels without being modified.

7. Oxidising Alcohols

Page 237 — Application Question

Q1 a)

b)

c)

Page 237 — Fact Recall Questions

Q1 Aldehydes have the functional group C=O and have one hydrogen atom and one R group attached to the carbon atom. Ketones have the functional group C=O and have two R groups attached either side of the carbon atom. Carboxylic acids have the functional group COOH.

Q2

Q3 Any two from: e.g. Fehling's solution / Benedict's solution / Tollens' reagent.

Exam-style Questions — pages 239-241

1 B *(1 mark)*

2 C *(1 mark)*

3.1 $C_6H_{12}O_{6(aq)} \rightarrow 2C_2H_5OH_{(aq)} + 2CO_{2(g)}$ *(1 mark)*
The reaction needs to be carried out in the presence of yeast and at 30–40 °C *(1 mark)*.

3.2 Fermentation uses renewable resources to produce ethanol and so will become more important as the amount of crude oil decreases *(1 mark)*.

3.3 The hydration of ethene by steam is carried out at 300 °C and at a pressure of 60 atm *(1 mark)*. It also needs a solid phosphoric(V) acid catalyst *(1 mark)*.

3.4

(4 marks, 1 mark for each correct curly arrow and 1 mark for the structure of the final product.)

3.5 A biofuel is a fuel that's made from biological material that's recently died *(1 mark)*.

3.6 Carbon dioxide goes into crops during photosynthesis:
$6CO_2 + 6H_2O \rightarrow C_6H_{12}O_6 + 6O_2$ *(1 mark)*
Taking the glucose that is produced in photosynthesis and fermenting it produces ethanol and carbon dioxide:
$C_6H_{12}O_6 \rightarrow 2C_2H_5OH + 2CO_2$ *(1 mark)*
Burning the ethanol produced gives off water and carbon dioxide:
$2C_2H_5OH + 6O_2 \rightarrow 4CO_2 + 6H_2O$ *(1 mark)*
In these three balanced equations, 6 moles of CO_2 go into the system, and 6 moles of CO_2 come out. So ethanol is thought of as a carbon neutral fuel *(1 mark)*.

3.7 There are still carbon emissions if you consider the whole ethanol production process *(1 mark)*. For example, the machinery used to produce the ethanol fuel may be powered by fossil fuels which release CO_2 into the atmosphere when they're burnt *(1 mark)*.

3.8 Any two of: e.g. they aren't carbon neutral and the manufacturing of them could still use fossil fuels / fertilisers used to grow the crops needed to make biofuels produce nitrous oxide which contributes to the greenhouse effect / deforestation takes place to make room for crops *(1 mark for each correct statement up to 2 marks)*.

3.9 E.g. it uses farmable land to produce fuel instead of food, and where food is scarce this could be a problem *(1 mark)*.

4.1 The student could shake the alkene with bromine water *(1 mark)*. The solution will turn from orange to colourless if a carbon-carbon double bond is present *(1 mark)*.

4.2 $C_6H_{12} + HBr \rightarrow C_6H_{13}Br$ *(1 mark)*

4.3

(1 mark)

4.4 This isomer is the major product of the reaction because it's formed when the reaction proceeds via the most stable carbocation intermediate *(1 mark)*. For the major product the reaction goes via a tertiary (3°) carbocation *(1 mark)* and for the minor product the reaction goes via a secondary (2°) carbocation *(1 mark)*.

4.5

(1 mark)

5.1 A monomer is an alkene molecule that is used to make a polymer *(1 mark)*.

5.2 tetrafluoroethene *(1 mark)*

5.3 Poly(tetrafluoroethene) is saturated (it only has single bonds in the carbon chain) *(1 mark)* and its main carbon chain is non-polar *(1 mark)*.

5.4 It makes the polymer more bendy/flexible *(1 mark)*.

6.1 butan-1-ol *(1 mark)*

6.2 potassium dichromate(VI) *(1 mark)*

6.3 Gently heat *(1 mark)* excess butan-1-ol with the oxidising agent in distillation apparatus *(1 mark)*. The aldehyde, butanal, is distilled off as soon as it forms as it passes up a fractionating column and through a condenser *(1 mark)*.

6.4 $C_4H_9OH + [O] \longrightarrow C_4H_8O + H_2O$ *(1 mark)*

You can also have the mark if you used the full structural formulas here.

6.5 She could test the unknown product with Fehling's/ Benedict's solution *(1 mark)*. As it is an aldehyde, the solution will go from a deep blue colour to a brick-red colour *(1 mark)*. She could also test the product with Tollens' reagent *(1 mark)*. The aldehyde would make a silver mirror coating form on the inside of the testing apparatus *(1 mark)*.

6.6

$$H-\overset{\overset{\displaystyle H}{|}}{\underset{\underset{\displaystyle H}{|}}{C}}-\overset{\overset{\displaystyle OH}{|}}{\underset{\underset{\displaystyle CH_3}{|}}{C}}-\overset{\overset{\displaystyle H}{|}}{\underset{\underset{\displaystyle H}{|}}{C}}-H$$

(1 mark)

Section 4: Organic Analysis

1. Tests for Functional Groups

Page 245 — Application Questions

Q1 Tollens' reagent is reduced to silver when warmed with an aldehyde, so the compound must be an aldehyde.

Q2 No reaction is seen between ketones and Benedict's solution. Therefore the test tube containing the ketone must be the one that doesn't produce a precipitate with Benedict's solution. So the ketone is compound B.

Q3 a) The potassium dichromate(VI) solution would change from orange to green.
   b) The limewater would turn cloudy.

Q4 E.g. first warm a small sample of solution from each test tube with a few drops of Tollens' reagent/Fehling's solution/ Benedict's solution. Propanal will give a silver mirror/ brick-red precipitate. No reaction will be seen with propanone or propanoic acid.
   Next add a small spatula of solid sodium carbonate to samples of the two remaining unknown solutions. The propanoic acid will fizz, producing carbon dioxide gas, which will turn limewater cloudy when bubbled through it. Propanone will not react with calcium carbonate.
   You could do these two steps the other way around if you wanted to — identifying the carboxylic acid first using the carbonate test, then using Tollens' reagent, Fehling's solution or Benedict's solution to identify the aldehyde and the ketone.

Q5 a) Potassium dichromate(VI) shows the same colour change (orange to green) when it reacts with both primary and secondary alcohols.
   b) Either: Add acidified potassium dichromate(VI) to both samples and heat them in distillation apparatus. Collect the products of both reactions. Add Fehling's/ Benedict's solution / Tollens' reagent to both and warm them. The primary alcohol will have been oxidised to an aldehyde and will produce a brick red precipitate / silver mirror. The secondary alcohol will have been oxidised to a ketone and will not react with Fehling's/ Benedict's solution / Tollens' reagent.
   Or: Add acidified potassium dichromate(VI) to both samples and heat them under reflux. Collect the products of both reactions. Add sodium carbonate to both. The primary alcohol will have been oxidised to a carboxylic acid and so it will begin to fizz.

(If you collect the gas produced and bubble it through limewater, the limewater will turn cloudy.)
The secondary alcohol will have been oxidised to a ketone, which will not react with the sodium carbonate (so it will not fizz).

Page 245 — Fact Recall Questions

Q1 Brick-red.

Q2 Put 2 cm^3 of 0.10 mol dm^{-3} silver nitrate solution in a test tube. Add a few drops of dilute sodium hydroxide solution. A light brown precipitate should form. Then, add drops of dilute ammonia solution until the brown precipitate dissolves completely.

Q3 The orange/brown bromine water would decolourise.

2. Mass Spectrometry

Page 247 — Application Questions

Q1 a) At lower resolution, all three of these molecules would appear to have the same molecular mass.
   $M_r (C_3H_6O) = (3 \times 12) + (6 \times 1) + 16 = 58$
   $M_r (C_3H_8N) = (3 \times 12) + (8 \times 1) + 14 = 58$
   $M_r (C_4H_{10}) = (4 \times 12) + (10 \times 1) = 58$
   b) $M_r (C_3H_6O)$
   $= (3 \times 12.0000) + (6 \times 1.0078) + 15.9949 = 58.0417$
   $M_r (C_3H_8N)$
   $= (3 \times 12.0000) + (8 \times 1.0078) + 14.0031 = 58.0655$
   $M_r (C_4H_{10}) = (4 \times 12.0000) + (10 \times 1.0078) = 58.0780$
   The molecular formula is C_3H_8N.

Q2 Find the precise molecular mass of each compound.
   M_r of butanoic acid
   $= (4 \times 12.0000) + (8 \times 1.0078) + (2 \times 15.9949) = 88.0522$
   M_r of pentan-1-ol
   $= (5 \times 12.0000) + (12 \times 1.0078) + 15.9949 = 88.0885$
   M_r of pentan-3-one
   $= (5 \times 12.0000) + (10 \times 1.0078) + 15.9949 = 86.0729$
   M_r of hexane = $(6 \times 12.0000) + (14 \times 1.0078) = 86.1092$
   So the compounds in the mixture are pentan-1-ol and hexane.

3. Infrared Spectroscopy

Page 250 — Application Questions

Q1 a) A (~3000 cm^{-1}) — O–H (carboxylic acid)
   B (~1700 cm^{-1}) — C=O
   b)

$$H-\overset{\overset{\displaystyle H}{|}}{\underset{\underset{\displaystyle H}{|}}{C}}-\overset{\overset{\displaystyle H}{|}}{\underset{\underset{\displaystyle H}{|}}{C}}-\overset{\overset{\displaystyle O}{||}}{C}-O-H$$

The mass of the carboxylic acid group (COOH) is 45 (12 + 16 + 16 + 1). The M_r of the molecule is 74, so the rest of the molecule has a mass of 74 – 45 = 29. This corresponds to an ethyl group (CH_3CH_2), so the molecule must be propanoic acid.

Q2 E.g. There is a strong, sharp peak at about 1700 cm^{-1}, this indicates that a C=O bond is present in the molecule.

Page 250 — Fact Recall Questions

Q1 A beam of IR radiation is passed through a sample of a chemical. The IR radiation is absorbed by the covalent bonds in the molecules, increasing their vibrational energy. Bonds between different atoms absorb different frequencies of IR radiation. Bonds in different places in a molecule absorb different frequencies too. The frequencies where they absorb IR radiation are plotted to give an IR spectrum.

Q2 1000 cm^{-1} – 1550 cm^{-1}

Exam-style Questions — pages 252-255

1.1 The IR spectrum of molecule A has a peak at around 1650 cm⁻¹, which corresponds to a C=C double bond in an alkene / doesn't contain a peak corresponding to O–H bonds in an alcohol *(1 mark)*.

So molecule **A** is:

(1 mark)

The IR spectrum of molecule B shows a strong, broad peak at around 3400 cm⁻¹. This corresponds to O–H bonds in an alcohol *(1 mark)*.

So molecule **B** is:

(1 mark)

The first thing you need to here is to work out what different molecules you could make by reacting 1-bromopropane with OH⁻ ions. Once you've drawn the two possible products (an alcohol and an alkene), you get the rest of the marks for working out which spectrum matches which product.

1.2 Molecule A is propene *(1 mark)*.
Molecule B is propan-1-ol *(1 mark)*.

1.3 Molecule A is produced by reacting 1-bromopropane with ethanol and potassium/sodium hydroxide under reflux *(1 mark)*.
Molecule B is produced by reacting 1-bromopropane with water and potassium/sodium hydroxide under reflux *(1 mark)*.

2 Water vapour is the most effective greenhouse gas *(1 mark)*. The infrared spectrum for water vapour shows that, out of the three gases, water vapour absorbs the most energy in the infrared region of the electromagnetic spectrum *(1 mark)*.

3 Compound A must be ethanol (a primary alcohol) since it is oxidised by potassium dichromate(VI) solution, but does not react with calcium carbonate or Tollens' reagent *(1 mark)*. Compound B must be butanal (an aldehyde) since it reacts with Tollens' reagent, a test for aldehydes, to produce a silver mirror *(1 mark)*. Therefore, compound **C** must be propanoic acid. This fits with the observations — propanoic acid is a carboxylic acid so reacts with calcium carbonate to produce carbon dioxide, which turns limewater cloudy *(1 mark)*.

4.1

(1 mark)

4.2

(1 mark)

4.3 The IR spectra of propanal and propanone would be very similar/it would be hard to tell the difference between the spectra of propanal and propanone as they both only contain C=O, C–C and C–H bonds *(1 mark)*.

4.4 The relative molecular masses of propanal and propanone are the same, so high resolution mass spectroscopy could not distinguish between them *(1 mark)*.

4.5 E.g. Use Benedict's/Fehling's solution *(1 mark)*. Benedict's/Fehling's solution will produce a brick-red precipitate when warmed with propanal, but not propanone *(1 mark)*.

OR Use Tollens' reagent *(1 mark)*. Tollens' reagent will produce a silver mirror when warmed with propanal, but not propanone *(1 mark)*.
Care should be taken when heating aldehydes and ketones as they are flammable — a water bath should be used instead of a naked flame. You should also always wear safety goggles and a lab coat to prevent any irritant reagents splashing into your eyes or onto your skin *(1 mark)*.

5.1 E.g. Spectrum X shows a peak just below 3000 cm⁻¹, probably for C–H bonds, but no other peaks corresponding to specific bonds. This suggests that one of the compounds is an alkane.
Alkanes with molecular formula C_5H_{12} have $M_r = (5 × 12.0) + (12 × 1.0) = 72$, which could be A or B. Find the precise molecular mass of C_5H_{12}: $(5 × 12.0000) + (12 × 1.0078) = 72.0936$ — i.e. compound B.
Spectrum Y has a peak at just over 1700 cm⁻¹, which suggests a C=O bond. There's no O–H/C–O peak for a carboxylic acid, but it could be an aldehyde or a ketone. The molecular formula could be C_4H_8O, which has $M_r = (4 × 12.0) + (8 × 1.0) + 16.0 = 72$, so check the precise molecular mass of C_4H_8O:
$(4 × 12.0000) + (8 × 1.0078) + 15.9949 = 72.0573$ — i.e. compound A.
Spectrum Z has a peak at about 1650 cm⁻¹. This could be caused by the C=C bond in an alkene.
Alkenes with molecular formula C_5H_{10} have $M_r = (5 × 12.0) + (10 × 1.0) = 70$, which could be C. Check by finding the precise molecular mass of C_5H_{10}:
$(5 × 12.0000) + (10 × 1.0078) = 70.0780$ — i.e. compound C.
So compound A is C_4H_8O, which gives spectrum **Y**.
Compound B is C_5H_{12}, which gives spectrum **X**.
Compound C is C_5H_{10}, which gives spectrum **Z**.
(8 marks available in total: 1 mark each for a correct analysis of the three spectra, 1 mark for each correct molecular formula and 2 marks for matching all three compounds to the correct spectra, otherwise 1 mark for matching one compound to the correct spectrum.)
You might have done things in a different order here — e.g. if you had a hunch about what the molecular formulas of the compounds were, you could have used the precise molecular masses to confirm them first, then matched them up to the IR spectra.

5.2 **A** is either an aldehyde or a ketone with molecular formula C_4H_8O. It doesn't have a branched carbon chain, so it must be either butanal or butanone *(1 mark for either)*.
B is a straight-chain alkane with molecular formula C_5H_{12}, so it must be pentane *(1 mark)*.
C is a straight-chain alkene with molecular formula C_5H_{10}. That means it's pentene. You don't know where the double bond is, so it could be pent-1-ene or pent-2-ene *(1 mark for either, allow 1 mark for pentene)*.

5.3 The infrared spectrum of every compound has a unique 'fingerprint region' between 1000 cm⁻¹ and 1550 cm⁻¹. You can compare spectra X, Y and Z against spectra for the suggested identities. If the suggestions are correct, the fingerprint regions will match *(1 mark)*.
In case you're wondering, the spectra here are actually for pentane (X), butanone (Y) and pent-1-ene (Z).

Glossary

Accurate result
A result that's really close to the true answer.

Activation energy
The minimum amount of kinetic energy that particles need to have in order to react when they collide.

Addition polymer
A long chain molecule (polymer) formed by an addition reaction.

Alcohol
A substance with the general formula $C_nH_{2n+1}OH$.

Aldehyde
A substance with the general formula $C_nH_{2n}O$ which has a hydrogen and one alkyl group attached to the carbonyl carbon atom.

Alkaline earth metal
An element in Group 2 of the periodic table.

Alkane
A hydrocarbon with the general formula C_nH_{2n+2}.

Alkene
A hydrocarbon with the general formula C_nH_{2n}, containing at least one carbon-carbon double bond.

Anomalous result
A result that doesn't fit in with the pattern of the other results in a set of data.

Atom
A neutral particle made up of protons and neutrons in a central nucleus and electrons orbiting the nucleus.

Atom economy
A measure of the proportion of reactant atoms that become part of the desired product in a balanced chemical reaction.

Atomic number
The number of protons in the nucleus of an atom. Also called proton number.

Avogadro constant
6.02×10^{23} — the number of particles in 1 mole of a substance.

B

Barium chloride test
Test that uses acidified barium chloride to test for sulfate ions in solution.

Barium meal
A suspension of barium sulfate swallowed by a patient before an X-ray in order to show up the structure of their oesophagus, stomach or intestine.

Benedict's solution
A deep blue solution containing Cu^{2+} ions, which are reduced to a brick-red precipitate of Cu_2O when warmed with an aldehyde, but stays blue when warmed with a ketone.

Biofuel
A fuel that's made from biological material that's recently died.

Bond enthalpy
The energy required to break a bond between two atoms.

C

Calorimetry
Method of finding out how much energy is given out or taken in by a reaction, by measuring the temperature change that takes place during the reaction.

Carbocation
An organic ion containing a positively charged carbon atom.

Carbonyl compound
A compound that contains a carbon-oxygen double bond.

Carboxylic acid
A substance which has a COOH group attached to the end of a carbon chain.

Catalyst
A substance that increases the rate of a reaction by providing an alternative reaction pathway with a lower activation energy. The catalyst is chemically unchanged at the end of the reaction.

Categoric data
Data that can be sorted into categories.

Causal link
The relationship between two variables where a change in one variable causes a change in the other.

Chain isomer
An organic molecule that contains the same atoms and functional groups as another molecule but has a different arrangement of the carbon skeleton.

Charge cloud
An area in an atom or molecule where there's a high chance of finding an electron pair.

Chloroalkane
An alkane with one or more hydrogen atoms substituted for chlorine atoms.

Closed system
A system where nothing can get in or out.

Collision theory
The theory that a reaction will not take place between two particles unless they collide in the right direction and with at least a certain minimum amount of kinetic energy.

Complete combustion
Burning a substance completely in oxygen to produce carbon dioxide and water only.

Continuous data
Data that can have any value on a scale.

Control variable
A variable that is kept constant in an experiment.

Co-ordinate bond
A covalent bond formed when one atom provides both of the shared electrons. Also called a dative covalent bond.

Correlation
The relationship between two variables.

Covalent bond
A pair of electrons shared between two atoms. Both nuclei are attracted electrostatically to the shared electrons.

Cracking
Breaking long-chain alkanes into smaller hydrocarbons.

Crude oil
A mixture consisting mainly of alkane hydrocarbons that can be separated into different fractions.

Curly arrow
An arrow used in reaction mechanism diagrams to show the movement of a pair of electrons.

Cycloalkane
A type of alkane where the carbon atoms form a ring, with two hydrogen atoms attached to each carbon.

Dative covalent bond
A covalent bond formed when one atom provides both of the shared electrons. Also called a co-ordinate bond.

Dehydration
A reaction where water is eliminated.

Dependent variable
The variable that you measure in an experiment.

Dichromate(VI) ion
An oxidising agent, used to test for the presence of primary or secondary alcohols. Orange dichromate(VI) ions ($Cr_2O_7^{2-}$) turn to green chromium(III) ions (Cr^{3+}) ions in the presence of primary or secondary alcohols.

Dipole
A difference in charge between two atoms caused by a shift in the electron density in a bond.

Discrete data
Data that can only take certain values.

Displacement reaction
A reaction where a more reactive element pushes out a less reactive element and takes its place.

Displayed formula
A way of representing a molecule that shows how all the atoms are arranged and all the bonds between them.

Disproportionation
When an element is both oxidised and reduced in a single chemical reaction.

Dynamic equilibrium
In a reversible reaction dynamic equilibrium is reached when the concentrations of the reactants and products are constant, and the forward and backward reactions are going at the same rate.

E-isomer
A stereoisomer of an alkene that has the two highest priority groups on opposite sides of the carbon-carbon double bond.

Electron
A subatomic particle with a relative charge of −1 and a relative mass of 1/2000, located in orbitals around the nucleus.

Electron configuration
The number of electrons an atom or ion has and how they are arranged.

Electronegativity
The ability of an atom to attract the bonding electrons in a covalent bond.

Electrophile
An electron-pair acceptor.

Electrophilic addition
A reaction mechanism where a C=C double bond in an alkene opens up and atoms are added to the carbon atoms.

Electrospray ionisation
A method of producing ions for analysis in a mass spectrometer by applying high pressure and high voltage to a sample of a substance.

Elimination reaction
A reaction mechanism in which a molecule loses atoms or groups of atoms.

Empirical formula
A formula that gives the simplest whole number ratio of atoms of each element in a compound.

Endothermic reaction
A reaction that absorbs energy (ΔH is positive).

Energy level
A region of an atom with a fixed energy that contains electrons orbiting the nucleus. Also known as a shell.

Enthalpy change
The energy transferred in a reaction at constant pressure.

Equilibrium constant, K_c
A ratio worked out from the concentration of the products and reactants once a reversible reaction has reached equilibrium.

Exothermic reaction
A reaction that gives out energy (ΔH is negative).

E/Z isomerism
A type of stereoisomerism that is caused by the restricted rotation about a carbon-carbon double bond. Each of the carbon atoms must have two different groups attached.

Fehling's solution
A deep blue Cu^{2+} complex, which reduces to a brick-red Cu_2O precipitate when warmed with an aldehyde, but stays blue with a ketone.

Fingerprint region
The region between 1000 cm^{-1} and 1550 cm^{-1} on an infrared spectrum. It's unique to a particular compound.

First ionisation energy
The energy needed to remove 1 electron from each atom in 1 mole of gaseous atoms to form 1 mole of gaseous 1+ ions.

Fractional distillation
A method of separating crude oil fractions using their boiling points.

Free radical
A particle with an unpaired electron, written like this: Cl• or •Cl.

Functional group
The group of atoms that is responsible for the characteristic reactions of a molecule (e.g. OH for alcohols, COOH for carboxylic acids, C=C for alkenes).

Functional group isomer
A molecule with the same molecular formula as another molecule, but with the atoms arranged into different functional groups.

Gas constant
A constant used in the ideal gas equation. It has the symbol R, and it's value is 8.31 J K^{-1} mol^{-1}.

General formula
An algebraic formula that can describe any member of a family of compounds.

Giant covalent structure
A structure consisting of a huge network of covalently bonded atoms. Sometimes called macromolecular structures.

Giant ionic lattice structure
A regular repeated structure made up of oppositely charged ions held together by electrostatic attraction.

Giant metallic lattice structure
A regular structure consisting of closely packed positive metal ions in a sea of delocalised electrons.

Greenhouse effect
The trapping of energy from the Sun that has been absorbed and re-emitted by the Earth, by certain gases in the Earth's atmosphere.

Greenhouse gas
A gas that contributes to the greenhouse effect by absorbing energy in the infrared region of the electromagnetic spectrum.

Group
A column in the periodic table.

Half-equation
An equation that shows oxidation or reduction — one half of a full redox equation.

Halide
A negative ion of a halogen.

Halogen
An element in Group 7 of the periodic table.

Halogenoalkane
An alkane with at least one halogen atom in place of a hydrogen atom.

Hess's Law
The total enthalpy change for a reaction is independent of the route taken.

Homologous series
A family of organic compounds that have the same general formula and similar chemical properties.

Hydrocarbon
A molecule that only contains hydrogen and carbon atoms.

Hydrogen bonding
The strongest intermolecular force. It occurs when polarised covalent bonds cause hydrogen atoms to form weak bonds with lone pairs of electrons on the fluorine, nitrogen or oxygen atoms of other molecules.

Hydrolysis reaction
A reaction where molecules are split apart by water molecules (which are themselves split apart).

Hypothesis
A suggested explanation for a fact or observation.

Ideal gas equation
The ideal gas equation is $pV = nRT$. It allows you to find the number of moles in a volume of gas at any temperature and pressure.

Incomplete combustion
Burning a substance in a poor supply of oxygen to produce carbon monoxide, water and sometimes carbon and carbon dioxide.

Independent variable
The variable that you change in an experiment.

Infrared (IR) spectroscopy
An analytical technique used to identify the functional groups present in a molecule by measuring the vibrational frequencies of its bonds.

Intermediate
A short-lived, reactive molecule that occurs in the middle of a step-wise reaction mechanism.

Intermolecular forces
Forces between molecules, e.g. van der Waals forces, permanent dipole-dipole forces and hydrogen bonding.

Ion
A charged particle formed when one or more electrons are lost or gained by an atom or molecule.

Ionic bond
An electrostatic attraction between positive and negative ions in a lattice.

Ionic equation
An equation which only shows the reacting particles of a reaction involving ions in solution.

Ionisation
The removal (or addition) of one or more electrons from an atom or molecule, resulting in an ion forming.

Ionisation energy
The energy needed to remove 1 electron from each atom or ion in 1 mole of gaseous atoms or ions.

Isomer
A molecule with the same molecular formula as another molecule, but with the atoms arranged in a different way.

Isotope
An atom with the same number of protons as another atom but a different number of neutrons.

Ketone
A substance with the general formula $C_nH_{2n}O$ which has two alkyl groups attached to the carbonyl carbon atom.

Le Chatelier's principle
A theory that states that if there's a change in concentration, pressure or temperature, the equilibrium position will move to help counteract the change.

Lone pair (of electrons)
An unshared pair of electrons in the outer shell of an atom. Also called a non-bonding pair of electrons.

Mass number
The total number of protons and neutrons in the nucleus of an atom.

Mass spectrometry
An analytical technique that gives information on relative mass and relative abundance of atoms or molecules in a sample.

Mass spectrum
A chart produced by a mass spectrometer which can give you information about the relative masses and relative abundances of particles in a sample.

Maxwell-Boltzmann distribution
A theoretical model that describes the distribution of kinetic energies of molecules in a gas.

Mean bond enthalpy
An average value for the bond enthalpy of a particular bond over the range of compounds it is found in.

Metallic bond
The attraction between delocalised electrons and a lattice of positive metal ions.

Model
A simplified picture or representation of a real physical situation.

Molar ratio
The ratio of the number of moles of each reactant and product in a balanced chemical equation.

Mole
The unit of amount of substance. One mole is equal to 6.02×10^{23} particles (the Avogadro constant).

Molecular formula
A way of representing molecules that shows the actual number of atoms of each element in a molecule.

Molecule
A group of two or more atoms bonded together with covalent bonds.

Monomer
A small molecule that is used to make a polymer.

Multiple covalent bond
A covalent bond that contains more than one shared pair of electrons.

Neutron
A subatomic particle with a relative charge of 0 and a relative mass of 1, located in the nucleus of an atom.

Nucleophile
An electron-pair donor.

Nucleophilic substitution reaction
A reaction mechanism where a nucleophile attacks a polar molecule and replaces a functional group in that molecule.

Nucleus
The central part of an atom or ion, made up of protons and neutrons.

Nomenclature
A fancy word for naming things, in particular organic compounds.

Orbital
A region of a sub-shell that contains a maximum of 2 electrons.

Ordered / ordinal data
Categoric data where the categories can be put in order.

Oxidation
Loss of electrons.

Oxidation state
The total number of electrons an element has donated or accepted. Also called an oxidation number.

Oxidising agent
Something that accepts electrons and gets reduced.

Ozone layer
A layer of ozone (O_3) found in the Earth's upper atmosphere which protects the Earth from ultraviolet radiation.

Percentage yield
A comparison between the amount of product that should form during a reaction and the amount that actually forms.

Period
A row in the periodic table.

Periodicity
The trends in the physical and chemical properties of elements as you go across the periodic table.

Permanent dipole-dipole forces
Intermolecular forces that exist because the difference in electronegativities in a polar bond causes weak electrostatic forces of attraction between molecules.

Petrochemical
Any compound that is made from crude oil (or any of its fractions).

Petroleum
A mixture consisting mainly of alkane hydrocarbons that can be separated into different fractions.

Photochemical reaction
A reaction started by ultraviolet light.

Polar bond
A covalent bond where a difference in electronegativity has caused a shift in electron density in the bond.

Polar molecule
A molecule containing polar bonds that are arranged so that the dipoles don't cancel each other out. This causes a permanent dipole across the whole molecule.

Polymer
A long molecule formed from lots of smaller molecules (monomers) joined together.

Position isomer
A molecule with the same skeleton and molecular formula as another molecule but with the functional group attached to a different carbon.

Precise result
Results where the data have a very small spread around the mean.

Prediction
A specific testable statement about what will happen in an experiment, based on observation, experience or a hypothesis.

Proton
A subatomic particle with a relative charge of +1 and a relative mass of 1, located in the nucleus of an atom.

Proton number
The number of protons in the nucleus of an atom. Also called atomic number.

Random error
An error introduced by a factor that you cannot control.

Redox reaction
A reaction where reduction and oxidation happen simultaneously.

Reducing agent
Something that donates electrons and gets oxidised.

Reduction
Gain of electrons.

Refluxing
A method for heating a reaction so that you can increase the temperature of an organic reaction to boiling without losing volatile solvents, reactants or products. Any vaporised compounds are cooled, condense and drip back into the reaction mixture.

Relative atomic mass, A_r
The average mass of an atom of an element on a scale where an atom of carbon-12 is exactly 12.

Relative formula mass
The average mass of a formula unit on a scale where an atom of carbon-12 is exactly 12.

Relative isotopic abundance
The relative amount of each isotope present in a sample of an element.

Relative isotopic mass
The mass of an atom of an isotope of an element on a scale where an atom of carbon-12 is exactly 12.

Relative molecular mass, M_r
The average mass of a molecule on a scale where an atom of carbon-12 is exactly 12.

Repeatable result
A result is repeatable if you can repeat an experiment multiple times and get the same result.

Reproducible result
A result is reproducible if someone else can recreate your experiment and get the same result you do.

Saturated molecule
A molecule that only has single carbon-carbon bonds.

Shell
A region of an atom with a fixed energy that contains electrons orbiting the nucleus.

Silver nitrate test
Test that uses silver nitrate solution to identify halide ions in solution.

Skeletal formula
A simplified organic formula which only shows the carbon skeleton and associated functional groups.

Standard conditions
100 kPa (about 1 atm) pressure and a stated temperature, usually 298 K.

Standard enthalpy change of combustion, $\Delta_c H^\circ$
The enthalpy change when 1 mole of a substance is completely burned in oxygen under standard conditions with all reactants and products in their standard states.

Standard enthalpy change of formation, $\Delta_f H^\circ$
The enthalpy change when 1 mole of a compound is formed from its elements in their standard states under standard conditions.

Standard enthalpy change of reaction, $\Delta_r H^\circ$
The enthalpy change when a reaction occurs in the molar quantities shown in the chemical equation, under standard conditions with all reactants and products in their standard states.

Standard solution
A solution that you know the exact concentration of.

State symbol
A symbol placed after a chemical in an equation to tell you what state of matter the chemical is in.

Stereoisomer
A molecule that has the same structural formula as another molecule, but has its atoms arranged differently in space.

Structural formula
A way of representing molecules that shows the atoms carbon by carbon, with the attached hydrogens and functional groups.

Structural isomer
A molecule with the same molecular formula as, but a different structural formula to another molecule (i.e. the atoms are connected in different ways).

Sub-shell
A sub-division of a shell (energy level). Sub-shells may be s, p, d or f sub-shells.

Substituted alkene
An alkene where one of the hydrogen atoms has been swapped for another atom or group.

Systematic error
An error introduced by the apparatus or method you use in an experiment.

Theoretical yield
The mass of product that should be formed in a chemical reaction.

Titration
A type of experiment used to find the concentration of a solution. It involves gradually adding one solution to a known volume of another until the reaction between the two is complete.

Tollens' reagent
A solution containing $[Ag(NH_3)_2]^+$. It's reduced to silver when warmed with an aldehyde, but not with a ketone. The silver will coat the inside of the apparatus to form a silver mirror.

Unsaturated molecule
A molecule with one or more carbon-carbon double bonds.

Valence shell electron pair repulsion theory
The theory that in a molecule lone pair/lone pair bond angles are the biggest, lone pair/bonding pair bond angles are the second biggest and bonding pair/bonding pair bond angles are the smallest.

Valid result
A result which answers the question it was intended to answer.

Van der Waals forces
A type of intermolecular force caused by temporary dipoles, which causes all atoms and molecules to be attracted to each other. Also called induced dipole-dipole forces or London forces.

Variable
A factor in an experiment or investigation that can change or be changed.

Yield
The amount of product you get from a reaction.

Z-isomer
A stereoisomer of an alkene that has the two highest priority groups on the same side of the carbon-carbon double bond.

Acknowledgements

Photograph Acknowledgements

Cover Photo **Laguna Design**/Science Photo Library, p 2 **Tek Image**/Science Photo Library, p 4 **Martyn F. Chillmaid**/Science Photo Library, p 9 **Gustoimages**/Science Photo Library, p 15 Science Photo Library, p 16 **Prof. Peter Fowler**/Science Photo Library, p 19 **Andrew Brookes, National Physical Laboratory**/Science Photo Library, p 21 **NASA**/Science Photo Library, p 24 **Food & Drug Administration**/Science Photo Library, p 30 **Andrew Lambert Photography**/Science Photo Library, p 38 **Andrew Lambert Photography**/Science Photo Library, p 41 **GIPhotostock**/Science Photo Library, p 47 **Charles D. Winters**/Science Photo Library, p 49 **Martyn F. Chillmaid**/Science Photo Library, p 50 **Andrew Lambert Photography**/Science Photo Library, p 53 **Martyn F. Chillmaid**/Science Photo Library, p 58 **Martyn F. Chillmaid**/Science Photo Library, p 69 **Charles D. Winters**/Science Photo Library, p 71 **Bill Beatty, Visuals Unlimited/**Science Photo Library, p 75 © **sarbiewski**/iStockPhoto.com, p 78 © **JeffreyRasmussen**/iStockPhoto.com, p 80 © **StasKhom/**iStockPhoto.com, p 81 © **JeffreyRasmussen**/iStockPhoto.com, p 82 **Dr Tim Evans**/Science Photo Library, p 88 **Marytn F. Chillmaid**/Science Photo Library, p 89 (top) **Clive Freeman/Biosym Technologies**/Science Photo Library, p 89 (bottom) **Clive Freeman/Biosym Technologies**/Science Photo Library, p 92 © **wertorer**/iStockPhoto.com, p 93 **Charles D. Winters**/Science Photo Library, p 94 (top) Science Photo Library, p 94 (bottom) **Andrew Lambert Photography**/Science Photo Library, p 95 **GIPhotostock**/Science Photo Library, p 104 **Charles D. Winters**/Science Photo Library, p 105 **Martyn F. Chillmaid**/Science Photo Library, p 115 (top) **Sheila Terry**/Science Photo Library, p 115 (bottom) Science Photo Library, p 117 **Emilio Segre Visual Archives/American Institute Of Physics**/Science Photo Library, p 126 (top) **Martyn F. Chillmaid**/Science Photo Library, p 126 (bottom) **Martyn F. Chillmaid**/Science Photo Library, p 128 **Martyn F. Chillmaid**/Science Photo Library, p 129 **Deloche**/Science Photo Library, p 137 **Martyn F. Chillmaid**/Science Photo Library, p 145 **Ria Novosti**/Science Photo Library, p 146 (top left) **Charles D. Winters**/Science Photo Library, p 146 (top right) **Charles D. Winters**/Science Photo Library, p 146 (bottom) **E. R. Degginger**/Science Photo Library, p 148 (top) **Martyn F. Chillmaid**/Science Photo Library, p 148 (bottom) **Andrew Lambert Photography**/Science Photo Library, p 149 (top) © **cerae**/iStockPhoto.com, p 149 (middle) **Charles D. Winters**/Science Photo Library, p 149 (bottom) **Charles D. Winters**/Science Photo Library, p 153 (top) **Charles D. Winters**/Science Photo Library, p 153 (bottom) **Martyn F. Chillmaid**/Science Photo Library, p 156 **Miriam Maslo**/Science Photo Library, p 159 (top) **Andrew Lambert Photography**/Science Photo Library, p 159 (middle) **Andrew Lambert Photography**/Science Photo Library, p 159 (bottom) **Charles D. Winters**/Science Photo Library, p 164 (top) **Andrew Lambert Photography**/Science Photo Library, p 164 (bottom) **Andrew Lambert Photography**/Science Photo Library, p 165 (top) **Andrew Lambert Photography**/Science Photo Library, p 165 (bottom left) **Andrew Lambert Photography**/Science Photo Library, p 165 (bottom right) **Andrew Lambert Photography**/Science Photo Library, p 166 **Trevor Clifford Photography**/Science Photo Library, p 171 **Laguna Design**/Science Photo Library, p 173 **Martyn F. Chillmaid**/Science Photo Library, p 176 **US Geological Survey**/Science Photo Library, p 179 **Nicolas Reusens**/Science Photo Library, p 180 Science Photo Library, p 183 **Faye Norman**/Science Photo Library, p 190 Science Photo Library, p 196 **Paul Rapson**/Science Photo Library, p 197 **Martyn F. Chillmaid/**Science Photo Library, p 199 (top) **Astrid & Hanns-Frieder Michler**/Science Photo Library, p 199 (bottom) **Simon Fraser**/Science Photo Library, p 202 **NASA/Goddard Space Flight Center**/Science Photo Library, p 210 **Andrew Lambert Photography**/Science Photo Library, p 216 **Andrew Lambert Photography**/Science Photo Library, p 223 **Astrid & Hanns-Frieder Michler**/Science Photo Library, p 228 **Andrew Lambert Photography/**Science Photo Library, p 231 (top) **Power and Syred**/Science Photo Library, p 231 (bottom) **Ed Young**/Science Photo Library, p 232 **Alex Bartel**/Science Photo Library, p 235 (top) © **ScantyNebula**/iStockPhoto.com, p 235 (bottom) **Andrew Lambert Photography**/Science Photo Library, p 236 **Martyn F. Chillmaid**/Science Photo Library, p 237 (top) **Andrew Lambert Photography**/Science Photo Library, p 237 (bottom) **Andrew Lambert Photography**/Science Photo Library, p 242 **Andrew Lambert Photography**/Science Photo Library, p 243 **Andrew Lambert Photography**/Science Photo Library, p 244 (top) **Andrew Lambert Photography**/Science Photo Library, p 244 (middle) Science Photo Library, p 244 (bottom) **Andrew Lambert Photography**/Science Photo Library, p 246 **Gustoimages**/Science Photo Library, p 250 **Science Source**/Science Photo Library, p 258 **Dr Tim Evans/**Science Photo Library, p 261 **Jon Stokes**/Science Photo Library, p 263 Science Photo Library.

Index